CORTINA METHOD

CONVERSATIONAL ITALIAN

IN 20 LESSONS

Cortina Method Books

FRENCH IN 20 LESSONS
SPANISH IN 20 LESSONS
GERMAN IN 20 LESSONS
ITALIAN IN 20 LESSONS
AMERICAN ENGLISH IN 20 LESSONS
MODERN GREEK IN 20 LESSONS
RUSSIAN IN 20 LESSONS
INGLÉS EN 20 LECCIONES
FRANCÉS EN 20 LECCIONES
INGLÊS EM 20 LIÇÕES
CONVERSATIONAL BRAZILIAN PORTUGUESE
CONVERSATIONAL JAPANESE
SPANISH CONVERSATIONAL GUIDE
SPANISH IN SPANISH
FRANÇAIS EN FRANÇAIS
ENGLISH IN ENGLISH
DEUTSCH AUF DEUTSCH
ITALIANO IN ITALIANO

CORTINA METHOD

CONVERSATIONAL ITALIAN IN 20 LESSONS

ILLUSTRATED

Intended for self-study and for use in schools

With a Simplified System of Phonetic Pronunciation

Based on the Method of

R. DIEZ DE LA CORTINA

UNIVERSITIES OF MADRID AND BORDEAUX
AUTHOR OF THE CORTINA METHOD
ORIGINATOR OF THE PHONOGRAPHIC METHOD OF
TEACHING LANGUAGES.

By
MICHAEL CAGNO

4TH EDITION
Completely Revised

CORTINA LEARNING INTERNATIONAL, INC.
Publishers • WESTPORT, CT 06880

Cataloging Information

Cortina Method Italian in 20 Lessons, intended for self-study and for use in schools; with a simplified system of phonetic pronunciation, by Michael Cagno, based on the method of R. Diez de la Cortina. New York, R. D. Cortina Co., 1977.

    336 p. illus. 21 cm.

    1. Italian language—Conversation and phrase books. 2. Italian language—Grammar. I. Title.

PC1112.5.C3 1977   458.242   54-14366
ISBN 0-8327-0005-3 (hardbound)
ISBN 0-8327-0013-4 (paperback)

Printed in the United States of America
9 8 7 6 5 4 3

Introduction

How a Knowledge of Italian Can Help You

NOW AS NEVER BEFORE alert Americans and other English-speaking people are learning the Italian language, and there are many reasons for the revival of interest in this most melodious and expressive tongue.

Italian has always been the language of the arts—of poetry, fiction, opera. Many of the great masterpieces of world literature were written in Italian—Dante's epic *Divine Comedy*, Boccaccio's lusty *Decameron*, Machiavelli's study of government, *The Prince*, the lyrics of Petrarch, to mention only a few. In recent years also there has been a great deal of literary activity in Italy and the many fine works written by such authors as Ignazio Silone, Alberto Moravia, Giuseppe Berto, Carlo Levi, and others make fascinating reading. With a knowledge of Italian these great works, old and new, now become available to you in the full flavor of the original language.

The very word "opera" is almost synonymous with the Italian language. An understanding of Italian will add a new dimension of pleasure when you hear such great musical masterpieces as Verdi's *La Traviata, Il Trovatore, Rigoletto, La Forza del Destino*, Donizetti's *Lucia*, Leoncavallo's *Pagliacci*, Puccini's *La Boheme, Madame Butterfly*, and *Tosca*.

Since World War II Italy has produced many great motion pictures which have been shown widely throughout the English-speaking world. Your understanding of Italian will enable you to enjoy to the fullest the fine nuances of the dialogue and the subtleties of character and humor instead of depending on the brief, often inadequate English subtitles.

Italy has always been a popular country with tourists, but now it is a "must" for anyone who visits Europe. Its great cities—Rome, Naples, Florence, and Milan—with their beautiful buildings, fascinating history, taste-tempting restaurants, and the enchanting countryside, make a visit to Italy a cherished memory. And when you visit Italy, you will find your knowledge of the native tongue a source of unending satisfaction and pleasure. You will be able to become more intimate with the Italian people, you will be welcomed as a cultured friend, not merely as a tourist. You will be invited into Italian homes. And you will find also that your knowledge of Italian saves you money when you deal with tradespeople, hotel keepers, ticket sellers, etc.

One should not forget also that Italy has become increasingly important as a commercial country. More and more people in the English-speaking countries are having business dealings with Italians. Italy now exports many products, including handicrafts, automobiles and machines, foods and wines, and, in turn, buys many products for import. Knowing how to deal with Italians in their native language is a decided advantage for businessmen and others who have commercial relations with Italy.

In short, your study of Italian will bring you many hours of pleasure in your cultural pursuits, and will also have numerous practical advantages.

Preface

IN 1882, THE CORTINA ACADEMY OF LANGUAGES was founded in the United States by Count Cortina. Besides engaging professors for all the modern languages (French, Spanish, German, Italian, and English) Count Cortina himself, personally, gave language instruction for many years. From this actual teaching experience, Professor Cortina developed a new simplified method that became an instant success. It has never been surpassed since. For the past 70-odd years the method has been constantly refined and improved from the Academy's long experience in teaching languages, and in terms of the changing needs of the present-day language student. It is now known all over the world as THE CORTINA METHOD.

Because of the success of and the demand for Cortina instruction from students who could not attend classes, the Academy was forced to publish Cortina lessons in book form. Well over two million Cortina language books have been sold, and they are a clear testimonial to the ease with which students have learned a new language through THE CORTINA METHOD.

Many thousands of students have learned a new language by this method at home, in their spare time. Many others have used THE CORTINA METHOD in schools and colleges throughout the United States and South America.

You may ask: "What is the secret of THE CORTINA METHOD's

success? How is it different from other ways to learn a language?" One of the main reasons is that the lessons are devoted to everyday topics which encourage the student to learn. The lessons begin with subjects that we all used as children when we learned our native tongue. For instance, right from the start, the first lessons teach you the same words that a child first speaks: *Mother, father, brother, sister,* as well as everyday words relating to meals, drinks, clothing, and so on. These words are easily put to use at once and are much more interesting than the abstract and academic words a student is usually asked to learn. Knowing that he can put these words to immediate use adds color and excitement to language study and keeps the interest of the student at a high level throughout his language-learning experience.

Features of This New Edition

The Editors have included two new features in this edition which will also be found of great help to the student:

First, the format of the lessons has been changed to allow for the inclusion of carefully chosen illustrations. The drawings have been arranged to highlight the subject matter of the lessons and thus will greatly aid the student in memorizing the foreign words through the graphic representation.

Second, a complete REFERENCE GRAMMAR has been appended at the back of the book so that the student may refer to any part of speech he wishes as he advances in his studies. The necessary grammar for the lessons is included in the footnotes, lesson by lesson, for the student's convenience.

In addition, practical bi-lingual dictionaries have been included which contain not only all of the words of the twenty lessons but also many other useful words as well.

How To Study

Language is habit. We are constantly expressing thoughts and ideas in speech, from habit, without paying any particular attention to the words, phrases, or idioms we use. When we say *"How do you do," "It's fine today," "I've had a wonderful trip,"* we do so spontaneously. We are merely repeating a speech pattern we have used so many times before that it has become automatic—a habit. Repetition, therefore, is the basis of language learning; and consequently it is extremely important that the student acquire the correct Italian pronunciation at the very beginning so that he learns the right speech habits.

For this purpose a basic feature of the CORTINA METHOD is the emphasis on *speaking* the language. At the outset we provide a GUIDE TO ITALIAN PRONUNCIATION. It explains how to pronounce Italian sounds, words, and phrases through simple phonetic symbols based on English spelling, with special explanations of how to articulate those sounds which occur only in the Italian language. In Lessons 1-16 the entire Italian vocabularies and conversations are transcribed in these symbols. Using them as a guide, the student will be able to read each entire lesson aloud, and he should do so as many times as necessary to be able to read the Italian text aloud easily and correctly. Through this practice, not only will the student attain fluency, but he will eventually be able to express his ideas in Italian just as easily and effortlessly as he does in English.

LESSON ARRANGEMENT. The lessons are arranged so that the student can follow them easily. For each of the first sixteen lessons there is (a) a vocabulary of important words of a general character, (b) a specific vocabulary covering the topic of the lesson, and (c) dialogues showing how these vocabularies are used in everyday conversation. To the right of each word or sentence is given the phonetic spelling so that the student can pronounce them correctly, and in the next column is given the English translation of the Italian text.

The student should start each lesson by memorizing as much of the general vocabulary as possible. Then, in turning to the conversation that follows, he will complete his mastery of these words by actually using them *to express ideas*. The conversational sentences should be read, making general reference to the translation of each sentence. *Learn* the thoughts that the Italian sentence conveys

9

rather than a word-for-word translation. The lesson has been mastered when the student can read the lesson aloud without reference to either the PRONUNCIATION or TRANSLATION columns.

The best way to express your thoughts in your new language is to try to use the basic speech patterns illustrated by the sentences of the lessons with a few variations as, for example, substituting one verbal form for another, and one noun for another, etc. Try also to imagine true-to-life situations and the way you would react to them conversationally, but don't try to learn too many basic speech patterns at once. Try to digest and master a few at a time.

Don't be afraid of making mistakes! It is only natural to make errors in spelling and grammar when you write down your translations. Your mistakes are really of great value to you, because they reveal your weak spots. Then you can eliminate them by consulting the grammar section and, of course, the spelling in the book. In this way, you see that when you are in doubt, it is actually of greater benefit to you to *guess wrong* than to *guess right*—because in the latter case you may not know *why* your solution is correct.

As you proceed from lesson to lesson, don't neglect to review, review, *and review again* the material of the previous lessons. Constant review and repetition will not only help you to retain what you have learned, but will also give you an ever firmer grasp of the language, enabling you at the end to use it spontaneously.

The last four lessons differ in form. On the assumption that the student has mastered the basic elements of Italian, they consist of dialogues (with footnotes) centering around topics of cultural, historical, and practical interest. All the words used are given in the ITALIAN-ENGLISH DICTIONARY in the back of the book.

The grammatical explanations in the FOOTNOTES are of great importance to the student and close attention should be paid to them. They also clear up many of the idiomatic difficulties and are very helpful because they give other illustrations of the language in actual use. For more elaborate grammatical explanation of any particular lesson the student can refer to the PLAN FOR STUDY which precedes the complete REFERENCE GRAMMAR.

Remember that there is no better way to learn a language than the way children learn—by speaking it. The CORTINA METHOD is based upon this principle with necessary modifications to adjust this natural method to the adult mind. With a little application you will have a lot of fun learning this way. What a satisfaction it will be to have *this important second language* at your command!

This book has been recorded to assist any student wishing to accelerate his progress and master the spoken language in the easiest manner. Please write R. D. Cortina Co., Suite 54, 136 W. 52 St. New York 10019, for free Sample Record and full information about this invaluable aid.

Table of Contents

REFERENCE
GRAMMAR

* § is the symbol for paragraph.

14

GUIDE TO

Italian Pronunciation

ITALIAN SPELLING IS highly phonetic; that is, letters and combinations of letters almost always represent the same sounds, as contrasted with English, where a single letter or combination of letters may represent three, four, or more sounds. For the student of Italian the phonetic character of Italian spelling means that he need merely familiarize himself with the basic sounds which the spellings stand for. From there he can proceed to pronounce almost any Italian word correctly.

In this book we use a simplified scheme of indicating the pronunciation of Italian letters and letter combinations. This is based on common English sounds wherever possible. The sounds in the following list should be learned first before proceeding to the lessons themselves. Syllable divisions are indicated by a hyphen (-) and accented syllables are printed in small capitals; thus, in the word *stanza*, meaning "room," the stress would fall on the first syllable, as indicated in "STAHN-tsah."

The Vowels

Vowels in Italian are pronounced fully and distinctly, and are never slurred.

ITALIAN SPELLING	SOUND	ITALIAN EXAMPLE	PHONETIC SYMBOL
a	Like the *a* in *far*.	scala (SKAH-lah) stairs	ah
e	Like the *e* in *let*, but slightly towards the *a* of *ate*.	pera (PEH-rah) pear	eh

19

Italian Spelling	Sound	Italian Example	Phonetic Symbol
i	Like the *i* of *machine*.	amico (ah-MEE-koh) friend	ee
o	Like the *o* of *fort*.	porto (POHR-toh) port	oh
u	Like the *oo* in *fool*.	muto (MOO-toh) mute	oo

The Consonants

b	As in English.	basta (BAH-stah) enough	b
c	1. Before *a, o,* and *u,* hard, like *k,* as in *cat*.	cane (KAH-neh) dog	k
	2. Before *e* and *i,* soft, like *ch,* as in *chin*.	cena (CHEH-nah) supper	ch
ch	Occurs only before *e* or *i,* to harden the *c* into a *k* sound.	anche (AHN-keh) also	k
	NOTE: When *chi* is followed by a vowel, the *i* is pronounced like a very light *y,* as in *cute, cure*.	chiave (KYAH-veh) key	ky
d	As in English, but with the tongue touching the upper teeth.	dove (DOH-veh) where	d
f	As in English.	fine (FEE-neh) end	f
g	1. Before *a, o,* and *u,* hard, as in *game, go*.	gamba (GAHM-bah) leg	g
	2. Before *e* and *i,* soft, as in *gentle, gem*.	gelo (JEH-loh) frost	j
gh	Occurs only before *e* and *i,* to harden the *g*.	righe (REE-geh) rulers	g
	NOTE: When *ghi* is followed by a vowel, the *i* is pronounced like a very light *y*.	ghiotto (GYOHT-toh) glutton	gy
gl	Usually pronounced like the *lli* in *billion* before *i*.	moglie (MOH-l'yeh) wife	l'y
	NOTE: In a very few words, *gli* has the same sound as in the English word *glib*.	glicerina (glee-cheh-REE-nah) glicerine negligente (neh-glee-JEHN-teh) negligent	gl
gn	Similar to, but stronger than the *ni* in *onion* and the *ny* in *canyon*.	agnello (ah-N'YEHL-loh) lamb	n'y

Italian Spelling	Sound	Italian Example	Phonetic Symbol
h	Always silent. It occurs in very few words.	hanno (AHN-noh) they have	—
[j]	Does not exist in the Italian alphabet.		
[k]	Does not exist in the Italian alphabet.		
l	As in English.	mela (MEH-lah) apple	l
m	As in English.	mano (MAH-noh) hand	m
n	As in English.	naso (NAH-soh) nose	n
p	As in English.	pane (PAH-neh) bread	p
qu	Like qu in quality, quick.	quindi (KWEEN-dee) therefore	kw
r	Trilled by vibrating the tongue slightly against the base of the upper front teeth.	Roma (ROH-mah) Rome	r
s	1. Unvoiced, as in sound.	solo (SOH-loh) alone	s
	2. Voiced, as in pose.	casa (KAH-zah) house	z
	NOTE A: Many Italians pronounce this sound not quite as a pure z, but with a slight leaning toward the unvoiced s.		
	NOTE B: At the beginning of a word, when s is followed by b, d, g, gh, l, m, n, r, or v, it is pronounced like z.	sbaglio (ZBAH-l'yoh) mistake sdegno (ZDEH-n'yoh) anger	
sc	1. Before e or i, like sh, as in shell.	scelta (SHEHL-tah) choice	sh
	2. Before a, o, u, and h, like sk, as in skill.	scala (SKAH-lah) stairs	sk
t	As in English, but with the tip of the tongue touching the upper teeth.	tale (TAH-leh) such	t
v	As in English.	voto (VOH-toh) vote	v
[w]	Does not exist in the Italian alphabet.		
x	Like the x in box. Rarely used, chiefly in words of Latin and Greek origin.		ks

ITALIAN SPELLING	SOUND	ITALIAN EXAMPLE	PHONETIC SYMBOL
[y]	Does not exist in the Italian alphabet.		
z	1. Unvoiced, like the *ts* in *pots.*	stanza (STAHN-tsah) room	ts
	2. Voiced, like the *ds* in *buds.*	pranzo (PRAHN-dzoh) dinner	dz

Diphthongs

A diphthong is a combination of two vowels pronounced as one syllable. There are three classes of diphthongs in Italian:

A. Those in which the first of the two vowels is stressed. We shall separate the two vowels by an apostrophe as a reminder that they are to be pronounced in one breath, without a break, even though the sound of the first vowel is stronger than the second:

ai	Similar to the *i* of *high.*	parlai (pahr-LAH'y) I spoke	AH'y
ao	Say "ah" and elide it to an "oh" sound.	Paolo (PAH'oh-loh) Paul	AH'oh
au	Similar to the "ow" of *cow.*	cauto (KAH'oo-toh) cautious	AH'oo
ea	No English equivalent. A combination of *eh* and *ah.*	idea (ee-DEH'ah) idea	EH'ah
ei	Like the *ay* in *day.*	lei (LAY) you	AY
eo	No English equivalent. A combination of *eh* and *oh.*	ebreo (eh-BREH'oh) Hebrew	EH'oh
eu	No English equivalent. A combination of *eh* and long *oo.*	neutro (NEH'oo-troh) neuter	EH'oo
ia	No English equivalent. A combination of *ee* and *ah.*	mia (MEE'ah) my	EE'ah
ie	No English equivalent. A combination of *ee* and *eh.*	bugie (boo-JEE'eh) lies	EE'eh
ii	No English equivalent. Like a drawn-out *ee* sound.	finii (fee-NEE'y) I finished	EE'y
io	No English equivalent. A combination of *ee* and *oh.*	Dio (DEE'oh) God	EE'oh

ITALIAN SPELLING	SOUND	ITALIAN EXAMPLE	PHONETIC SYMBOL
oe	No English equivalent. A combination of *oh* and *eh*.	eroe (eh-ROH'eh) hero	OH'eh
oi	Similar to the *oy* of *boy*.	noi (NOY) we	OY
ua	No English equivalent. A combination of long *oo* and *ah*.	sua (SOO'ah) his, her	oo'ah
ue	No English equivalent. A combination of long *oo* and *eh*.	due (DOO'eh) two	oo'eh
ui	Similar to the *ewy* of *chewy*, but without the "w" sound.	fui (FOO'y) I was	oo'y
uo	No English equivalent. A combination of long *oo* and *oh*.	duo (DOO'oh) duet	oo'oh

B. Those diphthongs in which the first of the individual vowel sounds is made part of the second, which gets the major part of the sound:

ia	No English equivalent. A combination of initial *y* and *ah*.	piatto (PYAHT-toh) dish	YAH
ie	Similar to the *ye* of *yet*, but more extended.	ieri (YEH-ree) yesterday	YEH
io	Similar to the *yo* of *yodel*.	biondo (BYOHN-doh) blonde	YOH
iu	Similar to *you*.	fiume (FYOO-meh) river	YOO
ua	Like the *wa* of *swallow*.	guanti (GWAHN-tee) gloves	WAH
ue	Like the *ue* of *quell*.	questo (KWEH-stoh) this	WEH
ui	Like the *uee* of *queen*.	quindici (KWEEN-dee-chee) fifteen	WEE
uo	Like the *uo* of *quote*.	uomo (WOH-moh) man	WOH

C. Those diphthongs in which neither vowel sound is stressed. These appear in unaccented syllables. They are indicated as in B above, but in lower case letters. Examples:

sedia (SEH-dyah) chair
vietato (vyeh-TAH-toh) forbidden
quindicina (kween-dee-CHEE-nah) fortnight

We shall not consider *ia, io,* and *iu* as diphthongs when they are preceded by *c* or *g* inasmuch as the *i* is used to give the letters *c* and *g* a soft sound, as explained above.

Triphthongs

A triphthong is a combination of three vowels pronounced as one syllable.

iei	A combination of initial *y* and *ay*.	miei (M'YAY) my	'YAY
uoi	A combination of *w* and *oy*.	tuoi (TWOY) your	WOY

Double Consonants

Double consonants in Italian have a stronger sound than single consonants. In our phonetic transcription, the first of the double consonants is written at the end of the preceding syllable. Examples:

pena (PEH-nah) pain;   **penna** (PEHN-nah) pen
caro (KAH-roh) dear;   **carro** (KAHR-roh) car, cart

A double *c* before *e* or *i* is pronounced like the *tch* in *watch*. A double *g* before *e* or *i* is pronounced like the *dg* in *budge*. In the phonetic system this sound is represented by *dj*. A double *z* is not indicated. The symbol for the single *z* is used.

Accent

In Italian the accented syllable is usually the next to the last one, called the penult:

tesoro (teh-ZOH-roh) treasure
trovare (troh-VAH-reh) to find

However, there are many words which do not follow this rule. Some words are accented on the final syllable, in which case they usually take a grave accent (`) on the vowel of that syllable:

facoltà (fah-kohl-TAH)   **pietà** (pyeh-TAH) pity

This accent mark is also used to distinguish between words of similar spelling but different meaning:

te you; **tè** tea   **la** the; **là** there
ancora (ahn-KOH-rah) yet;   **àncora** (AHN-koh-rah) anchor

Keep in mind that the stressed syllable in Italian has a longer and louder (almost explosive) sound than the others.

ITALIAN IN 20 LESSONS

Vocabularies and Conversations

Prima Lezione

Vocabolario per Questa Lezione   Vocabulary for This Lesson
(voh-kah-boh-LAH-ryoh pehr KWE-stah leh-TSYOH-neh)

io desidero[1] (EE'oh deh-ZEE-deh-roh)   I desire, I wish
desidera lei? (deh-ZEE-deh-rah LAY)   do you want, do you wish?
egli desidera (EH-l'yee deh-ZEE-deh-rah)   he wants, he wishes
molto (MOHL-toh)   much, a great deal, very
perfettamente (pehr-feht-tah-MEHN-teh)   perfectly
un'automobile (oon-ah'oo-toh-MOH-bee-leh)   an automobile

domani (doh-MAH-nee) tomorrow   partire (pahr-TEE-reh)   to leave
solo (SOH-loh)   alone   presto (PREH-stoh)   soon, early
con (kohn)   with   soltanto (sohl-TAHN-toh) only
ma (mah)   but   o (oh)   or
anche (AHN-keh)   also   bene (BEH-neh)   well

un[2] aeroplano (oon ah'eh-roh-   an airplane
  PLAH-noh)
un viaggio (oon vee-AH-djoh)   a trip
un piroscafo (oon pee-ROH-skah-foh) a boat

un po'[3] (oon POH)   a little, some
prende lei? (PREHN-deh LAY)   do you take?
io prendo (EE'oh PREHN-doh)   I take
gli[4] affari[5] (l'yee ahf-FAH-ree)   business
il[4] treno (eel TREH-noh)   the train
interessante (een-teh-rehs-SAHN-teh)   interesting
parlarlo[6] (pahr-LAHR-loh)   to speak it
la mattina (lah maht-TEE-nah)   the morning
imparare (eem-pah-RAH-reh)   to learn
abitare (ah-bee-TAH-reh)   to live, to dwell

il mio[7] (eel MEE'oh) my, mine   dove (DOH-veh)   where
la mia (lah MEE'ah)   my, mine   dov'è? (doh-VEH)   where is?
il suo[8] (eel soo'oh) your, his, her chi (kee)   who
la sua (lah soo'ah)   your, his, her   andare[9] (ahn-DAH-reh) to go
perchè (pehr-KEH)   because   che (keh)   that, which
perchè? (pehr-KEH)   why?   quando (KWAHN-doh)   when

26

(lah fah-MEE-l'yah)   **LA FAMIGLIA**   THE FAMILY

l' uomo (LWOH-moh)		the man		
uomini (WOH-mee-nee)		men		

la donna (lah DOHN-nah)	woman	**la figlia** (lah FEE-l'yah)	daughter	
il marito (eel mah REE-toh)	husband	**lo⁴ zio** (loh DZEE'oh)	uncle	
la moglie (lah MOH-l'yeh)	wife	**la zia** (lah DZEE'ah)	aunt	
il padre (eel PAH-dreh)	father	**il cugino** (eel koo-JEE-noh)	cousin *(m.)*	
la madre (lah MAH-dreh)	mother	**la cugina** (lah koo-JEE-nah)	cousin *(f.)*	
il figlio (eel FEE-l'yoh)	son			

il fratello (eel frah-TEHL-loh)	brother
la sorella (lah soh-REHL-lah)	sister
il cognato (eel koh-N'YAH-toh)	brother-in-law
la cognata (lah koh-N'YAH-tah)	sister-in-law
un bambino (oon bahm-BEE-noh)	a child *(m.)*
una bambina (OO-nah bahm-BEE-nah)	a child *(f.)*
un ragazzo (oon rah-GAH-tsoh)	a boy
una ragazza (OO-nah rah-GAH-tsah)	a girl
un ragazzino¹⁰ (oon rah-gah-TSEE-noh)	a little boy
una ragazzina (OO-nah rah-gah-TSEE-nah)	a little girl

signor (see-N'YOHR)	mister
signore (see-N'YOH-reh)	sir, gentleman
signori (see-N'YOH-reeh)	gentlemen

Le Nazionalità e Le Lingue • Nationalities and Languages
(leh nah-tsyoh-nah-lee-TAH eh leh LEEN-gweh)

NAZIONALITA	PAESE (country)	LINGUA
un italiano (ee-tah-LYAH-noh)	**Italia** (ee-TAH-lyah)	**l'italiano**
an Italian	Italy	Italian
un inglese (een-GLEH-zeh)	**Inghilterra** (een-gil-TEH-rah)	**l'inglese**
an Englishman	England	English
un francese (frahn-CHEH-zeh)	**Francia** (FRAHN-chah)	**il francese**
a Frenchman	France	French
un tedesco (teh-DEH-skoh)	**Germania** (jer-MAHN-yah)	**il tedesco**
a German	Germany	German
uno spagnuolo (spah-N'YWOH-loh)	**Spagna** (SPAH-n'yah)	**lo spagnuolo**
a Spaniard	Spain	Spanish
un belga (BEHL-gah)	**Belgio** (BEHL-joh)	
a Belgian	Belgium	
un russo (ROOS-soh)	**Russia** (ROO-s'yah)	**il russo**
a Russian	Russia	Russian
un americano (ah-meh-ree-KAH-noh)	**America** (ah-MEH-ree-kah)	**l'inglese**
an American	America	English

CONVERSATION

1 Io desidero . . .

2 Che desidera,[12] signore?

3 Io desidero parlare[13] italiano.

4 Chi desidera parlare italiano?

5 Egli desidera parlare italiano.

6 Lei[15] desidera parlare la lingua inglese?

7 Sì, signore, io desidero parlarla.[14]

8 Parla lei francese?[16]

9 Io parlo italiano e anche francese.

10 Desidera lei parlarmi[17] in italiano?

11 Io desidero molto parlarle,[18] ma io non[19] parlo italiano molto bene.

12 Lei parla inglese perfettamente.

13 No, signore, io lo[20] parlo un po' soltanto.

14 Perchè desidera imparare l'italiano lei?[15]

15 Perchè io desidero abitare in Italia.

FOOTNOTES: *1.* The infinitive of this verb is *desiderare,* a regular verb of the first conjugation. All first conjugation verbs end in *-are.* Here is the complete present tense: *io* (I) *desidero; tu* (you, familiar) *desideri; lei* (you, polite), *egli* (he), *ella* (she) *desidera; noi* (we) *desideriamo; voi* (you, familiar plural) *desiderate; loro* (you, polite plural), *essi* (they, masculine plural), *esse* (they, feminine plural) *desiderano.* There is only one form of the present in Italian. Thus, *io desidero* means "I wish," "I am wishing," "I do wish." *2. Un* (a, an) is one of the indefinite articles. The other indefinite articles are: *una, un'* (fem.); *uno* (masc.), before a singular noun beginning with *z* or *s-impura* (*s* followed by a consonant); *dei* (some, masc. pl.); *delle* (some, fem. pl.); *degli* (some, masc. pl.) before nouns beginning with *z, s'impura,* or a vowel. *3. Un po'* becomes *un po' di* when

PRONUNCIATION	TRANSLATION
1 EE'oh deh-ZEE-deh-roh ...	I wish ...
2 keh deh-ZEE-deh-rah, see-N'YOH-reh?	What do you wish, sir?
3 EE'oh deh-ZEE-deh-roh pahr-LAH-reh ee-tah-LYAH-noh.	I wish to speak Italian.
4 KEE deh-ZEE-deh-rah pahr-LAH-reh ee-tah-LYAH-noh?	Who wishes to speak Italian?
5 EH-l'yee deh-ZEE-deh-rah pahr-LAH-reh ee-tah-LYAH-noh.	He wishes to speak Italian.
6 LAY deh-ZEE-deh-rah pahr-LAH-reh lah LEEN-gwah een-GLEH-zeh?	Do you wish to speak the English language?
7 SEE, see-N'YOH-reh, EE'oh deh-ZEE-deh-roh pahr-LAHR-lah.	Yes, sir, I wish to speak it.
8 PAHR-lah LAY frahn-CHEH-zeh?	Do you speak French?
9 EE'oh PAHR-loh ee-tah-LYAH-noh eh AHN-keh frahn-CHEH-zeh.	I speak Italian and French also.
10 deh-ZEE-deh-rah LAY pahr-LAHR-mee een ee-tah-LYAH-noh?	Do you wish to speak to me in Italian?
11 EE'oh deh-ZEE-deh-roh MOHL-toh pahr-LAHR-leh, mah EE'oh nohn PAHR-loh ee-tah-LYAH-noh MOHL-toh BEH-neh.	I want very much to speak to you, but I don't speak Italian very well.
12 lay PAHR-lah een-GLEH-zeh pehr-feht-tah-MEHN-teh.	You speak English perfectly.
13 NOH, see-N'YOH-reh, EE'oh loh PAHR-lo oon POH sohl-TAHN-toh.	No, sir, I speak it only a little.
14 pehr-KEH deh-ZEE-deh-rah eem-pah-RAH-reh lee-tah-LYAH-noh lay?	Why do you wish to learn Italian?
15 pehr-KEH EE'oh deh-ZEE-deh-roh ah-bee-TAH-reh een ee-TAH-lyah.	Because I wish to live in Italy.

followed by a noun. *4.* The definite article "the" has several forms in Italian: *il* (masc.); *la* (fem.); *l'* (before a masc. or fem. noun beginning with a vowel); *lo* (before a masc. noun beginning with *z* or *s-impura*); *i* (masc. pl.); *le* (fem. pl.); *gli* (masc. pl. before *z*, *s-impura*, or a vowel). *5.* Note that "business" in Italian is plural. *6. Parlarlo* is a combination of *parlare* and *lo*. *Lo* is a direct object pronoun meaning "it" and is attached to the infinitive, which drops the final *e*. All other direct and indirect object pronouns, except *loro*, are likewise attached to the infinitive. See also Note 20. *7.* Notice that in Italian the words for "my" *(il mio, la mia, i miei, le mie)* are preceded by the definite article. However, *il* and *la* are omitted if the words *mio* or *mia* are used before a noun denoting a relative or a member of the family. Ex.: *mio padre, mia zia, mio figlio.* *8.* The possessive

16 Abita negli[21] Stati Uniti la sua famiglia?

17 No, signore, la mia famiglia abita nel[22] Canadà.

18 Dove abita sua sorella?

19 Mia sorella e mio fratello abitano nel[22] Belgio.

20 È italiana sua moglie?

21 No, signore, mia moglie è francese.[23]

22 È italiano suo figlio?

23 Sì, signore, mio figlio è italiano.

24 Chi è italiano?

25 Mio cugino è italiano.

26 Desidera andare in Italia?[15]

27 No, egli desidera andare negli Stati Uniti.

28 Prende[24] il treno per[25] andare in Francia?

29 No, per andare in Francia io prendo il piroscafo o l'aeroplano.

30 Desidera fare un viaggio[26] in automobile suo padre?

adjectives *il suo, la sua, i suoi, le sue* mean "your, his, her." The possessive adjective always agrees with the "thing" possessed. The definite articles *il* and *la* are omitted as explained in Note 7. *9. Andare* is an irregular verb and is not conjugated like *desiderare.* Its present tense is *io vado; tu vai; lei, egli, ella va; noi andiamo; voi andate; loro, essi, esse vanno.* *10.* The suffixes *-ino* and *-ina* are often used in Italian to denote smallness and grace. *11.* Nouns and adjectives denoting nationality or language are not capitalized in Italian. Nouns of countries are, however, capitalized. *12.* The word *lei* is omitted because the word *signore* makes the meaning clear. *13. Parlare* alone means "to speak;" therefore no preposition is needed before it. *14.* In questions, the subject (noun or pronoun) may be placed immediately after the verb or at the end of the sen-

16 AH-bee-tah NEH-l'yee STAH-tee OO-NEE-tee lah soo'ah fah-MEE-l'yah?

Does your family live in the United States?

17 NOH, see-N'YOH-reh, lah MEE'ah fah-MEE-l'yah AH-bee-tah nehl cah-nah-DAH.

No, sir, my family lives in Canada.

18 DOH-veh AH-bee-tah soo'ah soh-REHL-lah?

Where does your sister live?

19 MEE'ah soh-REHL-lah eh MEE'oh frah-TEHL-loh AH-bee-tah-noh nehl BEHL-joh.

My sister and my brother live in Belgium.

20 EH ee-tah-LYAH-nah soo'ah MOH-l'yeh?

Is your wife Italian?

21 NOH, see-N'YOH-reh, MEE'ah MOH-l'yeh EH frahn-CHEH-zeh.

No, sir, my wife is French.

22 EH ee-tah-LYAH-noh soo'oh FEE-l'yoh?

Is your son Italian?

23 SEE, see-N'YOH-reh, MEE'oh FEE-l'yoh EH ee-tah-LYAH-noh.

Yes, sir, my son is Italian.

24 kee EH ee-tah-LYAH-noh?

Who is Italian?

25 MEE'oh koo-JEE-noh EH ee-tah-LYAH-noh.

My cousin is Italian.

26 deh-ZEE-deh-rah ahn-DAH-reh een ee-TAH-lyah?

Does he wish to go to Italy?

27 NOH, EH-l'yee deh-ZEE-deh-rah ahn--DAH-reh NEH-l'yee STAH-tee OO-NEE-tee.

No, he wishes to go to the United States.

28 PREHN-deh eel TREH-noh pehr ahn-DAH-reh een FRAHN-chah?

Do you take the train to go to France?

29 NOH, pehr ahn-DAH-reh een FRAHN-chah EE'oh PREHN-doh eel pee-ROH-skah-foh oh lah'eh-roh-PLAH-noh.

No, to go to France I take the boat or the airplane.

30 deh-ZEE-deh-rah FAH-reh oon vee-AH-djoh een ah'oo-toh-MOH-bee-leh soo'oh PAH-dreh?

Does your father want to take an automobile trip (*literally,* a trip in automobile) ?

tence. However, sometimes it is left before the verb, the inflection of the voice indicating that it is a question. *15.* See Note 6. *16.* When the name of a language follows any form of the verb *parlare* the definite article is not used. All other verbs, however, require the article. *17. Mi* is both a direct and an indirect object pronoun. It means "me" or "to me." *18. Le* is an indirect object pronoun and means "to you" or "to her." *19.* In Italian a verb is made negative by putting *non* before it. *20. Lo* in this case means "it." (It also means "him.") It is a direct object pronoun. All direct and indirect object pronouns, except *loro,* precede any form of a verb except the infinitive (see Note 6), the present participle, and some forms of the imperative. *21. Negli* is a contraction of *in* and *gli.* Most masculine names of countries require the definite article after the preposition *in.*

31 Sì, signore, il viaggio in automobile è molto interessante.

32 Quando parte[27] il treno?

33 Il treno parte di[28] mattina.

34 Perchè desidera andare in Inghilterra?

35 Io desidero andarci[29] per affari.

36 Desidera andarci solo?

37 No, io desidero andarci con la mia famiglia.

38 Perchè desidera andarci con la sua famiglia?

39 Perchè io non desidero viaggiare solo.

40 Quando parte sua madre?

41 Mia madre desidera partire subito.

42 Mio zio abita in Inghilterra.

43 È inglese suo zio?

44 No, signore, egli è spagnuolo.

45 Mia zia è russa.

46 Parla ella la lingua russa?

47 Sì, la[30] parla. Parla lei il russo?

48 No, signore, ma è una lingua molto interessante.

49 Io desidero imparare l'inglese.

22. *Nel* is a contraction of *in* and *il. Canadà* is masculine. See Note 21. 23. Adjectives ending in *e* are both masculine and feminine. Those ending in *o* are masculine and form the feminine by changing *o* to *a.* 24. The infinitive of this verb is *prendere*, which is a verb of the second conjugation. The present tense is: *io prendo; tu prendi; lei, egli, ella prende; noi prendiamo; voi prendete; loro, essi, esse prendono.* 25. If "to" can be replaced by "in order to," it is translated as *per* before an infinitive. 26. *Fare un viaggio* is an idiom. Literally it means "to make a trip." *Fare* is an irregular verb. Its present tense is: *io faccio; tu fai; lei,*

31 SEE, see-N'YOH-reh, eel vee-AH-djoh een ah'oo-toh-MOH-bee-leh EH MOHL-to een-teh-rehs-SAHN-teh.

Yes, sir, the automobile trip is very interesting.

32 KWAN-doh PAHR-teh eel TREH-noh?

When does the train leave?

33 eel TREH-noh PAHR-teh dee maht-TEE-nah.

The train leaves in the morning.

34 pehr-KEH deh-ZEE-deh-rah ahn-DAH-reh een een-geel-TEHR-rah?

Why do you wish to go to England?

35 deh-ZEE-deh-roh ahn-DAHR-chee pehr ahf-FAH-ree.

I wish to go there on business (*lit.*, for business).

36 deh-ZEE-deh-rah ahn-DAHR-chee SOH-loh?

Do you wish to go there alone?

37 NOH, EE'oh deh-ZEE-deh-roh ahn-DAHR-chee kohn lah MEE'ah fah-MEE-l'yah.

No, I wish to go there with my family.

38 pehr-keh deh-ZEE-deh-rah ahn-DAHR-chee kohn lah soo'ah fah-MEE-l'yah?

Why do you wish to go there with your family?

39 pehr-KEH EE'oh nohn deh-ZEE-deh-roh vee-ah-DJAH-reh SOH-loh.

Because I don't wish to travel alone.

40 KWAHN-doh PAHR-teh soo'ah MAH-dreh.

When does your mother leave?

41 MEE'ah MAH-dreh deh-ZEE-deh-rah pahr-TEE-reh soo-bee-toh.

My mother wants to leave soon.

42 MEE'oh DZEE'oh AH-bee-tah een een-geel-TEHR-rah.

My uncle lives in England.

43 EH een-GLEH-zeh soo'oh DZEE'oh?

Is your uncle English?

44 NOH, see-N'YOH-reh, EH-l'yee EH span-N'YWOH-loh.

No, sir, he is Spanish.

45 MEE'ah DZEE'ah EH ROOS-sah.

My aunt is Russian.

46 PAHR-lah EHL-lah lah LEEN-gwah ROOS-sah?

Does she speak Russian?

47 SEE, lah PAHR-lah. PAHR-lah LAY eel ROOS-soh?

Yes, she speaks it (*lit.*, she it speaks). Do you speak Russian?

48 NOH, see-N'YOH-reh, mah EH oo-nah LEENN-gwah MOHL-toh een-teh-rehs-SAHN-teh.

No, sir, but it is a very interesting language.

49 EE'oh deh-ZEE-deh-roh eem-pah-RAH-reh leen-GLEH-zeh.

I want to learn English.

---

egli, ella fa; noi facciamo; voi fate; loro, essi, esse fanno. 27. The infinitive of this verb is *partire*, a regular verb of the third conjugation. The present tense is: *io parto; tu parti; lei, egli, ella parte; noi partiamo; voi partite; loro, essi, esse partono.* 28. *Di* means "of." Used with *mattina*, however, it means "in the." 29. *Ci* is an adverbial pronoun meaning "there," and, like other pronouns, it is attached to the infinitive. 30. *La* in this case means "it" (fem.). See Note 2.

Seconda Lezione

SECOND LESSON   (seh-KOHN-dah leh-TSYOH-neh)

Vocabolario per Questa Lezione

la sala da[1] pranzo (SAH-lah dah PRAHN-dzoh)		dining room
di buon'ora[2] (dee bwohn-OH-rah)		early
generalmente (jeh-neh-rahl-MEHN-teh)		ordinarily
accompagnare (ahk-kohm-pah-N'YAH-reh)		to accompany

dolce (DOHL-cheh)	sweet, soft	la tazza (TAH-tsah)	cup
amaro (ah-MAH-roh)	bitter	il gusto (GOO-stoh)	taste
c'è (cheh)	there is	ci sono (chee SOH-noh)	there are

mi dispiace[3] (mee dee-SPYAH-cheh)	I am sorry
vuole?[4] (VWOH-leh)	will you, do you want?
io devo[5] (EE'oh DEH-voh)	I must, I have to

grazie (GRAH-tsee'eh)	thank you	prima[7] (PREE-mah)	before
tardi (TAHR-dee)	late	dopo[7] (DOH-poh)	after
io bevo[6] (BEH-voh)	I drink	adesso (ah-DEHS-soh)	now
vendere (VEHN-deh-reh)	to sell	a (ah)	to, at
il prezzo (PREH-tsoh)	price	le piace? (leh PYAH-cheh)	do you like?
più (pyoo)	more	da (dah)	from
buono (BWOH-noh)	good	invece[8] (een-VEH-cheh)	instead

io posso[9] (POHS-soh)	I can, I may, I am able to
mi piace[10] (mee PYAH-cheh)	I like
abbastanza (ahb-bah-STAHN-tsah)	enough

il bicchiere (beek-KYEH-reh)	glass	il cappello (kahp-PEHL-loh)	hat
mangiare (mahn-JAH-reh)	to eat	comprare (kohm-PRAH-reh)	to buy
la via (lah VEE'ah)	street	preferire (preh-feh-REE-reh)	to prefer

34

I CIBI ed I PASTI

FOODS AND MEALS   (ee CHEE-bee ed ee PAH-stee)

il pasto (PAH-stoh)   meal
il pranzo[11] (PRAHN-dzoh)   dinner
la cena (CHEH-nah)   supper
la colazione (koh-lah-TSYOH-neh)   breakfast, lunch
la colazione del mezzogiorno   lunch
     (. . . dehl meh-dzoh-JOHR-noh)

l'acqua (LAHK-kwah)   water   la carne (KAHR-neh)   meat
il vino (VEE-noh)   wine   la pecora (PEH-koh-rah) sheep
il latte (LAHT-teh)   milk   il maiale (mah-YAH-leh) pork
il caffè (kahf-FEH)   coffee, cafe il bue (BOO'eh)   ox, beef
il tè (teh)   tea   la vitella (vee-TEHL-lah) veal

il pollo (POHL-loh)   chicken
il pollo arrosto (ahr-ROH-stoh)   roast chicken
il pollo alla cacciatora (kah-chah-TOH-rah)   chicken fricassee
l'agnello (lah-N'YEHL-loh)   lamb

la costoletta (koh-stoh-LEHT-tah)   chop
il castrato (kah-STRAH-toh)   mutton
l'arrosto (lahr-ROH-stoh)   roast
arrostito (ahr-roh-STEE-toh)   roasted
il prosciutto (proh-SHOOT-toh)   Italian ham
il burro (BOOR-roh)   butter

i legumi (leh-GOO-mee) vegetables   la torta (TOHR-tah)   cake, pie
duro (DOO-roh)   tough, hard fritto (FREET-toh)   fried
il brodo (BROH-doh)   thin soup   il pesce (PEH-sheh)   fish
il dolce (DOHL-cheh)   dessert   il pane (PAH-neh)   bread

ben cotto (behn KOHT-toh)   well cooked
la marmellata (mahr-mehl-LAH-tah)   jam
il panino[12] (pah-NEE-noh)   roll
il formaggio (fohr-MAH-djoh)   cheese
un uovo bollito (WOH-voh bohl-LEE-toh)   a soft-boiled egg
la verdura[13] (vehr-DOO-rah)   green vegetables
la frutta[14] (FROOT-tah)   fruit
lo zucchero (DZOOK-keh-roh)   sugar

la cioccolata (chohk-koh-LAH-tah)   chocolate
di ottima[15] qualità (dee OHT-tee-mah kwah-lee-TAH) of excellent quality
a prezzi moderati (ah PREH-tsee moh-deh-RAH-tee)   reasonably priced

CONVERSATION

1 Io faccio colazione.[16]

2 A che ora fa colazione lei?

3 Faccio[17] colazione di buon'ora.

4 In che[18] consiste generalmente la sua colazione?

5 La mia colazione generalmente consiste di una tazza di caffelatte[19] o di cioccolata, ed[20] un panino con marmellata.

6 Andiamo[21] nella sala da pranzo.

7 Desidera mangiare adesso o prima di partire?

8 Preferisco mangiare più tardi.[22]

9 Che cosa mangia a pranzo?

10 Il martedì,[23] generalmente, io mangio due costolette di vitella o di agnello ben cotte.

FOOTNOTES: *1. Lit.*, the hall for dinner. *2. Lit.*, of a good hour. This is an idiom. An idiom is a unique expression to which the general rules of grammar do not apply. An idiom is not to be translated literally. *3. Lit.*, it is displeasing to me. *4.* This is a form of the present of the verb *volere*, an irregular verb, whose present is: *io voglio; tu vuoi; lei, egli, ella vuole; noi vogliamo; voi volete; loro, essi, esse vogliono. 5.* This is a form of the verb *dovere*, an irregular verb, whose present is: *io devo, tu devi, lei deve, noi dobbiamo, voi dovete, loro devono.* NOTE: Inasmuch as the verb forms for *lei, egli, ella* and *loro, essi, esse* are the same, only the *lei* and *loro* forms will be given from now on. *6.* The infinitive of *bevo* is *bere*, but the present tense, which is regular, is conjugated from the old form *bevere. 7. prima* and *dopo* are followed by *di* when a noun, pronoun, or verb follows. *8. invece* is followed by *di* before a noun, pronoun, or verb. *9.* This is a form of *potere*, an irregular verb, whose present is: *io posso, tu puoi,*

PRONUNCIATION	TRANSLATION
1 EE'oh FAH-tchoh koh-lah-TSYOH-neh.	I have breakfast.
2 ah keh OH-rah fah koh-lah-TSYOH-neh LAY?	At what time do you have breakfast?
3 EE'oh FAH-tchoh koh-lah-TSYOH-neh dee bwoh-NOH-rah.	I have breakfast early.
4 een keh kohn-SEE-steh jeh-neh-rahl-MEHN-teh lah soo'ah koh-lah-TSYOH-neh?	What does your breakfast generally consist of (*lit.*, in)?
5 lah MEE'ah koh-lah-TSYOH-neh jeh-neh-rahl-MEHN-teh kohn-SEE-steh dee oo-nah TAH-tsah dee kahf-feh-LAHT-teh oh dee chok-koh-LAH-tah, ed oon pah-NEE-noh kohn mahr-mehl-LAH-tah.	My breakfast generally consists of a cup of coffee with milk, or chocolate and a roll with jam.
6 ahn-DYAH-moh NEHL-lah SAH-lah dah PRAHN-dzoh.	Let us go into the dining room.
7 deh-ZEE-deh-rah mahn-JAH-reh ah-DEHS-soh oh PREE-mah dee pahr-TEE-reh?	Do you wish to eat now or before leaving?
8 preh-feh-REE-skoh mahn-JAH-reh PYOO TAHR-dee.	I prefer to eat later.
9 keh KOH-zah MAHN-jah ah PRAHN-dzoh?	What do you have for dinner (*lit.*, eat at dinner) ?
10 eel mahr-teh-DEE, jeh-neh-rahl-MEHN-teh EE'oh MAHN-joh DOO'eh koh-stoh-LEHT-teh dee vee-TEHL-lah oh dee ah-N'YEHL-loh behn KOHT-teh.	On Tuesdays, ordinarily, I eat two veal or lamb chops well done (*lit.*, cooked).

lei può, noi possiamo, voi potete, loro possono. *10. Lit.*, it is pleasing to me. *11.* Normally *il pranzo* is the noon meal. However, if it is not a complete dinner the expression *colazione* or *colazione del mezzogiorno* is used. *12. Panino* is a diminutive form of *pane* (bread). *Lit.*, it means "little bread." *13. Verdura* is a generic word to indicate any green vegetable or vegetables. *14. La frutta* means "the fruit" or "fruits of a tree." In a figurative sense *il frutto* and *i frutti* are used. *15. Ottimo* (fem. *ottima*) is the absolute superlative form of *buono.* See Reference Grammar. *16. Fare colazione* is an idiom. *17.* Notice the omission of the subject pronoun *io.* Subject pronouns are often omitted in Italian. *18. In che lit.* means "in what." *19. Caffelatte* is composed of *caffè* and *latte.* Notice *caffè* loses its accent mark. In Italian accents are used only on the final vowel of a word. *20.* The conjunction *e* usually becomes *ed* before a vowel. *21.* This is the *noi* form of the imperative of *andare.* The personal pronouns are omitted in the

11 A mezzogiorno io non faccio un pranzo[24] completo. Mangio soltanto un uovo[25] bollito ed un po' di verdura, o del[26] prosciutto con insalata.

12 Non le piace[27] la carne di maiale?[28]

13 Sì, ma preferisco[29] il castrato.[30]

14 Posso offrirle del pollo arrosto? Questo pollo è molto tenero.

15 Grazie, ma prima prenderò[31] un po' di minestrone[32] invece dell'[33] antipasto.[34]

16 Questo arrosto di bue non è molto tenero.

17 Il pesce, invece, è veramente squisito.

18 Che desidera a pranzo?

19 Carne, insalata, pane e burro.[35]

20 E poi?

21 Non so.[36] Che cosa mi consiglia lei?

---

imperative.   *22. Più tardi* is a comparative form. In Italian the comparative is formed by adding *più* (more) or *meno* (less) before an adverb or an adjective. *23.* Before days of the week *il* means "on." It indicates habitual occurrence. *24. Faccio un pranzo* is an idiom. The verb *pranzare* may be used instead. *25.* The plural of *l'uovo* is *le uova.*   *26. del* is a contraction of *di* and *il.* It means "some" or "of the."   *27.* Literal meaning of *le piace* is "it is pleasing to you." It also means "she likes."   *28. Lit.,* meat of pig.   *29. Preferisco* is a form of the present of *preferire,* a regular *-isco* verb of the third conjugation (see Reference Grammar). The present is: *io preferisco, tu preferisci, lei preferisce, noi preferiamo, voi preferite, loro preferiscono. 30. Il castrato.* Notice that the definite article is used when a noun is used in a general sense.   *31.* This is a

11 ah meh-dzoh-JOHR-noh EE'oh nohn FAH-choh oon PRAHN-dzoh kohm-PLEH-toh. MAHN-joh sohl-TAHN-toh oon WOH-voh bohl-LEE-toh ed oon POH dee vehr-DOO-rah, oh dehl proh-SHOOT-toh kohn een-sah-LAH-tah.

At noon I don't have a complete dinner. I eat only a boiled egg and some green vegetables, or some Italian ham with salad.

12 nohn leh PYAH-cheh lah KAHR-neh dee mah-YAH-leh?

Don't you like pork?

13 SEE, mah preh-feh-REE-skoh eel kah-STRAH-toh.

Yes, but I prefer mutton.

14 POHS-soh ohf-FREER-leh dehl POHL-loh ahr-ROH-stoh? KWEH-stoh POHL-loh EH MOHL-toh TEH-neh-roh.

May I offer you some roast chicken? This chicken is very tender.

15 GRAH-tsyeh, mah PREE-mah prehn-deh-ROH oon POH dee mee-neh-STROH-neh een-VEH-cheh dehl-lahn-tee-PAH-stoh.

Thank you, but first I shall have some minestrone soup instead of the appetizer.

16 KWEH-stoh ahr-ROH-stoh dee BOO'-eh nohn EH MOHL-toh TEH-neh-roh.

This roast beef is not very tender.

17 eel PEH-sheh, een-VEH-cheh, EH veh-rah-MEHN-teh skwee-ZEE-toh.

The fish, on the other hand, is really delicious.

18 keh deh-ZEE-deh-rah ah PRAHN-dzoh?

What do you wish to have for dinner?

19 KAHR-neh, een-sah-LAH-tah, PAH-neh eh BOOR-roh.

Meat, salad, bread and butter.

20 eh POY?

And then? (What next?)

21 nohn SOH. keh KOH-zah mee kohn-SEE-l'yah LAY?

I don't know. What do you suggest (*lit.*, What do you advise me)?

---

form of the future of *prendere: io prenderò, tu prenderai, lei prenderà, noi prenderemo, voi prenderete, loro prenderanno.* The endings, *erò, erai, erà, eremo, erete, eranno,* are the same for all regular verbs of the first and second conjugations. 32. *Minestrone* is a very thick soup made with several vegetables. 33. *Dell'* is a contraction of *di* and *l'* and means "some" or "of the." 34. *Antipasto* (*lit.,* before meal) is a delectable dish usually consisting of lettuce, tomato, peppers, beets, salami, anchovies, cheese, etc. 35. The partitive articles such as "some, any," etc., are often omitted for the sake of simplicity, especially when words are used in a series. 36. *So* is a form of the irregular verb *sapere,* whose present is: *io so, tu sai, lei sa, noi sappiamo, voi sapete, loro sanno.* 37. *Abbiamo* is a form of the irregular verb *avere* whose present is: *io ho, tu hai, lei ha, noi abbiamo, voi*

22 Abbiamo[37] del formaggio fresco e piccante, della frutta secca e dei pasticcini.

23 Preferisco pane e formaggio.

24 Desidera del tè?

25 No, dopo il pasto preferisco prendere una tazza di caffè.

26 Beve vino durante il pasto?

27 Generalmente bevo un bicchiere di vino e un bicchier[38] d'acqua.

28 È abbastanza dolce il caffè, o è ancora un po' amaro?

29 È abbastanza dolce, grazie.

30 Vuole accompagnarmi a teatro[39] dopo il pranzo?

31 Mi dispiace moltissimo doverla lasciare, ma debbo[40] comprare un cappello.

32 In questa strada c'è una buona cappelleria.

33 Si vendono[41] dei[42] buoni cappelli là?

34 Sì, signore, i cappelli sono di ottima qualità ed i prezzi ragionevoli.[43]

---

avete, loro hanno. 38. The final e is often dropped for the sake of euphony. 39. A teatro. An idiom. It means "to the theater." 40. Debbo is an alternate form for devo. See Note 5. 41. Si vendono is an impersonal expression. Vendono agrees with cappelli. Lit., are good hats sold there. 42. Dei is a contraction of

22 ahb-BYAH-moh dehl fohr-mah-DJOH FREH-skoh eh peek-KAHN-teh, DEHL-lah FROOT-tah SEHK-kah eh day pah-stee-CHEE-nee.

We have some fresh, sharp cheese, dry fruit, and pastry.

23 preh-feh-REE-skoh PAH-neh eh fohr-mah-DJOH.

I prefer bread and cheese.

24 deh-ZEE-deh-rah dehl TEH?

Do you want tea?

25 NOH, DOH-poh eel PAH-stoh preh-feh-REE-skoh PREHN-deh-reh oo-nah TAH-tsah dee kahf-FEH.

No, after the meal I prefer to have (*lit.,* take) a cup of coffee.

26 BEH-veh VEE-noh doo-RAHN-teh eel PAH-stoh?

Do you drink wine with your meal (*lit.,* during the meal)?

27 jeh-neh-rahl-MEHN-teh BEH-voh oon beek-KYEH-reh dee VEE-noh eh oon beek-KYEHR DAHK-kwah.

Ordinarily I drink a glass of wine and a glass of water.

28 EH ahb-bah-STAHN-tsah DOHL-cheh eel kahf-FEH, oh EH ahn-KOH-rah oon POH ah-MAH-roh?

Is the coffee sweet enough, or is it still a little bitter?

29 EH ahb-bah-STAHN-tsah DOHL-cheh, GRAH-tsyeh.

It is sweet enough, thank you.

30 vwoh-leh ahk-kohm-pah-N'YAHR-mee ah teh-AH-troh DOH-poh eel PRAHN-dzoh?

Do you wish to go to the theater with me (*lit.,* accompany me)?

31 mee dee-SPYAH-cheh mohl-TEES-see-moh doh-VEHR-lah lah-SHAH-reh, mah DEHB-boh kohm-PRAH-reh oon kahp-PEHL-loh.

I am very sorry I have to leave you, but I must buy a hat.

32 een KWEH-stah STRAH-dah CHEH oo-nah BWOH-nah kahp-pehl-leh-REE-ah.

In this street there is a good hat store.

33 see VEHN-doh-noh day BWOH-nee kahp-PEHL-lee LAH?

Do they sell good hats there?

34 SEE, see-N'YOH-reh, ee kahp-PEHL-lee SOH-noh dee OHT-tee-mah kwah-lee-TAH ed ee PREH-tsee rah-joh-NEH-voh-lee.

Yes, sir. The hats are of excellent quality and the prices reasonable.

---

di and *i.* It means "some" or "of the." adjectives in Italian follow the noun they modify and agree with it in gender and number. 43. *Ragionevoli* is an adjective. Most

Terza Lezione

THIRD LESSON (TEHR-tsah leh-TSYOH-neh)

Vocabolario per Questa Lezione

quanto costa? (KWAHN-toh KOH-stah)		how much does it cost?
a buon mercato[1] (ah BWOHN mehr-KAH-toh)		cheap, inexpensive
aver bisogno di[2] (ah-VEHR bee-ZOH-n'yoh dee)		to need
è necessario[3] (EH neh-chehs-SAH-ryoh)		it is necessary
non è vero[4]? (nohn EH VEH-roh)		is it not so?
beninteso (behn-een-TEH-zoh)		of course

il denaro (deh-NAH-roh)	money
costare (koh-STAH-reh)	to cost
caro (KAH-roh)	dear, expensive

il giorno (JOHR-noh)	day	**buona sera** (BWOH-nah ...)	good evening
buon[5] **giorno** (bwohn ...)	good day, hello	**la notte** (NOHT-teh)	night
la sera (SEH-rah)	evening	**buona notte** (BWOH-nah ...)	good night
la serata[6] (seh-RAH-tah)	evening, evening party		

il negozio (neh-GOH-tsyoh)	store
il passeggio (pahs-SEH-djoh)	the walk, walking
cupo (KOO-poh)	dark, deep (in reference to color)
differente[7] (deef-feh-REHN-teh)	different
elegante (eh-leh-GAHN-teh)	elegant, stylish
ecco (EHK-koh)	here is, there is, here are, there are

alto (AHL-toh)	high, tall	**lungo** (LOON-goh)	long
basso (BAHS-soh)	low, short	**lo stesso** (STEHS-soh)	same
corto (KOHR-toh)	short	**troppo** (TROHP-poh)	too much
largo (LAHR-goh)	large, wide	**alcuni** (ahl-KOO-nee)	some (m.)
stretto (STREHT-toh)	narrow, tight	**alcune** (ahl-KOO-neh)	some (f.)

42

VESTIARIO e CALZATURE

CLOTHING AND FOOTWEAR   (veh-stee'AH-ryoh eh kahl-tsah-TOO-reh)

il vestito (veh-STEE-toh)	suit	la veste (VEH-steh)	dress
la giacca (JAHK-kah)	jacket	il guanto (GWAHN-toh)	glove
la manica (MAH-nee-kah)	sleeve	la maglia (MAH-l'yah)	sweater
la calza (KAHL-tsah)	stocking	la pelle (PEHL-leh)	leather, skin
la scarpa (SKAHR-pah)	shoe	la seta (SEH-tah)	silk

il cappello (kahp-PEHL-loh)	hat
il berretto (behr-REHT-toh)	cap
la cravatta (krah-VAHT-tah)	necktie
la camicia (kah-MEE-chah)	shirt
il panciotto (pahn-CHOHT-toh)	vest
i calzoni (kahl-TSOH-nee)	trousers
il soprabito (soh-PRAH-bee-toh)	overcoat

il polsino (pohl-SEE-noh)	cuff (of a shirt)
il fazzoletto (fah-tsoh-LEHT-toh)	handkerchief
il calzino (kahl-TSEE-noh)	sock
la pantofola (pahn-TOH-foh-lah)	slipper
la gonnella (gohn-NEHL-lah)	skirt
la camicetta (kah-mee-CHEHT-tah)	blouse

l'impermeabile (leem-pehr-meh-AH-bee-leh)	raincoat
la biancheria intima[8] (byahn-keh-REE'ah EEN-tee-mah)	underwear
le mutande (moo-TAHN-deh)	underwear, shorts
la sottana (soht-TAH-nah)	slip, petticoat
la panciera (pahn-CHYEH-rah)	girdle
il reggipetto (reh-djee-PEHT-toh)	brassiere
la borsetta (bohr-SEHT-tah)	handbag
il portamonete[9] (pohr-tah-moh-NEH-teh)	change purse
l'abito a giacca (LAH-bee-toh ah JAHK-kah)	tailored suit (for a woman)
il tessuto (tehs-SOO-toh)	cloth, fabric
la stoffa (STOHF-fah)	material, cloth

il cotone (koh-TOH-neh)	cotton	il tacco (TAHK-koh)	heel
la lana (LAH-nah)	wool	il colore (koh-LOH-reh)	color
il feltro (FEHL-troh)	felt	analogo (ah-NAH-loh-goh)	matching
la suola (SWOH-lah)	sole	il velo (VEH-loh)	veil

CONVERSATION

1 Buon giorno, signore. Buona sera, signora. Buona notte, bambino mio.

2 Di che cosa parlavano[10] quando io sono entrato?[11]

3 Parlavamo di vestiario e di calzature.

4 Lei ha[12] un vestito che le sta[13] a pennello.[14]

5 Grazie. La stoffa è buona, ma la giacca mi sembra troppo lunga ed il panciotto troppo corto.

6 Le vanno bene[15] i calzoni?

7 Sì, i calzoni mi vanno benissimo.

8 Ho bisogno d'un[16] soprabito, d'un cappello e d'un paio[17] di guanti.

9 In questo negozio può[18] comprare tutto quello di cui[19] ha bisogno: cravatte, fazzoletti, camicie e calzini.

10 Ha anche bisogno di mutande?

FOOTNOTES: *1. A buon mercato* is an idiom. *Mercato* means "market."   *2. Aver bisogno di*, "to have need of," is an idiom. The word *di* is used when a noun, pronoun, or verb follows.   *3. È necessario*—"it is necessary." The word *it* is not translated when it is the subject of a verb.   *4.* The Italian expression *non è vero* is used to translate such English expressions as "isn't it true," "isn't that so," "aren't we," etc. The expected answer is "yes."   *5. Buon* is one of the adjectives which normally precedes the noun. Notice that *buono* becomes *buon* before a singular masculine noun.   *6. La serata* instead of *la sera* is used to express the duration of the evening, or the events which took place in the course of the evening. *7.* Adjectives which end in *e* are both masculine and feminine.   *8. La biancheria intima. Lit.*, the intimate linens.   *9. Portamonete* is composed of the words *porta* (carries) and *monete* (coins).   *10.* This is a form of the imperfect of the

PRONUNCIATION	TRANSLATION
1 bwohn JOHR-noh, see-N'YOH-reh. BWOH-nah SEH-rah, see-N'YOH-rah. BWOH-nah NOHT-teh, bahm-BEE-noh MEE'oh.	Good day, sir. Good evening, madam. Good night, my child.
2 dee keh COH-zah pahr-LAH-vah-noh KWAHN-doh EE'oh SOH-noh ehn-TRAH-toh?	What were you talking about when I came in?
3 pahr-lah-VAH-moh dee veh-stee' AH-ryoh eh dee kahl-tsah-TOO-reh.	We were talking about clothes and footwear.
4 lay AH oon veh-STEE-toh keh leh STAH ah pehn-NEHL-loh.	You have a suit which fits you perfectly.
5 GRAH-tsyeh. lah STOHF-fah EH BWOH-nah, mah lah JAHK-kah mee SEHM-brah TROHP-poh LOON-gah ed eel pahn-CHOHT-toh TROHP-poh KOHR-toh.	Thank you. The material is good, but the coat seems too long to me, and the vest too short.
6 leh VAHN-noh BEH-neh ee kahl-TSOH-nee?	Do the trousers fit you well?
7 SEE, ee kahl-TSOH-nee mee VAHN-no beh-NEES-see-moh.	Yes, the trousers fit me very well.
8 oh bee-ZOH-n'yoh doon soh-PRAH-bee-toh, doon kahp-PEHL-loh eh doon PAH-yoh dee GWAHN-tee.	I need an overcoat, a hat, and a pair of gloves.
9 een KWEH-stoh neh-GOH-tsyoh PWOH kohm-PRAH-reh TOOT-toh KWEHL-loh dee KOOy ah bee-ZOH-n'yoh: krah-VAHT-teh, fah-tsoh-LEHT-tee, kah-MEE-cheh eh kahl-TSEE-nee.	In this store you can buy everything you need: neckties, handkerchiefs, shirts, and socks.
10 ah AHN-keh bee-ZOH-n'yoh dee moo-TAHN-deh?	Do you need underwear also?

first conjugation: *io parlavo, tu parlavi, lei parlava, noi parlavamo, voi parlavate, loro parlavano.* For the use of this tense see Reference Grammar.   *11.* This is a form of the present perfect *(passato prossimo).* It is used to express an action which took place recently. *Entrare* is one of the few verbs which takes the present of *essere* (to be) as an auxiliary. The great majority of verbs take instead the present of *avere* (to have). See Note 12.   *12.* This is a form of the present of *avere: io ho, tu hai, lei ha, noi abbiamo, voi avete, loro hanno.* REMINDER: the *h* is silent. *13. Sta* is a form of the irregular verb *stare* (to stay), whose present is: *io sto, tu stai, lei sta, noi stiamo, voi state, loro stanno.*   *14. Le sta a pennello* is an idiom and requires the indirect object. *Le* therefore is an indirect object pronoun, meaning "to you" The word *pennello* means "a painter's brush."   *15. Le vanno bene* is an idiom, and requires the indirect object.   *16. d'un* is a contraction of *di un.* The

11 Sì, ne[20] ho bisogno.

12 I polsini di questa camicia sono troppo lunghi.[21]

13 Desidero comprare un abito a giacca per mia moglie.

14 Che tessuto preferisce?

15 Preferisco un buon tessuto che non costi[22] troppo.

16 Desidera una gonnella ed una camicetta analoghe?

17 Beninteso. Le preferisco di un colore unito, ma cupo.

18 Abbiamo degli[23] abiti da[24] sera e dei vestiti da[24] passeggio molto eleganti.

19 Quanto costa questo cappello di feltro?

20 Questo cappello è caro, ma questo berretto è a buon mercato.

21 La signorina Borgese desidera comprare una sottana e delle[25] calze, non è vero?

22 Sì, ed ho anche bisogno di una panciera e di un reggipetto.

---

apostrophe is used in lieu of the first vowel to avoid two vowels coming together. This process is called apocopation. *17.* The plural of *paio* is *paia.* Ex: *due paia di scarpe*—"two pairs of shoes." *18.* *Può* is a form of the irregular verb *potere,* whose present is: *io posso, tu puoi, lei può, noi possiamo, voi potete, loro possono.* *19. Di cui ha bisogno. Lit.,* of which you have need. *Cui* is always preceded by a preposition, unless it means "whose,"—in which case it is preceded by the definite article. Ex.: *Il signore il cui figlio è qui*—"The gentleman whose son is here."

11 SEE neh oh bee-ZOH-n'yoh.

Yes, I need some.

12 ee pohl-SEE-nee dee KWEHS-tah kah-MEE-chah SOH-noh TROHP-poh LOON-gee.

The cuffs of this shirt are too long.

13 deh-ZEE-deh-roh kohm-PRAH-reh oon AH-bee-toh ah JAHK-kah pehr MEE'ah MOH-l'yeh.

I wish to buy a tailored suit for my wife.

14 keh tehs-soo-toh preh-feh-REE-sheh?

What material do you prefer?

15 preh-feh-REE-skoh oon BWOHN tehs-soo-toh keh nohn KOH-stee TROHP-poh.

I prefer a good material which is not too expensive.

16 deh-ZEE-deh-rah oo'nah gohn-NEHL-lah ed oo-nah kah-mee CHEHT-tah ah-NAH-loh-geh?

Do you wish a matching skirt and blouse?

17 beh-neen-TEH-zoh. leh preh-feh-REE-skoh dee oon koh-LOH-reh oo-NEE-toh mah KOO-poh.

Of course. I prefer them in the same color, but deep.

18 ahb-BYAH-moh DEH-l'yee AH-bee-tee dah SEH-rah eh day veh-STEE-tee dah pahs-SEH-djoh MOHL-toh eh-leh-GAHN-tee.

We have some very elegant evening dresses and street clothes.

19 KWAHN-toh KOH-stah KWEH-stoh kahp-PEHL-loh dee FEHL-troh?

How much does this felt hat cost?

20 KWEH-stoh kahp-PEHL-loh EH KAH-roh, mah KWEH-stoh behr-REHT-toh eh ah BWOHN mehr-KAH-toh.

This hat is expensive, but this cap is cheap.

21 lah see-n'yoh-REE-nah bohr-JEH-zeh deh-ZEE-deh-rah kohm-PRAH-reh oo-nah soht-TAH-nah eh DEHL-leh KAHL-tseh, nohn eh VEH-roh?

Miss Borgese wishes to buy a slip and some stockings, doesn't she?

22 SEE, ed oh AHN-keh bee-ZOH-n'yoh dee oo-nah pahn-CHEH-rah eh dee oon reh-djee-PEHT-toh.

Yes, and I also need a girdle and a brassiere.

---

20. *Ne* is a direct object pronoun meaning "of it, of them, some, some of it, some of them." Like other direct object pronouns it precedes the verb. 21. Words ending in *go* and *ga* normally take an *h* before the *e* or *i* of the plural. 22. *Costi* is a form of the present subjunctive of *costare*. The subjunctive in this case is used after an indefinite antecedent. See Reference Grammar. 23. *degli* is a contraction of *di* and *gli* and means "some" or "of the." 24. *da sera* (for use in the evening); *da passeggio* (used for walking). This is a special use of the word *da,* which nor-

23 Può dirmi dove posso comprare delle scarpe?

24 C'è un negozio di calzature all'angolo di questa strada che ha un vasto assortimento.

25 La signora Bianchi desidera comprare delle scarpe da ballo con tacchi[26] alti e suole sottili.[27]

26 E noi vogliamo comprare un paio di scarpe da passeggio e delle pantofole.

27 Queste scarpe sono un po' troppo strette. Potrebbe darmene un altro paio di un numero[28] più grande?

28 Certo, signora. Eccole.[29] Queste le vanno molto bene.

29 Desidera una borsetta in pelle?

30 Sì, vorrei[30] una borsetta con un portamonete per gli spiccioli,[31] perchè non ho dove metterli.[32]

---

mally means "from" or "at" (person's home, office, shop, etc.). 25. *delle* is a contraction of *di* and *le* and means "some" or "of the." 26. *Tacchi* is the plural of *tacco*. A great many words ending in *co* change to *chi* in the plural. 27. The singular of *sottili* is *sottile*. Nouns and adjectives ending in *e* change *e* to *i* to form the plural. 28. *Numero* ordinarily means "number." In this case it means

23 PWOH DEER-mee DOH-veh POS-soh kohm-PRAH-reh DEEHL-leh SKAHR-peh?

Can you tell me where I can buy some shoes?

24 CHEH oon neh-GOH-tsyoh dee kahl-tsah-TOO-reh ahl-LAHN-goh-loh dee KWEH-stah STRAH-dah keh ah oon VAH-stoh ahs-sohr-tee-MEHN-toh.

There is a shoe store at the corner of this street which has a large assortment.

25 lah see-N'YOH-rah BYAHN-kee deh-ZEE-deh-rah kohm-PRAH-reh DEHL-leh SKAHR-peh dah BAHL-loh kohn TAHK-kee AHL-tee eh SWOH-leh soht-TEE-lee.

Mrs. Bianco wishes to buy some dancing shoes with high heels and thin soles.

26 eh noy voh-L'YAH-moh kohm-PRAH-reh oon PAH-yoh dee SKAHR-peh dah pahs-SEH-djoh eh DEHL-leh pahn-TOH-foh-leh.

And we want to buy a pair of walking shoes and some slippers.

27 KWEH-steh SKAHR-peh SOH-noh oon POH TROHP-poh STREHT-teh. poh-TREHB-beh DAHR-meh-neh oon AHL-troh PAH-yoh dee oon NOO-meh-roh PYOO GRAHN-deh?

These shoes are a little too tight. Could you give me another pair a size larger?

28 CHEHR-toh, see-N'YOH-rah. EHK-koh-leh. KWEH-steh leh VAHN-noh MOHL-toh BEH-neh.

Of course, madam. Here they are. These fit you very well.

29 deh-ZEE-deh-rah oo-nah bohr-SEHT-tah een PEHL-leh?

Do you wish a leather handbag (lit., a handbag in leather)?

30 SEE, vohr-RAY oo-nah bohr-SEHT-tah kohn oon pohr-tah-moh-NEH-teh pehr l'yee SPEE-tchoh-lee, pehr-KEH nohn oh DOH-veh MEHT-tehr-lee.

Yes, I should like a handbag with a purse for my change, because I don't have a place to put it (lit., I don't have where to put them).

___

"size." 29. Eccole—"here they are" (lit., here are they). The le is a direct object pronoun. 30. Vorrei is a form of the conditional of the verb volere (to want). 31. Spiccioli is always used in the plural. 32. Non ho dove metterli. Notice the idiomatic construction of this sentence.

Quarta Lezione

Vocabolario per Questa Lezione

domani mattina (doh-MAH-nee maht-TEE-nah)	tomorrow morning
domani sera (doh-MAH-nee SEH-rah)	tomorrow evening
per piacere (pehr pyah-CHEH-reh)	please
vuole avere la bontà[1]	will you be kind enough
(VWOH-leh ah-VEH-reh lah bohn-TAH)	
trovarsi[2] (troh-VAHR-see)	to be, to be located
un chilo[3], **un chilogrammo** (kee-loh-GRAHM-moh)	a kilogram

imbarcarsi (eem-bahr-KAHR-see)	to embark, sail
l'arrivo (lahr-REE-voh)	arrival
la partenza (pahr-TEHN-tsah)	departure
visitare (vee-zee-TAH-reh)	to visit
veramente (veh-rah-MEHN-teh)	really, truly

si trova (see TROH-vah)	is located	**il tempo** (TEHM-poh)	time,
subito (soo-bee-toh)	quickly		weather
allora (ahl-LOH-rah)	then	**a tempo** (ah TEHM-poh)	on time
pesare (peh-ZAH-reh)	to weigh	**il corso** (KOHR-soh)	boulevard
già (JAH)	already	**valido** (VAH-lee-doh)	valid

un aeroporto (ah'eh-roh-POHR-toh)	an airport
atterrare (aht-tehr-RAH-reh)	to land
decollare (deh-kohl-LAH-reh)	to take off (aviation)
non ancora (ahn-KOH-rah)	not yet

la piazza (PYAH-tsah)	square	**sapere** (sah-PEH-reh)	to know
il nord (NOHRD)	north		(how)
primo (PREE-moh)	first	**io so** (SOH)	I know
presto (PREH-stoh)	soon	**il paese** (pah-EH-zeh)	country
altro (AHL-troh)	other	**poichè** (poy-KEH)	since
		pronto (PROHN-toh)	ready

50

MEZZI DI TRASPORTO

MEANS OF TRANSPORTATION (MEH-dzee dee trah-SPOHR-toh)

il treno (TREH-noh)	train
la stazione (stah-TSYOH-neh)	station
il biglietto (bee-L'YEHT-toh)	ticket
la carrozza (kahr-ROH-tsah)	railroad car
la ferrovia[4] (fehr-roh-VEE'ah)	railroad
l'orario (loh-RAH-ree'oh)	timetable

il bagaglio (bah-GAH-l'yee)	baggage
la ricevuta dei bagagli (lah ree-cheh-voo-tah . . .)	baggage check
or lo scontrino (skohn-TREE-noh)	
depositare (deh-poh-zee-TAH-reh)	to check, deposit
il deposito dei bagagli (deh-POH-zee-toh . . .)	baggage room

lo scompartimento (skohm-pahr-tee-MEHN-toh)	compartment
andata e ritorno[5] (ahn-DAH-tah eh ree-TOHR-noh)	round-trip
un'agenzia di viaggi (oo-nah-jehn-TSEE'ah dee VYAH-djee)	a travel agency
un autobus (AH'oo-toh-boos)	a bus
prenotare (preh-noh-TAH-reh)	to reserve
lo sportello dei biglietti (loh spohr-TEHL-loh DAY bee-L'YEHT-tee) or la biglietteria (bee-l'yeht-teh-REE'ah)	ticket window

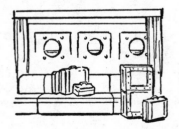

il baule (bah-oo-leh)	trunk
la valigia (vah-LEE-jah)	valise
il vapore (vah-POH-reh)	steamboat
la cabina (kah-BEE-nah)	cabin
il porto (POHR-toh)	port
il molo (MOH-loh)	pier
il pilota (pee-LOH-tah)	pilot
il tram, tranvai (TRAHM, TRAHN-vah'y)	street car
la bicicletta (bee-chee-KLEH-tah)	bicycle

il motore (moh-TOH-reh)	motor
un tassì (tahs-SEE)	a taxi

CONVERSATION

1 Mi vuol[6] dire dov'è la stazione, per piacere?

2 Ci sono diverse stazioni. Dove deve andare?

3 Devo andare a Milano.

4 Per[7] andare a Milano deve prendere il treno alla Stazione Centrale.

5 A che ora parte il primo treno?

6 Il primo treno parte di mattina[8] presto.

7 Allora bisognerà[9] prendere un tassì per arrivare più presto, perchè gli autobus passano raramente a quell'ora.

8 Sono pronti i suoi bagagli?

9 Sì, le mie valigie ed i miei bauli sono già alla stazione.

10 Vuole avere la bontà di dirmi dov'è la biglietteria?

11 Quanto costa un biglietto di terza classe[10] per Milano, andata e ritorno?

FOOTNOTES: *1. Lit.,* "will you have the kindness." *Bontà* is followed by the word *di* before the infinitive. *2. Trovarsi* is a reflexive verb. *Lit.,* it means "to find oneself." The present tense is: *io mi trovo, tu ti trovi, lei si trova, noi ci troviamo, voi vi trovate, loro si trovano.* The reflexive pronouns always precede the verb, except when the infinitive form is used, in which case the reflexive pronouns are attached to it. Almost any verb can be made reflexive if it makes sense. At times the Italian expression may be reflexive whereas the English equivalent

PRONUNCIATION	TRANSLATION
1 mee VWOHL DEE-reh doh-VEH lah stah-TSYOH-neh, pehr pyah-CHEH-reh?	Will you please tell me where the station is.
2 chee SOH-noh dee-VEHR-seh stah-TSYOH-nee. DOH-veh DEH-veh ahn-DAH-reh?	There are several stations. Where must you go?
3 DEH-voh ahn-DAH-reh ah mee-LAH-noh.	I must go to Milan.
4 . . . PREHN-deh-reh eel TREH-noh AHL-lah stah-TSYOH-neh chehn-TRAH-leh.	To go to Milan you must take the train at the Central Station.
5 ah keh OH-rah PAHR-teh eel PREE-moh TREH-noh?	At what time does the first train leave?
6 . . . PAHR-teh dee maht-TEE-nah PREH-stoh . . .	The first train leaves early in the morning.
7 ahl-LOH-rah bee-zoh-n'yeh-RAH PREHN-deh-reh oon tahs-SEE pehr ahr-ree-VAH-reh PYOO PREH-stoh, pehr-KEH l'yee AH'oo-toh-boos PAHS-sah-noh rah-rah-MEHN-teh ah kwehl-LOH-rah.	Then we will have to take a taxi to arrive early, because the buses run infrequently at that hour.
8 SOH-noh PROHN-tee ee SWOY bah-GAH-l'yee?	Is your baggage ready?
9 SEE, leh MEE'eh vah-LEE-jeh ed ee M'YAY bah-oo-lee SOH-noh JAH AHL-lah stah-TSYOH-neh.	Yes, my suitcases and my trunks are already at the station.
10 vwoh-leh ah-VEH-reh lah bohn-TAH dee DEER-mee doh-VEH lah bee-l'yeht-teh-REE'ah?	Will you kindly tell me where the ticket office is?
11 KWAHN-toh KOH-stah oon bee-L'YEHT-toh dee TEHR-tsah KLAHS-seh pehr mee-LAH-noh, ahn-DAH-tah eh ree-TOHR-noh?	How much does a third class round-trip ticket to (*lit.,* for) Milan cost?

is not, as in this case. See Reference Grammar.   3. A kilogram is a little over two pounds, and is the standard weight in Italy.   4. *Ferrovia* is composed of two words: *ferro* and *via. Lit.* "road of iron."   5. *Andata e ritorno* is an idiom. *Lit.* "going and returning."   6. *Vuol* is *vuole* without the final *e*, which is usually dropped before another verb for the sake of euphony.   7. *Per* before an infinitive means "in order to."   8. *Di mattina* is an idiom which means "in the morning." Likewise we have *di giorno, di sera, di notte,* etc.   9. *Bisognerà* is a form of the

12 Per quanto tempo è valido questo biglietto?

13 Un biglietto di andata e ritorno è valido per trenta giorni.

14 Dov'è il deposito di bagagli?[11] Voglio depositare i miei bauli.

15 Mi vuol dare, per piacere, lo scontrino dei miei bagagli?

16 Ecco la sua ricevuta, signora Bianchi.

17 Quanto pesa il mio baule?

18 Il suo baule pesa cinquanta chili.

19 Mettiamoci in vettura[12] poichè il treno sta per[13] partire.

20 Ecco un buon sedile in uno scompartimento di terza. Per favore,[14] ha l'orario ferroviario?

21 No, ma so che il treno arriverà[15] domani mattina alle[16] otto.

22 Allora arriveremo in tempo per prendere il vapore.

23 Ha prenotato[17] la[18] cabina?

---

future of *bisognare*. This verb is normally used only in the third person. *10.* There are three classes on Italian trains. The third class is the least expensive. *11.* The singular of *bagagli* is *bagaglio*. Words ending in *io* drop the *o* in the plural, unless the *i* is stressed, in which case you change *o* to *i*. Ex.: *zio* (uncle), *zii*. *12.* In a general sense *vettura* means any sort of conveyance. In reference to a train it means "a railroad car." *13. Stare per* is an idiom meaning "to be about to." *14. Per favore* is used interchangeably with *per piacere*. *15. Arriverà* is a future form of *arrivare: io arriverò, tu arriverai, lei arriverà, noi arriveremo, voi arriverete, loro arriveranno*. All first and second conjugation regular verbs form

12 pehr KWAHN-toh TEHM-poh EH VAH-lee-doh KWEH-stoh bee-L'YEHT-toh?

For how long (*lit.,* how much time) is this ticket valid?

13 ... ahn-DAH-tah eh ree-TOHR-noh EH VAH-lee-doh pehr TREHN-tah JOHR-nee.

A round-trip ticket is valid for thirty days.

14 doh-VEH eel deh-POH-zee-toh dee bah-GAH-l'yee? VOH-l'yoh deh-poh-zee-TAH-reh ee M'YAY bah-oo-lee.

Where is the baggage room? I want to check my trunks.

15 mee VWOHL DAH-reh ... skohn-tree-noh day M'YAY bah-GAH-l'yee?

Will you please give me my baggage check.

16 EHK-koh lah SOO'ah ree-cheh-voo-tah, see-N'YOH-rah BYAHN-kee.

Here is your check, Mrs. Bianchi.

17 KWAHN-toh PEH-zah eel MEE'oh bah-oo-leh?

How much does my trunk weigh?

18 eel SOO'oh bah-oo-leh PEH-zah cheen-KWAHN-tah KEE-lee.

Your trunk weighs fifty kilograms.

19 meht-TYAH-moh-chee een veht-TOO-rah poy-KEH eel TREH-noh stah pehr pahr-TEE-reh.

Let's get on the train since it is about to leave.

20 EHK-koh oon BWOHN seh-DEE-leh een OO-noh skohm-pahr-tee-MEHN-toh dee TEHR-tsah. pehr fah-VOH-reh, ah loh-RAH-ryoh fehr-roh-VYAH-ryoh?

Here is a good seat in a third-class compartment. Do you have the timetable, please?

21 NOH, mah SOH keh eel TREH-noh ahr-ree-veh-RAH doh-MAH-nee maht-TEE-nah AHL-leh OHT-toh.

No, but I know that the train will arrive tomorrow morning at eight.

22 ahl-LOH-rah ahr-ree-veh-REH-moh een TEHM-poh pehr PREHN-deh-reh eel vah-POH-reh.

Then we shall arrive on time to take the boat.

23 ah preh-noh-TAH-toh lah kah-BEE-nah?

Have you reserved a cabin?

---

the future in the same manner; that is, by adding the endings *erò, erai, erà, eremo, erete, eranno* to the stem of the verb.   *16. Alle* is a contraction of *a* and *le.* In Italian the definite article is used before the hours, whereas in English it is not. *17. Ha prenotato* is a form of the present perfect of *prenotare.* The past participle of the first conjugation verbs ends in *ato* and is preceded by the present of the auxiliary verb *avere.* See Note 11, Lesson 3.   *18.* The definite article is used before *cabina* because in this case it refers to a definite cabin, your cabin.

24 Non ancora, ma spero tro-varne[19] una libera[20] anche senza prenotazione.

25 Il signor Bianchi va a Londra in aereo.[21]

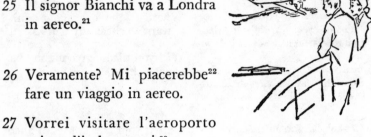

26 Veramente? Mi piacerebbe[22] fare un viaggio in aereo.

27 Vorrei visitare l'aeroporto prima d'imbarcarmi.[23]

28 Benissimo. Visiteremo l'aeroporto da dove partono gli aeroplani transatlantici.

---

19. Like the other object pronouns *ne* is attached to the infinitive. *20. Libera* normally means "free." In this case it means "available." *21.* It is common use to say *in aereo* rather than *in aeroplano*. *22. Piacerebbe* is a form of the condi-

24 nohn ahn-KOH-rah, mah SPEH-roh troh-VAHR-neh OO-nah LEE-beh-rah AHN-keh SEHN-tsah preh-noh-tah-TSYOH-neh.

Not yet, but I hope to find one available even without a reservation.

25 eel see-N'YOHR BYAHN-kee vah ah LOHN-drah een ah-EH-reh'oh.

Mr. Bianchi is going to London by plane.

26 veh-rah-MEHN-teh? mee pyah-cheh-REHB-beh FAH-reh oon VYAH-djoh een ah-EH-reh'oh.

Really? I should like to take a trip by *(lit.,* in) plane.

27 vohr-RAY vee-zee-TAH-reh lah'eh-roh-POHR-toh PREE-mah deem-bahr-KAHR-mee.

I should like to visit the airport before sailing.

28 beh-NEES-see-moh. vee-zee-teh-REH-moh lah'eh-roh-POHR-toh dah DOH-veh PAHR-tohnoh l'yee ah'eh-roh-PLAH-nee trahn-saht-LAHN-tee-chee.

Very well. We shall visit the airport from which *(lit.,* where) the transatlantic planes leave.

---

tional of *piacere.* This verb is used mostly in the third person.   *23. Imbarcarmi* is a reflexive verb. Like other pronouns *mi* (myself) is attached to the infinitive.

5 Quinta Lezione

Vocabolario per Questa Lezione

sa lei? (sah LAY)	do you know?	una volta (VOHL-tah)	once, one time
quale (KWAH-leh)	which	il doppio (DOHP-pyoh)	double
spesso (SPEHS-soh)	often	fino a (FEE-noh ah)	up to, until, as far as
più (PYOO)	more		
meno[1] (MEH-noh)	less	ci (CHEE)	there (place already mentioned)
tanto (TAHN-toh)	so much, as much		
contare (kohn-TAH-reh)	to count	là (LAH)	there

il quaderno (kwah-DEHR-noh) — notebook
la prima volta (PREE-mah . . .) — the first time
l'ultima volta (LOOL-tee-mah . . .) — the last time
press'a poco[2] (prehs-sah-POH-koh) — just about
una quindicina (kween-dee-CHEE-nah) — two weeks, (lit., fifteen days)
una ventina (vehn-TEE-nah) — about twenty
un centinaio (chehn-tee-NAH'yoh) — about a hundred

I NUMERI CARDINALI

THE CARDINAL NUMBERS (ee NOO-meh-ree kahr-dee-NAH-lee)

0. zero (DZEH-roh)
1. uno (OO-noh), una (OO-nah)
2. due (DOO'eh)
3. tre (TREH)
4. quattro (KWAHT-troh)
5. cinque (CHEEN-kweh)
6. sei (SAY)
7. sette (SEHT-teh)

8. otto (OHT-toh)
9. nove (NOH-veh)
10. dieci (DYEH-chee)
11. undici (OON-dee-chee)
12. dodici (DOH-dee-chee)
13. tredici (TREH-dee-chee)
14. quattordici (kwaht-TOHR-dee-chee)
15. quindici (KWEEN-dee-chee)

58

I NUMERI CARDINALI

(CONTINUED)

16. sedici (SEH-dee-chee)
17. diciassette (dee-chahs-SEHT-teh)
18. diciotto (dee-CHOHT-toh)
19. diciannove (dee-chahn-NOH-veh)
20. venti (VEHN-tee)
21. ventuno (vehn-TOO-noh)
22. ventidue (vehn-tee-DOO'eh)
23. ventitrè (vehn-tee-TREH)
24. ventiquattro (. . . KWAHT-troh)
25. venticinque (. . . -CHEEN-kweh)
26. ventisei (vehn-tee-SAY)
27. ventisette (vehn-tee-SEHT-teh)

28. ventotto (vehn-TOHT-toh)
29. ventinove (vehn-tee-NOH-veh)
30. trenta (TREHN-tah)
31. trentuno (trehn-TOO-noh)
32. trentadue (trehn-tah-DOO'eh)
40. quaranta (kwah-RAHN-tah)
50. cinquanta (cheen-KWAHN-tah)
60. sessanta (sehs-SAHN-tah)
70. settanta (seht-TAHN-tah)
80. ottanta (oht-TAHN-tah)
90. novanta (noh-VAHN-tah)

100. cento[3] (CHEHN-toh)
101. cento uno (CHEHN-toh OO-noh)
123. cento ventitrè (.. vehn-tee-TREH)

200. duecento (doo'eh-CHEHN-toh)
210. duecento dieci (. . . DYEH-chee)
400. quattrocento (kwaht-troh . . .)

869. ottocento sessantanove
1000. mille[4]
1492. mille quattrocento novantadue
2000. due mila[5]

7900. sette mila novecento
50,000. cinquanta mila
100,000. cento mila
1,000,000. un milione[6]

I Numeri Ordinali

THE ORDINAL NUMBERS   (ee NOO-meh-ree ohr-dee-NAH-lee)

primo (PREE-moh)   first
secondo (seh-KOHN-doh) second
terzo (TEHR-tsoh)   third
quarto (KWAHR-toh)   fourth
quinto (KWEEN-toh)   fifth

sesto (SEH-stoh)   sixth
settimo (SEHT-tee-moh) seventh
ottavo (oht-TAH-voh)   eighth
nono (NOH-noh)   ninth
decimo (DEH-chee-moh) tenth

undicesimo[7] (oon-dee-CHEH-zee-moh)   eleventh
dodicesimo (doh-dee-CHEH-zee-moh)   twelfth

Le Frazioni

THE FRACTIONS   (leh frah-TSYOH-nee)

la metà (meh-TAH), mezzo (MEH-dzoh)   half
un terzo (oon TEHR-tsoh)   a third
un quarto (oon KWAHR-toh)   one fourth
tre quarti (TREH KWAHR-tee)   three quarters
un quindicesimo (oon kween-dee-CHEH-zee-moh) one fifteenth

CONVERSATION

1 Sa[8] contare lei?

2 Sì, so contare.

3 Vuole contare, per piacere?

4 Sì. Uno, due, tre, quattro, cinque.

5 Lei ha contato da uno a cinque.

6 Sa[8] contare da uno a cento la signorina Romano?

7 Sì, signore, io so contare da uno a cento.

8 Quali[9] sono i numeri ordinali, signor Lanza?

9 I numeri ordinali sono: primo, secondo, terzo, quarto, quinto, eccetera.

10 Ho dieci libri. Quanti libri ha lei?

11 Ne[10] ho la metà. Ne ho cinque.

12 Allora lei ha tanti[11] libri quanti[11] ne ho io, non è vero?

13 No, io ho meno libri di[12] lei.

14 La signorina Ferrara ha tre cappelli ed io non ne ho che[13] uno.

15 Ella ha più cappelli di me.[14]

FOOTNOTES: *1. Più* and *meno* are followed by *di* before a number, a noun, or a pronoun. *2. Press'a poco* is an idiom. *3. Cento* (one hundred) does not take *un* before it. *Cento* does not change its form. *4. Mille* (one thousand) does not take *un* before it. *5.* Note that the plural of *mille* is *mila.*

PRONUNCIATION	TRANSLATION
1 sah kohn-TAH-reh LAY?	Do you know how to count?
2 SEE, EE'oh soh kohn-TAH-reh.	Yes, I know how to count.
3 vwoH-leh kohn-TAH-reh, pehr pyah-CHEH-reh?	Will you count, please?
4 SEE. oo-noh, DOO'eh, TREH, KWAHT-troh, CHEEN-kweh.	Yes. One, two, three, four, five.
5 LAY ah kohn-TAH-toh dah oo-noh ah CHEEN-kweh.	You have counted from one to five.
6 sah kohn-TAH-reh dah oo-noh ah CHEHN-toh lah see-n'yoh-REE-nah roh-MAH-noh?	Does Miss Romano know how to count from one to one hundred?
7 SEE, see-n'yoH-reh, EE'oh soh kohn-TAH-reh dah oo-noh ah CHEHN-toh.	Yes, sir, I know how to count from one to one hundred.
8 KWAH-lee soH-noh ee NOO-meh-ree ohr-dee-NAH-lee, see-n'yOHR LAHN-tsah?	What are the ordinal numbers, Mr. Lanza?
9 . . . PREE-moh, seh-KOHN-doh, TEHR-tsoh, KWAHR-toh, KWEEN-toh, eh-CHEH-teh-rah.	The ordinal numbers are: first, second, third, fourth, fifth, etc.
10 EE'oh OH DYEH-chee LEE-bree. KWAHN-tee LEE-bree AH LAY?	I have ten books. How many books have you?
11 EE'oh neh OH lah meh-TAH. neh OH CHEEN-kweh.	I have half as many (*lit.*, the half of them). I have five.
12 ahl-LOH-rah lay AH TAHN-tee LEE-bree KWAHN-tee neh OH EE'oh, nohn EH VEH-roh?	Then you have as many books as I, don't you (*lit.*, isn't that true)?
13 NOH, EE'oh OH MEH-noh LEE-bree dee LAY.	No, I have fewer (*lit.*, less) books than you.
14 lah see-n'yoh-REE-nah fehr-RAH-rah AH TREH kahp-PEHL-lee ed EE'oh NOHN neh OH keh oo-noh.	Miss Ferrara has three hats and I have only one.
15 EHL-lah AH PYOO kahp-PEHL-lee dee MEH.	She has more hats than I.

---

6. Note that *un milione*, unlike *cento* and *mille*, does take *un* in front of it.
7. Beginning with *undici*, the ordinal numbers in Italian are formed by dropping the final vowel of the number and adding *-esimo*. However, numbers ending in *trè* drop the accent but not the *e*. Ex.: *ventitrè* becomes *ventitreesimo*.   *8.* Any

16 Una volta io ho comprato una ventina di camicie.

17 E perchè tante?[15] La prossima volta non ne compri[16] tante.

18 L'ultima volta che[17] sono[18] stato[19] a Torino ho comprato un bel[20] vestito in quella bella[20] città.

19 Io sono stato a Torino almeno venti volte.

20 Questa volta voglio andare a Genova.

21 Un biglietto ferroviario per la Svizzera[21] costa il doppio di quello per Bologna, non è vero?

22 Sì, press'a poco. E il viaggio da Genova a Venezia costa quasi lo stesso che[22] un viaggio a Firenze.

---

form of *sapere* followed by an infinitive means "to know how." 9. The singular of *quali*, an interrogative adjective, is *quale* (masc. and fem.). *Quale* and *quali* are also interrogative pronouns. 10. *Ne*, meaning "of it, of them, some, any, etc." is never omitted in Italian, whereas its English equivalent often is omitted. 11. *Tanto* and *quanto* are used in the comparative of equality. They agree with the noun to which they refer. 12. The word "than" is usually translated by *di* before a noun, pronoun, or number. 13. *Non* ... (verb) ... *che* is an idiomatic expression meaning "only." *Soltanto, solo,* or *solamente* can be used instead of *non* ...*che*. 14. *Me* is a pronoun which follows a preposition, unlike the direct and indirect object pronouns. Pronouns unrelated to the verb are called disjunctive pronouns. See Reference Grammar. 15. Notice that *tante* agrees with *camicie,*

16 OO-na VOHL-tah EE'oh OH kohm-PRAH-toh OO-nah vehn-TEE-nah dee kah-MEE-cheh.

Once I bought about twenty shirts.

17 eh pehr-KEH TAHN-teh? lah PROHS-see-mah VOHL-tah NOHN neh KOHM-pree TAHN-teh.

And why so many? Next time don't buy so many.

18 LOOL-tee-mah VOHL-tah keh SOH-noh STAH-toh ah toh-REE-noh oh kohm-PRAH-toh oon behl veh-STEE-toh een KWEHL-lah BEHL-lah cheet-TAH.

The last time I went to Turin I bought a fine suit in that beautiful city.

19 EE'oh SOH-noh STAH-toh ah toh-REE-noh ahl-MEH-noh VEHN-tee VOHL-teh.

I have been in Turin at least twenty times.

20 KWEH-stah VOHL-tah VOH-l'yoh ahn-DAH-reh ah JEH-noh-vah.

This time I want to go to Genoa.

21 oon bee-L'YEHT-toh fehr-roh-VYAH-ryoh pehr lah ZVEE-tseh-rah KOH-stah eel DOHP-pyoh dee KWEHL-loh pehr boh-LOH-n'yah, nohn EH VEH-roh?

A railroad ticket for Switzerland costs twice as much (*lit.*, double) as one (*lit.*, that) for Bologna, doesn't it?

22 SEE, prehs-sah-POH-koh. eh eel VYAH-djoh dah JEH-noh-vah ah veh-NEH-tsyah KOH-stah KWAH-zee loh STEHS-soh keh oon VYAH-djoh ah fee-REHN-tseh.

Yes, just about. And the trip from Genoa to Venice costs almost as much (*lit.*, the same) as a trip to Florence.

---

which is feminine plural. 16. *Compri* is the *lei* form of the imperative of *comprare*. 17. The relative pronoun *che* (that) is never omitted in Italian, as it frequently is in English. 18. *Sono* is a form of the present of *essere* (to be): *io sono, tu sei, lei è, noi siamo, voi siete, loro sono.* 19. *Sono stato* is a form of the present perfect of *essere,* which takes its own present tense as an auxiliary. In verbs conjugated with *essere* the past participle agrees with the subject. Ex.: *ella è stata* (she has been or was). 20. *bel* is used before a singular masculine noun if it does not begin with *z, s-impura,* or *a vowel.* The feminine form is always *bella.* 21. *La Svizzera* (Switzerland): In Italian names of countries are preceded by the definite article. 22. *Che* is used here in a comparative of equality, and means "as."

 Sesta Lezione

Vocabolario per Questa Lezione

il freddo (FREHD-doh)	the cold	il sole (SOH-leh)	the sun
fa freddo[1] (fah . . .)	it (the weather) is cold	ieri (YEH-ree)	yesterday
		l'altro ieri (LAHL-troh...)	day before
il caldo (KAHL-doh)	the heat		yesterday

fa caldo (fah KAHL-doh)   it (the weather) is warm, hot
fa bel[2] tempo (fah behl TEHM-poh)   the weather is fine
dopodomani (doh-poh-doh-MAH-nee)   the day after tomorrow
la giornata (johr-NAH-tah)   the day (in its duration)

oggi (OH-djee)	today	mite (MEE-teh)	mild
domani (doh-MAH-nee)	tomorrow	durare (doo-RAH-reh)	to last
l'alba (LAHL-bah)	dawn	nè ... nè (NEH ... NEH)	neither... nor

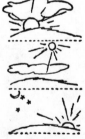

il levar del sole[3] (leh-VAHR dehl SOH-leh)   sunrise
il mattino (maht-TEE-noh)   morning
mezzogiorno (meh-dzoh-JOHR-noh)   noon
il pomeriggio (poh-meh-REE-joh)   afternoon
il tramonto (trah-MOHN-toh)   sunset
il sole tramonta (SOH-leh trah-MOHN-tah)   the sun is setting
mezzanotte (fem.) (meh-dzah-NOHT-teh)   midnight

la settimana (seht-tee-MAH-nah)   week
la settimana scorsa[4] (seht-tee-MAH-nah SKOHR-sah)   last week
la settimana prossima[4] (. . . PROHS-see-mah)   next week
il mese prossimo (MEH-zeh PROHS-see-moh)   next month
il mese scorso (. . . SKOHR-soh)   last month
un giorno di vacanza[5] (oon JOHR-noh dee vah-KAHN-tsah)   a holiday
il clima[6] (KLEE-mah)   climate

64

I GIORNI · I MESI · LE STAGIONI[7]

THE DAYS, THE MONTHS,
THE SEASONS

(ee JOHR-nee, ee MEH-zee,
leh stah-JOH-nee)

I GIORNI

lunedì[8] (loo-neh-DEE)	Monday	venerdì (veh-nehr-DEE)	Friday
martedì (mahr-teh-DEE)	Tuesday	sabato (SAH-bah-toh)	Saturday
mercoledì (mehr-koh-leh-DEE)	Wednesday	domenica (doh-MEH-nee-kah)	Sunday
giovedì (joh-veh-DEE)	Thursday		

I MESI

gennaio (jehn-NAH-yoh)	January	settembre (seht-TEHM-breh)	September
febbraio (fehb-BRAH-yoh)	February		
marzo (MAHR-tsoh)	March	ottobre (oht-TOH-breh)	October
aprile (ah-PREE-leh)	April		
maggio (MAH-djoh)	May	novembre (noh-VEHM-breh)	November
giugno (JOO-n'yoh)	June		
luglio (LOO-l'yoh)	July	dicembre (dee-CHEHM-breh)	December
agosto (ah-GOH-stoh)	August		

LE STAGIONI

la primavera[9] (lah pree-mah-VEH-rah)	spring
l'estate (fem.) (leh-STAH-teh)	summer
l'autunno (lah'oo-TOON-noh)	autumn
l'inverno (leen-VEHR-noh)	winter

il tempo (TEHM-poh)	weather
fa cattivo tempo (kaht-TEE-voh . . .)	the weather is bad
il sole brilla (eel SOH-leh BREEL-lah)	the sun is shining
il mese (MEH-zeh)	month
l'anno (LAHN-noh)	year
il secolo (SEH-koh-loh)	century
il riposo (ree-POH-zoh)	rest (repose)
si compone (see kohm-POH-neh)	is composed, it is composed
cominciare (koh-meen-CHAH-reh)	to begin
che cosa è? (keh KOH-zah EH)	what is?
cioè (choh'EH)	that is, that is to say

CONVERSATION

1 Come si compone la giornata?

2 La giornata si compone del mattino,[10] del pomeriggio e della sera.

3 Il mattino dura fino a mezzogiorno. Il pomeriggio dura fino al tramonto.

4 Quando comincia la sera?

5 Generalmente parlando, la sera comincia dopo il tramonto.

6 Che cosa è l'alba?

7 L'alba è il primo chiarore[11] dopo la notte, e precede lo spuntar del sole.[12]

8 Quanti giorni ci sono in una settimana?

9 La settimana è composta[13] di sette giorni.

10 Quale giorno della settimana è questo?

11 Oggi è lunedì,[14] che è il primo giorno della settimana. L'ultimo giorno della settimana è domenica, che è un giorno di vacanza e di riposo.

12 Che giorno sarà domani?

FOOTNOTES: *1. Fa* (from the verb *fare*) is here used impersonally. *Lit.*, "it makes cold." This impersonal form is used in several expressions relating to the weather. *2. Bel* (beautiful) is the form used before a singular masculine noun. After a noun it becomes *bello*. The feminine form is always *bella.* *3. Lit.,* the rising of

PRONUNCIATION	TRANSLATION
1 KOH-meh see kohm-POH-neh lah johr-NAH-tah?	How is the day divided (*lit.*, composed)?
2 ... dehl maht-TEE-noh, dehl poh-meh-REE-djoh eh DEHL-lah SEH-rah.	The day is composed of the morning, the afternoon, and the evening.
3 eel maht-TEE-noh DOO-rah FEE-noh ah meh-dzoh-JOHR-noh. eel poh-meh-REE-djoh DOO-rah FEE-noh ahl trah-MOHN-toh.	The morning lasts until noon. The afternoon lasts until sunset.
4 KWAHN-doh koh-MEEN-chah lah SEH-rah?	When does the evening begin?
5 jeh-neh-rahl-MEHN-teh pahr-LAHN-doh, lah SEH-rah koh-MEEN-chah DOH-poh ...	Generally speaking, the evening begins after sunset.
6 keh KOH-zah EH LAHL-bah?	What is dawn?
7 LAHL-bah EH eel PREE-moh kyah-ROH-reh DOH-poh lah NOHT-teh, eh preh-CHEH-deh loh spoon-TAHR dehl SOH-leh.	Dawn is the first light after the night and precedes sunrise.
8 KWAHN-tee JOHR-nee chee SOH-noh een OO-nah seht-tee-MAH-nah?	How many days are there in a week?
9 lah seht-tee-MAH-nah EH kohm-POH-stah dee SEHT-teh JOHR-nee.	The week is composed of seven days.
10 KWAH-leh JOHR-noh DEHL-lah seht-tee-MAH-nah EH KWEH-stoh?	What day of the week is this?
11 OH-djee EH loo-neh-DEE, keh EH eel PREE-moh ... LOOL-tee-moh ... doh-MEH-nee-kah, ... dee vah-KAHN-tsah eh dee ree-POH-zoh.	Today is Monday, which is the first day of the week. The last day of the week is Sunday, which is a day of vacation and rest.
12 keh JOHR-noh sah-RAH doh-MAH-nee?	What day will it be tomorrow?

the sun. *4.* The words *scorsa* and *prossima* may either follow or precede the noun. *5.* Lit., a day of vacation. *6.* Although the great majority of words ending in *a* are feminine, there are several that are masculine. *Clima* is one of these. *7.* Days, months, and seasons are not capitalized in Italian. *8.* The days

13 Domani sarà martedì e dopodomani sarà mercoledì.

14 È stato mercoledì ieri?

15 No, signore, è stata[15] domenica e l'altro ieri è stato[15] sabato.

16 Mi può dire come si divide l'anno?

17 L'anno si divide in dodici mesi.

18 Che mese è questo?

19 Questo è il mese di settembre, il mese prossimo sarà ottobre, ed il mese scorso è stato [16] agosto.

20 Qual'è il primo mese dell'anno?

21 Il primo mese dell'anno è gennaio.

22 Quante stagioni ci sono in un anno?

23 L'anno ha quattro stagioni: la primavera, l'estate, l'autunno e l'inverno.

24 Quali sono i mesi della primavera?

25 I mesi della primavera sono: marzo, aprile e maggio.

---

of the week are masculine, except *domenica*, which is feminine. *9.* The names of the seasons require the definite article before them. *10. Il mattino* or *la mattina*. The masculine form is more properly used when referring to the light, or atmospheric conditions, or when used figuratively, as in *il mattino della vita* (the morning of life). *11. Chiarore* is a synonym for *luce* (fem.). *12. Lo*

13 doh-MAH-nee sah-RAH mahr-teh-DEE eh doh-poh-doh-MAH-nee sah-RAH mehr-koh-leh-DEE.

Tomorrow will be Tuesday and the following day (*lit.,* after tomorrow) will be Wednesday.

14 EH STAH-toh mehr-koh-leh-DEE YEH-ree?

Was yesterday Wednesday?

15 . . . EH STAH-tah doh-MEH-nee-kah, eh LAHL-troh YEH-ree eh STAH-toh SAH-bah-toh.

No, sir, it was Sunday, and the day before (*lit.,* the other yesterday) was Saturday.

16 mee PWOH DEE-reh KOH-meh see dee-VEE-deh LAHN-noh?

Can you tell me how the year is divided?

17 LAHN-noh see dee-VEE-deh een DOH-dee-chee MEH-zee.

The year is divided into twelve months.

18 keh MEH-zeh EH KWEH-stoh?

What month is this?

19 KWEH-stoh EH eel MEH-zeh dee seht-TEHM-breh, eel MEH-zeh PROHS-see-moh sah-RAH oht-TOH-breh ed eel MEH-zeh SKOHR-soh eh STAH-toh ah-GOH-stoh.

This is the month of September, next month will be October, and last month was August.

20 kwah-LEH eel PREE-moh MEH-zeh dehl-LAHN-noh?

Which is the first month of the year?

21 eel PREE-moh MEH-zeh dehl-LAHN-noh EH jehn-NAH-yoh.

The first month of the year is January.

22 KWAHN-teh stah-JOH-nee chee SOH-noh een oon AHN-noh?

How many seasons are there in a year?

23 LAHN-noh ah KWAHT-troh stah-JOH-nee: lah pree-mah-VEH-rah, leh-STAH-teh, lah'oo-TOON-noh eh leen-VEHR-noh.

The year has four seasons: spring, summer, autumn, and winter.

24 KWAH-lee SOH-noh ee MEH-zee DEHL-lah pree-mah-VEH-rah?

What are the months of spring?

25 . . . MAHR-tsoh, ah-PREE-leh eh MAH-djoh.

The months of spring are: March, April, and May.

---

spuntar del sole literally means "the appearing of the sun." *13. È composta* is a synonym for *si compone.* *14.* In Italy Monday is considered the first day of the week. *15.* See Note 19, Lesson 5. *16.* The present perfect is used here because *il mese scorso* is a recent occurrence.

26 Fa bel tempo o cattivo tempo in questa stagione?

27 Nella primavera generalmente fa bel tempo ed il clima è mite, cioè non fa nè troppo freddo, nè troppo caldo.

28 Quali sono i mesi dell'estate?

29 I mesi dell'estate sono: giugno, luglio e agosto.

30 Fa freddo in questa stagione?

31 No, signore, d'estate fa sempre caldo.

32 Quanti anni ci sono in un secolo?

33 In un secolo ci sono cento anni.

26 fah behl TEHM-poh oh kaht-TEE-voh TEHM-poh een KWEH-stah stah-JOH--neh?	Is the weather good or bad in this season?
27 . . . jeh-neh-rahl-MEHN-teh fah behl TEHM-poh ed eel KLEE-mah EH MEE-teh, choh'EH nohn fah NEH TROHP-poh FREHD-doh NEH TROHP-poh KAHL-doh.	In the spring the weather is generally good and the climate is mild, that is to say, it's neither too cold nor too hot.
28 KWAH-lee SOH-noh ee MEH-zee dehl-leh-STAH-teh?	What are the months of summer?
29 . . . JOO-n'yoh, LOO-l'yoh eh ah-GOH-stoh.	The months of summer are: June, July, and August.
30 fah FREHD-doh een KWEH-stah stah-JOH-neh?	Is it cold in this season?
31 NOH, see-N'YOH-reh, deh-STAH-teh fah SEHM-preh KAHL-doh.	No, sir, in the summer (*lit.*, of summer) it is always hot.
32 KWAHN-tee AHN-nee chee SOH-noh een oon SEH-koh-loh?	How many years are there in a century?
33 . . . CHEHN-toh AHN-nee.	In a century there are one hundred years.

Settima Lezione

Vocabolario per Questa Lezione

un amico (ah-MEE-koh) a friend *(masc.)*
un'amica (ah-MEE-kah) a friend *(fem.)*
nuovo (NWOH-voh) new
ancora (ahn-KOH-rah) yet, still

infatti (een-FAHT-tee) in fact
troppo (TROHP-poh) too, too much
si chiama[1] (KYAH-mah) is called, his (her) name is
pulire (poo-LEE-reh) to clean

l'indirizzo (leen-dee-REE-tsoh) — address
per meno (pehr MEH-noh) — for less
un agente di polizia[2] — a policeman
(ah-JEHN-teh dee poh-lee-TSEE-ah)
un carabiniere[3] (kah-rah-bee-NYEH-reh) — a military policeman

riparare (ree-pah-RAH-reh) to repair
esaminare (eh-zah-mee-NAH-reh) to examine
sostituire (soh-stee-too'EE-reh) to replace
indicare (een-dee-KAH-reh) to indicate, point
caricare (kah-ree-KAH-reh) to wind (a watch)

c'è un guasto (CHEH oon GWAH-stoh) — there is something out of order

a servirla![4] (sehr-VEER-lah) — at your service!
bisogna che (bee-ZOH-n'yah keh) — it is necessary that
il resto (REH-stoh) — the rest, remainder

rotto (ROHT-toh) broken
sporco (SPOHR-koh) dirty
scusi! (SKOO-zee) excuse me!
va bene! (vah BEH-neh) all right!

caro (KAH-roh) dear, expensive
fra, tra (frah, trah) between, among

72

L'OROLOGIO · L'ORA

THE WATCH, THE TIME (loh-roh-LOH-joh, LOH-rah)

l'orologio (loh-roh-LOH-joh) — watch, clock
un orologio da[5] polso (dah POHL-soh) — a wrist watch
un orologio a[6] pendolo (ah PEHN-doh-loh) — a wall clock (pendulum)
un orologio a[6] sveglia (ah ZVEH-l'yah) — an alarm clock
un orologio d'oro[7] (DOH-roh) — a gold watch
un orologio da[5] tasca (dah TAH-skah) — a pocket watch

un orologiaio (oh-ro-loh-JYAH-yoh) — a watchmaker
un'orologeria (oo-noh-roh-loh-jeh-REE-ah) — a watchmaker's shop
il quadrante (kwah-DRAHN-teh) — face (of a watch)
la lancetta (lahn-CHEHT-tah) — hand (of a watch)
il meccanismo (mehk-kah-NEE-zmoh) — movement

il secondo (seh-KOHN-doh) — second
il minuto (mee-NOO-toh) — minute
l'ora (LOH-rah) — hour

il vetro (VEH-troh) — glass, crystal
la molla (MOHL-lah) — spring
il rubino (roo-BEE-noh) — ruby, jewel

va[8] bene (vah BEH-neh) — it is right (of a watch)
suonare (swoh-NAH-reh) — to ring, strike (the hour)

va avanti (vah ah-VAHN-tee) — it is fast (of a watch)
va[8] indietro (vah een-DYEH-troh) — it is slow (of a watch)
non funziona (nohn foon-TSYOH-nah) — it is out of order
si è fermato[9] (see EH fehr-MAH-toh) — it has stopped

CHE ORA È?

WHAT TIME IS IT? (keh OH-rah EH)

È l'una[10] (EH LOO-nah) — It is one o'clock.
Sono le due[10] (SOH-noh leh DOO'eh) — It is two o'clock.

Sono le quattro precise[11] (... preh-CHEE-zeh) — It is four o'clock sharp.
È l'una e mezzo[12] (EH LOO-nah eh MEH-dzoh) — It is half past one.
Sono le cinque e mezzo (... MEH-dzoh) — It is half past five.
È l'una e un quarto[12] (... oon KWAHR-toh) — It is a quarter past one.

È l'una meno un quarto — It is quarter to one.
Sono le dieci meno un quarto — It is a quarter to ten.
Sono le undici meno cinque[13] — It is five to eleven.
Sono le sei e dieci[12] — It is ten after six.

CONVERSATION

1 Scusi, signore, mi può dire che ora è, per piacere?

2 Certo, signore. Sono le due e venti.

3 Sono già le tre?

4 Sì, sono le tre precise.

5 Non è ancora l'una meno un quarto.

6 Infatti, non sono ancora le tre.

7 Non sono ancora suonate le quattro?

8 Sì, Pietro, le quattro sono suonate poco fa.[14] Il suo orologio non va bene. Credo che vada[15] cinque minuti avanti.

9 Il mio orologio, invece, va un quarto d'ora indietro.

10 È rotto?

11 Credo.[16] Si è fermato. Ci dev'essere un guasto e dovrò portarlo da[17] un orologiaio.

12 L'ha caricato?

13 Sì, ma è sporco e bisognerà farlo pulire.

FOOTNOTES: *1. Si chiama,* from the reflexive verb *chiamarsi. Lit.,* "calls himself, herself, or yourself." 2. *Lit.* "an agent of the police." 3. The *carabinieri* are members of a police corps attached to the army. A fine physique is a prerequisite. The dress uniforms of the *caribinieri* are very impressive. 4. *Lit.,* "to serve you." *5. Da polso, da tasca.* This is a special use of the word *da.* See Note 25, Lesson 3.

PRONUNCIATION	TRANSLATION
1 SKOO-zee, see-N'YOH-reh, mee PWOH DEE-reh keh OH-rah EH, pehr pyah-CHEH-reh?	Pardon me, sir, can you please tell me what time it is?
2 CHEHR-toh, see-N'YOH-reh. SOH-noh leh DOO'eh eh VEHN-tee.	Certainly, sir. It is twenty after two.
3 SOH-noh JAH leh TREH?	Is it three o'clock already?
4 SEE, SOH-noh leh TREH preh-CHEE-zeh.	Yes, it is three o'clock sharp.
5 nohn EH ahn-KOH-rah LOO-nah MEH-noh oon KWAHR-toh.	It isn't a quarter to one yet.
6 een-FAHT-tee, nohn SOH-noh ahn-KOH-rah leh TREH.	In fact, it is not yet three o'clock.
7 nohn SOH-noh ahn-KOH-rah swoh-NAH-teh leh KWAHT-troh?	Hasn't four o'clock struck yet?
8 SEE, PYEH-troh, . . . POH-koh FAH. eel SOO'oh oh-roh-LOH-joh nohn vah BEH-neh. KREH-doh keh VAH-dah CHEEN-kweh mee-NOO-tee ah-VAHN-tee.	Yes, Peter, four o'clock struck a short while ago. Your watch isn't right. I think it is five minutes fast.
9 eel MEE'oh oh-roh-LOH-joh, een-VEH-cheh, vah oon KWAHR-toh DOH-rah een-DYEH-troh.	My watch, instead, is a quarter of an hour slow.
10 EH ROHT-toh?	Is it broken?
11 KREH-doh. see EH fehr-MAH-toh. chee deh-VEHS-seh-reh oon GWAH-stoh eh doh-VROH pohr-TAHR-loh dah oon oh-roh-loh-JAH'yoh.	I think so. It has stopped. It must be out of order and I shall have to take it to a watch-maker.
12 LAH kah-ree-KAH-toh?	Have you wound it up?
13 SEE, mah eh SPOHR-koh eh bee-zoh-n'yeh-RAH FAHR-loh poo-LEE-reh.	Yes, but it is dirty and it will have to be cleaned.

See also Reference Grammar. *6. A pendolo, a sveglia.* This is a special use of the word *a*, meaning "with". *7. d'oro (di oro)*, "of gold." See Note 21, Lesson 3. *8. Va* (goes). This is an idiomatic use of word *va* in connection with the functioning of a watch. *9. Si è fermato* is a form of the present perfect of the reflexive verb *fermarsi*, which is intransitive. *Fermare* (not reflexive) is transitive. Ex.: *Io fermo*

14 Dove c'è un buon orologiaio che non faccia[18] pagare[19] troppo?

15 In Via Nazionale, numero duecento quaranta.[20]

16 Come si chiama quest'orologiaio?

17 Si chiama Pelloni.

18 Se non mi sbaglio[21] il[22] 240 è vicino al Palazzo della Mostra.

19 Precisamente, signore. È tra Piazza Esedra ed il Tunnel.

20 Scusi, c'è il[23] signor Pelloni?

21 A servirla, signore. In che posso esserle utile?

22 Un mio amico mi ha dato il suo indirizzo. Vuole avere la bontà di ripararmi quest'orologio?

23 Certo, ma bisogna che prima l'esamini.[24]

24 Quando sarà[25] pronto? Quanto mi costerà?

25 Sarà pronto fra[26] cinque giorni, e le costerà mille lire.

---

la macchina (I stop the car.)   *10.* In telling time the whole hour is mentioned first, preceded by the definite article.   *11. precise,* as an adjective, agrees with *le quattro (ore* understood).   *12.* "Half past, a quarter after," and any number of minutes after the hour are preceded by the word *e   13.* "A quarter to" or any number of minutes before the hour are preceded by the word *meno.   14. Poco fa* is an idiom meaning "a short while ago." The word *fa* means "ago" when used with words expressing periods of time.   *15. Vada* is a form of the present subjunctive of *andare.* The verb *credo (credere)* requires the subjunctive. See Reference Gram-

14 DOH-veh CHEH oon BWOHN oh-roh-loh-JAH'yoh keh nohn FAH-tchah pah-GAH-reh TROHP-poh?

Where is there a good watchmaker who doesn't charge too much?

15 een VEE'ah nah-tsyoh-NAH-leh, NOO-meh-roh doo'eh-CHEHN-toh kwah-RAHN-tah.

At 240 Via Nazionale.

16 KOH-meh see KYAH-mah kweh-stoh-roh-loh-JAH'yoh?

What's the name of this watchmaker?

17 see KYAH-mah pehl-LOH-nee.

His name is Pelloni.

18 seh NOHN mee ZBAH-l'yoh eel doo' eh-CHEHN-toh kwah-RAHN-tah EH vee-CHEE-noh ahl pah-LAH-tsoh DEHL-lah MOH-strah.

If I am not mistaken, 240 is near the Palazzo della Mostra.

19 preh-chee-zah-MEHN-teh, see-N'YOH-reh, EH trah PYAH-tsah eh-ZEH-drah ed eel TOON-nehl.

Exactly, sir. It is between Piazza Esedra and the Tunnel.

20 SKOO-zee, CHEH eel see-n'YOHR pehl-LOH-nee?

Pardon me, is Mr. Pelloni in?

21 ah sehr-VEER-lah, see-N'YOH-reh een KEH POHS-soh EHS-sehr-leh OO-tee-leh?

At your service, sir. What can I do for you?

22 oon MEE'oh ah-MEE-koh mee ah DAH-toh eel soo'oh een-dee-REE-tsoh. vwoh-leh ah-VEH-reh lah bohn-TAH dee ree-pah-RAHR-mee kweh-stoh-roh-LOH-joh?

A friend of mine has given me your address. Would you be good enough to repair this watch for me?

23 CHEHR-toh, mah bee-ZOH-n'yah keh PREE-mah leh-ZAH-mee-nee.

Certainly, but I must examine it first.

24 KWAHN-doh sah-RAH PROHN-toh? KWAHN-toh mee koh-steh-RAH?

When will it be ready? How much will it cost me?

25 ... frah CHEEN-kweh JOHR-nee, eh leh koh-steh-RAH MEEL-leh LEE-reh.

It will be ready in five days, and it will cost you one thousand lire.

---

mar. *16. Credo,* used alone and referring to something previously mentioned, means "I think so." *17.* The word *da,* as mentioned in Note 25, Lesson 3, means "to or at somebody's place," the nature of the place not being specified. *18. Faccia* is a form of the present subjunctive of *fare.* An indefinite antecedent requires the subjunctive. *Orologiaio* is the indefinite antecedent because it does not refer to a specific watchmaker. *19. Faccia pagare* is an idiom. *Lit.,* "makes pay." *20.* In Italian, when mentioning an address, the number follows the street. *21. Se non mi sbaglio* is a form of the reflexive verb *sbagliarsi.* *22. Il (numero* under-

26 Mi sembra caro. Non potrebbe farmelo[27] per meno?

27 Impossibile, signore. La molla è rotta e dovrò sostituirla.

28 È in buone condizioni il resto del meccanismo?

29 Sì, signore, ma, come vede, dovrò sostituire anche il vetro.

30 Va bene. Arrivederla a giovedì, signore.

31 Ha lei degli orologi d'oro?

32 Sì, mia moglie ne ha uno da polso, d'oro.

33 Costano molto gli orologi con diamanti?

34 Un orologio con diamanti costa sempre[28] caro.

35 Mi può dire quanti minuti ci sono in un'ora?

36 In un'ora ci sono sessanta minuti, e in un minuto sessanta secondi.

37 Che cosa indica l'ora in un orologio?

38 Le due lancette indicano l'ora sul quadrante degli orologi.

39 La lancetta piccola indica le ore, e la lancetta grande indica i minuti.

_____

stood) 240. **23.** The definite article is required before the title of a person, but is omitted when addressing the person. **24.** *Esamini* is a subjunctive form required by *bisogna che*. See Reference Grammar. **25.** Future of *essere: io sarò, tu sarai, lei sarà, noi saremo, voi sarete, loro saranno.* **26.** *Fra* means "in" or

26 mee SEHM-brah KAH-roh. nohn poh-TREHB-beh FAHR-meh-loh pehr MEH-noh?

It seems a little expensive to me. Couldn't you do it for less?

27 eem-pohs-SEE-bee-leh . . . MOHL-lah EH ROHT-tah eh doh-VROH soh-stee-too'EER-lah.

Impossible, sir. The spring is broken and I shall have to replace it.

28 EH een BWOH-neh kohn-dee-TSYOH-nee eel REH-stoh dehl mehk-kah-NEEZ-moh?

Is the rest of the movement in good condition?

29 SEE, see-N'YOH-reh, mah KOH-meh VEH-deh, doh-VROH soh-stee-too'-EE-reh AHN-keh eel VEH-troh.

Yes, sir, but, as you see, I shall have to replace the glass also.

30 vah BEH-neh. ahr-ree-veh-DEHR-lah ah joh-veh-DEE, see-N'YOH-reh.

Very well. I'll see you Thursday, sir.

31 AH lay DEH-l'yee oh-roh-LOH-jee DOH-roh?

Do you have any gold watches (*lit.*, watches of gold)?

32 SEE, MEE'ah MOH-l'yeh neh ah oo-no dah POHL-soh, DOH-roh.

Yes, my wife has a gold wrist watch.

33 KOH-stah-noh MOHL-toh l'yee oh-roh-LOH-jee kohn dee'ah-MAHN-tee?

Are diamond watches (*lit.*, watches with diamonds) very expensive?

34 oon oh-roh-LOH-joh kohn dee'ah-MAHN-tee KOH-stah SEHM-preh KAH-roh.

A diamond watch is always expensive.

35 mee PWOH DEE-reh KWAHN-tee mee-NOO-tee chee SOH-noh een oon-OH-rah?

Can you tell me how many minutes there are in an hour?

36 . . . sehs-SAHN-tah mee-NOO-tee, eh een oon mee-NOO-toh sehs-SAHN-tah seh-KOHN-dee.

In an hour there are sixty minutes, and in a minute sixty seconds.

37 keh KOH-zah EEN-dee-kah LOH-rah een oon oh-roh-LOH-joh?

What indicates the time on a watch?

38 leh DOO'eh lahn-CHEHT-teh EEN-dee-kah-noh LOH-rah sool kwah-DRAHN-teh DEH-l'yee oh-roh-LOH-jee.

The two hands indicate the time on the face of a watch (*lit.*, of the watches).

39 lah lahn-CHEHT-tah PEEK-koh-lah EEN-dee-kah leh OH-reh, eh lah lahn-CHEHT-tah GRAHN-deh EEN-dee-kah ee mee-NOO-tee.

The small hand indicates the hours, and the large hand indicates the minutes.

"within" when used in connection with expressions of time.   *27. Farmelo—melo* (it to me) is a double pronoun attached to the infinitive. See Reference Grammar. *28. Sempre* is an adverb of time. In Italian adverbs follow the verb.

Ottava Lezione

Vocabolario per Questa Lezione

stabilire (stah-bee-LEE-reh)	to establish
felicissimo (feh-lee-CHEES-see-moh)	very happy
nel frattempo (nehl fraht-TEHM-poh)	in the meantime
dappertutto (dahp-pehr-TOOT-toh)	everywhere
senza dubbio (SEHN-tsah DOOB-byoh)	without doubt
il testimonio (teh-stee-MOH-nyoh)	witness
comprare (kohm-PRAH-reh)	to buy
all'ingrosso[1] (ahl-leen-GROHS-soh)	wholesale
al minuto[1] (mee-NOO-toh)	retail
qualsiasi (kwahl-SEE'ah-zee)	any, no matter which
congelare (kohn-jeh-LAH-reh)	to freeze

i prodotti (proh-DOHT-tee)	products
l'olio (LOH-lyoh)	oil
il grano (GRAH-noh)	wheat
le banane (bah-NAH-neh)	bananas
la lana (LAH-nah)	wool

sto bene[2] (stoh BEH-neh)	I am well	**sperare** (speh-RAH-reh)	to hope
sto male[2] (stoh MAH-leh)	I am ill	**vendere** (VEHN-deh-reh)	to sell
felice (feh-LEE-cheh)	happy	**sbrigare** (zbree-GAH-reh)	to settle,
come va?[3] (koh-meh VAH)	how is?		regulate

80

IL COMMERCIO

Trade   (kohm-MEHR-choh)

il cambio (KAHM-byoh)   exchange
il commerciante (kohm-mehr-CHAN-teh)   merchant
lo sportello (spohr-TEHL-loh)   pay-window
il guadagno (gwah-DAH-n'yoh)   profit
il dirigente (dee-ree-JEHN-teh)   manager
la succursale (sook-koor-SAH-leh)   branch (of a firm)

la rata (RAH-tah)   rate
la tratta (TRAHT-tah)   draft
i valori (vah-LOH-ree)   securities
la merce (MEHR-cheh)   merchandise
gli affari (ahf-FAH-ree)   business
il danaro (dah-NAH-roh)   money
la banca (BAHN-kah)   bank
la casa (KAH-zah)   house, firm
la ditta (DEET-tah)   firm   firmare (feer-MAH-reh)   to sign
prestare (preh-STAH-reh)   to lend   la firma (FEER-mah)   signature
il prestito (preh-STEE-toh) loan   il notaio (noh-TAH-yoh) notary

le restrizioni (reh-stree-TSYOH-nee)   restrictions
le transazioni (trahn-sah-TSYOH-nee)   transactions
in contanti[1] (een kohn-TAHN-tee)   for cash
a credito (ah KREH-dee-toh)   on credit
importare (eem-pohr-TAH-reh)   to import
esportare (eh-spohr-TAH-reh)   to export

il tabacco (tah-BAHK-koh)   tobacco
lo[4] stagno (STAH-n'yoh)   tin
lo[4] zucchero (DZOOK-keh-roh)   sugar
il petrolio (peh-TROH-lyoh)   petroleum
l'ananasso (lah-nah-NAHS-soh)   pineapple
il pompelmo (pohm-PEHL-moh)   grapefruit
l'uva (LOO-vah)   grapes
i fichi (FEE-kee)   figs

le arachidi (leh ah-RAH-kee-dee)   peanuts
la noce di cocco (NOH-cheh dee KOHK-koh)   cocoanut
il cuoio or la pelle (KWOH-yoh, PEHL-leh)   leather
la carne congelata (KAHR-neh kohn-jeh-LAH-tah)   frozen meat
il vino bianco (VEE-noh BYAHN-koh)   white wine
il vino rosso (VEE-noh ROHS-soh)   red wine

CONVERSATION

1 Come sta, caro signore? Sono felicissimo di[5] vederla.

2 Molto bene, grazie; e lei?

3 Non c'è male,[6] grazie.

4 Conta rimanere a lungo[7] a Roma?

5 No, signore. Mi fermerò[8] alcuni mesi soltanto, perchè son[9] venuto per[10] affari.

6 E come vanno le cose negli[11] Stati Uniti? Senza dubbio lei sarà di ritorno[12] prima della primavera.

7 Sì, signore, e nel frattempo spero poter sbrigare tutti i miei affari.

8 Ha intenzione di[13] fare delle importazioni?[14]

9 Vorrei importare caffè, tabacco, zucchero, lana e qualche[15] varietà di frutta.

10 Intende[13] importare questi prodotti da tutte le regioni mediterranee?

FOOTNOTES: *1. All'ingrosso, al minuto,* and *in contanti* are idioms. *2. Sto bene, sto male* are idioms. The infinitive is *stare bene (male).* *3. Come va* literally means "how goes it?" *4.* A reminder that *lo* (the) is used before masculine nouns (singular) beginning with *z* or *s-impura.* *5.* Infinitives depending on adjectives are often preceded by *di.* *6. Non c'è male* is an idiom. *7. A lungo* after an infinitive means "a long time." *8.* See Note 9, Lesson 7. *9. Venire* is one of the verbs that takes *essere* as an auxiliary. *10. Per affari* literally means "for busi-

PRONUNCIATION	TRANSLATION
1 KOH-meh STAH, KAH-roh see-N'YOH-reh? SOH-noh feh-lee-CHEES-see-moh dee veh-DEHR-lah.	How are you, my dear sir? I am very happy to see you.
2 MOHL-toh BEH-neh, GRAH-tsyeh; eh LAY?	I am very well, thank you; and you?
3 nohn CHEH MAH-leh, GRAH-tsyeh.	Not bad, thank you.
4 KOHN-tah ree-mah-NEH-reh ah LOON-goh ah ROH-mah?	Do you expect to remain in Rome a long time?
5 NOH, see-N'YOH-reh. mee fehr-meh-ROH ahl-KOO-nee MEH-zee sohl-TAHN-toh, pehr-KEH sohn veh-NOO-toh pehr ahf-FAH-ree.	No, sir. I am going to stay only a few months, because I came on business.
6 eh KOH-meh VAHN-noh leh KOH-seh NEH-l'yee STAH-tee OO-NEE-tee? SEHN-tsah DOOB-byoh lay sah-RAH dee ree-TOHR-noh PREE-mah DEHL-lah pree-mah-VEH-rah.	And how are things in the United States? Undoubtedly you will be back before spring.
7 ... nehl fraht-TEHM-poh SPEH-roh poh-TEHR zbree-GAH-reh TOOT-tee ee M'YAY ahf-FAH-ree.	Yes, sir, and in the meantime I hope to be able to settle all my affairs.
8 AH een-ten-TSYOH-neh dee FAH-reh DEHL-leh eem-pohr-tah-TSYOH-nee?	Do you intend to do importing?
9 vohr-RAY eem-pohr-TAH-reh kahf-FEH, tah-BAHK-koh, DZOOK-keh-roh, LAH-nah eh KWAHL-keh vah-ryeh-TAH dee FROOT-tah.	I should like to import coffee, tobacco, sugar, wool, and some varieties of fruit.
10 een-TEHN-deh eem-pohr-TAH-reh KWEH-stee proh-DOHT-tee dah TOOT-teh leh reh-JOH-nee meh-dee-tehr-RAH-neh'eh?	Do you intend to import these products from all the Mediterranean regions?

---

ness."   *11. Negli* is a contraction of *in* and the definite article *gli*.   *12. Sarà di ritorno* is an idiom.   *13.* Normally an infinitive depending on a noun is introduced by *di*. Compare sentences 8 and 10.   *14. Delle importazioni.* The plural is used because it refers to different products to be imported.   *15.* The word *qualche* is always singular. The word that follows is, of course, singular also.

11 Un po' dappertutto. Dall'Egitto[16] riceverò tabacco, cotone, zucchero e legumi; e dalla Grecia, uva e fichi.[17]

12 E che cosa riceverà dall'Italia e da altri paesi?

13 Dall'Italia riceverò arance, limoni ed olio d'oliva; dall'Algeria banane e pompelmi; dalla Tunisia, grano; dal Marocco, cuoio; e dal Senegal, arachidi e noci di cocco.

14 Ha intenzione di vendere in contanti o a credito?[18]

15 A certi commercianti aprirò[19] un credito a breve scadenza,[18] oppure farò[20] con loro uno scambio[21] di prodotti.

16 Come conta[22] impiantare questo commercio?

17 La mia idea è di[13] aprire una succursale della mia ditta a Milano, dove metterò mio fratello come dirigente.

18 Non avrà[23] egli bisogno di una procura da parte della sua ditta per legalizzare le operazioni?

---

16. *Dall'* is a contraction of *da* (from) and *l'*. Remember that in Italian names of countries are preceded by the definite article.   17. The singular of *fichi* is *fico*. 18. *A credito* and *a breve scadenza* are idioms.   19. Future of the third conjugation verb *aprire: io aprirò, tu aprirai, lei aprirà, noi apriremo, voi aprirete, loro*

11 oon POH dahp-pehr-TOOT-toh.
dahl-leh-JEET-toh ree-cheh-veh-ROH tah-BAHK-koh, koh-TOH-neh, DZOOK-keh-roh eh leh-GOO-mee; eh DAHL-lah GREH-chah, oo-vah eh FEE-kee.

12 eh keh KOH-zah ree-cheh-veh-RAH dahl-lee-TAH-lyah eh dah AHL-tree pah-EH-zee?

13 ...ree-che-veh-ROH ah-RAHN-cheh, lee-MOH-nee ed OH-lyoh doh-LEE-vah; dahl-lahl-jeh-REE'ah bah-NAH-neh eh pohm-PEHL-mee; DAHL-lah too-nee-ZEE'ah, GRAH-noh; dahl mah-ROHK-koh, KWOH-yoh; eh dahl seh-neh-GAHL, ah-RAH-kee-dee eh NOH-chee dee KOHK-koh.

14 AH een-tehn-TSYOH-neh dee VEHN-dereh een kohn-TAHN-tee oh ah KREH-dee-toh?

15 ah CHEHR-tee kohm-mehr-CHAHN-tee ah-pree-ROH oon KREH-dee-toh ah BREH-veh skah-DEHN-tsah, ohp-POO-reh fah-ROH kohn LOH-roh oo-noh SKAHM-byoh dee proh-DOHT-tee.

16 KOH-meh KOHN-tah eem-pyahn-TAH-reh KWEH-stoh kohm-MEHR-choh?

17 lah MEE'ah ee-DEH'ah EH dee ah-PREE-reh oo-nah sook-koor-SAH-leh DEHL-lah MEE'ah DEET-tah ah mee-LAH-noh, DOH-veh meht-teh-ROH MEE'oh frah-TEHL-loh KOH-meh dee-ree-JEHN-teh.

18 nohn ah-VRAH EH-l'yee bee-ZOH-n'yoh dee oo-nah proh-KOO-rah dah PAHR-teh DEHL-lah soo'ah DEET-tah pehr leh-gah-lee-DZAH-reh leh oh-peh-rah-TSYOH-nee?

A little from everywhere. From Egypt I shall receive tobacco, cotton, sugar, and legumes; and from Greece, grapes and figs.

And what will you receive from Italy and other countries?

From Italy I shall receive oranges, lemons, and olive oil *(lit.,* oil of olives) ; from Algeria, bananas and grapefruit; from Tunisia, wheat; from Morocco, leather; and from Senegal, peanuts and cocoanuts.

Do you intend to sell for cash or on credit?

To certain merchants I shall extend short term credit, or else I shall make an exchange of products with them.

How do you expect to establish this business *(lit.,* commerce)?

My idea is to open a branch of my firm in Milan, which my brother will manage *(lit.,* where I shall put my brother as a manager).

Will he not need a power of attorney on behalf *(lit.,* from the part of) of your company to legalize his transactions *(lit.,* operations) ?

---

apriranno. 20. Future of the irregular verb *fare: io farò, tu farai, lei farà, noi faremo, voi farete, loro faranno.* 21. Do not confuse the words *scambio,* which means "any kind of exchange," and *cambio,* which means "rate of exchange." 22. *Conta,* from the verb *contare,* "to count." Before an infinitive, as in this case, it

19 Naturalmente. Ne avrà bisogno per poter comprare e vendere a nome[24] della mia ditta.

20 Per redigere una procura a chi[25] bisogna[26] rivolgersi?

21 Bisogna farla redigere da un notaio e davanti a[27] due testimoni.

22 Qual'è la rata di cambio oggi?

23 Oggi il cambio è molto favorevole.

24 Potrei riscuotere in dollari una lettera di cambio?

25 Al momento ci sono delle restrizioni sui valori e sulla circolazione estera; ma credo che potrà riscuotere una tratta in moneta italiana in qualsiasi banca in Italia.

26 Vorrei anche esportare dei prodotti in Turchia. Che ne[28] pensa lei?

27 Ottima idea!

---

also means "to expect." *23.* Future of *avere: io avrò, tu avrai, lei avrà, noi avremo, voi avrete, loro avranno.* *24.* A *nome di,* idiom meaning "in the name of." *25. Chi* is an interrogative pronoun and refers only to persons. *26. Bisogna* is

19 nah-too-rahl-MEHN-teh. neh ah-VRAH bee-ZOH-n'yoh pehr poh-TEHR kohm-PRAH-reh eh VEHN-deh-reh ah NOH-meh DEHL-lah MEE'ah DEET-tah.

Naturally. He will need one in order to be able to buy and sell in the name of my company.

20 pehr reh-DEE-jeh-reh oo-nah proh-KOO-rah ah KEE bee-ZOH-n'yah ree-VOHL-jehr-see?

To whom must one go (*lit.,* turn to) in order to draw up a power of attorney?

21 . . . FAHR-lah reh-DEE-jeh-reh dah oon noh-TAH'yoh eh dah-VAHN-tee ah DOO'eh teh-stee-MOH-nee.

It must be drawn up by a notary and before two witnesses.

22 kwah-LEH lah RAH-tah dee KAHM-byoh OH-djee?

What is the rate of exchange today?

23 OH-djee eel KAHM-byoh EH MOHL-toh fah-voh-REH-voh-leh.

Today the exchange is very favorable.

24 poh-TRAY ree-SKWOH-teh-reh een DOHL-lah-ree oo-nah LEHT-teh-rah dee KAHM-byoh?

Could I cash a letter of exchange in dollars?

25 ahl moh-MEHN-toh chee SOH-noh DEHL-leh reh-stree-TSYOH-nee SOO'y vah-LOH-ree eh SOOL-lah cheer-koh-lah-TSYOH-neh EH-steh-rah; mah KREH-doh keh poh-TRAH ree-SKWOH-teh-reh oo-nah TRAHT-tah een moh-NEH-tah ee-tah-LYAH-nah een kwahl-SEE'ah-zee BAHN-kah een ee-TAH-lyah.

At present there are some restrictions on foreign securities and currency; but I believe you can cash a draft in Italian money in any bank of Italy.

26 vohr-RAY AHN-keh eh-spohr-TAH-reh day proh-DOHT-tee een toor-KEE'ah. keh neh PEHN-sah LAY?

I should like to export some products to (*lit.,* in) Turkey. What do you think?

27 OHT-tee-mah ee-DEH'ah!

Excellent idea!

an impersonal expression and means "must." *27. Davanti* requires the preposition *a* before a noun or pronoun. *28. Ne* (of it) cannot be omitted in Italian.

9 Nona Lezione

Vocabolario per Questa Lezione

apparecchiare la tavola (ahp-pah-rehk-KYAH-reh . . .)	to set the table
il coperto (koh-PEHR-toh)	place setting
mettere il coperto[1] (MEHT-teh-reh . . .)	to set the place

l'argenteria (lahr-jehn-tee-REE'ah)	silverware
la tovaglia (toh-VAH-l'yah)	tablecloth
il tovagliolo[2] (toh-vah-L'YOH-loh)	napkin
il piattino (pyaht-TEE-noh)	saucer
la tazza (TAH-tsah)	cup
una tazza di caffè (kahf-FEH)	a cup of coffee
il coltello (kohl-TEHL-loh)	knife
la forchetta (fohr-KEHT-tah)	fork
il cucchiaio (kook-KYAH-yoh)	spoon
il cucchiaino (kook-kyah-EE-noh)	teaspoon

la tavola (TAH-voh-lah)	the table
il piatto (PYAHT-toh)	plate, dish
salato (sah-LAH-toh)	salty, salted
crudo (KROO-doh)	raw
subito (soo-bee-toh)	quickly, immediately

il bicchiere (beek-KYEH-reh)	glass
un bicchiere di latte (. . . LAHT-teh)	a glass of milk
un bicchiere di vino (. . . VEE-noh)	a glass of wine
un bicchiere d'acqua (. . . DAHK-kwah)	a glass of water

la bottiglia (boht-TEE-l'yah)	bottle
la caraffa (kah-RAHF-fah)	the decanter, pitcher
la caffettiera (kahf-feht-TYEH-rah)	coffee pot
la zuccheriera (dzook-keh-RYEH-rah)	sugar bowl
al contrario (ahl kohn-TRAH-ryoh)	on the contrary
insipido (een-SEE-pee-doh)	tasteless

88

IL RISTORANTE · I CIBI

THE RESTAURANT, FOOD   (eel ree-stoh-RAHN-teh, ee CHEE-bee)

il cameriere (kah-meh-RYEH-reh)	waiter
la lista delle vivande (LEE-stah DEHL-leh vee-VAHN-deh)	menu
la lista dei vini (. . . day VEE-nee)	wine list
il conto (KOHN-toh)	check, bill
la mancia (MAHN-chah)	tip

il cibo (CHEE-boh)	food
il pasto (PAH-stoh)	meal
la pietanza (pyeh-TAHN-tsah)	the course (of a dinner)
l'antipasto (lahn-tee-PAH-stoh)	appetizer

il brodo (BROH-doh)	soup
il pane (PAH-neh)	bread
il panino (pah-NEE-noh)	roll
l'aceto (lah-CHEH-toh)	vinegar
il sale (SAH-leh)	salt

il pepe (PEH-peh)	pepper	la torta (TOHR-tah)	cake
il burro (BOOR-roh)	butter	il gelato (jeh-LAH-toh)	ice cream
la salsa (SAHL-sah)	sauce	il dolce (DOHL-cheh)	dessert

il minestrone (mee-neh-STROH-neh)	vegetable soup (thick)
la bistecca (bee-STEHK-kah)	steak
al sangue (ahl SAHN-gweh)	rare (of meat)
il filetto (fee-LEHT-toh)	filet, filet mignon
una frittata (freet-TAH-tah)	an omelet
gli spaghetti (spah-GEHT-tee)	spaghetti
il condimento (kohn-dee-MEHN-toh)	seasoning
le patate (pah-TAH-teh)	potatoes
le patate fritte (. . . FREET-teh)	fried potatoes
il purè di patate (poo-REH dee . . .)	mashed potatoes
il pomodoro (poh-moh-DOH-roh)	tomato

la salsa di pomodori (SAHL-sah dee . . .)	tomato sauce
la salsa piccante (. . . peek-KAHN-teh)	spicy (sharp) sauce
la lattuga (laht-TOO-gah)	lettuce
l'insalata (leen-sah-LAH-tah)	salad
l'acqua con ghiaccio (LAHK-kwah kohn GYAH-tchoh)	ice water

CONVERSATION

1 Mi può dire, per piacere, dove posso trovare un buon ristorante?

2 In Via Marche o in Via Sicilia ci sono molti ristoranti dove si mangia[3] bene.

3 Vorrebbe[4] accompagnarmi?

4 Con gran piacere.

5 Sediamoci[5] a questa tavola. Il cameriere ha messo il coperto proprio ora.[6]

6 Questa tavola è coperta da[7] una tovaglia bianca.

7 E che cosa c'è sopra la tavola?

8 Sopra la tavola ci sono le posate: forchette, cucchiai e coltelli. Ci sono anche delle salviette, una caraffa d'acqua con ghiaccio e molti bicchieri.

9 Chiamiamo[8] il cameriere.

10 Cameriere, la lista delle vivande e dei vini, per piacere.

11 Desidero una bistecca con purè di patate e dei piselli ed un'insalata verde.

FOOTNOTES: *1. Lit.*, to put the cover. 2. *Tovagliolo* may also be spelled *tovagliuolo*. *3. Si mangia* is an impersonal expression. Lit., one eats. *4. Vorrebbe* is the *lei* form of the conditional of *volere*. *5. Sediamoci* is the *noi* form of the imperative of the reflexive verb *sedersi*. Direct, indirect, and reflexive pronouns are also attached to the *tu, noi,* and *voi* forms of the affirmative imperative. See Reference Grammar. *6. Proprio ora* is an idiom. It means "just,

PRONUNCIATION	TRANSLATION
1 mee PWOH DEE-reh, pehr pyah-CHEH-reh, DOH-veh, POHS-soh troh-VAH-reh oon BWOHN ree-stoh-RAHN-teh?	Can you please tell me where I can find a good restaurant?
2 een VEE'ah MAHR-keh oh een VEE'-ah see-CHEE-lyah chee SOH-noh MOHL-tee reeh-stoh-RAHN-tee DOH-veh see MAHN-jah BEH-neh.	On Via Marche or Via Sicilia there are many good restaurants where you eat well (*lit.,* where one eats well).
3 vohr-REHB-beh ahk-kohm-pah-N'YAHR-mee?	Would you like to accompany me?
4 kohn GRAHN pyah-CHEH-reh.	With great pleasure.
5 seh-DYAH-moh-chee ah KWEH-stah TAH-voh-lah. eel kah-meh-RYEH-reh ah MEHS-soh eel koh-PEHR-toh PROH-pryoh OH-rah.	Let's sit at this table. The waiter has just set it.
6 KWEH-stah TAH-voh-lah EH koh-PEHR-tah dah oo-nah toh-VAH-l'yah BYAHN-kah.	This table is covered with a white tablecloth.
7 eh keh KOH-zah CHEH SOH-prah lah TAH-voh-lah?	What is there on the table?
8 . . . leh poh-ZAH-teh: fohr- KEHT-teh, kook-KYAH'y eh kohl-TEHL-lee. chee SOH-noh AHN-keh DEHL-leh sahl-VYEHT-teh, oo-nah kah-RAHF-fah DAHK-kwah kohn GYAH-choh eh MOHL-tee beek-KYEH-ree.	On the table is the silverware: forks, spoons, and knives. There are also the napkins, a pitcher of ice water (*lit.,* water with ice), and several glasses.
9 kyah-MYAH-moh eel kah-meh-RYEH-reh.	Let's call the waiter.
10 . . . LEE-stah DEHL-leh vee-VAHN-deh eh day VEE-nee, pehr pyah-CHEH-reh.	Waiter, the menu and the wine list, please.
11 . . . bee-STEHK-kah kohn poo-REH dee pah-TAH-teh eh day pee-ZEHL-lee, ed oon-een-sah-LAH-tah VEHR-deh.	I would like a steak with mashed potatoes and peas, and a green salad.

just now, a while ago." 7. *Da,* which normally means "from" or "at," means "with" in this case. 8. *Chiamiamo* is the *noi* form of the imperative of *chiamare.* Notice that the *noi* form of the imperative in all cases is the same as the *noi* form of the present. 9. *Al sangue* is an idiom. *Sangue* means "blood." 10. *Si dice* is the impersonal form of the present of the irregular verb *dire.* 11. *Mi porti* is the *lei* form of the imperative of *portare.* Notice that the pronoun *mi* follows

12 Non mi piace la carne troppo cotta; la preferisco al sangue.[9]

13 Si dice[10] che la carne al sangue sia più nutriente, non è vero?

14 Mi porti[11] del pollo arrosto e mezza bottiglia di vino rosso, il migliore.

15 Vuol mettere lei stesso il sale, l'olio e l'aceto nella sua insalata?

16 Sì, a meno che[12] non sia[13] già condita.

17 Questa pietanza è un po' salata.[14]

18 È strano! Al contrario, a me[15] sembra che non ci sia[16] sale abbastanza.

19 Non ho molto appetito perchè ho fatto colazione molto tardi, alle undici. Adesso vorrei soltanto una frittata con un po' di prosciutto.

20 Mi dia[17] il bricco,[18] per piacere. Voglio prendere un po' di caffè in questa tazza.

21 Ecco la zuccheriera; metta lei[19] lo zucchero.

22 Cameriere, il conto, per piacere. Quanto è?

the general rule of preceding the verb. See Note 5 above. *12.* An idiom. *13. Sia* is the subjunctive of *essere.* The subjunctive is required after the adverbial phrase *a meno che.* See Reference Grammar. *14. Salata* (salty, salted). This word also means "expensive" in a figurative sense. *15. Me* is a disjunctive pronoun used

12 nohn mee PYAH-cheh lah KAHR-neh TROHP-poh KOHT-tah; lah preh-feh-REE-skoh ahl SAHN-gweh.

I don't like meat too well done; I prefer it rare.

13 see DEE-cheh keh . . . SEE'ah PYOO noo-tree-EHN-teh, nohn EH VEH-roh?

They say that rare meat is more nutritious, don't they?

14 mee POHR-tee dehl POHL-loh ahr-ROH-stoh eh MEH-dzah boht-TEE-l'yah dee VEE-noh ROHS-soh, eel mee-L'YOH-reh.

Bring me some roast chicken and a half bottle of red wine, the best.

15 VWOHL MEHT-teh-reh lay STEHS-soh eel SAH-leh, LOH-lyoh eh lah-CHEH-toh NEHL-lah soo'ah een-sah-LAH-tah?

Do you wish to put salt, oil, and vinegar in your salad yourself?

16 SEE, ah MEH-noh keh nohn SEE'ah JAH kohn-DEE-tah.

Yes, unless it is already seasoned.

17 KWEH-stah pyeh-TAHN-tsah EH oon POH sah-LAH-tah.

This dish is a little salty.

18 EH STRAH-noh! ahl kohn-TRAH-ryoh ah MEH SEHM-brah keh NOHN chee SEE'ah SAH-leh ahb-bah-STAHN-tsah.

That's strange! On the contrary, it seems to me that there is not enough salt.

19 nohn oh MOHL-toh ahp-peht-TEE-toh pehr-KEH oh FAHT-toh koh-lah-TSYOH-neh MOHL-toh TAHR-dee, AHL-leh OON-dee-chee. ah-DEHS-soh vohr-RAY sohl-TAHN-toh oo-nah freet-TAH-tah kohn oon POH dee proh-SHOOT-toh.

I am not very hungry *(lit.,* I don't have much appetite) because I had breakfast very late, at eleven. Now I would like to have just an omelet with some Italian ham.

20 mee DEE'ah eel BREEK-koh, pehr pyah-CHEH-reh. VOH-l'yoh PREHN-deh-reh oon POH dee kahf-FEH een KWEH-stah TAH-tsah.

Will you please let me have *(lit.,* give me) the coffee pot? I would like to have *(lit.,* take) some coffee in this cup.

21 EHK-koh lah dzook-keh-RYEH-rah; MEHT-tah LAY loh DZOOK-keh-roh.

Here is the sugar bowl; help yourself to *(lit.,* you put) the sugar.

22 kah-meh-RYEH-reh, eel KOHN-toh, . . . KWAHN-toh EH?

Waiter, the check, please. How much is it?

---

instead of the indirect object pronoun *mi* for emphasis. *16. Sia* is the subjunctive of *essere,* here required by the impersonal expression *mi sembra.* *17. Mi dia* is the *lei* form of the imperative of *dare.* See Note 11. *18. Bricco,* synonym for *caffettiera,* is the more elegant word for "coffee pot," when serving at the table.

23 Ecco, signore. Ottocento cinquanta lire. Le porterò subito il resto.

24 Va bene. Lasciamo una mancia al cameriere.

25 Dopo questo pranzo luculliano[20] non crede lei che dovremmo[21] fare una passeggiata?[22]

26 Mi farebbe[23] molto piacere.[24]

---

19. *Lei* is used for emphasis after the imperative *metta*. The word *stesso* after *lei* is understood. 20. The word *luculliano* derives from *Lucullus (Lucullo)* a Roman general and consul, famous for, among other things, the sumptuous banquets he gave. The expression *un pranzo luculliano* is still in common use

23 EHK-koh, see-N'YOH-reh. oht-toh-CHEHN-toh cheen-KWAHN-tah LEE-reh. leh pohr-teh-ROH soo-bee-toh eel REH-stoh.

Here it is, sir. Eight hundred fifty lire. I shall bring you the change immediately.

24 vah BEH-neh. lah-SHYAH-moh oo-nah MAHN-chah ahl kah-meh-RYEH-reh.

Very well. Let's leave a tip for the waiter.

25 DOH-poh KWEH-stoh PRAHN-dzoh loo-kool-LYAH-noh nohn KREH-deh LAY keh doh-VREHM-moh FAH-reh oo-nah pahs-seh-DJAH-tah?

After this sumptuous dinner don't you think we ought to go for a walk?

26 mee fah-REHB-beh MOHL-toh pyah-CHEH-reh.

It would please me very much.

---

after two thousand years. *21. Dovremmo* is the *noi* form of the conditional of *dovere*. *22. Fare una passeggiata* is an idiom: "to take a walk." *23. farebbe* is the impersonal third person of the conditional of *fare*. *24. Lit.,* it would be very pleasing to me.

10 Decima Lezione

Vocabolario per Questa Lezione

scegliere (SHEH-l'yeh-reh)	to choose
delle volte (DEHL-leh VOHL-teh)	at times
qualche volta (KWAHL-keh VOHL-tah)	sometimes
un invitato (een-vee-TAH-toh)	a guest

accendere (ah-CHEHN-deh-reh)	to light
spegnere (SPEH-n'yeh-reh)	to extinguish
arredare (ahr-reh-DAH-reh)	to furnish
il giardino (jahr-DEE-noh)	garden
la fontana (fohn-TAH-nah)	fountain

a destra (ah DEH-strah)	to the right
a sinistra (ah see-NEE-strah)	to the left
comodo (KOH-moh-doh)	comfortable
la casa (KAH-zah)	house
lo studio (STOO-dyoh)	study
lo stile (STEE-leh)	style
l'aiuto (lah-YOO-toh)	help

un vano, una camera[1] (VAH-noh, KAH-meh-rah)	a room
il palazzo (pah-LAH-tsoh)	building, palace
l'appartamento (lahp-pahr-tah-MEHN-toh)	apartment
il cortile (kohr-TEE-leh)	inner court, courtyard
la periferia (peh-ree-feh-REE'ah)	suburbs
il vasellame (vah-zehl-LAH-meh)	china
la luce elettrica (... eh-LEHT-tree-kah)	electric light
l'elettricità (leh-leht-tree-chee-TAH)	electricity
la finestra (fee-NEH-strah)	window

96

LA CASA · LA MOBILIA

The House, the Furniture   (lah KAH-zah, lah moh-BEE-lyah)

il primo piano (PREE-moh PYAH-noh)   first floor
il pianterreno (pyahn-tehr-REH-noh)   ground floor
il piano superiore (PYAH-noh soo-peh-RYOH-reh)   upper floor

la scala (SKAH-lah)   stairway
il salotto (sah-LOHT-toh)   living room
il bagno[2] (BAH-n'yoh)   bathroom, bath
la cucina (koo-CHEE-nah)   kitchen
il letto (LEHT-toh)   bed
la coperta (koh-PEHR-tah)   blanket
il cuscino (koo-SHEE-noh)   pillow
il divano (dee-VAH-noh)   sofa
la sedia (SEH-dyah)   chair

l'ascensore (lah-shehn-SOH-reh)   elevator
la biblioteca (bee-blee'oh-TEH-kah)   library
la sala da[3] pranzo (SAH-lah dah PRAHN-dzoh) dining room
la camera da[3] letto (KAH-meh-rah dah LEHT toh) bedroom
il lenzuolo[4] (lehn-TSWOH-loh)   bed sheet
l'armadio (lahr-MAH-dyoh)   closet
la toletta (toh-LEHT-tah)   dressing table
il cassettone (kahs-seht-TOH-neh)   bureau
il tappeto (tahp-PEH-toh)   rug

il gas (gahs)   gas   il lavabo (lah-VAH boh)   washstand
la luce (LOO-cheh)   light   la vasca (VAH-skah)   bathtub
la porta (POHR-tah)   door   lo specchio (SPEHK-kyoh)   mirror
la chiave (KYAH-veh)   key   le tendine (tehn-DEE-neh)   curtains
il quadro (KWAH-droh)   picture   il mobile (MOH-bee-leh)   piece of
il legno (LEH-n'yoh)   wood   furniture

il frigorifero (free-goh-REE-feh-roh)   refrigerator
la stufa (STOO-fah)   stove, kitchen range
il gabinetto (gah-bee-NEHT-toh)   toilet
l'asciugamano (lah-shyoo-gah-MAH-noh)   towel
la lampada (LAHM-pah-dah)   lamp
la lampadina (lahm-pah-DEE-nah)   bulb
il paralume (pah-rah-LOO-meh)   lamp shade

CONVERSATION

1 Io abito in città. Dove abitano loro?

2 Noi abitiamo alla periferia.

3 Di quanti piani[5] è la loro[6] casa?

4 Noi abitiamo in un palazzo di tre piani, senza contare il pianterreno.

5 Quanti vani ci sono nel loro appartamento.

6 Il nostro appartamento si compone di sette vani: il salotto, la sala da pranzo, due camere da letto, la cucina, il bagno e lo studio.

7 Bisogna salire[7] le scale per venire da[8] loro?

8 Niente affatto! C'è un ascensore.

9 Ha arredato lei stesso l'appartamento, signor Conti?

10 Sì, ma naturalmente mia moglie m'ha aiutato a[9] scegliere la mobilia, che è di stile moderno.

11 Se non le dà[10] molto disturbo, mi piacerebbe molto vedere l'arredamento del suo appartamento.

FOOTNOTES: *1*. When referring to a specific room the word *camera* or *stanza* is always used. *2. Il bagno* or *la stanza da bagno*. *3*. The word *da* indicates use. See Note 25, Lesson 3. *4*. The plural of *il lenzuolo* is *le lenzuola (fem.)*.

PRONUNCIATION	TRANSLATION
1 EE'oh AH-bee-toh een cheet-TAH. DOH-veh AH-bee-tah-noh LOH-roh?	I live in the city. Where do you live?
2 NOY ah-bee-TYAH-moh AHL-lah peh-ree-feh-REE'ah.	We live in the suburbs.
3 dee KWAHN-tee PYAH-nee EH lah LOH-roh KAH-zah?	How many floors are there in your house?
4 . . . pah-LAH-tsoh dee treh PYAH-nee, SEHN-tsah kohn-TAH-reh eel pyahn-tehr-REH-noh.	We live in a three-story building, not counting the ground floor.
5 KWAHN-tee VAH-nee chee SOH-noh nehl LOH-roh ahp-pahr-tah-MEHN-toh?	How many rooms are there in your apartment?
6 eel NOH-stroh . . . kohm-POH-neh dee SEHT-teh VAH-nee: eel sah-LOHT-toh, lah SAH-lah dah PRAHN-dzoh, DOO'eh KAH-meh-reh dah LEHT-toh, lah koo-CHEE-nah, eel BAH-n'yoh eh loh STOO-dyoh.	Our apartment has seven rooms: the living room, the dining room, two bedrooms, the kitchen, the bathroom, and the study.
7 bee-ZOH-n'yah sah-LEE-reh leh SKAH-leh pehr veh-NEE-reh dah LOH-roh?	Do you have to climb the stairs to get to your place?
8 NYEHN-teh ahf-FAHT-toh! CHEH oon ah-shehn-SOH-reh.	Not at all! There is an elevator.
9 AH ahr-reh-DAH-toh lay STEHS-soh lahp-pahr-tah-MEHN-toh, see-N'YOHR KOHN-tee?	Did you furnish the apartment yourself, Mr. Conti?
10 SEE, mah MEE'ah MOH-l'yeh mah ah-yoo-TAH-toh ah SHEH-l'yeh-reh lah moh-BEE-lyah keh EH dee STEE-leh moh-DEHR-noh.	Yes, but naturally my wife helped me to choose the furniture, which is modern (*lit.,* of modern style) .
11 seh nohn leh DAH MOHL-toh dee-STOOR-boh, mee pyah-cheh-REHB-beh veh-DEH-reh lahr-reh-dah-MEHN-toh dehl soo'oh ahp-pahr-tah-MEHN-toh.	If it is no bother to you (*lit.,* gives you no bother) , I should like very much to see how your apartment is furnished (*lit.,* the arrangement of).

5. *Lit.,* of how many floors. 6. *Loro* besides being a subject personal pronoun meaning "you" (polite plural) is a possessive adjective or pronoun meaning "your, yours (polite plural), their, theirs." As a possessive *loro* requires the definite article

12 Tutt'altro![11] Mi farebbe molto piacere. Entriamo prima nel[12] salotto.

13 Ecco un divano, due poltrone, diverse piccole tavole con le lampade ed una graziosa raccolta di quadri.

14 Molto bello! Ed i mobili,[13] come vede, sono di mogano, che è un legno tanto[14] bello quanto[14] solido.

15 Qual'è l'arredamento della camera da letto?

16 Il letto, il cassettone, la toletta, l'armadio a specchio ed il comodino che sono di noce. L'armadio ed il cassettone sono forniti di due grandi specchi.

17 Sono autentici persiani questi tappeti?

18 No, sono di fabbricazione italiana, ma di buona qualità.

19 Andiamo nella sala da pranzo, per piacere. La tavola è grande perchè a volte abbiamo degli invitati. Ci sono in tutto dodici sedie ed una credenza dove mettiamo il servizio da tavola e l'argenteria.

---

before it, even when followed by a noun indicating a relative or member of the family. *Loro* is invariable. *7. Salire* is an irregular verb. Its present is: *io salgo, tu sali, lei sale, noi saliamo, voi salite, loro salgono.* *8.* See Note 17, Lesson 7. *9. Aiutare* is one of the verbs that take *a* to introduce a dependent infinitive. *10. Dà* (gives) from the present of *dare,* an irregular verb: *io do, tu dai, lei dà, noi diamo, voi date, loro danno.* Notice that *dà* has an accent, to distinguish it from the word *da* (from, at). *11. Tutt'altro!* An idiom: "anything but!" *12. Entrare* is an intransitive verb and requires the preposition *in,* which contracts with the definite article. *13. Mobili* is a collective noun used in the plural. The singular *mobile,* is used when referring to a single piece of furniture. It literally means

12 toot-AHL-troh! mee fah-REHB-beh.
. . . ehn-TRYAH-moh PREE-mah
nehl sah-LOHT-toh.

13 EHK-koh oon dee-VAH-noh, DOO'eh
pohl-TROH-neh, dee-VEHR-seh
PEEK-koh-leh TAH-voh-leh kohn
leh LOH-roh LAHM-pah-deh ed
oo-nah grah-TSYOH-zah rahk-
KOHL-tah dee KWAH-dree.

14 MOHL-toh BEHL-loh! ed ee MOH-
bee-lee, KOH-meh VEH-deh, SOH-
noh dee MOH-gah-noh, keh EH
oon LEH-n'yoh TAHN-toh BEHL-
loh KWAHN-toh SOH-lee-doh.

15 kwah-LEH lahr-reh-dah-MEHN-toh
DEHL-lah KAH-meh-rah dah LEHT-
toh?

16 eel LEHT-toh, eel kahs-seht-TOH-
neh, lah toh-LEHT-tah, lahr-MAH-
dyoh ah SPEHK-kyoh ed eel koh-
moh-DEE-noh keh SOH-noh dee
NOH-cheh. . . . SOH-noh fohr-NEE-
tee dee DOO'eh GRAHN-dee SPEHK-
kyee.

17 SOH-noh ah'oo-TEHN-tee-chee
pehr-SYAH-nee KWEH-stee tahp-
PEH-tee?

18 . . . fahb-bree-kah-TSYOH-neh ee-
tah-LYAH-nah, mah dee BWOH-nah
kwah-lee-TAH.

19 ahn-DYAH-moh NEHL-lah SAH-lah
dah PRAHN-dzoh, pehr pyah-CHEH-
reh. lah TAH-voh-lah EH GRAHN-
deh pehr-KEH ah VOHL-teh ahb-
BYAH-moh DEH-l'yee een-vee-TAH-
tee. chee SOH-noh een TOOT-toh
DOH-dee-chee SEH-dyeh ed oo-nah
kreh-DEHN-tsah DOH-veh meht-
TYAH-moh eel sehr-VEE-tsyoh dah
TAH-voh-lah eh lahr-jehn-teh-
REE'ah.

On the contrary! That would
please me very much. Let's first
enter (into) the living room.

Here are a sofa, two armchairs,
several small tables with lamps,
and a lovely collection of pictures.

Very beautiful! And the furniture, as you see, is of mahogany,
which is a wood as beautiful as
it is strong.

What are the furnishings of the
bedroom?

The bed, the bureau, the dressing table, the wardrobe with a
mirror, and the night table,
which are of walnut. The wardrobe and the bureau have (*lit.*,
are furnished with) two large
mirrors.

Are these authentic Persian rugs?

No, they are of Italian manufacture, but of good quality.

Let's go into the dining room, if
you please. The center table is
large because at times we have
guests. There are in all twelve
chairs and a buffet where (*lit.*,
in which) we put the table
service and the silverware.

"movable." *14.* "as . . . as . . ." is a comparative of equality. See Note 11, Lesson 5.
15. Com'è (come è) used in an exclamatory sentence requires an inverted word
order, i.e. the verb before the subject. *16. Più . . . più.* An idiom: "the more . . .
the more." *17. Guardare* means "to look" and "to look at." *18. Nostro* is

20 Com'è[15] grande la sua cucina! Più[16] la guardo,[17] più[16] mi piace.

21 Infatti, è così spaziosa che qualche volta consumiamo qui i nostri[18] pasti. Abbiamo un frigorifero ed una stufa elettrica, e l'acquaio per lavare i piatti.

22 Posso vedere la stanza da bagno?

23 Faccia[19] come se fosse[20] a casa sua.[21] Il sapone e gli[22] asciugamani sono a sinistra del lavabo, accanto alla vasca.

---

both a possessive adjective and a possessive pronoun. Its different forms are: *il nostro, la nostra, i nostri, le nostre.* 19. *Faccia, lei* form of the imperative of *fare.* 20. *Fosse, lei* form of the imperfect subjunctive of *essere.* Subjunctive is required

20 koh-MEH GRAHN-deh lah soo'ah koo-CHEE-nah! PYOO lah GWAHR-doh, PYOO mee PYAH-cheh.

How large your kitchen is! The more I look at it, the more I like it.

21 een-FAHT-tee, EH koh-ZEE spah-TSYOH-zah keh KWAHL-keh VOHL-tah kohn-soo-MYAH-moh KWEE ee NOH-stree PAH-stee. ahb-BYAH-moh oon free-goh-REE-feh-roh ed oo-nah STOO-fah eh-LEHT-tree-kah, eh lahk-KWAH'yoh pehr lah-VAH-reh ee PYAHT-tee.

Indeed, it is so spacious that sometimes we eat (consume) our meals here. We have a refrigerator and an electric stove, and a sink for (to wash) the dishes.

22 POHS-soh veh-DEH-reh lah STAHN-tsah dah BAH-n'yoh?

May I see the bathroom?

23 FAH-tchah KOH-meh seh FOHS-seh ah KAH-zah soo'ah. eel sah-POH-neh eh l'yee ah-shyoo-gah-MAH-nee SOH-noh ah see-NEE-strah dehl lah-VAH-boh, ahk-KAHN-toh AHL-lah VAH-skah.

Make yourself at home. The soap and towels are to the left of the washstand, beside the bathtub.

---

by *faccia,* which implies a wish or a command. See Reference Grammar.   *21. A casa sua* is an idiom. Likewise *a casa mia, a casa nostra,* etc.   22. In a series of nouns the definite article is used before each noun.

11 Undicesima Lezione

Vocabolario per Questa Lezione

una corrente d'aria[1] (kohr-REHN-teh DAH-ryah)	a draft
un raffreddore (raf-frehd-DOH-reh)	a cold
prendere un raffreddore (PREHN-deh-reh oon . . .)	to catch a cold

un soffio (SOHF-fyoh)	a breath
un soffio d'aria (. . . DAH-ryah)	a breath of air
si soffoca (see SOHF-foh-kah)	it is suffocating
al disopra (ahl dee-SOH-prah)	above
al disotto (ahl dee-SOHT-toh)	below
acuisce (ah-koo'EE-sheh)	intensifies
indicare (een-dee-KAH-reh)	to indicate, point
piacevole (pyah-CHEH-voh-leh)	agreeable, pleasant

avvicinarsi (ahv-vee-chee-NAHR-see)	to draw near
si avvicina (see ahv-vee-CHEE-nah)	it draws near
l'ombra (LOHM-brah)	the shade, the shadow

l'aria (LAH-ryah)	air
laggiù (lah-DJOO)	down there
la paura (pah-oo-rah)	fear
il grado (GRAH-doh)	degree
umido (oo-mee-doh)	humid, damp
aprire (ah-PREE-reh)	to open

fa fresco[2] (fah FREH-skoh)	it is cool
ho paura or **temo** (oh pah-oo-rah, TEH-moh)	I am afraid

104

CHE TEMPO FA?

How is the Weather?   (keh TEHM-poh FAH)

in ascesa[3] (een ah-SHEH-zah)   rising
in discesa (een dee-SHEH-zah)   dropping
centigrado[4] (chehn-TEE-grah-doh)   centigrade
la temperatura (tehm-peh-rah-TOO-rah)   temperature
il termometro (tehr-MOH-meh-troh)   thermometer
il barometro (bah-ROH-meh-troh)   barometer

piovere (PYOH-veh-reh) to rain
piove (PYOH-veh)   it is raining
la pioggia (PYOH-djah) the rain
nevicare   to snow
    (neh-vee-KAH-reh)
nevica (NEH-vee-kah)   it is snowing
la neve (NEH-veh)   the snow
il lampo (LAHM-poh)   lightning
il tuono (TWOH-nah)   thunder

un acquazzone (ahk-kwah-TSOH-neh)   a shower (rain)
a torrenti (ah tohr-REHN-tee)   pouring
le soprascarpe[5] (soh-prah-SKAHR-peh)   rubbers
l'ombrello or il parapioggia (ohm-BREHL-loh,   umbrella
    pah-rah-PYOH-djah)

il tempo è mite (. . .MEE-teh)   it (the weather) is mild
tira vento[6] (TEE-rah VEHN-toh)   it is windy
lampeggia (lahm-PEH-djah)   it is lightning
tuona (TWOH-nah)   it is thundering
c'è nebbia[7] (CHEH NEHB-byah)   it is foggy
il tempo è nuvoloso (. . . noo-voh-   it is cloudy, overcast
    LOH-zoh)

la tempesta (tehm-PEH-stah)   storm
l'uragano (loo-rah-GAH-noh)   hurricane
l'umidità (loo-mee-dee-TAH)   humidity
c'è umidità (CHEH oo-mee-dee-TAH)   it is damp, humid
il ghiaccio (GYAH-tchoh)   ice
c'è fango[7] (CHEH FAHN-goh)   it is muddy

la nebbia (NEHB-byah)   fog   il gelo (JEH-loh)   frost
la nuvola (NOO-voh-lah)   cloud   si gela (see JEH-lah)   it is freezing
il clima (KLEE-mah)   climate   il fango (FAHN-goh)   mud

Conversation

1 Che tempo fa?[8]

2 Il tempo è meraviglioso. Fa bel tempo.

3 Apra,[9] per piacere, la finestra e veda[10] che tempo fa.

4 C'è un bel sole, ma fa molto freddo.

5 Quanti gradi abbiamo? La temperatura è sopra o sotto zero?

6 Il termometro segna quattro gradi sotto zero.

7 Credo che avremo[11] cattivo tempo. Il barometro indica pioggia.

8 Il barometro è in discesa. Temo che avremo una tempesta di neve.[12]

9 Guardi come lampeggia! L'uragano[13] s'avvicina. Tira già un forte vento.

10 Qual'è la temperatura massima in Italia?

11 In linea generale,[14] si può dire che il clima dell'Italia Settentrionale sia simile a quello di Nuova York, ma è più mite.

12 Com'è il clima dell'Italia Meridionale?

FOOTNOTES: *1. Lit.,* a current of air. 2. See Note 1, Lesson 6. *3.* Idioms. *4.* In Italy the temperature is measured in degrees centigrade. *5.* The words *le calosce* or *le galosce* may be used in lieu of *soprascarpe. 6. Tira vento* is an idiom. *Lit.,* the wind is pulling. 7. Lit., there is fog, there is humidity, there is

PRONUNCIATION	TRANSLATION

1 keh TEHM-poh FAH?

How is the weather?

2 eel TEHM-poh EH meh-rah-vee-L'YOH-zoh. FAH behl TEHM-poh.

The weather is wonderful. The weather is fine.

3 AH-prah, pehr pyah-CHEH-reh, lah fee-NEH-strah eh VEH-dah keh TEHM-poh FAH.

Please open the window and see how the weather is.

4 CHEH oon behl SOH-leh, mah fah MOHL-toh FREHD-doh.

There is a beautiful sun, but it is very cold.

5 KWAHN-tee GRAH-dee ahb-BYAH-moh? lah tehm-peh-rah-TOO-rah EH SOH-prah oh SOHT-toh DZEH-roh?

What is the temperature (*lit.,* how many degrees do we have) ? Is the temperature above or below zero?

6 eel tehr-MOH-meh-troh SEH-n'yah KWAHT-troh GRAH-dee SOHT-toh DZEH-roh.

The thermometer shows (indicates) four degrees below zero.

7 KREH-doh keh ah-VREH-moh kaht-TEE-voh TEHM-poh; eel bah-ROH-meh-troh EEN-dee-kah PYOH-djah.

I think we are going to have some bad weather; the barometer indicates rain.

8 . . . dee-SHEH-zah. TEH-moh keh ah-VREH-moh oo-nah tehm-PEH-stah dee NEH-veh.

The barometer is falling (*lit.,* is in descent) ; I am afraid we are going to have a snowstorm.

9 GWAHR-dee KOH-meh lahm-PEH-djah! loo-rah-GAH-noh sahv-vee-CHEE-nah. TEE-rah JAH oon FOHR-teh VEHN-toh.

Look how it's lightning! A hurricane is approaching; there is already a strong wind.

10 kwah-LEH lah tehm-peh-rah-TOO-rah MAHS-see-mah een ee-TAH-lyah?

What is the maximum temperature in Italy?

11 een LEE-neh'ah jeh-neh-RAH-leh, see PWOH DEE-reh keh eel KLEE-mah dehl-lee-TAH-lyah seht-tehn-tree'oh-NAH-leh SEE'ah SEE-mee-leh ah KWEHL-loh dee NWOH-vah YOHRK mah EH PYOO MEE-teh.

Generally speaking, one can say that the climate of northern Italy is similar to that of New York, but it is milder.

12 koh-MEH eel KLEE-mah dehl-lee-TAH-lyah meh-ree-dyoh-NAH-leh?

How is the climate of southern Italy?

---

mud.   *8. Lit.,* What weather does it make?   *9.* Imperative of *aprire.*   *10.* Imperative of *vedere.*   *11.* Notice the omission of the word *del,* meaning "some." *12. Lit.,* a storm of snow.   *13.* Notice the peculiar use of the definite article before *uragano,* as compared to the indefinite article in the English translation.

13 Durante l'estate fa molto caldo, ma d'inverno il clima è mite, quasi simile a quello della California. Non nevica quasi mai,[15] e piove poco.

14 Sulla Costa Ligure la temperatura è spesso di[16] venti o venticinque gradi centigradi, anche in inverno. Anche lì il clima è simile a quello[17] della California.

15 Sarà[18] molto piacevole nell'inverno.

16 Ah, sì! Mi piacerebbe[19] passare[20] l'inverno in uno dei luoghi incantevoli che si trovano sulla Costa Ligure.

17 Crede che pioverà oggi?

18 Il tempo è nuvoloso, ma credo che faccia[21] troppo freddo per piovere. Probabilmente avremo del gelo, e il tempo minaccia una tempesta di neve.

19 Infatti, nevica già. Dovrebbe mettere l'impermeabile prima di uscire,[22] perchè un parapioggia non le servirebbe a nulla.

20 Ha le soprascarpe?[23]

---

14. Idiom. *Linea* means "line."   *15.* Notice that the Italian expression for "never" is: *non* before the verb, and *mai* after the verb. The word *mai* alone means "never" when used without a verb.   *16.* Notice the idiomatic use of the word *di* (of). *17. Quello* is a demonstrative pronoun. The other forms are: *quella, quelli, quelle.* *18. Sarà* is future of probability.   *19. Piacerebbe* is the impersonal third person of the conditional of *piacere.*   *20. Passare* means "to spend" when used in connection with a noun implying duration of time. Otherwise it means "to pass."

13 doo-RAHN-teh leh-STAH-teh fah MOHL-toh KAHL-doh, mah deen-VEHR-noh eel KLEE-mah EH MEE-teh, KWAH-zee SEE-mee-leh ah KWEHL-loh DEHL-lah kah-lee-FOHR-nyah. nohn NEH-vee-kah KWAH-zee MAH'y, eh PYOH-veh POH-koh.

During the summer it is very hot, but in winter the climate is mild, almost similar to that of California. It hardly ever snows (*lit.*, it snows almost never), and there is little rain (*lit.*, rains little).

14 SOOL-lah KOH-stah LEE-goo-reh lah tehm-peh-rah-TOO-rah EH SPEHS-soh dee VEHN-tee oh vehn-tee-CHEEN-kweh GRAH-dee chehn-TEE-grah-dee, AHN-keh een een-VEHR-noh. AHN-keh LEE eel KLEE-mah EH SEE-mee-leh ah KWEHL-loh DEHL-lah kah-lee-FOHR-nyah.

On the Ligurian Coast the temperature is often twenty or twenty-five degrees centigrade, even in winter. There too the climate is similar to that of California.

15 sah-RAH MOHL-toh pyah-CHEH-voh-leh nehl-leen-VEHR-noh.

It is probably very pleasant in winter.

16 AH, SEE! mee pyah-cheh-REHB-beh pahs-SAH-reh leen-VEHR-noh een oo-noh day LWOH-gee een-kahn-TEH-voh-lee keh see TROH-vah-noh SOOL-lah KOH-stah LEE-goo-reh.

Oh, yes! I would like to spend the winter in one of the enchanting places (that are found) on the Ligurian Coast.

17 KREH-deh keh pyoh-veh-RAH OH-djee?

Do you think it will rain today?

18 . . . noo-voh-LOH-zoh, mah KREH-doh keh FAH-tchah TROHP-poh FREHD-doh pehr PYOH-veh-reh. proh-bah-beel-MEHN-teh ah-VREH-moh dehl JEH-loh, eh eel TEHM-poh mee-NAH-tchah oo-nah tehm-PEH-stah dee NEH-veh.

The weather is cloudy, but I think it is too cold for rain (to rain). We shall probably have some frost, and a snowstorm is threatening.

19 een-FAHT-tee, NEH-vee-kah JAH. doh-VREHB-beh MEHT-teh-reh leem-pehr-meh'AH-bee-leh PREE-mah dee oo-SHEE-reh, pehr-KEH oon pah-rah-PYOH-djah nohn leh sehr-vee-REHB-beh ah NOOL-lah.

In fact, it's snowing already. You ought to put on your raincoat before going out, for an umbrella would be useless to you (*lit.*, would serve you to nothing).

20 AH leh soh-prah-SKAHR-peh?

Do you have your rubbers?

---

21. Faccia is the subjunctive of *fare,* required by the word *credo.* See Reference Grammar.   *22.* In Italian, after a preposition, the verb is used in the infinitive.   *23.* Notice the omission of the possessive adjective before *soprascarpe.* This is done because *soprascarpe* is a personal article.   *24. Troppa* is an adjective here, and agrees with *umidità.* When *troppo* is an adverb it is invariable. The same applies to the word *molto.*

21 Non ha mai fatto un freddo simile durante tutto l'inverno.

22 Non crede lei che faccia troppo caldo?

23 Il caldo è soffocante. Non c'è un soffio d'aria.

24 C'è troppa[24] umidità, e l'umidità acuisce tanto il freddo quanto il caldo.

21 nohn ah MAH'y FAHT-toh oon FREHD-doh SEE-mee-leh doo-RAHN-teh TOOT-toh leen-VEHR-noh.

22 nohn KREH-deh LAY keh FAH-tchah TROHP-poh KAHL-doh?

23 eel KAHL-doh EH sohf-foh-KAHN-teh. nohn CHEH oon SOHF-fyoh DAH-ryah.

24 cheh TROHP-pah oo-mee-dee-TAH, eh loo-mee-dee-TAH ah-koo'EE-sheh TAHN-toh eel FREHD-doh KWAHN-toh eel KAHL-doh.

It has never been so cold during the whole winter.

Don't you think that it is too hot?

The heat is stifling. There isn't a breath of air.

There is too much humidity, and the humidity intensifies the heat as well as the cold.

 Dodicesima Lezione

Vocabolario per Questa Lezione

la bontà (bohn-TAH)		kindness, goodness
avere la bontà di (ah-VEH-reh . . . dee)		to have the kindness to
la cintura (cheen-TOO-rah)		belt
la vita (VEE-tah)		waistline (*also* life)
il colletto (kohl-LEHT-toh)		collar
la varietà (vah-ryeh-TAH)		variety

largo (LAHR-goh)	large, wide
stretto (STREHT-toh)	tight, narrow
nuovo (NWOH-voh)	new
ciò (CHOH)	that
cucire (koo-CHEE-reh)	to sew
tagliare (tah-L'YAH-reh)	to cut

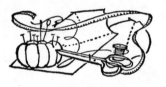

senz'altro[1] (sehn-TSAHL-troh)	without fail
precisamente (preh-chee-zah-MEHN-teh)	precisely
dopo di ciò (DOH-poh dee CHOH)	after that

provare (proh-VAH-reh)	to try, try on	usare (OO-ZAH-reh)	to use, employ
mettere (MEHT-teh-reh)	to put, put on	coprire (koh-PREE-reh)	to cover

aggiungere (ah-DJOON-jeh-reh)	to add
la stoffa or il tessuto (STOHF-fah, tehs-soo-toh)	material
dimenticare (dee-mehn-tee-KAH-reh)	to forget

il colore (koh-LOH-reh)	the color	giallo (JAHL-loh)	yellow
bianco (BYAHN-koh)	white	verde (VEHR-deh)	green
nero (NEH-roh)	black	marrone (mahr-ROH-neh)	brown
rosso (ROHS-soh)	red	grigio (GREE-joh)	gray
celeste (cheh-LEH-steh) or azzurro (ah-DZOOR-roh)			blue

112

IL SARTO · LA SARTA · LA MODA

THE TAILOR, THE DRESSMAKER,
FASHION

(eel SAHR-toh, lah SAHR-tah,
lah MOH-dah)

la sartoria (sahr-toh-REE-ah)	tailor shop
la macchina (MAHK-kee-nah)	machine
la macchina da² cucire (... dah koo-CHEE-reh)	sewing machine
le forbici (FOHR-bee-chee)	scissors
il modello (moh-DEHL-loh)	pattern

le guarnizioni (gwahr-nee-TSYOH-nee)	trimmings
la cucitura (koo-chee-TOO-rah)	seam, sewing
il merletto (mehr-LEHT-toh)	lace
il bottone (boht-TOH-neh)	button
l'ago (LAH-goh)	needle
il filo (FEE-loh)	thread

un vestito (veh-STEE-toh)	a suit
confezionare un vestito (kohn-feh-tsyoh-NAH-reh ...)	to make a suit
la misura (mee-ZOO-rah)	measure, measurement
prendere la misura (PREHN-deh-reh ...)	to take the measurement

un pezzo (PEH-tsoh)	a piece
il cotone (koh-TOH-neh)	cotton
la lana (LAH-nah)	wool
la seta (SEH-tah)	silk
la flanella (flah-NEHL-lah)	flannel
il lino (LEE-noh)	linen
il velluto (vehl-LOO-toh)	velvet
il crespo (KREH-spoh)	crepe
il nastro (NAH-stroh)	ribbon

una giacca (JAHK-kah)	a jacket, coat
una giacca larga (... LAHR-gah)	a loose jacket
una giacca aderente (... ah-deh-REHN-teh)	a close-fitting jacket
a colore³ (ah-koh-LOH-reh)	colored

variare (vah-RYAH-reh)	to vary	il braccio (BRAH-tchoh)	the arm
lo stile (loh STEE-leh)	style	il fianco (FYAHN-koh)	the hip
la moda (MOH-dah)	fashion	la manica (MAH-nee-kah)	sleeve
attuale (aht-too'AH-leh)	present, actual		
il collo (KOHL-loh)	neck	il metro (MEH-troh)	meter
		il ricamo (ree-KAH-moh)	embroidery

CONVERSATION

1 Signorina Del Vecchio, vuole avere la bontà di dirci di quanti pezzi si compone una veste da[4] donna?

2 Normalmente si compone di due pezzi: del busto e della gonna. Ma ci sono anche delle vesti ad[5] un solo pezzo.

3 Benissimo,[6] signorina. E come si chiama la parte della veste che copre il braccio?

4 Si chiama manica. La parte della veste che aderisce al collo si chiama colletto, e la parte al di sopra dei fianchi[7] dove si usa mettere la cintura si chiama vita.

5 Come si usano[8] adesso le maniche?[9]

6 Per le maniche la moda varia spesso. Delle volte si portano molto corte o molto lunghe[9]; delle volte sono larghe[9] o molto strette.

7 Di che si fanno le vesti?

FOOTNOTES: *1*. An idiom.   *2*. *Da* implies use See Note 25, Lesson 3.   *3*. *A colore* is an idiom.   *4*. Special use of the word *da*. In this case it means "to be used by."   *5*. *a* often adds a *d* before a vowel. Here, used idiomatically, it means "in."   *6*. *Benissimo* is the absolute superlative form of *bene*.   *7*. The singular of *fianchi* is *fianco*.   *8*. *Usano*, impersonal form of *usare*, agrees with *maniche*. *9*. A reminder that nouns and adjectives ending in *-ca* and *-ga* take an *h* before the plural ending.   *10*. *Cui* is a relative pronoun. See Note 19, Lesson 3.

PRONUNCIATION	TRANSLATION
1 see-n'yoh-REE-nah dehl VEHK-kyoh, VWOH-leh ah-VEH-reh lah bohn-TAH dee DEER-chee dee KWAHN-tee PEH-tsee see kohm-POH-neh oo-nah VEH-steh dah DOHN-nah?	Miss Del Vecchio, will you be good enough to tell us of how many pieces a woman's dress is made?
2 nohr-mahl-MEHN-teh see kohm-POH-neh dee DOO'eh PEH-tsee; dehl BOO-stoh eh DEHL-lah GOHN-nah. mah chee SOH-noh AHN-keh DEHL-leh VEH-stee ahd oon SOH-loh PEH-tsoh.	Usually it consists of two pieces: the bodice and the skirt. But there are also dresses in a single piece.
3 beh-NEE-see-moh . . . KOH-meh see KYAH-mah lah PAHR-teh . . . keh KOH-preh eel BRAH-tchoh?	Very good, Miss. And what is the part of the dress that covers the arm called?
4 . . . MAH-nee-kah . . . ah-deh-REE-sheh ahl KOHL-loh see KYAH-mah kohl-LEHT-toh, . . . FYAHN-kee DOH-veh see OO-zah MEHT-teh-reh lah cheen-TOO-rah . . . VEE-tah.	It is called the sleeve. The part of the dress which is fitted to the neck is called the collar, and the part above the hips, where it is customary to put the belt, is called the waist.
5 KOH-meh see OO-zah-noh ah-DEHS-soh leh MAH-nee-keh?	How are sleeves being worn now?
6 . . . MOH-dah VAH-ryah SPEHS-soh. DEHL-leh VOHL-teh see POHR-tah-noh MOHL-toh KOHR-teh oh . . . LOON-geh; DEHL-leh VOHL-teh SOH-noh LAHR-geh oh MOHL-toh STREHT-teh.	For sleeves the style often varies. Sometimes they are worn very short or very long; sometimes they are wide or very narrow.
7 dee KEH see FAHN-noh leh VEH-stee?	Of what are dresses made?

---

11. Note the generic use of the definite article. *12. S'intende di cucito* is an idiom. Notice reflexive form of the verb. *13.* The infinitive of *occorrono* is *occorrere,* used only in the third person. *14.* A meter is 39.37 inches. It is the standard measurement of length in Italy. *15. Si taglia* and *si cuce* are impersonal expressions. *16.* The word *a* is used idiomatically before *mano* and *macchina.* It means "by." *17. Suppongo* is a form of the present of the irregular verb *supporre.* For other forms see table of irregular verbs. *18. Si prova* is a reflexive

8 C'è una grande varietà di stoffe di cui[10] si possono fare, ma le più comuni sono la[11] seta, la lana ed il cotone. Poi c'è il crespo, il rayon, la flanella, il lino, il velluto, e tante altre ancora.

9 Lei s'intende di cucito,[12] non è vero?

10 Sì, signore, abbastanza per confezionare i miei vestiti con l'aiuto d'un modello.

11 Mi vuol dire come si fa una veste?

12 Con piacere. Occorrono[13] tre metri[14] o più di stoffa, che si taglia[15] con le forbici, seguendo il modello e le misure, e poi si cuce[15] con l'ago infilato col cotone o con la seta. Certe cuciture si fanno a[16] mano, altre a[16] macchina.

13 Dopo di ciò suppongo[17] che lei si prova[18] la veste per vedere se le va bene.

14 Precisamente. Poi si aggiungono le guarnizioni che consistono in merletti, ricami, nastri e bottoni a colore.

verb. It means "try on yourself." *19. Comprarsi* is a reflexive verb and means "to buy for himself." *20. -ci* is a pronoun referring to a place already mentioned,

8 CHEH OO-nah GRAHN-deh vah-ryeh-TAH dee STOHF-feh dee KOO'y see POHS-soh-noh FAH-reh, mah leh PYOO koh-MOO-nee SOH-noh lah SEH-tah, lah LAH-nah ed eel koh-TOH-neh. POY CHEH eel KREH-spoh, eel rah-YOHN, lah flah-NEHL-lah, eel LEE-noh, eel vehl-LOO-toh, eh TAHN-teh AHL-treh ahn-KOH-rah.

There is a great variety of materials of which they can be made, but the most common are silk, wool, and cotton. There are also crepe, rayon, flannel, linen, velvet, and many others.

9 lay seen-TEHN-deh dee koo-CHEE-toh, nohn EH VEH-roh?

You know how to sew, don't you (lit., you understand about sewing)?

10 SEE, see-N'YOH-reh, ahb-bah-STAHN-tsah pehr kohn-feh-tsyoh-NAH-reh ee M'YAY veh-STEE-tee kohn lah-YOO-toh doon moh-DEHL-loh.

Yes, sir, enough to make my own dresses with the aid of a pattern.

11 mee VWOHL DEE-reh KOH-meh see FAH OO-nah VEH-steh?

Will you tell me how a dress is made?

12 kohn pyah-CHEH-reh. ohk-KOHR-roh-noh treh MEH-tree oh PYOO dee STOHF-fah, keh see TAH-l'yah kohn leh FOHR-bee-chee seh-GWEHN-doh eel moh-DEHL-loh eh leh mee-zoo-reh. eh POY see KOO-cheh kohn LAH-goh een-fee-LAH-toh kohl koh-TOH-neh oh kohn lah SEH-tah. CHEHR-teh koo-chee-TOO-reh see FAHN-noh ah MAH-noh, AHL-treh ah MAHK-kee-nah.

With pleasure. You need (lit., are necessary) three or more yards of material, which is cut with the scissors, following the pattern and the measurements, and then it is sewn with a needle threaded with cotton or silk. Some sewing (lit., certain sewings) is done by hand and some (others) by machine.

13 DOH-poh dee CHOH soop-POHN-goh keh lay see PROH-vah lah VEH-steh pehr veh-DEH-reh seh leh vah BEH-neh.

After that I suppose you try the dress on to see if it fits you well.

14 preh-chee-zah-MEHN-teh. POY see ah-DJOON-goh-noh leh gwahr-nee-TSYOH-nee keh kohn-SEE-stoh-noh een mehr-LEHT-tee, ree-KAH-mee, NAH-stree eh boht-TOH-nee ah koh-LOH-reh.

Exactly. Then you add the trimmings, which consist of lace, embroidery, ribbons, and colored buttons.

and is attached to the imperative *andiamo.* It means "to have made for myself."

21. This is a peculiar use of *farmi.*
22. Imperative form of *dimenticare.* In

15 Avrà bisogno di questo danaro suo marito?

16 Ne avrà bisogno immediatamente, perchè oggi deve comprarsi[19] un vestito.

17 Da chi intende farsi confezionare il suo vestito?

18 Dal sarto all'angolo di Via Veneto. Il signor Leoni è un ottimo sarto.

19 Allora andiamoci.[20] Ecco suo marito.

20 Buon giorno, signor Leoni. Desidero farmi[21] un vestito.

21 Vuole avere la bontà di mostrarmi gli ultimi arrivi di tessuti?

22 Voglio un vestito fatto su misura, poichè gli abiti già confezionati non mi vanno mai bene.

23 Mi permetta di prendere le sue misure. Vuole una giacca larga o aderente?

24 La preferisco larga e comoda, e non dimentichi[22] che il vestito mi occorre per la prossima settimana.

25 Cercherò[23] di farglielo[24] trovare pronto senz'altro martedì o, al più tardi,[25] mercoledì.

---

verbs ending in *-care* and *-gare* an *h* is inserted between the stem of the verb and the ending when the ending is or begins with *e* or *i*. See Reference Grammar. *23.* From the future of *cercare*. See Note 22 above. *24.* *-glielo* is a double pro-

15 ah-VRAH bee-ZOH-n'yoh dee KWEH-stoh dah-NAH-roh soo'oh mah-REE toh?

Will your husband need this money?

16 . . . eem-meh-dyah-tah-MEHN-teh, pehr-keh OH-djee DEH-veh kohm-PRAHR-see oon veh-STEE-toh.

He will need it immediately, because today he must buy a suit (for himself).

17 dah KEE een-TEHN-deh FAHR-see kohn-feh-tsyoh-NAH-reh eel soo'-oh veh-STEE-toh?

By whom does he intend to have his suit made?

18 dahl SAHR-toh ahl-LAHN-goh-loh dee VEE'ah VEH-neh-toh. eel see-N'YOHR leh'OH-nee EH oon OHT-tee-moh SAHR-toh.

By the tailor at the corner of Via Veneto. Mr. Leoni is an excellent tailor.

19 ahl-LOH-rah ahn-DYAH-moh-chee. EHK-koh soo'oh mah-REE-toh.

Then let's go there. Here is your husband.

20 BWOHN JOHR-noh . . . deh-ZEE-deh-roh FAHR-mee oon veh-STEE-toh.

Good day, Mr. Leoni. I wish to have a suit made.

21 vwoH-leh ah-VEH-reh lah bohn-TAH dee moh-STRAHR-mee l'yee OOL-tee-mee ahr-REE-vee dee tehs-soo-tee?

Will you have the kindness to show me the latest (arrivals of) fabrics?

22 voH-l'yoh oon veh-STEE-toh FAHT-toh soo mee-zoo-rah, poy-KEH l'yee AH-bee-tee JAH kohn-feh-tsyoh-NAH-tee nohn mee VAHN-noh MAH'y BEH-neh.

I want a suit made to order (*lit.,* on measurement) because ready-made suits never fit me well.

23 mee pehr-MEHT-tah dee PREHN-deh-reh leh soo'eh mee-zoo-reh. vwoH-leh oo-nah JAHK-kah LAHR-gah oh ah-deh-REHN-teh?

Allow me to take your measurements. Do you want the jacket loose or tight-fitting?

24 lah preh-feh-REE-skoh LAHR-gah eh KOH-moh-dah, eh nohn dee-MEHN-tee-kee keh . . . mee oh-KOH-reh pehr lah PROHS-see-mah seht-tee-MAH-nah.

I prefer it loose and comfortable, and don't forget that I need the suit next week.

25 chehr-keh-ROH dee FAHR-l'yeh-loh troh-VAH-reh PROHN-toh sehn-TSAHL-troh mahr-teh-DEE oh, ahl PYOO TAHR-dee, mehr-koh-leh-DEE.

I shall try to have it ready for you (*lit.,* make you find it) without fail Tuesday or, at the latest, Wednesday.

---

noun attached to the infinitive. See Reference Grammar.   *25. Al più tardi* is an idiom.

13 Tredicesima Lezione

Vocabolario per Questa Lezione

una vettura (veht-TOO-rah)		a car, carriage
un'automobile[1] (oo-nah'oo-toh-MOH-bee-leh)		an automobile
il veicolo (veh-EE-koh-loh)		vehicle
una passeggiata (pahs-seh-DJAH-tah)		a walk
fare una passeggiata[2] (FAH-reh . . .)		to take a walk
andare a passeggio[2] (ahn-DAH-reh ah pahs-SEH-djoh)		to go for a walk

il mare (MAH-reh)	sea	**dormire** (dohr-MEE-reh)	to sleep
il lido (LEE-doh)	seashore	**alzarsi** (ahl-TSAHR-see)	to get up
la spiaggia (SPYAH-djah)	beach	**sedersi** (seh-DEHR-see)	to sit down
l'orlo (LOHR-loh)	edge	**la gente** (JEHN-teh)	people
tanto (TAHN-toh)	so, so much	**il pedone** (peh-DOH-neh)	pedestrian

il costume da[3] **bagno** (koh-STOO-meh dah BAH-n'yoh)	bathing suit
fare i bagni[2] (FAH-reh ee BAH-n'yee)	to go bathing
la radio (RAH-dyoh)	radio
la televisione (teh-leh-vee-ZYOH-neh)	television
andare a letto (ahn-DAH-reh ah LEHT-toh)	to go to bed
addormentarsi (ahd-dohr-mehn-TAHR-see)	to fall asleep
svegliarsi (zveh-L'YAHR-see)	to awaken
lavarsi (lah-VAHR-see)	to wash (oneself)
vestirsi (veh-STEER-see)	to dress (oneself)

a sua disposizione[4] (ah soo'ah dee-spoh-zee-TSYOH-neh)	at your service
prego (PREH-goh)	I beg of you (please) ; don't mention it (after "thank you")
arrivederci (ahr-ree-veh-DEHR-chee)	until we meet again (familiar form)
arrivederla (ahr-ree-veh-DEHR-lah)	until we meet again (polite form)

120

IN CITTA

IN TOWN   (een cheet-TAH)

un edificio (eh-dee-FEE-choh)   a building
il palazzo di giustizia (. . . joo-STEE-tsyah) court house
un ospedale (oh-speh-DAH-leh)   a hospital
il municipio (moo-nee-CHEE-pyoh)   city hall
il mercato (mehr-KAH-toh)   the market

il teatro (teh'AH-troh)   theater
una scuola (SKWOH-lah)   a school
una chiesa (KYEH-zah)   a church
una banca (BAHN-kah)   a bank
il parco (PAHR-koh)   park
la piazza (PYAH-tsah)   square
l'angolo (LAHN-goh-loh)   corner

la posta (POH-stah)   post office, mail
l'ufficio postale (loof-FEE-choh poh-   post office
    STAH-leh)
la stazione (stah-TSYOH-neh)   station
la via (VEE-ah)   avenue, street
la strada (STRAH-dah)   street, road
il corso (KOHR-soh)   boulevard
il marciapiede (mahr-chah-PYEH-deh)   sidewalk
la caserma (kah-ZEHR-mah)   police station
il traffico (TRAHF-fee-koh)   traffic

il cinema (CHEE-neh-mah)   motion picture house
la pellicola or il film (pehl-LEE-koh-lah,   film, motion picture
    FEELM)
un abitante (ah-bee-TAHN-teh)   an inhabitant
presentare (preh-zehn-TAH-reh)   to introduce, present
fare la conoscenza (. . . koh-noh-SHEHN-tsah) to make the acquaintance
la dogana (doh-GAH-nah)   customs house
il doganiere (doh-gah-NYEH-reh)'   customs officer

CONVERSATION

1 A che ora è andato a letto iersera,[5] che dorme ancora?

2 Sono andato a letto molto tardi ed ho dormito un po' più del solito.

3 Non[6] mi son[7] potuto addormentare fino alle quattro del mattino.

4 La mia domestica non mi ha chiamato e mi sono[7] svegliato proprio adesso.[8]

5 Si accomodi, prego. Mi alzo,[9] mi lavo e mi vesto subito.

6 Eccomi.[10] Son già pronto ed ai suoi ordini.[11]

7 Possiamo uscire quando le fa comodo.[12]

8 Dove vuole che andiamo?

9 Se vuole, possiamo andare a fare una passeggiata a Villa Borghese.

10 Preferirei[13] visitare alcuni edifici pubblici: i fori romani, una scuola, un ufficio postale, un mercato, una chiesa ed il municipio.

11 Che magnifica idea! E dopo andremo a teatro o al cinema. In questa piazza c'è un cinema dove si proiettano le migliori[14] pellicole.

FOOTNOTES: *1. Automobile* is feminine, therefore the indefinite article is *un'*.
2. Idioms. *3.* If you don't remember this use of *da* see Note 25, Lesson 3.
4. A synonym of *a sua disposizione* is *ai suoi ordini*, both idioms. *5. Iersera* or

PRONUNCIATION	TRANSLATION
1 ah keh OH-rah EH ahn-DAH-toh ah LEHT-toh yehr-SEH-rah, keh DOHR-meh ahn-KOH-rah?	At what time did you go to bed last night, that you are still sleeping?
2 . . . MOHL-toh TAHR-dee ed oh dohr-MEE-toh oon POH PYOO dehl SOH-lee-toh.	I went to bed very late and I have slept a little more than usual.
3 nohn mee SOHN poh-TOO-toh ahd-dohr-mehn-TAH-reh FEE-noh AHL-leh KWAHT-troh dehl maht-TEE-noh.	I wasn't able to fall asleep until four in the morning.
4 lah MEE'ah doh-MEH-stee-kah nohn mee ah kyah-MAH-toh eh mee SOH-noh zveh-L'YAH-toh PROH-pryoh ah-DEHS-soh.	My maid didn't call me and I have just awakened.
5 see ahk-KOH-moh-dee, PREH-goh. mee AHL-tsoh, mee LAH-voh, eh mee VEH-stoh soo-bee-toh.	Make yourself comfortable, I beg of you. I shall get up, wash, and dress at once.
6 EHK-koh-mee. sohn JAH PROHN-toh ed ah'y swoy OHR-dee-nee.	Here I am. I am ready and at your service.
7 pohs-SYAH-moh OO-SHEE-reh KWAHN-doh leh fah KOH-moh-doh.	We can go out whenever you wish.
8 DOH-veh vwoH-leh keh ahn-DYAH-moh?	Where do you suggest (*lit.*, want) we go?
9 . . . FAH-reh oo-nah pahs-seh-DJAH-tah ah VEEL-lah bohr-GEH-zeh.	If you wish, we can go for a walk in Villa Borghese.
10 preh-feh-ree-RAY vee-zee-TAH-reh ahl-KOO-nee eh-dee-FEE-chee POOB-blee-chee: ee FOH-ree roh-MAH-nee, oo-nah SKWOK-lah, oon oof-FEE-choh poh-STAH-leh, oon mehr-KAH-toh, oo-nah KYEH-zah ed eel moo-nee-CHEE-pyoh.	I would rather (*lit.*, prefer to) visit some public buildings: the Roman Forums, a school, a post office, a market, a church, and the city hall.
11 keh mah-N'YEE-fee-kah ee-DEH'ah! eh DOH-poh ahn-DREH-moh ah teh-AH-troh oh ahl CHEE-neh-mah. een KWEH-stah PYAH-tsah CHEH oon CHEE-neh-mah DOH-veh see proh-YEHT-tah-noh leh mee-L'YOH-ree pehl-LEE-koh-leh.	What a splendid idea! And afterwards we shall go to the theater or to the movies. On this square there is a motion picture house where the best films are shown.

ieri sera. 6. See Note 19, Lesson 1. 7. *Son,* same as *sono.* Reflexive verbs require the auxiliary *essere* in all compound tenses. 8. *Proprio adesso* means literally "just now." 9. The present is often used in Italian to indicate immediate

12 Più edifici visiterò, meglio[15] conoscerò la città.

13 Come regola bene il traffico quell'agente di polizia! Ci sono sempre tanti veicoli per le strade e tanti pedoni sui marciapiedi che sarà[16] difficile regolare[17] il traffico.

14 Roma ha molti abitanti. Molte delle sue strade sono larghe ed alberate. I suoi sette colli sono pittoreschi e storici.[18]

15 Debbo andare alla banca per cambiare i miei dollari.

16 Il cambio non è molto alto. Mi dispiace non poterla[19] accompagnare. L'aspetterò dalla[20] sarta.

17 Vuole avere la gentilezza di presentarmi a questa signora prima di andarsene?

18 Con piacere. La[21] presenterò immediatamente.

19 Mia cara amica, le voglio presentare la signora Menichini.

20 Signora, sono fortunatissima di fare la sua conoscenza.

21 Il piacere è mio, signora, perchè ho spesso sentito parlare[22] di lei.

---

future. *10.* See Note 29, Lesson 3. *11. Lit.,* at your orders. *12. Quando le fa comodo* is an idiom. *Lit.,* when it makes you comfortable. *13. Preferirei* (*io* form) is the conditional of *preferire*. *14. Migliori* (sing., *migliore*) is the relative superlative of *buono*. Like other adjectives it agrees in gender and number

12 PYOO eh-dee-FEE-chee vee-zee- teh-ROH. MEH-l'yoh koh-noh-sheh-ROH lah cheet-TAH.

The more buildings I visit (*lit.*, shall visit) the better I shall know the city.

13 KOH-meh REH-goh-lah BEH-neh eel TRAHF-fee-koh kwehl-lah-JEHN-teh dee poh-lee-TSEE'ah! chee SOH-noh SEHM-preh TAHN-tee veh-EE-koh-lee pehr leh STRAH-deh eh TAHN-tee peh-DOH-nee SOO'y mahr-chah-PYEH-dee keh sah-RAH dee-FEE-chee-leh. . . .

How well that policeman directs (*lit.*, regulates) traffic! There are always so many vehicles in the streets and so many pedestrians on the sidewalks that it must be difficult to direct the traffic.

14 ROH-mah ah MOHL-tee ah-bee-TAHN-tee . . . LAHR-geh ed ahl-beh-RAH-teh. ee SWOY SEHT-teh KOHL-lee SOH-noh peet-toh-REH-skee eh STOH-ree-chee.

Rome has many inhabitants. Many of its streets are wide and lined with trees. Its seven hills are picturesque and historical.

15 DEHB-boh ahn-DAH-reh ahl-lah-BAHN-kah pehr kahm-BYAH-reh ee M'YAY DOHL-lah-ree.

I must go to the bank to exchange my dollars.

16 eel KAHM-byoh nohn EH MOHL-toh AHL-toh. mee dee-SPYAH-cheh nohn poh-TEHR-lah ahk-kohm-pah-N'YAH-reh. lah-speht-teh-ROH DAHL-lah SAHR-tah.

The rate of exchange isn't very high. I am sorry I can't accompany you. I shall wait for you at the dressmaker's.

17 vwoH-leh ah-VEH-reh lah jehn-tee-LEH-tsah dee preh-zehn-TAHR-mee ah KWEH-stah see-N'YOH-rah PREE-mah dee ahn-DAHR-seh-neh?

Will you have the kindness to introduce me to this lady before leaving?

18 kohn pyah-CHEH-reh. lah preh-zehn-teh-ROH eem-meh-dyah-tah-MEHN-teh.

With pleasure. I shall introduce you at once.

19 MEE'ah KAH-rah ah-MEE-kah, leh voH-l'yoh preh-zehn-TAH-reh . . . meh-nee-KEE-nee.

My dear friend, may I present Mrs. Menichini.

20 . . . fohr-too-nah-TEES-see-mah dee FAH-reh lah soo'ah koh-noh-SHEHN-tsah.

Madam, I am very happy (fortunate) to make your acquaintance.

21 . . . oh SPEHS-soh sehn-TEE-toh pahr-LAH-reh dee LAY.

The pleasure is mine, for I have often heard of you.

with the noun is modifies. *15. Meglio* is the irregular comparative of *bene.* *16. Sará* in this case is future of probability. See Reference Grammar. *17. Regolare* literally means "to regulate." *18. Storico* is one of the words ending in *co* which does not add an *h* after the *c* in the plural. *19.* The direct object

22 Rimarrà a lungo in città?

23 Non molto tempo. Intendo passare[23] l'estate al lido. M'hanno detto che ad Anzio c'è una spiaggia bellissima.

24 Ed anche molti divertimenti. Ci[24] vado anch'io, e sarò molto felice di farle[25] da guida.[26]

25 Lei è molto gentile, ed io le sarò molto riconoscente.

26 Sarò a sua disposizione. Intanto le auguro buon viaggio.

27 Grazie. Arrivederla,[27] signora. A presto.[28]

---

pronoun *la* could be attached to the infinitive *accompagnare* instead of *potere* (to be able to). *20. Dalla* is a contraction of *da* and *la*. *21.* This direct object pronoun *la* is both masculine and feminine (polite singular). *22. Sentito parlare di* is an idiom. It means "heard someone speak of." *23.* See Note 20, Lesson 11. *24.* See Note 19, Lesson 12. In this case *ci* precedes the verb. *25.* The *le* of *farle*

22 ree-mahr-RAH ah LOON-goh een cheet-TAH?

Will you remain long in the city?

23 . . . een-TEHN-doh pahs-SAH-reh leh-STAH-teh ahl LEE-doh. MAHN-noh DEHT-toh keh ahd AHN-tsyoh CHEH oo-nah SPYAH-djah behl-LEES-see-mah.

Not long (*lit.*, much time). I expect to spend the summer at the seashore. I have been told (*lit.*, they have told me) that at Anzio there is a very beautiful beach.

24 ed AHN-keh MOHL-tee dee-vehr-tee-MEHN-tee. chee VAH-doh ahn-KEE'oh, eh sah-ROH MOHL-toh feh-LEE-cheh dee FAHR-leh dah GWEE-dah.

And also many amusements. I am going there also and I shall be very happy to be your guide.

25 lay EH MOHL-toh jehn-TEE-leh, ed EE'oh leh sah-ROH . . . ree-koh-noh-SHEHN-teh.

You are very kind, and I shall be very grateful to you.

26 . . . soo'ah dee-spoh-zee-TSYOH-nneh. een-TAHN-toh leh AH'oo-goo-roh BWOHN VYAH-djoh.

I shall be at your service. Meanwhile I wish you a pleasant trip.

27 GRAH-tsyeh. ahr-ree-veh-DEHR-lah, see-N'YOH-rah. ah PREH-stoh.

Thank you. Good-bye, madam. See you soon.

---

is an indirect object pronoun. 26. *Farle da guida* is an idiom. It means "to act as a guide to you." 27. *Arrivederla* is an idiom. It means "good-bye, until we meet again." The familiar form is *arrivederci*. 28. *A presto* is an idiom. It means "until soon." Likewise *a domani, a lunedì,* etc.

14 Quattordicesima Lezione

Vocabolario per Questa Lezione

il campanello (kahm-pah-NEHL-loh)	door bell
suoni[1] il campanello! (SWOH-nee . . .)	ring the bell!
un pochino (poh-KEE-noh)	a very little bit
ogni ora (OH-n'yee OH-rah)	every hour
io ho fretta[2] (EE'oh oh FREHT-tah)	I am in a hurry

un tassì (tahs-SEE)	a taxi	quanto (KWAHN-toh)	how much
grave (GRAH-veh)	serious, grave	salire (sah-LEE-reh)	to go up
		abitare (ah-bee-TAH-reh)	to live, reside
meglio (MEH-l'yoh)	better		

chiuda[3] lo sportello! (KYOO-dah)	close the door
faccia presto[4]! (FAH-tchah PREH-stoh)	hurry up
da questa parte[2] (dah-KWEH-stah PAHR-teh)	this way
a domicilio (doh-mee-CHEE-lyoh)	at home, to the house

peggio[5] (PEH-djoh)	worse
ritorni![6] (ree-TOHR-nee)	come back
entri![6] (EHN-tree)	come in

la testa or il capo (TEH-stah, KAH-poh)	head
l'autista (lah'oo-TEE-stah)	driver, chauffeur
libero (LEE-beh-roh)	free, unoccupied

domandare (doh-mahn-DAH-reh)	to ask
mi mostri[6]! (mee-MOH-stree)	show me
si fermi![6] (see FEHR-mee)	stop
nuovamente (nwoh-vah-MEHN-teh)	again
si accomodi! (see ahk-KOH-moh-dee)	make yourself comfortable, sit down
favorisca![7] (fah-voh-REE-skah)	come, come in

DAL MEDICO

AT THE DOCTOR'S   (dahl MEH-dee-koh)

il dottore[8] (doht-TOH-reh)   doctor
la clinica (KLEE-nee-kah)   doctor's office, clinic
la sala d'aspetto (SAH-lah dah-SPEHT-toh)   waiting room
l'onorario (loh-noh-RAH-ryoh)   fee
il polso (POHL-soh)   pulse
tastare il polso (tah-STAH-reh . . .)   to feel the pulse

la visita (VEE-zee-tah)   visit
la lingua (LEEN-gwah)   tongue
un' infermiera (een-   a nurse
  fehr-M'YEH-rah)
la febbre (FEHB-breh)   fever

le vertigini (vehr-TEE-jee-nee)   dizziness
ho le vertigini[2] (oh . . .)   I am dizzy
i sintomi (ee SEEN-toh-mee)   the symptoms
la ricetta (ree-CHEHT-tah)   prescription
la medicina (meh-dee-CHEE-nah)   medicine
la farmacia (fahr-mah-CHEE'ah)   drug store, pharmacy
la pillola (PEEL-loh-lah)   pill
un' aspirina (ah-spee-REE-nah)   an aspirin tablet

mi sento bene[9] (mee SEHN-toh BEH-neh)   I feel well
si sente male?[9] (see SEHN-teh MAH-leh)   do you feel ill, sick?
avere una buona cera[2] (ah-VEH-reh oo-nah   to look well
  BWOH-nah CHEH-rah)
io ho un mal di testa[2] (EE'oh OH oon MAHL   I have a headache
  dee TEH-stah)
il dolore (eel doh-LOH-reh)   pain

CONVERSATION

1 Che cosa ha?[10] Non ha un'ottima cera oggi.

2 Non mi sento bene. Non ho più[11] appetito e vorrei farmi visitare da un medico.

3 Quanto prende il dottor[12] Valdengo per una visita a domicilio?

4 Non so, ma dato che abita molto lontano, il suo onorario sarà[13] alto.

5 In questo caso prenderemo un tassì per recarci[14] alla sua clinica.

6 Verrò[15] con lei molto volentieri. Ecco un tassì.

7 Autista, è libera la sua vettura?[16]

8 Sì, signori; dove vogliono andare?

9 Ci porti al numero tredici di Via Pietro Borsiero, dalla parte di Piazza Mazzini. Chiuda lo sportello per piacere.

10 Faccia presto ed avrà una buona mancia.

11 Ecco l'indirizzo. Si fermi. Noi scendiamo qui.

12 Suoni il campanello.

FOOTNOTES: *1.* Imperative of *suonare* (*lei* form). First conjugation verbs form the third person singular of the imperative by adding *i* to the stem. The ending of

PRONUNCIATION	TRANSLATION
1 keh KOH-zah AH? nohn AH OHT-tee-mah CHEH-rah OH-djee.	What is the matter with you? You don't look too well today.
2 nohn mee SEHN-toh BEH-neh. nohn oh PYOO ahp-peh-TEE-toh eh vohr-RAY FAHR-mee vee-zee-TAH-reh dah oon MEH-dee-koh.	I don't feel well. I have no (more) appetite and I should like to see a doctor (*lit.*, make a doctor visit me).
3 KWAHN-toh PREHN-deh eel doht-TOHR vahl-DEHN-goh pehr oo-nah VEE-zee-tah ah doh-mee-CHEE-lyoh?	How much does Dr. Valdengo charge (*lit.*, take) for a house call (*lit.*, visit at home).
4 nohn SOH, mah DAH-toh keh AH-bee-tah MOHL-toh lohn-TAH-noh, eel soo'oh oh-noh-RAH-ryoh sah-RAH AHL-toh.	I don't know, but since he lives very far from here, his fee is probably high.
5 . . . KAH-zoh prehn-deh-REH-moh oon tas-SEE pehr reh-KAHR-chee . . . KLEE-nee-kah.	In that case we shall take a taxi (to go) to his office.
6 vehr-ROH kohn lay MOHL-toh voh-lehn-TYEH-ree. EHK-koh oon tahs-SEE.	I shall gladly come with you. Here is a taxi.
7 ah'oo-TEE-stah, EH LEE-beh-rah lah soo'ah veht-TOO-rah?	Driver, is your cab free?
8 SEE, see-N'YOH-ree; DOH-veh VOH-l'yoh-noh ahn-DAH-reh?	Yes, gentlemen. Where do you wish to go?
9 chee POHR-tee ahl NOO-meh-roh TREH-dee-chee dee VEE'ah PYEH-troh bohr-SYEH-roh, DAHL-lah PAHR-teh dee PYAH-tsah mah-TSEE-nee. KYOO-dah loh spohr-TEHL-loh, . . .	Take us to 13 Pietro Borsiero Avenue, in the direction of Mazzini Square. Will you please close the door?
10 FAH-tchah PREH-stoh ed ah-VRAH oo-nah BWOH-nah MAHN-chah.	Hurry, and you will get a good tip.
11 EHK-koh leen-dee-REE-tsoh. see FEHR-mee. noy shehn-DYAH-moh KWEE.	Here is the address. Stop. We are getting off here.
12 SWOH-nee eel kahm-pah-NEHL-loh.	Ring the bell

the third person plural is *ino*. 2. An idiom. 3. Imperative of *chiudere*. Second and third conjugation verbs form the third person singular of the imperative by

13 È in casa il dottor Valdengo?

14 Entrino nella sala d'aspetto, per piacere. S'accomodino. Il dottore verrà a momenti.

15 Buon giorno, signori. Favoriscano da questa parte, per piacere.

16 Da quanto tempo[17] non si sente[18] bene?

17 Da ieri. Sudavo quando sono uscito[19] da teatro e ho preso un brutto raffreddore.

18 Mi lasci tastare il polso.[20] Mi mostri la lingua.[20]

19 Dottore, crede lei che i sintomi siano[21] gravi?

20 No, signore; nulla di grave. Mi sembra che abbia un po' di febbre.[22] Mi lasci misurare la[23] temperatura.

21 Ho un forte mal di testa e le vertigini.

22 Prenda[7] queste pillole per calmare il dolore.

23 Si sente meglio?

24 Nè meglio, nè peggio.

---

adding *a* to the stem. The ending of the third person plural is *ano*. The endings of the *isco* verbs are: *isca* and *iscano*.   4. *Fare presto* is an idiom.   5. *Peggio* is the comparative of *male*.   6. See Note 1 above.   7. See Note 3 above. 8. *Dottore* and *medico* are synonyms, but *dottore* must be used in direct address or when the name is mentioned. In the latter case the final *e* is dropped. 9. *Sentirsi bene* and *sentirsi male* are idioms. Note that the verb is reflexive.

13 EH een KAH-zah eel doht-TOHR vahl-DEHN-goh?

Is Dr. Valdengo in (*lit.,* in the house)?

14 EHN-tree-noh NEHL-lah SAH-lah dah-SPEHT-toh . . . sahk-KOH-moh-dee-noh. eel doht-TOH-reh vehr-RAH ah moh-MEHN-tee.

Come (enter) into the waiting room, please. Make yourselves comfortable. The doctor will come in a few moments.

15 . . . fah-voh-REE-skah-noh dah KWEH-stah PAHR-teh. . . .

Good day, gentlemen. Come this way, please.

16 dah KWAHN-toh TEHM-poh nohn see SEHN-teh BEH-neh?

Since when have you been indisposed?

17 dah YEH-ree. SOO-DAH-voh KWAHN-doh SOH-noh OO-SHEE-toh dah teh'AH-troh eh oh PREH-zoh oon BROOT-toh rahf-frehd-DOH-reh.

Since yesterday. I was perspiring when I came out of the theater and I caught a nasty (ugly) cold.

18 mee LAH-shee tah-STAH-reh eel POHL-soh. mee MOH-stree lah LEEN-gwah.

Let me feel your pulse. Show me your tongue.

19 doht-TOH-reh, KREH-deh lay keh ee SEEN-toh-mee SEE'ah-noh GRAH-vee?

Doctor, do you think the symptoms are serious?

20 . . . NOOL-lah dee GRAH-veh. mee SEHM-brah keh AHB-byah oon POH dee FEHB-breh. mee LAH-shee mee-zoo-RAH-reh lah tehm-peh-rah-TOO-rah.

No, sir; nothing serious. It seems to me that you have a slight fever. Let me take (measure) your temperature.

21 oh oon FOHR-teh MAHL dee TEH-stah eh leh vehr-TEE-jee-nee.

I have a violent headache and I feel dizzy.

22 PREHN-dah KWEH-steh PEEL-loh-leh pehr kahl-MAH-reh eel doh-LOH-reh.

Take these pills to soothe the pain.

23 see SEHN-teh MEH-l'yoh?

Do you feel better?

24 NEH MEH-l'yoh, NEH PEH-djoh.

Neither better, nor worse.

---

10. Lit., what have you? This is a special use of the verb *avere* and implies that something is wrong. *11. Non* . . . *più,* a special negative, meaning "no longer."
12. The definite article is used before a title, but it is omitted in direct address.
13. Sarà is future of probability. *14.* The infinitive is *recarsi* (to take oneself to).
15. Future of *venire: io verrò, tu verrai, lei verrà, noi verremo, voi verrete, loro verranno. 16. Vettura* in this case means "cab." See Note 12, Lesson 4. *17. Da*

25 In questo caso le prescrivo questa ricetta, che porterà subito alla farmacia. Prenda un cucchiaio di questa medicina ogni due ore.

26 Se non si sente meglio ritorni[6] nuovamente fra tre giorni, e proveremo qualche altra medicina più efficace.

quanto tempo. Lit., since how much time. *Da* before an expression implying duration of time means "since" or "for." *18.* Note that *si sente* is present tense. In Italian an action which began in the past but continues in the present is expressed by the present tense. *19. Uscire* is one of the verbs that takes *essere* as an auxiliary verb. *20.* Notice the omission of the possessive adjective, which

25 . . . KAH-soh leh preh-SKREE-voh KWEH-stah ree-CHEHT-tah, keh pohr-teh-RAH soo-bee-toh . . . fahr-mah-CHEE'ah . . . koo-KYAH'-yoh . . . meh-dee-CHEE-nah OH-n'yee DOO'eh OH-reh.

In that case I shall give (*lit.*, prescribe) you this prescription, which you will take to the drug store right away. Take a spoonful of this medicine every two hours.

26 seh nohn see SEHN-teh MEH-l'yoh ree-TOHR-nee nwoh-vah-MEHN-teh frah treh JOHR-nee, eh proh-veh-REH-moh KWAHL-keh AHL-trah meh-dee-CHEE-nah PYOO ehf-fee-KAH-cheh.

If you don't feel better, come back in three days, and we shall try more effective medication.

---

in Italian is normally omitted with parts of the body and articles of clothing. Usually the indirect object is used instead. Ex: *mi lavo le mani* (I wash my hands. *Lit.*, I wash the hands to me.)   21. Subjunctive after *credere*, a verb of doubt. See Reference Grammar.   22. *Lit.*, some fever.   23. The possessive *sua* is omitted because it can only mean "your temperature."

15 Quindicesima Lezione

Vocabolario per Questa Lezione

i conforti moderni (kohn-FOHR-tee moh-DEHR-nee)	modern conveniences
dà su[1] (DAH SOO)	it faces, looks out on
voglio sistemarmi (VOH-l'yoh see-steh-MAHR-mee)	I want to get settled
affittare (ahf-feet-TAH-reh)	to rent

si paga (see PAH-gah)	one pays	**firmato** (feer-MAH-toh)	signed
la veduta (veh-DOO-tah)	view	**capire** (kah-PEE-reh)	to understand

una quindicina[2] (kween-dee-CHEE-nah)	a fortnight, two weeks
in anticipo (ahn-TEE-chee-poh)	in advance
a[3] **giornata** (johr-NAH-tah)	by the day
a[3] **settimana** (seht-tee-MAH-nah)	by the week
mensilmente (mehn-seel-MEHN-teh)	monthly
a[3] **mese** (MEH-zeh)	by the month

fin da ora[4] (feen dah OH-rah)	beginning now
fra[5] **un'ora** (frah oo-NOH-rah)	in an hour
oggi stesso (OH-djee STEHS-soh)	this very day
oggi ad otto[2] (... ahd OHT-toh)	a week from today

entri pure! (EHN-tree POO-reh)	come right in!
debbo avvertirla (DEHB-boh ahv-vehr-TEER-lah)	I must warn (inform) you
non importa (nohn eem-POHR-tah)	it doesn't matter
per me fa lo stesso[4] (pehr MEH fah loh STEHS-soh)	it's all the same to me
il pagamento (pah-gah-MEHN-toh)	the payment
si mangia alla carta[6] (see MAHN-jah AHL-lah KAHR-tah)	one eats à la carte
s'intende (seen-TEHN-deh)	of course, it's understood

136

IN CERCA D'UN ALLOGGIO · ARTICOLI DA TOLETTA

IN SEARCH OF LODGING
TOILET ARTICLES

(een CHEHR-kah doon ahl-LOH-djoh, ahr-TEE-koh-lee dah toh-LEHT-tah)

un albergo (ahl-BEHR-goh)	a hotel
la pensione (pehn-SYOH-neh)	board, boarding house
una pensione completa (. . . kohm-PLEH-tah)	room and board
una camera ammobiliata (. . . ahm-moh-bee-LYAH-tah)	a furnished room
il riscaldamento centrale (ree-skahl-dah-MEHN-toh chehn-TRAH-leh)	central heating
la pigione (pee-JOH-neh)	rent

la doccia (DOH-tchah)	shower
la spugna (SPOO-n'yah)	sponge
il sapone (sah-POH-neh)	soap
la crema (KREH-mah)	cream
la cipria (CHEE-pree'ah)	powder

la spazzola (SPAH-tsoh-lah)	the brush
il pettine (PEHT-tee-neh)	comb
il dentifricio (dehn-tee-FREE-choh)	tooth paste
lo spazzolino (spah-tsoh-LEE-noh)	tooth brush
il rasoio (rah-ZOH-yoh)	razor
la lametta (lah-MEHT-tah)	razor blade
crema da barba (KREH-mah dah BAHR-bah)	shaving cream
il profumo (proh-FOO-moh)	perfume
il rossetto (roh-SEHT-toh)	the lipstick

l'acqua corrente (LAHK-kwah kohr-REHN-teh)	running water
l'acqua calda (. . . KAHL-dah)	hot water, warm water
l'acqua fredda (. . . FREHD-dah)	cold water

CONVERSATION

1 Debbo trovare un albergo oggi stesso.

2 Vuole una camera ammobiliata?

3 Preferirei tre stanze vuote per fare il salotto, la camera da letto ed il bagno.

4 Entri pure. Le mostrerò ciò che[7] lei desidera.

5 Preferisce un salotto che dia[8] sulla strada o sul mare?

6 Preferisco quello che dà sul mare.

7 Non importa che la camera da letto dia[9] sulla strada o sul mare.

8 Qual'è il prezzo di questa camera?

9 Qual'è il prezzo di questo appartamento?

10 Affitta al mese, a settimana, o a giornata?[10]

11 Quanto costa la pensione completa?

12 Si mangia alla carta?

13 Voglio prendere in affitto[11] una grande camera ammobiliata.

14 Debbo avvertirla che si paga in anticipo.

FOOTNOTES:　1. Dare su is an idiom.　2. In common parlance, una quindicina means two weeks, exactly fourteen days. Similarly otto giorni means a week. Thus the expression oggi ad otto means "a week from today."　3. This is a special

PRONUNCIATION	TRANSLATION
1 DEHB-boh troh-VAH-reh oon ahl-BEHR-goh OH-djee STEHS-soh.	I must find a hotel this very day.
2 VWOH-leh OO-nah KAH-meh-rah ahm-moh-bee-LYAH-tah?	Do you want a furnished room?
3 preh-feh-ree-RAY treh STAHN-tseh VWOH-teh pehr FAH-reh eel sah-LOHT-toh, lah KAH-meh-rah dah LEHT-toh ed eel BAH-n'yoh.	I should prefer three unfurnished (*lit.*, empty) rooms for (to make) the living room, the bedroom, and the bathroom.
4 EHN-tree POO-reh. Leh moh-streh-ROH CHOH keh lay deh-ZEE-deh-rah.	Come right in. I'll show you what you wish.
5 preh-feh-REE-sheh oon sah-LOHT-toh keh DEE'ah SOOL-lah STRAH-dah oh sool MAH-reh.	Do you prefer a living room that faces the street or the sea?
6 preh-feh-REE-skoh KWEHL-loh keh DAH sool MAH-reh.	I prefer the one that faces the sea.
7 nohn eem-POHR-tah keh lah KAH-meh-rah dah LEHT-toh DEE'ah SOOL-lah STRAH-dah oh sool MAH-reh.	It doesn't matter whether the bedroom faces the street or the sea.
8 kwah-LEH eel PREH-tsoh dee KWEH-stah KAH-meh-rah?	What is the price of this room?
9 kwah-LEH eel PREH-tsoh dee KWEH-stoh ahp-pahr-tah-MEHN-toh?	What is the price of this apartment?
10 ahf-FEET-tah ahl MEH-zeh, ah seht-tee-MAH-nah oh ah johr-NAH-tah?	Do you rent by the month, by the week, or by the day?
11 KWAHN-toh KOH-stah lah pehn-SYOH-neh kohm-PLEH-tah?	What is the cost of room and board?
12 see MAHN-jah AHL-lah KAHR-tah?	Are the meals (*lit.*, does one eat) a la carte?
13 VOH-l'yoh PREHN-deh-reh een ahf-FEET-toh OO-nah GRAHN-deh KAH-meh-rah ahm-moh-bee-LYAH-tah.	I want to rent a large furnished room.
14 DEHB-boh ahv-vehr-TEER-lah keh see PAH-gah een ahn-TEE-chee-poh.	I must inform you that you pay in advance.

use of the word *a*, meaning "by." *4. Fin da ora* and *fa lo stesso* are idioms. *5.* The word *fra* means *in* or *within* when used in connection with words implying duration of time. *6. Alla carta* is an adaptation of the French expression *à la*

15 Capisco,[12] ma io preferisco[12] pagare a settimana.

16 Mi dispiace, ma qui si paga[13] mensilmente, e non posso affittare ad altre condizioni.

17 In questo caso la pagherò[14] in anticipo ogni due settimane. Questo è tutto quello che[15] posso permettermi.[16]

18 Nella camera, s'intende, c'è un lavabo.

19 Sì, signore, le nostre camere hanno tutti i conforti moderni: gas, elettricità, riscaldamento centrale, acqua corrente, fredda e calda.

20 Benissimo. Voglio sistemarmi al più presto possibile[17] e, se vuole, prendo[18] la camera fin da ora.

21 Fra un'ora i miei bagagli saranno qui.

22 Ecco il pagamento per la prima quindicina. Vuole avere la bontà di darmi una ricevuta?

23 Ecco la ricevuta firmata. La prego di prenderne visione.[19]

---

carte. 7. The word "what" must be translated *ciò che* when it means "that which." 8. *Dia* is the third person subjunctive of *dare.* The subjunctive is required here by the indefinite antecedent *un salotto.* See Reference Grammar. *9.* This sub-

15 kah-PEE-skoh, mah EE'oh preh-feh-REE-skoh pah-GAH-reh ah seht-tee-MAH-nah.

I understand, but I prefer to pay by the week.

16 mee dee-SPYAH-cheh, mah KWEE see PAH-gah mehn-seel-MEHN-teh, eh nohn POHS-soh ahf-feet-TAH-reh ahd AHL-treh kohn-dee-TSYOH-nee.

I am sorry, but payments must be made monthly, and I cannot make any other arrangement (*lit.,* I cannot rent at other conditions).

17 een KWEH-stoh KAH-zoh lah pah-geh-ROH een ahn-TEE-chee-poh OH-n'yee DOO'eh seht-tee-MAH-neh . . . POHS-soh pehr-MEHT-tehr-mee.

In this case I will pay every two weeks in advance. This is all I can afford.

18 . . . seen-TEHN-deh, CHEH oon lah-VAH-boh.

In the room, of course, there is a wash basin.

19 . . . AHN-noh TOOT-tee ee kohn-FOHR-tee moh-DEHR-nee: GAHS, eh-leht-tree-chee-TAH, ree-skahl-dah-MEHN-toh chehn-TRAH-leh, AHK-kwah kohr-REHN-teh, FREHD-dah eh KAHL-dah.

Yes, sir, our rooms have all the modern conveniences: gas, electricity, central heating, hot and cold running water.

20 beh-NEES-see-moh. VOH-l'yoh see-steh-MAHR-mee ahl PYOO PREH-stoh pohs-SEE-bee-leh, eh, seh vwoH-leh, PREHN-doh lah KAH-meh-rah feen dah OH-rah.

Very well. I want to get settled as soon as possible, and, if you wish, I will take the room as of now.

21 frah OO-NOH-rah ee M'YAY bah-GAH-l'yee sah-RAHN-noh KWEE.

My baggage will be here in an hour.

22 EHK-koh eel pah-gah-MEHN-toh pehr lah PREE-mah kween-dee-CHEE-nah. vwoH-leh ah-VEH-reh lah bohn-TAH dee DAHR-mee OO-nah ree-cheh-voo-tah?

Here is the payment for the first two weeks. Will you be good enough to give me a receipt?

23 . . . feer-MAH-tah. lah PREH-goh dee PREHN-dehr-neh vee-ZYOH-neh.

Here is the signed receipt. Please read it.

junctive form is required by the impersonal expression *non importa.* See Reference Grammar.   *10. A giornata* instead of *al giorno.* See Note 6, Lesson 3.   *11. Prendere in affitto* literally means "to take for rent." *In affitto* is an idiom.   *12. -isco*

24 "Ricevuta[20] dal signor Tal dei Tali la somma di lire trentamila per alloggio e pensione per quindici giorni nello stabile sito a Via Veneto numero cento ottantatrè, Roma, il primo giugno."

25 Le ore dei pasti sono: colazione alle sette e trenta; pranzo da mezzogiorno alle tredici[21]; cena dalle diciannove alle ventuno precise.

26 Per piacere, mi mostri la stanza da bagno.

27 Eccola.[22] Come può vedere ci sono degli asciugamani, una doccia, una spugna, ed un armadietto a muro per il pettine, la spazzola, il profumo, crema a base di olio, cipria, dentifricio, ecc.

---

verbs. See Note 27, Lesson 2. *13. Si paga* is an impersonal expression meaning "one pays." *14.* See Note 23, Lesson 12. *15. Quello che* is the same as *ciò che.* *16. Posso permettermi* literally means "I can allow myself." *17. Lit.,* at the earliest possible. *18.* See Note 10, Lesson 13. *19. Prenderne visione* is an

24 ree-cheh-voo-tah dahl see-N'YOHR tahl day TAH-lee lah SOHM-mah dee LEE-reh trehn-tah-MEE-lah pehr ahl-LOH-djoh eh pehn-SYOH-neh pehr KWEEN-dee-chee JOHR-nee NEHL-loh STAH-bee-leh SEE-toh ah VEE'ah VEH-neh-toh NOO-meh-roh CHEHN-toh oht-tahn-tah-TREH, ROH-mah, eel PREE-moh JOO-n'yoh.

"Received from Mr. So and So the sum of 30,000 lire for room and board for two weeks in the building located at No. 183 Via Veneto, Rome, June 1st."

25 leh OH-reh day PAH-stee SOH-noh: koh-lah-TSYOH-neh AHL-leh SEHT-teh eh TREHN-tah; PRAHN-dzoh dah meh-dzoh-JOHR-noh AHL-leh TREH-dee-chee; CHEH-nah DAHL-leh dee-chan-NOH-veh AHL-leh vehn-TOO-noh.

Meal hours are: breakfast at seven thirty, dinner from noon to one, and supper from seven to nine P.M. sharp.

26 pehr pyah-CHEH-reh, mee MOH-stree lah STAHN-tsah dah BAH-n'yoh.

Please show me the bathroom.

27 EHK-koh-lah. KOH-meh PWOH veh-DEH-reh chee SOH-noh, DEH-l'yee ah-shoo-gah-MAH-nee, oo-nah DOH-chah, oo-nah SPOO-n'yah, ed oon ahr-mah-DYEHT-toh ah MOO-roh pehr eel PEHT-tee-neh, lah SPAH-tsoh-lah, eel proh-FOO-moh, KREH-mah ah BAH-zeh dee OH-lyoh, CHEE-pryah, dehn-tee-FREE-choh, eh-TCHEH-teh-rah.

Here it is. As you can see, there are some towels, a shower, a sponge, and a small wall cabinet for a comb, brush, perfume, cold cream, powder, toothpaste, etc.

---

idiom meaning literally "to take vision of it." 20. The past participle *ricevuta* agrees with *somma*, which is feminine. 21. In Italy the twenty-four hour clock is used in official announcements and in timetables to avoid ambiguity. It is also used, but not exclusively, in conversation. 22. See Note 29, Lesson 3.

16 Sedicesima Lezione

Vocabolario per Questa Lezione

la posta aerea (POH-stah ah'EH-reh'ah)	air mail
per via aerea (pehr VEE'ah ...)	by air mail
la carta da[1] lettere (KAHR-tah dah LEHT-teh-reh)	letter paper
nel cuore della città (nehl KWOH-reh DEHL-lah cheet-TAH)	in the center (heart) of the city

la carta (KAHR-tah)	paper
la gomma (GOHM-mah)	eraser
la penna (PEHN-nah)	pen
il lapis,[2] la matita[2] (LAH-pees, mah-TEE-tah)	pencil
la riga (REE-gah)	ruler

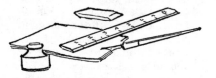

la penna stilografica (... stee-loh-GRAH-fee-kah)	fountain pen
la carta sugante (KAHR-tah soo-GAHN-teh)	blotter
l'inchiostro (leen-KYOH-stroh)	ink
il calamaio (kah-lah-MAH'yoh)	inkwell
la carta geografica (... jeh'oh-GRAH-fee-kah)	map
un opuscolo (oh-POO-skoh-loh)	a pamphlet
la cartoleria (kahr-toh-leh-REE'ah)	stationary store

riscuotere (ree-SKWOH-teh-reh)	to cash
aspettare a lungo[3] (ah-speht-TAH-reh ah LOON-goh)	to wait a long time
la corrispondenza (kohr-ree-spohn-DEHN-tsah)	correspondence
sbrigare la corrispondenza (zbree-GAH-reh ...)	to write (attend to) the correspondence
la maggior parte (mah-DJOHR PAHR-teh)	larger part, most

144

RELAZIONI COMMERCIALI

COMMERCIAL RELATIONS (reh-lah-TSYOH-nee kohm-mehr-CHAH-lee)

l'agenzia (lah-jehn-TSEE'ah)	agency
all'estero[4] (ahl-LEH-steh-roh)	abroad
al giorno d'oggi (ahl JOHR-noh DOH-djee)	nowadays
conservare agli atti (kohn-sehr-VAH-reh AH-l'yee AHT-tee)	keep on record
fare affari (FAH-reh ahf-FAH-ree)	to do business
un libretto di assegni (lee-BREHT-toh dee ahs-SEH-n'yee)	a check book
la sede centrale (SEH-deh chehn-TRAH-leh)	main office
occupato (ohk-koo-PAH-toh)	busy

la macchina da scrivere (MAHK-kee-nah dah SKREE-veh-reh)	typewriter
scrivere a macchina[5] (SKREE-veh-reh ah . . .)	to typewrite
il foglio di carta (FOH-l'yoh . . .)	sheet of paper
la busta (BOO-stah)	envelope
la lettera (LEHT-teh-rah)	letter

l'indirizzo (een-dee-REE-tsoh)	address
il sigillo (see-JEEL-loh)	seal
il bollo (BOHL-loh)	stamp, rubber stamp
il giornale (johr-NAH-leh)	journal
il libro mastro (LEE-broh MAH-stroh)	ledger
il libro di cassa (. . . dee KAHS-sah)	cash book

la contabilità (kohn-tah-bee-lee-TAH)	accounting
un rappresentante (rahp-preh-zehn-TAHN-teh)	representative, agent
la polizza di carico (POH-lee-tsah dee KAH-ree-koh)	bill of lading
la copia (KOH-pyah)	copy, duplicate
in duplice copia (een DOO-plee-cheh . . .)	in duplicate

CONVERSATION

1 Cosa[6] ha fatto di bello[7] oggi?

2 Ha lavorato molto?

3 Sì, siamo stati[8] molto occupati[9] a sbrigare la corrispondenza con le nostre agenzie in tutta l'Europa ed in Oriente.

4 Hanno scritto le lettere in italiano?

5 Alcune. Ma la maggior parte le abbiamo scritte[10] in francese poichè, come lei sa, il francese si parla in quasi tutte le capitali europee, specialmente nei paesi in cui[11] la propria lingua non è molto conosciuta all'estero: per esempio, la Rumenia,[12] la Polonia, la Ceco-Slovacchia, l'Egitto e la Turchia.

6 Scrivono le lettere a macchina?

7 Sì, al giorno d'oggi tutta la corrispondenza d'affari viene scritta a macchina, e generalmente in duplice copia per conservarne[13] una agli atti.

8 Hanno delle relazioni commerciali con l'Argentina?

9 Sì, e facciamo affari anche col Brasile.

FOOTNOTES: *1. Lit.*, paper for letters. The word *da* in this case implies "use." 2. It is equally common to say *la matita* instead of *il lapis*.   *3. A lungo,* see

PRONUNCIATION	TRANSLATION

1 KOH-sah ah FAHT-toh dee BEHL-loh OH-djee?

What have you accomplished today?

2 ah lah-voh-RAH-toh MOHL-toh?

Have you done much work?

3 SEE, SYAH-moh . . . ohk-koo-PAH-tee ah zbree-GAH-reh lah kohr-ree-spohn-DEHN-tsah . . . ah-jehn-TSEE'eh een TOOT-tah leh'oo-ROH-pah ed een oh-ree-EHN-teh.

Yes, we have been very busy attending to the correspondence with our agencies throughout Europe and the Orient.

4 AHN-noh SKREET-toh leh LEHT-teh-reh een ee-tah-LYAH-noh?

Did you write the letters in Italian?

5 ahl-KOO-neh. mah lah mah-DJOHR PAHR-teh leh ahb-BYAH-moh SKREET-teh een frahn-CHEH-zeh poy-KEH, . . . see PAHR-lah een KWAH-zee TOOT-teh leh kah-pee-TAH-lee eh'oo-roh-PEH'eh, speh-chahl-MEHN-teh nay pah'EH-zee een KOO'y lah PROH-pryah LEEN-gwah . . . koh-noh-SHYOO-tah ahl-LEH-steh-roh; pehr eh-ZEHM-pyoh lah roo-meh-NEE'ah, lah poh-LOH-nyah, la cheh-koh-sloh-VAHK-kyah, leh-JEET-toh eh lah toor-KEE'ah.

Some. But we wrote most (*lit.,* the larger part) of them in French because, as you know, French is spoken in nearly all European capitals, especially in the countries whose (own) language is not very well known abroad; for example, Rumania, Poland, Czechoslovakia, Egypt, and Turkey.

6 SKREE-voh-noh leh LEHT-teh-reh ah MAHK-kee-nah?

Do you typewrite your letters?

7 SEE, ahl JOHR-noh DOH-djee TOOT-tah lah kohr-ree-spohn-DEHN-tsah dahf-FAH-ree VYEH-neh SKREET-tah ah MAHK-kee-nah . . . DOO-plee-cheh KOH-pyah pehr kohn-sehr-VAHR-neh oo-nah AH-l'yee AHT-tee.

Yes, nowadays all business correspondence is (*lit.,* comes) typewritten, and usually in duplicate in order to keep one copy on record.

8 . . . reh-lah-TSYOH-nee kohm-mehr-CHAH-lee kohn lahr-jehn-TEE-nah?

Have you business relations with Argentina?

9 SEE, eh fah-TCHAH-moh ahf-FAH-ree AHN-keh kohl brah-ZEE-leh.

Yes, and we also do business in Brazil.

Note 7, Lesson 8.   *4.* Idiom.   *5. Lit.,* to write by machine.   *6.* The interrogative "what" is translated by *che cosa* in Italian, but *che* or *cosa* are frequently

10 Voglio riscuotere una tratta. Ho bisogno di dollari americani ed io non ho che[14] sterline.

11 A proposito, ho perduto il mio libretto[15] di assegni.[16]

12 Dobbiamo andare alla banca immediatamente?

13 Sì, dobbiamo andarci subito, perchè le banche[17] chiudono alle tre precise.

14 Quando deve spedire questi articoli?

15 Bisogna spedire[18] subito la merce?

16 Non vuole prima mandare un cablogramma al suo rappresentante?

17 No, una lettera aerea sarà sufficiente. La riceverà lunedì.

18 Debbo scrivere anche al mio rappresentante ad[19] Atene.

19 Quando parte la posta per la Grecia? Bisogna aspettare a lungo?

20 Il piroscafo parte una volta la[20] settimana, ma c'è un servizio aereo quotidiano.

21 Fa molti affari con i Paesi Bassi?

used alone. *7. Fare qualche cosa di bello. Lit.,* to do something nice. *8. Essere* takes its own present as an auxiliary. In verbs conjugated with *essere* the past participle agrees with the subject. *Stati* agrees with *noi,* understood. *9. Occupato*

10 voh-l'yoh ree-skwoh-teh-reh oo-nah traht-tah. oh bee-zoh-n'yoh dee dohl-lah-ree ah-meh-ree-kah-nee ed ee'oh nohn oh keh stehr-lee-neh.

I want to cash a draft. I need American dollars and I have only pounds sterling.

11 ah proh-poh-zee-toh, oh pehr-doo-toh eel mee'oh lee-breht-toh dee ahs-seh-n'yee.

By the way, I have lost my check book.

12 dohb-byah-moh ahn-dah-reh ahl-lah bahn-kah eem-meh-dyah-tah-mehn-teh?

Must we go to the bank at once?

13 . . . ahn-dahr-chee soo-bee-toh . . . bahn-keh kyoo-doh-noh ahl-leh treh preh-chee-zeh.

Yes, we have to go there right away because banks close at three o'clock sharp.

14 kwahn-doh deh-veh speh-dee-reh kweh-stee ahr-tee-koh-lee?

When do you have to send these articles?

15 bee-zoh-n'yah speh-dee-reh soo-bee-toh lah mehr-cheh?

Must the merchandise be shipped right away?

16 nohn vwoh-leh pree-mah mahn-dah-reh oon kah-bloh-grahm-mah ahl soo'oh rahp-preh-zehn-tahn-teh?

Don't you want to first send a cablegram to your representative?

17 . . . ah'eh-reh'ah sah-rah soof-fee-chyehn-teh. lah ree-cheh-veh-rah loo-neh-dee.

No, an air mail letter will suffice. He will receive it on Monday.

18 dehb-boh skree-veh-reh ahl mee'-oh rahp-preh-zehn-tahn-teh ahd ah-teh-neh.

I must also write to my representative in Athens.

19 kwahn-doh pahr-teh lah poh-stah pehr lah greh-chyah? bee-zoh-n'yah ah-speht-tah-reh ah loon-goh?

When does the mail leave for Greece? Will it be necessary to wait long?

20 eel pee-roh-skah-foh pahr-teh oo-nah vohl-tah lah seht-tee-mah-nah, mah cheh oon sehr-vee-tsyoh ah'eh-reh'oh ᵗkwoh-tee-dyah-noh.

The boat leaves once a week, but there is plane service every day.

21 fah mohl-tee ahf-fah-ree kohn ee pah'eh-zee bahs-see?

Do you do much business with the Low Countries?

---

takes *a* to introduce an infinitive.   10. *Scritte* agrees with *le,* which refers to *lettere.* The past participle of verbs conjugated with the auxiliary *avere* agrees with the preceding direct object.   11. See Note 19, Lesson 3.   12. A reminder

22 Recentemente ho venduto molta merce in[21] Olanda e nel[21] Belgio.

23 In questo caso dovrebbe aprire una succursale a[19] Parigi, non le pare?

24 Sì, intendo aprire la sede centrale nel cuore della città, vicino alla Borsa,[22] il quindici di questo mese.

that names of countries are preceded by the definite article. *13.* The *ne* of *conservarne* refers to *copia.* *14.* See Note 13, Lesson 5. *15. Libretto* is a diminutive of *libro.* *-etto* is a diminutive suffix. *16. Libretto di assegni. Lit.,* little book of checks. *17.* The singular of *banche* is *banca.* *18. Spedire* means "to send;" also "to ship." *19.* "In" before the name of a city is usually translated

22 reh-chehn-teh-MEHN-teh ... MEHR-cheh een oh-LAHN-dah eh .nehl BEHL-joh.

23 . . . doh-VREHB-beh ah-PREE-reh oo-nah sook-koor-SAH-leh ah pah-REE-jee . . . PAH-reh?

24 SEE, een-TEHN-doh ah-PREE-reh lah SEH-deh chehn-TRAH-leh nehl KWOH-reh DEHL-lah cheet-TAH, vee-CHEE-noh AHL-lah BOHR-sah, eel KWEEN-dee-chee dee KWEH-stoh MEH-zeh.

Recently I sold a great deal of merchandise in Holland and Belgium.

In that case you ought to open a branch in Paris, don't you think?

Yes, I intend to open the main office in the center of the city, near the Stock Exchange, the fifteenth of this month.

---

by *a* (*ad* before a vowel). *20.* The definite article is used idiomatically here. *21.* Feminine nouns of countries, not modified by an adjective, do not take the definite article after the preposition *in*. Thus we have here *in Olanda* (fem.) and *nel Belgio* (masc.). But: *nella bella Olanda* (in beautiful Holland). *22. Borsa* basically means "purse;" also "scholarship."

17 Diciasettesima Lezione

IN CASA DI ALCUNI AMICI A NAPOLI

(Carlo e Maria Smith sbarcano a Napoli per iniziare il loro viaggio di nozze. Dopo il controllo della dogana incontrano, all'uscita, il professore Di Giacomo, vecchio amico di Carlo, che li conduce all'albergo, e servirà loro da guida durante la loro permanenza a Napoli.)

CARLO: Mia cara sposina,[1] eccoci[2] a Napoli. Che impressione ti ha fatto il golfo di questa antica e storica città?

MARIA: Magnifica! Sembra proprio un sogno. La scena dell' arrivo è ancora più bella di come la immaginavo. Ardo dal[3] desiderio di visitare tutti i bei luoghi di questa incantevole parte dell'Italia.

CARLO: Il tuo desiderio sarà presto appagato. Intanto mettiamoci in fila[4] qui per il controllo della dogana.[5]

MARIA: Chi sa quanto tempo ci vorrà[6] per sbrigarci!

CARLO: Non molto. Il controllo della dogana è quasi una formalità. Abbiamo tutte le nostre valigie? Non abbiamo dimenticato nulla a bordo?[7]

MARIA: Nulla. Oh, a proposito,[8] dov'è il tuo orologio da polso?

CARLO: Il mio orologio? È qui. No, non c'è. Accidempoli![9] Dov'è? L'avrò dimenticato[10] nella cabina. Corro a cercarlo. *(Sta per allontanarsi, ma Maria lo ferma.)*

FOOTNOTES: *1. Sposina* is a diminutive for *sposa* (wife, bride). *2. Eccoci:* "Here we are." *3. Dal* in this case means "with the." *4.* An idiom: "Let's stand on line." *5. Controllo della dogana:* "customs inspection." *6. Quanto tempo ci vorrà:* "How long will it take?" *Vorrà* is future of *volere*, an irregular verb. See Table of Irregular Verbs. *7. A bordo:* "on board." *8.* An idiom:

MARIA: Calmati, calmati, amor mio. Ecco il tuo orologio. Lo avevi veramente dimenticato. Meno male[11] che ci sono io che penso a tutto, altrimenti un giorno o l'altro dimenticheresti anche la testa.

CARLO: Adesso non esageriamo. Tuttavia sono molto felice di averti con me. Ecco il doganiere.

DOGANIERE: Vuole avere la bontà di aprire le valigie, signore?

CARLO: Certo. (*Apre le valigie.*) Ecco fatto.[12]

DOGANIERE: Ha tabacco, articoli di seta o altre cose da[13] dichiarare?

CARLO: Sì, ho venti pacchetti di sigarette. Il resto consiste di biancheria ed altri oggetti per uso personale. Ho anche una macchina fotografica, una macchina cinematografica e quindici rulli di pellicole. Debbo pagare la tassa?

DOGANIERE: No, signore, può chiudere le valigie. Auguri a lei ed alla sua signora per una felice permanenza in Italia.

CARLO (*chiudendo le valigie*): Accetta[14] una sigaretta?

DOGANIERE: Con piacere, signore. Non si può rifiutare una buona sigaretta americana. Tante grazie.

MARIA: Ci siamo sbrigati presto. E adesso possiamo veramente dire che siamo in Italia.

CARLO: Proprio così,[15] adorata. Sei felice?

MARIA: Immensamente. (*Additando un signore che gesticola con la mano.*) Oh, guarda quel signore, sembra che chiami[16] te.

"by the way." 9. *Accidempoli* is an interjection signifying surprise and annoyance. Translate it any way you wish. 10. *Avrò dimenticato* is future of probability. See Reference Grammar. 11. *Meno male* is an idiom: "It's a good thing!" 12. *Ecco fatto!:* "It's done!" 13. This is a special use of the word *da.* See Reference Grammar. 14. "Will you accept . . ." 15. *Proprio così:* "Exactly."

CARLO: Infatti! È il professore Di Giacomo. Professore!

PROFESSORE: Caro Capitano Smith! Che[17] piacere di rivederla! (*Cordiale abbraccio.*)

CARLO: È un gran piacere anche per me di rivedere lei, caro professore. Mi permetta di presentarle la mia signora.[18]

PROFESSORE: Fortunatissimo, signora.

MARIA: Il piacere è mio, professore.

CARLO (*a Maria*): Ebbi la fortuna di fare la conoscenza del professor Di Giacomo quando ero[19] a Napoli durante la guerra. Come vedi, mi chiama ancora "capitano." Ben presto[20] si stabilì fra noi una grande amicizia. Gli promisi[21] che saremmo venuti in Italia per il nostro viaggio di nozze . . .[22]

PROFESSORE: Ed ha mantenuto la promessa. Bravissimo! Intanto, cari sposini, prendiamo il tassì che già aspetta. (*Tutti e tre entrano nel tassì.*) Andiamo prima all'albergo. Ho prenotato per loro una bellissima camera con tutti i conforti moderni ai quali loro americani sono abituati.

MARIA: Le siamo immensamente grati, professore.

PROFESSORE: Le assicuro che è un vero piacere per me potervi[23] essere utile. E se mi permette, signora, le debbo dire che lei è proprio come la immaginavo. Suo marito, allora suo fidanzato, non faceva che[24] parlarmi di lei. Poveretto,[25] soffriva molto per lei, e debbo confessare che aveva ben ragione.[26] Non avrebbe potuto fare una scelta migliore.

MARIA: Grazie, professore. Lei è molto galante.

CARLO: La galanteria, mia cara, è parte di ogni italiano.

PROFESSORE: Colgo questa occasione per augurare loro una lunga e felice vita insieme. Possa il loro cammino essere sempre cosparso di fiori e di felicità infinita.

MARIA E CARLO: Grazie, professore.

PROFESSORE: E adesso, se mi permettono, dirò loro che cosa

---

16. Chiami is subjunctive of *chiamare.* It is required here by the impersonal expression *mi sembra.* See Reference Grammar.   *17. Che* in exclamations is translated as "what a."   *18.* In speaking of one's wife or of somebody else's wife, the word *signora* is often used instead of *moglie.*   *19. Ero* is imperfect of *essere.* For complete tense See Reference Grammar.   *20. Ben presto:* "At once."

faremo stasera. Io li accompagnerò all'albergo, e poi ritornerò alle sei.

CARLO: La prego, professore, di non darsi troppo disturbo per noi.

PROFESSORE: Disturbo? Tutt'altro,[27] amici cari. È un vero piacere per me e per mia moglie che li aspetta a braccia aperte.[28]

CARLO: A proposito, come sta[29] la sua cara e gentile signora?

PROFESSORE: Benissimo. Li aspetta con ansia. Dunque, questa sera ci faranno l'onore[30] di cenare con noi. E dopo cena andremo al San Carlo.

MARIA: Che idea stupenda! E che cosa si dà[31] stasera al San Carlo?

PROFESSORE: La Boheme.

MARIA: Questa è una vera fortuna. La nostra visita in Italia incomincia proprio bene.

PROFESSORE: Ecco l'albergo. (*Scendono dal tassì. Il professore paga l'autista.*) Li accompagno fino alla loro camera e poi li lascio. So che vogliono rimanere soli.

CARLO: La sua compagnia non ci dà mai disturbo.[32] Nel pomeriggio andremo a zonzo[33] per le vie della città. Prima di tutto,[34] però, dovrò cambiare alcuni dollari in lire italiane.

PROFESSORE: Questo sarà molto facile farlo, perchè l'ufficio dell'American Express si trova[35] qui vicino.

CARLO: Benissimo. Allora, caro professore, arrivederla a stasera.

MARIA: Arrivederla, professore, ed abbia la bontà di porgere i nostri cordiali saluti alla sua gentile signora.

PROFESSORE: Grazie. Lo farò con piacere. A stasera.[36] (*Strette di mano.*)

IN CASA DEL PROFESSORE DI GIACOMO

(*La signora Lucia, moglie del professore, accoglie gli sposini.*)

PROFESSORE: Mia cara Lucia, ho l'onore di presentarti la simpatica signora Smith.

---

21. *Promisi* is past definite of irregular verb *promettere.* 22. *Viaggio di nozze:* "Honeymoon trip." 23. *Potervi. Vi* is a direct object pronoun attached to the infinitive. 24. *Non . . .* (verb) *. . . che* means "only." 25. *Poveretto* is a diminutive of *povero.* In this case it means "poor thing!" 26. *Aveva ben ragione:* "He was well justified." *Avere ragione* is an idiom meaning "to be right." The

LUCIA: Molto, molto felice di conoscerla. E tu, caro Carlo, abbracciami.

CARLO: Con gioia! (*L'abbraccia.*) Sa bene che per me lei è come una seconda madre. Non è affatto[37] cambiata. Anzi, posso dire che è ancora più bella di prima.

LUCIA: So che lo dici per galanteria, ma non mi dispiace.[38] Attento, però. Non dimenticare che tua moglie e mio marito sono presenti.

CARLO: Non hanno alcuna ragione di essere gelosi.

PROFESSORE: E infatti, non lo siamo. Vero, signora Smith?

MARIA: Verissimo. Però ho notato che sua moglie dà del tu[39] a mio marito. . . .

LUCIA: Ah, ah! Che cosa dicevo[40] io poco fa?[41]

PROFESSORE: Per mia moglie suo marito è come se fosse un figlio.

MARIA: Lo so, lo so, io non penso male affatto. Però chi dà del tu a mio marito deve dare del tu anche a me. Quindi per lei e per sua moglie io sono Maria, e non la signora Smith.

PROFESSORE: Che incantevole creatura!

---

opposite is *avere torto:* "to be wrong." 27. *Tutt'altro:* "On the contrary." 28. *A braccia aperte* is an idiom meaning *"with open arms."* *Aperte* is the past participle of *aprire,* and in this case it agrees with *braccia,* which is feminine plural. 29. *Come sta?:* "How is?" The verb *stare* is used in expressions relating to health. 30. *Ci faranno l'onore:* "Will do us the honor." 31. *Si dà* is an impersonal expression. The infinitive is *dare,* which is irregular. 32. *Non ci dà mai disturbo:* "Never inconveniences us." 33. *Andare a zonzo* is an idiom

Lucia: Con piacere, Maria. E dimmi, cara, come va[42] che parli italiano così bene?

Maria: I miei genitori sono nati[43] in Italia, e quindi a casa mia si parla sempre in italiano. Naturalmente l'ho studiato anche a scuola.

Professore: Ho notato che Carlo lo parla perfettamente adesso, mentre quando era qui alcuni anni fa, lo parlava con un po' di difficoltà.

Carlo: L'ho studiato anch'io all'università; e poi, la mia cara sposina, insiste perchè fra noi si parli sempre in italiano.

Domestica: La cena è servita!

Professore: Benissimo. Dunque, a tavola.[44] Avete appetito?

(*Tutti si seggono. Di tanto in tanto la domestica porta le diverse pietanze.*)

Carlo: Non esito a dire che ho una fame da lupo.[45] La lunga passeggiata che abbiamo fatto lungo Via Caracciolo ed altre belle strade mi ha dato un ottimo appetito.

Maria: Debbo confessare che anch'io sono ben disposta a fare onore all'eccellente cena che la signora ha preparato.

Lucia: Non puoi ancora dire se la cena sia eccellente o no.

Maria: Oh, non posso averne[46] alcun dubbio. Mio marito mi ha parlato diverse volte degli eccellenti pasti che lei gli preparava quando era qui.

Professore: Quanto tempo vi tratterrete[47] a Napoli?

Carlo: Una diecina di giorni,[48] credo. C'è molto da vedere da queste parti.

Maria: Prima di tutto vorrei andare all' isola di Capri, per vedere la famosa Grotta Azzurra.

Carlo: Sarai accontentata.

Maria: Una giornata la passeremo a Pompei.

Professore: Sì, bisogna visitare anche Pompei, la città che

---

meaning "to go strolling about." *34. Prima di tutto:* "before everything else." *35. Si trova:* "is located." *36.* An idiom: "See you tonight!" *37. Non . . . affatto:* "Not at all!" *38. Non mi dispiace:* "I don't mind it." *39. Dare del tu* means "to thee and thou;" that is, to use the familiar form of address. *40. Dicevo* is imperfect of irregular verb *dire.* *41. Poco fa:* "a short while ago; just now." *Fa* (from the verb *fare*) means "ago" when used in expressions indicating elapsed time. *42. Come va:* "How come?" *43. Nati* is past participle of *nascere* (to be

circa duemila anni fa fu completamente sepolta dalla lava della più terribile eruzione del Vesuvio che la storia ricordi.[49] Come

sapete, da tanti anni vi si fanno scavi[50] e già una buona parte dell'antica città è venuta di nuovo[51] alla luce ed ha rivelato lo splendore della civilità e del lusso di venti secoli fa.

CARLO: Ti sarà concesso di visitare anche Pompei. Naturalmente bisognerà salire anche sul Vesuvio. Io sono già stato sulla cima di questo famoso vulcano ed ho piacere di rivedere lo spetta-colo magnifico, il panorama incantevole che si offre agli occhi del viaggiatore dalla cima di questa montagna.

MARIA: Ti sarà concesso. Posso venire con te?

CARLO: Credo di sì.[52]

MARIA: Grazie, signor[53] comandante! E così, dopo averlo tanto desiderato, salirò finalmente sulla funicolare[54] del Vesuvio, resa famosa[55] dalla bella canzonetta "Funiculì — Funiculà".

LUCIA: Vi piacciono[56] le canzoni napoletane?

MARIA: Immensamente. Come lei sa, molte canzoni napole-tane come "O'Marì," "O Sole Mio," "Santa Lucia," "Torna a Sorrento," e tante altre ancora sono conosciute in tutto il mondo e si cantano in moltissime lingue. La musica di queste canzoni è così dolce, così melodiosa, e spesso così appassionata[57] che scende direttamente al cuore.

PROFESSORE: Sono sicuro che vi piacerebbe assistere alla festa di Piedigrotta in onore della Madonna. Questa è la festa delle

born). Here it agrees with *genitori.*   *44. A tavola:* "Let's sit at the table." The verb is understood.   *45. Ho una fame da lupo:* "I am hungry as a wolf," an idiomatic expression.   *46. Averne. Ne* is attached to the infinitive *avere,* and means "about it."   *47. Vi tratterrete* is future of *trattenersi,* which is conjugated like *tenere.*   *48. Una diecina di giorni:* "About ten days."   *49.* This eruption took place in the year 79 A.D. and completely buried the towns of Pompei (Pompeii) Stabia, and Ercolano (Herculaneum).   *50.* The excavations, which began in the

canzoni, ed in questa occasione viene scelta la più bella canzone dell'anno.

MARIA: Mi piacerebbe veramente. Quando si celebra questa festa?

LUCIA: Il sette di settembre.

CARLO: Faremo tutto il possibile di trovarci di nuovo a Napoli per questa festa.

PROFESSORE: Andrete anche a Sorrento, immagino.

CARLO: Senza dubbio. E lì andremo anche a fare i bagni,[58] e, se possibile, vorrei andare anche a pescare per alcune ore.

PROFESSORE: Ti piace la pesca?

MARIA: Mio marito è molto appassionato[59] della pesca. Sono andata diverse volte con lui, e adesso piace anche a me.

LUCIA: Immagino che abbiate intenzione di visitare tutta l'Italia.

CARLO: Se non tutta, una buona parte di sicuro.

PROFESSORE: Quanto tempo contate di rimanere in Italia?

_____

year 1748, are a major attraction for tourists. *51.* An idiom: "again." *52. Credo di sì:* "I think so." Likewise, *credo di no* means "I don't think so." *53.* Do not translate the word *signor,* which in Italian is often used in direct address before a title or profession, for the sake of politeness. *54.* The *Funicolare,* cable car, which goes to the summit of Mt. Vesuvius, offers a panorama of breathtaking beauty. *55. Resa famosa:* "made famous." *56.* The verb *piacere* is mostly used in the third person singular and plural. The direct object of the English

MARIA: Otto o dieci settimane. Quando lasceremo Napoli andremo a Roma.

CARLO: Non prima di avere fatto una breve visita a Taormina, in Sicilia, mia cara. Non sono ancora stato a Taormina, e sono molto desideroso di vedere questo luogo che tutti definiscono[60] il paradiso dei turisti.

MARIA: Come vuoi[61] tu, amor mio. Ovunque andrai ti seguirò. Se vuoi passeremo lì tre o quattro giorni. Va bene così? Lo sai che per te io sono disposta a fare qualunque sacrificio.

CARLO: Non si può negare[62] che questo sia[63] veramente un grandissimo sacrificio!

PROFESSORE: E adesso, miei cari, prepariamoci per il teatro. (Tutti si alzano da tavola.) Sono quasi le otto, e la rappresentazione comincia alle otto e mezzo precise. (Guarda l'orologio.)

MARIA: Allora sbrighiamoci. Non voglio perdere una sola nota della bellissima musica di Puccini. Sono veramente ansiosa di vedere il San Carlo che, dicono, sia uno dei più bei teatri d'opera del mondo.

LUCIA: Vedo che siamo tutti pronti. Andiamo.

PROFESSORE: E il tassì?

LUCIA: La domestica ha telefonato mezz'ora fa. Dovrebbe già essere alla porta.

---

sentence becomes the subject of *piacere,* and the subject becomes an indirect object. Thus the sentence: *Vi piacciono le canzoni?* (Do you like the songs?) becomes: "are the songs pleasing to you?" In the compound tenses the auxiliary *essere* is used. Example: *Mi è piacciuto quel libro.* (I liked that book). 57. "Full of feeling." 58. An idiom: "To go bathing." 59. "Passionately fond." 60. *Che tutti definiscono:* "Which everybody calls." 61. "As you wish." *Vuoi* is

PROFESSORE: C'è infatti, e l'autista ha annunciato la sua presenza suonando la tromba della macchina.[64] Maria, posso avere l'onore di offrirti il braccio?[65]

MARIA: Con piacere.

CARLO: Professore, questa volta non se la passa liscia,[66] perchè io do il braccio alla sua signora, e così siamo pari. (*Tutti escono.*)

---

present of the irregular verb *volere.*   62. An impersonal verb: "one cannot deny." 63. *Sia:* present subjunctive of *essere.*   64. *Macchina* is often used instead of *automobile.*   65. *Il braccio:* "your arm." With parts of the body the possessive adjective is usually omitted in Italian. See Reference Grammar.   66. *Non se la passa liscia* is an idiomatic expression. It means, "You won't get away with it."

18 Diciottesima Lezione

NELLA CITTÀ ETERNA

ALL'USCITA DELLA STAZIONE DI TERMINI

CARLO: Autista, è libera la sua vettura?

AUTISTA: Sì, signore; entrino pure. Dove vogliono andare?

CARLO: Ci porti all'Albergo Flora. Sa dov'è?

AUTISTA: Eh, si figuri[1]! È vicino a Villa Borghese.[2] È un ottimo albergo. Hanno fatto la prenotazione?

CARLO: Sì, abbiamo telegrafato da Napoli. Non vada[3] troppo veloce. Cammin facendo[4] vogliamo incominciare ad ammirare le bellezze di questa incantevole città. Anzi, invece di andare direttamente all'albergo, la prego di passare per il Colosseo.

AUTISTA: Sarà servito,[5] signore.

MARIA: Amor mio, mi sembra proprio di sognare! Questa è la grande, l'immortale, l'incantevole Roma, che per secoli dominò il mondo, portando ovunque civiltà e cultura.

CARLO: Guarda là, a sinistra, cara. Che cosa vedi?

MARIA: Quella grande cupola non può essere che[6] la Cupola di San Pietro, il capolavoro dell'immortale Michelangelo.

CARLO: Sai che Michelangelo aveva fatto prima la cupola del Duomo di Firenze. Il grande artista era orgoglioso di quella meravigliosa cupola, e nell'ammirarla ancora una volta[7] prima di partire[8] per Roma, sai cosa disse?[9]

FOOTNOTES: *1. Si figuri:* "You can imagine." *2. Villa Borghese:* One of the most beautiful parks in Rome. *3. Vada* is imperative of *andare.* *4.* "On the way." *5. Sarà servito:* "as you wish." *6.* See Note 24, Lesson 17. *7.* Idiom: "once more." *8.* After a preposition the Italian verb is in the infinitive. *9.*

MARIA: Credo di sì,[10] ma non voglio toglierti il piacere di dirmelo.

CARLO: Allora te lo dico: "A Roma vado a far la tua sorella ..."

MARIA: ". . . Più grande sì, ma non di te più bella."

CARLO: C'è molto, ma molto da vedere[11] a Roma. Per farci una buona idea[12] di Roma dovremmo[13] rimanerci almeno un mese.

MARIA: Purtroppo ciò non sarà possibile, mio caro sposo, ma credo che potremo rimanerci due settimane. Che ne dici?[14]

CARLO: Come vuoi, cara. Ma bisogna fare un programma che ci permetterà[15] di vedere più che sia possibile.[16] Certo che Roma merita una visita più lunga che le altre città. In primo luogo,[17] Roma è capitale della Repubblica Italiana.[18] Poi è la più grande città d'Italia, ed una delle più belle del mondo.

MARIA: Va bene; stasera faremo il nostro itinerario.

CARLO: Ecco il Colosseo, Maria. Che te ne pare?

MARIA: Meraviglioso, imponente! Per me questo è il primo segno visibile dell'antica gloria di Roma. Mi sembra già di essere trasportata ai tempi dell'antichità. Posso quasi ricostruire nella mia mente lo splendore dell'antica Roma.

CARLO: Questa è la Via dei Fori Imperiali. Qui, a sinistra c'è l'antico Foro Romano, laggiù, vedi, c'è la bella Piazza Venezia.

MARIA: Dobbiamo visitare con cura tutti questi luoghi, e, naturalmente, ci toccherà fare molta strada a piedi.[19]

CARLO: E già! Non c'è altro mezzo.[20] Per visitare questi luoghi come si deve[21] bisognerà camminare molto.

MARIA: Bisognerà alzarci presto la mattina[22] e incominciare le nostre peregrinazioni di buon'ora.[23]

Disse is past definite of irregular verb *dire.* 10. See Note 52, Lesson 17. 11. "There is a great deal to see." 12 "To get a good idea." 13. Conditional of irregular verb *dovere.* 14. "What do you say (about it)?" 15. Future instead of subjunctive because a definite future action is indicated. 16. "As much as

CARLO: Ben detto, mia cara. E sai che faremo dopo la colazione del mezzogiorno?

MARIA: Continueremo a girare.

CARLO: Ti sbagli.[24] Faremo come fanno i romani. La maggior parte[25] di essi vanno a letto per un paio d'ore dopo la colazione, per riposarsi e per sfuggire al caldo.[26] "Paese che vai, usanze che trovi."[27] Andremo a letto anche noi, e verso le quattro del pomeriggio continueremo il nostro itinerario.

MARIA: Forse hai ragione. Non vale la pena[28] di stancarci troppo. Ecco il nostro albergo. (Carlo e Maria scendono dalla vettura.)

CARLO: Autista, quanto le dobbiamo?

AUTISTA: Seicento cinquanta lire, signore.

CARLO: Va bene. (Gli dà il denaro.) Ecco settecento lire. Tenga[29] il resto.

AUTISTA: Mille grazie,[30] signore.

(Gli sposini entrano nell'albergo.)

DIRETTORE DELL'ALBERGO: Ben venuti,[31] signori.[32]

CARLO: Io sono il signor Carlo Smith, e questa è la mia signora.

DIRETTORE: Abbiamo ricevuto la prenotazione e le abbiamo riservata una bella camera al[33] secondo piano. Alberto, porta le valigie dei signori nella camera trentadue. Intanto, vuole avere la bontà di mostrarmi il passaporto e di firmare sul registro?[34]

CARLO: Certo. (Firma sul registro.) Deve firmare anche mia moglie?

_____

possible." Sia is subjunctive because più has the superlative force of il più. 17. In primo luogo: "in the first place." 18. Italy was a monarchy up to 1946 when, as the result of a plebiscite, it became a republic. 19. "We shall have to walk a great deal." In this sentence we actually have three idioms: ci toccherà, fare strada, a piedi. 20. "There is no other way." 21. "As one should." 22. "In the morning." 23. "Early." Literally, at a good hour. 24. "You are mistaken." The infinitive is sbagliarsi. 25. La maggior parte: "most." Lit., the greater part.

DIRETTORE: Non è necessario. Ecco la chiave. C'è anche un messaggio per lei.

CARLO: Grazie. (Apre la busta e legge il biglietto. Poi rivolgendosi a Maria.) Indovina di chi è questo messaggio?

MARIA: Preferisco non indovinare. Forse qualche tua vecchia fiamma?

CARLO: Macchè[35]! È della signorina Borgese, la nipote del professore Di Giacomo.

MARIA: Ah, benissimo. Il professore ci disse che avrebbe[36] informata sua nipote della nostra venuta a Roma.

CARLO: La signorina Borgese ci prega di telefonarle appena possibile dopo il nostro arrivo. (Al direttore.) C'è telefono[37] nella nostra camera?

DIRETTORE: Sì, signore. Se permettono li accompagno io stesso.

CARLO: Grazie. Molto gentile.[38]

MARIA: Hai il numero del telefono della signorina?

CARLO: Sì, è scritto[39] qui nel biglietto. È meglio che telefoni subito. (Prende il telefono.) Pronto! Mi dia il 60-345, per piacere . . . Pronto! . . . Signorina Borgese? . . . Sono proprio io, Carlo Smith . . . Sì, siamo arrivati all'albergo pochi minuti fa . . . Ma certo, venga pure[40] quando le fa comodo.[41] Mia moglie ed io non vediamo l'ora di conoscerla . . . Alle cinque? . . . Benissimo, l'attendiamo con ansia. Arrivederla a presto!

MARIA: Ammiro il tuo entusiasmo, caro.

CARLO: Ma . . .

MARIA: Non è necessario che dica[42] niente, Non ti allarmare. Se la signorina è gentile come lo zio sono sicura che anche a Roma avremo un'ottima guida.

---

26. "To escape the heat." Per means "in order to." 27. "When in Rome do as the Romans do." Notice the literal meaning of this saying in this instance. 28. Idiom: "It is not worth while." 29. Imperative of irregular verb tenere. 30. "Thanks a million." Lit., a thousand thanks. 31. "Welcome." 32. Notice that, even though the majordomo is welcoming a lady and a gentleman, he uses the masculine plural form signori. 33. Here al means "on." 34. Lit., to sign on the register. 35. Macchè!: "Not at all!" 36. Conditional of avere. 37. "Is

QUALCHE ORA DOPO NELLA CAMERA DELL'ALBERGO FLORA

(Squillo[43] del telefono.)

MARIA: Vuoi rispondere tu?

CARLO: Va bene, rispondo io. Sarà[44] la signorina Borgese. Pronto![45] . . . Ma sì, sì, salga pure.[40] *(A Maria.)* Ho indovinato. *(Apre la porta.)* Cara signorina, non so dirle quanto sono felice di conoscerla. Questa è Maria, mia moglie.

MARIA: Sono anch'io felicissima di fare la sua conoscenza. *(Strette di mano.[46])*

SIGNORINA BORGESE: È una immensa gioia anche per me. Lo zio mi ha scritto una lunghissima lettera parlandomi di loro. Io mi metto a loro completa disposizione. Ho molto tempo disponibile e, se vogliono, li accompagnerò con piacere dovunque desiderino[47] andare.

CARLO: Cara signorina, è superfluo dirle che per noi questa è una vera fortuna. Ma si accomodi, prego.

MARIA: Accettiamo con entusiasmo la sua gentile offerta. Siamo sicuri che lei conosce ogni angolo di Roma.

SIG.NA BORGESE: Come loro certamente conoscono New York. Mi sono permessa di portare loro una guida di Roma. È la migliore che esista,[48] e c'è anche una pianta ben dettagliata della città. Loro sanno benissimo che per visitare con cura tutta Roma non basterebbero diversi mesi. Quindi, dato che[49] la loro permanenza qui sarà di un paio di settimane al massimo,[50] così

there a telephone?" Notice the omission of the indefinite article in the Italian sentence. *38.* "You are very kind." *Lei è* is understood. *39.* Past participle of irregular verb *scrivere.* *40.* The word *pure* is often used for emphasis. It is not to be translated. *41.* "When it is suitable to you." *42.* Subjunctive of irregular verb *dire.* *43. Squillo:* "ring, ringing." *44.* Future of probability. *45.*

almeno mi ha scritto lo zio, se permettono, darò loro un consiglio.

CARLO: Ma dica, dica pure,[40] cara signorina.

SIG.NA BORGESE: Ecco. In questa guida sono tracciati diversi itinerari. La esaminino attentamente e facciano una lista dei luoghi che in ispecial[51] modo desiderano vedere.

MARIA: L'idea è eccellente, e noi gliene siamo molto grati. Questa sera passeremo qualche oretta[52] a fare i nostri piani. Però ho già in mente che cosa desidero fare la prima giornata.

CARLO: Scommetto che lo so. Vuoi vedere San Pietro ed il Vaticano.

MARIA: Come hai fatto a indovinarlo?[53]

CARLO: Eh! Ne hai parlato tanto!

SIG.NA BORGESE: Non potrebbero incominciare in modo migliore. San Pietro è la più bella chiesa del mondo.

MARIA: Ed è logico e naturale che questa basilica si trovi a Roma che è il centro del Cristianesimo.

CARLO: So che a Roma ci sono moltissime chiese, tutte bellissime.

SIG.NA BORGESE: Ciò è verissimo. In questa città ci sono più di quattrocento chiese, ma le più importanti, oltre a quella di San Pietro, sono le basiliche di San Paolo, di San Giovanni in Laterano e di Santa Maria Maggiore. Queste chiese, i palazzi dei papi ed i numerosi musei che spero avranno occasione di visitare, ricordano e tracciano le origini, lo sviluppo e lo splendore del Cristianesimo.

This is the Italian way of saying "Hello!" when answering the telephone. 46. "Handshakes." 47. *Desiderino* is subjunctive. It is required by the indefinite adverb *dovunque*. 48. Subjunctive after a relative superlative. 49. "Inasmuch as." 50. "At the most." 51. A variation of the word *speciale*. Nouns beginning with *s-impura* often take an *i* at the beginning, when the preceding word ends in

MARIA: Gli italiani sono quasi tutti cattolici e molto religiosi, non è vero?

SIG.NA BORGESE: Sì, la grandissima maggioranza sono cattolici. Ma le altre religioni sono tollerate ed hanno i loro fedeli.

CARLO: Le due più grandi feste, indubbiamente, sono quelle di Natale e di Pasqua.

SIG.NA BORGESE: Verissimo. Lei non può immaginare l'immensa folla che si raduna nella chiesa e nell'immensa piazza di San Pietro la notte di Natale[54] per sentire la Messa di mezzanotte, celebrata dal Papa. Naturalmente, anche le altre chiese sono molto affollate. Molta affluenza di pubblico c'è anche nelle chiese durante la Settimana Santa, specialmente il Sabato Santo, cioè la vigilia di Pasqua, che è il giorno della Risurrezione. Tutti i fedeli vengono ad adorare Gesù Cristo risorto, mentre da tutte le chiese squillano allegramente le campane, suonando a festa.

MARIA: Sarà uno spettacolo meraviglioso. Una mia amica mi ha parlato di un'usanza molto simpatica che ha luogo in molte città d'Italia il giorno di Pasqua.

SIG.NA BORGESE: Quale?

MARIA: Prima di incominciare il pranzo pasquale[55] il padre di famiglia benedice la tavola e la famiglia con un ramo d'olivo, e poi tutti si danno[56] il bacio della pace.

SIG.NA BORGESE: Già. E poi sperano che la pace sia duratura.

CARLO: Signorina, mia moglie ed io siamo molto desiderosi di vedere il Papa. È possibile?

SIG.NA BORGESE: Sì. Non è facile ottenere un'udienza speciale, ma Sua Santità[57] concede spesso delle udienze a gruppi di persone che desiderano vederlo. Sono sicura che il loro desiderio sarà appagato. Forse ciò potrà avverarsi[58] domani stesso. Dato che

---

a consonant.   52. "A few hours." *Oretta* is a diminutive of *ora*, and implies pleasure.   53. How did you guess it?"   54. *Notte di Natale:* "Christmas Eve." 55. "Easter dinner." *Pasquale* is an adjective derived from *Pasqua.*   56. "Give each other."   57. "His Holiness."   58. "May come true."   59. *Urbino:* birthplace of Raffael (Raphael).   60. *"Il Giudizio Universale,"* "The Last Judgment";

andremo a San Pietro, visiteremo il Vaticano, specialmente i Musei Vaticani, dove si trovano le più preziose e complete raccolte di antichità del mondo; le quattro Stanze di Raffaello, in cui vedranno le sublimi creazioni d'arte dell'immortale pittore di Urbino;[59] e la Cappella Sistina, dove vedranno le opere d'arte dei più grandi artisti del Cinquecento: del Ghirlandaio, del Botticelli, del Perugino, e sopratutto di Michelangelo.

CARLO: Se non mi sbaglio è proprio nella Cappella Sistina che potremo ammirare i famosi affreschi di Michelangelo: Il Giudizio Universale,[60] La Creazione[60] ed il Diluvio Universale.[60]

SIG.NA BORGESE: Esattamente.

MARIA: E poi, se non siamo troppo stanchi, mi piacerebbe visitare, sia pure di sfuggita,[61] la Biblioteca Vaticana che è senza dubbio la più interessante e ricca del mondo, perchè, a quanto mi è stato detto,[62] racchiude i libri più rari e più belli.

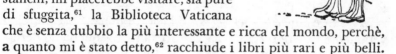

CARLO: Mi dica, per piacere, signorina, se il popolo italiano è contento della Conciliazione tra il Governo Italiano e la Santa Sede[63] avvenuta nel 1929.

SIG.NA BORGESE: In gran parte sì. Come lei indubbiamente sa, quando nel 1870 l'unificazione d'Italia poteva dirsi quasi completa, il Papa rifiutò di cedere Roma a Vittorio Emanuele, benchè il popolo volesse che Roma fosse la capitale del nuovo regno d'Italia. Così, il 20 settembre 1870, le truppe italiane occuparono Roma e ne fecero la capitale. Il Papa allora, in segno di protesta, si rinchiuse come prigioniero nel Vaticano, e nè lui, nè i suoi successori ne uscirono più fino all'undici febbraio 1929, giorno in cui fu firmato il Patto del Laterano.[64] Fino a quel giorno si

---

"La Creazione," "The Creation"; "Il Diluvio Universale", "The Flood." *61. Sia pure di sfuggita:* "Even if I do it hastily." 62. "From what I have heard." *63. La Santa Sede:* "The Holy See." 64. The Lateran Treaty." *65. Tanto . . . quanto:* "as . . . as." *66. Nacque* (was born) is past definite of *nascere.* 67 *Nome di battesimo:* "first name." *Lit.,* name of baptism. *68. Tante e tante*

può dire che uno stato di guerra esistesse tra la Santa Sede ed il Governo d'Italia. Ciò non piaceva al popolo, che era tanto patriottico quanto[65] religioso. Così nacque[66] il più piccolo stato del mondo che è senza dubbio uno dei più importanti.

CARLO: Maria, signorina Borgese . . .

SIG.NA BORGESE: Mi chiami semplicemente Rosella, che è il mio nome di battesimo.[67]

CARLO: Va bene. Rosella, Maria sentite: mi è venuta un'idea brillante.

MARIA: Un'idea brillante? È possibile?

CARLO: Non scherziamo! Dunque, ecco la mia idea. Dato che abbiamo tante e tante[68] cose da fare e da vedere a Roma, non sarebbe meglio prendere in noleggio[69] un'automobile per il periodo di tempo che resteremo qui?

SIG.NA BORGESE: Non si può negare che l'idea sia eccellente. Sicuro che è possibile. Credo che sia il mezzo migliore e forse il più economico per visitare tutti i luoghi[70] della città.

MARIA: Ammetto anch'io che l'idea è buona. Così potremo veramente vedere tutta Roma, la parte antica e quella moderna.

SIG.NA BORGESE: Giustissimo. Non debbono lasciare questa città portando con loro, come fanno tanti altri turisti, l'impressione che Roma sia soltanto una città antica. Roma è anche una città molto moderna, con nuovi quartieri residenziali, nuove vie bellissime, larghe ed alberate, nuovi parchi e monumenti. Il più imponente e meraviglioso di questi monumenti è quello di Vittorio Emanuele Secondo,[71] che fu il primo Re d'Italia. Probabilmente sanno che al centro di questo monumento c'è la tomba del Milite Ignoto.[72]

MARIA: Mi piacerebbe visitare anche le famose Catacombe[73] in cui si riunivano segretamente i Cristiani.

SIG.NA BORGESE: Le Catacombe sono molto interessanti. Allora dovranno visitare anche le Fosse Ardeatine, scena di una delle più orrende stragi dell' epoca moderna.

"so many."   69. Prendere in noleggio: "to rent."   70. Luoghi is plural of luogo (place).   71. Victor Emanuel II (1820-1878) was the first king of United Italy. 72. "Unknown Soldier."   73. The miles and miles of Catacombs in Rome are of great interest to tourists. It was there that the early Christians held their secret

CARLO: Lo so. Purtroppo fu lì che 335 detenuti politici[74] italiani furono, per rappresaglia, orribilmente trucidati dai tedeschi nel 1944.

MARIA: Ciò è molto doloroso. Beh,[75] che facciamo adesso?

CARLO: Adesso usciamo. Facciamo una bella passeggiata e poi andremo a cena. Vuol concederci il piacere della sua compagnia, Rosella?

SIG.NA BORGESE: Molto volentieri. L'avverto però che domani sera verranno[76] a pranzo a casa mia. I miei genitori sono molto desiderosi di conoscerli.

MARIA: Non possiamo rifiutare un'offerta così gentile.

SIG.NA BORGESE: Domani sera conosceranno anche il mio fidanzato.

CARLO: Benissimo. E forse, se il suo fidanzato avrà tempo, potrà[77] accompagnarci anche lui nelle nostre peregrinazioni per la Città Eterna. (Escono tutti e tre.[78])

---

meetings and performed their rituals. *74.* "Political prisoners." *75. Beh* is an exclamation meaning *"well! so!"* *76.* Future of *venire.* *77.* Future of *potere.* *78. Tutti e tre:* "the three of them." Likewise, *tutti e due:* "both."

19 Diciannovesima Lezione

FIRENZE, CULLA DELLE ARTI

IN UNA PIAZZA DI FIRENZE

CARLO: Mia cara Maria, ti debbo confessare una cosa.

MARIA: Grave?

CARLO: Molto.

MARIA: Ti ascolto. E quando avrai finito confesserò io una cosa a te.

CARLO: Ho appetito. Anzi, ho una fame da lupo.

MARIA: Ah, ah, ah!

CARLO: Che cosa c'è da ridere?

MARIA: Rido perchè questo è proprio quello che[1] volevo confessarti. Ho fame anch'io.

CARLO: Allora è inutile aspettare oltre.[2] Vedo un ristorante da quel lato della piazza. Andiamoci.[3]

MARIA: Andiamoci.

AL RISTORANTE

CAMERIERE: Buon giorno, signori. Una tavola per due?

CARLO: Sì.

CAMERIERE: Si vogliono accomodare qui?

CARLO: Sì, va bene qui. *(Carlo e Maria siedono ad una tavola.)*

CAMERIERE: Vino bianco o rosso?

CARLO: Riguardo al vino ci rimettiamo a lei.[4] Mi piace un

FOOTNOTES: 1. *Proprio quello che:* "exactly what." 2. *Aspettare oltre:* "to wait any longer." 3. The *ci* of *andiamoci* means "there." 4. *Ci rimettiamo a lei:* "We leave it to you." 5. "Leave it to me!" 6. *Secondo quello che . . . :* "According to what . . ." 7. *Lista delle vivande:* "Menu." *Lit.*, list of the victuals.

172

buon bicchiere di vino, ma debbo ammettere che non sono un buon conoscitore.

CAMERIERE: Allora lascino fare a me[5] che sarò ben lieto di consigliarli secondo quello che[6] desiderano mangiare. Ecco la lista delle vivande.[7] Ritornerò fra[8] pochi minuti.

(Un signore che è seduto alla tavola vicina si alza e si avvicina. Si chiama Gianni Pascolo.)

PASCOLO: Chiedo loro scusa di[9] questa intrusione.

CARLO: Ma si figuri![10] Non ci disturba affatto.

PASCOLO: Non ho potuto fare a meno[11] di avvicinarmi sentendoli parlare. Loro sono indubbiamente americani.

CARLO: Sì, signore.

PASCOLO: Non l'ho capito dal parlare perchè lei parla perfettamente l'italiano; ma lei e la sua signora hanno quel certo non so che[12] che distingue gli americani dagli altri forestieri.

MARIA: Lei è molto gentile, signore.

PASCOLO: Grazie, signora. Dunque, stavo per dire[13] che non appena mi sono convinto che sono americani mi ha invaso una certa nostalgia.

CARLO: Come mai?[14]

PASCOLO: Ecco, mi spiego. Ma prima permettano che mi presenti: Gianni Pascolo, ingegnere.

CARLO: Tanto piacere di conoscerla. Io sono Carlo Smith, e questa è mia moglie.

PASCOLO: Fortunatissimo.

MARIA: Piacere.

CARLO: Adesso che ci conosciamo vuole avere la bontà di sedersi alla nostra tavola?

PASCOLO: Lo faccio con piacere. Grazie infinite.

---

8. *Fra:* "within." 9. I apologize for . . ." 10. See Note 1, Lesson 18. 11. "I couldn't help . . ." 12. "That certain something." 13. "I was about to say . . ." 14. How come?" 15. *Minestrone* is a very thick soup prepared with an assortment of vegetables (celery, onion, cabbage, etc.) and legumes (beans, lentils, etc.)

MARIA: Poco fa lei parlava di nostalgia. È evidente che è stato in America.

PASCOLO: Proprio così, cara signora. Due anni, due bellissimi anni in cui ebbi occasione di conoscere, di ammirare e anche di amare la loro bella patria.

CAMERIERE: Hanno deciso, signori?

CARLO: Sì. Per incominciare ci porti un po' d'antipasto: prosciutto, olive, sedani, eccetera.

CAMERIERE: Benissimo. E poi? Vogliono del brodo di pollo, del minestrone?[15]

CARLO: No. Poi porti costolette d'agnello con contorno[16] di spinaci per la signora, una bistecca con purè di patate per me, e quello che desidera l'ingegnere Pascolo.

CAMERIERE: Oh, quanto all'ingegnere io so benissimo che cosa vuole senza che me lo dica. Oggi è giovedì, quindi un quarto di pollo arrosto. Vero, ingegnere?

PASCOLO: Vero. Ormai questo caro cameriere conosce le mie abitudini. E, senti, Gianni, porta anche una bottiglia di vecchio Chianti.

MARIA: A proposito di vino,[17] ho notato che ogni volta che entriamo in un ristorante la prima cosa che il cameriere ci domanda è se vogliamo vino bianco o rosso.

PASCOLO: Già. E glielo spiego. Quasi tutti gli italiani bevono il vino durante i pasti, anche se molto modesti, consistenti in una minestra,[18] pane e formaggio. L'italiano deve avere il suo bicchiere di vino. È un'abitudine. Si dice che il buon vino faccia venire buoni pensieri. Le debbo[19] dire, però, che beviamo con moderazione.

CARLO: Il buon vino fa venire buoni pensieri. Mi piace questa espressione. Già, perchè, anche volendo, gli italiani non potrebbero bere del cattivo vino, perchè in Italia è tutto buono.

PASCOLO: Come trovano[20] la nostra Firenze?

MARIA: Divinamente bella. È innegabile che dal punto di

---

and is flavorfully seasoned.   *16.* "Side dish."   *17. A proposito di vino:* "talking of wine."   *18.* Same as *minestrone,* but with fewer ingredients.   *19. Debbo* or *devo,* present of irregular verb *dovere.*   *20. Come trovano:* "How do you like . . ."   *21. Non per nulla:* "That's why." *Lit.,* Not for nothing.   *22.* "The cradle of

vista culturale Firenze è la più importante città, non solo d'Italia, ma del mondo.

CARLO: Non per nulla[21] Firenze è chiamata "la culla delle arti."[22] Chi non sa che per oltre tre secoli questà città fu il centro della cultura mondiale? Ci sono tanti tesori d'arte che l'intera città può considerarsi un vero museo.

PASCOLO: Debbo dirle con orgoglio che ha ragione. Nessuna città ha dato al mondo tanti geni quanti ne[23] ha dati Firenze. E se non tutti questi grandi uomini nacquero[24] qui, quasi tutti vi[25] studiarono e vi lavorarono: Dante, Petrarca, Boccaccio, Machiavelli, Leonardo da Vinci, Michelangelo, Della Robbia, Brunelleschi e tanti, tanti altri ancora. Fu proprio qui che, dopo il periodo di decadenza intellettuale del Medio Evo, ebbe origine il Rinascimento, il luminoso periodo che va dal quindicesimo al sedicesimo secolo, epoca che diede al mondo un nuovo, luminoso indirizzo nel campo delle arti, delle scienze, della letteratura e della politica. E anche tutt'oggi,[26] Firenze continua a essere il centro delle industrie artistiche.

CARLO: Ha ragione, caro ingegnere. Firenze ci ha affascinati completamente.

MARIA: Abbiamo trascorse[27] delle ore indimenticabili ammirando estasiati i tesori artistici della Galleria degli Uffizi, del Palazzo Pitti, e di quel capolavoro d'architettura medioevale ch'è il Palazzo Vecchio. Tutto è arte a Firenze. Il Campanile di Giotto è indescrivibilmente bello.

PASCOLO: Immagino che hanno già visitato il Ponte Vecchio[28] con le sue piccole, ma graziose botteghe.

MARIA: Ah, sì. Ed abbiamo comprato lì, per ricordo, diversi oggetti d'argento ed in cuoio sbalzato.[29] Dei ricordi bellissimi. Adesso vorrei comprare dei buoni libri. So bene che posso comprarli dovunque, ma preferisco comprarli qui, a Firenze. Quali libri mi consiglia di comprare, ingegnere?

PASCOLO: Immagino che non vorrà[30] comprarne troppi, dato che devono viaggiare. Ma siccome lei è amante della letteratura,

---

arts."   23. Omit this *ne* (of them) in translation.   24. Plural of *nacque*, which is past definite of *nascere*.   25. *Vi*: "here."   26. *Tutt'oggi*: "nowadays."   27. Past participle of *trascorrere*: "to spend (time)."   28. The Ponte Vecchio (Old Bridge), which crosses the Arno River, is lined with quaint little shops where for

le consiglio di acquistare prima di tutto la "Divina Commedia" di Dante Alighieri.

MARIA: Ho già una copia della "Divina Commedia," ma in formato piccolo. Adesso vorrei[31] comprarne una in formato grande, quella con le illustrazioni di Botticelli. Per me la "Divina

Commedia" è l'opera più bella e più completa che esista. Pochi momenti fa si parlava del Ponte Vecchio. Se non erro,[32] fu proprio su questo ponte che Dante un giorno incontrò Beatrice e se ne innamorò. Dante non sposò Beatrice, ma ella rimase per sempre la donna ideale del suo cuore e della sua mente, e divenne l'ispirazione della "Divina Commedia."

PASCOLO: E a lei dedicò anche una bella poesia! Ricorda come comincia?

"Tanto gentile e tanto onesta pare
La donna mia quand'ella altrui saluta."

Poi le consiglio di comprare "Il Principe," di Machiavelli, in cui l'autore insegna come un principe deve governare, dipinge con esattezza gli eventi dei suoi tempi, e lancia la prima voce invocante la liberazione dell'Italia dal giogo straniero. Un altro libro che non dovrebbe mancare[33] nella sua biblioteca è il bellissimo romanzo di Manzoni, "I Promessi Sposi." Anche Manzoni, in questo libro, accende nel cuore degli italiani il fervente desiderio di vedere l'Italia libera e unita. Ancora un libro che le consiglio è il "Decamerone," del Boccaccio. In questa divertente raccolta di cento novelle il più grande prosatore di quell'epoca dipinge meravigliosamente gli usi e costumi dei suoi tempi.

CARLO: La prima cosa che faremo questo pomeriggio sarà di comprare tutti questi libri.

---

over 500 years goldsmiths and silversmiths have practiced their art. Longfellow, who loved Italy, pays tribute to this picturesque landmark of medieval Florence in his poem, "The Old Bridge." 29. Florence is famous for, among other things,

MARIA: Ho anche diverse altre cosette[34] da comprare: profumo, dentifricio, cipria, eccetera.

PASCOLO: C'è un'ottima profumeria poco distante da qui, in Via degli Speziali. E, perdonino ancora una volta la mia audacia. Posso domandare loro che cosa intendono fare stasera?

MARIA: Ma non parli di audacia. Noi siamo molto felici di questo piacevole incontro, e la consideriamo già un buon amico.

PASCOLO: Molto gentile, signora.

CARLO: Per stasera non abbiamo ancora niente in programma.

PASCOLO: Ottimamente bene![35] Loro amano la musica?

MARIA: È il mio debole.[36]

PASCOLO: E allora li prego di concedermi l'onore ed il piacere di averli come miei ospiti al Politeama,[37] dove si dà un magnifico concerto di musica sinfonica.

CARLO: Accettato, caro ingegnere. Noi ci tratterremo qui tre o quattro giorni ancora, e spero che almeno una di queste sere sarà lei nostro ospite.

PASCOLO: Con immenso piacere. Grazie infinite.

MARIA: Ingegnere, ci parli, per piacere, di alcune feste per cui Firenze è tanto famosa. La Festa del Grillo, per esempio.

PASCOLO: Ah, sì, È una festa divertentissima che ha luogo alle Cascine,[38] per celebrare il ritorno della primavera. La gioia e l'allegrezza dei fiorentini in questa occasione è grandissima.

MARIA: Sarà un gran divertimento per i fiorentini, ma che c'entra il grillo?[39]

PASCOLO: Per un' antica usanza tutti portano un grillo in una piccolissima gabbia. Si dice che il grillo porti fortuna. Dopo la festa, però, i poveri grilli vengono messi in libertà, e questa è una fortuna per loro.

CARLO: Meno male. Così sono tutti felici.

---

its artistic objects of silver and embossed leather.   *30.* Future of irregular verb *volere.* Here it indicates probability.   *31.* Conditional of *volere.*   *32.* "If I am not mistaken."   *33.* "Should not be missing."   *34.* Diminutive of *cose* (things).

PASCOLO: Dato che loro americani sono amanti dello sport, sono sicuro che piacerebbe loro di assistere ad un'altra festa bellissima: il Calcio Fiorentino. Due squadre, una rappresentante gli abitanti di "qua dell'Arno," e l'altra gli abitanti di "là dell' Arno," giocano due partite di calcio: una la prima domenica di maggio e la seconda il ventiquattro giugno. Tutti i giocatori portano costumi del Rinascimento. Questa è un'altra occasione in cui i fiorentini si divertono un mondo. Ma questa festa ha anche un significato storico.

MARIA: Veramente? Quale?

PASCOLO: Nel 1530, durante una guerra, Firenze era stata assediata e un giorno, mentre i nobili fiorentini giocavano una partita di calcio, i nemici incominciarono a far fuoco[40] sulla città. Ma per dimostrare il loro coraggio i fiorentini continuarono la loro partita.

CARLO: Molto interessante. E giacchè si parla di feste, debbo confessare che ce n'è una alla quale, in ispecial modo[41] mi piacerebbe di assistere: la Festa del Palio che ha luogo a Siena.

PASCOLO: A, sì, questa è una festa veramente meravigliosa che attrae numerosi turisti. Consiste in una corsa di dieci cavalli, rappresentanti le dieci Contrade della città. La corsa si svolge[42] proprio sulla piazza maggiore della città. C'è una magnifica parata prima della corsa, e tutti quelli che vi partecipano indossano costumi medioevali. L'intera città è decorata di fiori e di bandiere. La gioia e l'entusiasmo degli abitanti, e anche dei forestieri,

---

35. "Fine!" 36. "It's my weakness!" 37. The *Politeama* is a magnificent concert hall in Florence. 38. The *Cascine* is a beautiful park in Florence. 39. *Che c'entra il grillo?*: "What has the cricket got to do with it?" 40. *Far fuoco*: "to

non hanno limiti. Il cavallo vincitore viene portato in chiesa per ricevere la benedizione. Questa festa ha luogo il due luglio e si ripete il sedici agosto.

CARLO: Magnifico! Questa è una vera fortuna. Che ne dici, Maria? Possiamo prolungare la nostra visita qui di quattro giorni ancora?

MARIA: Perchè no? Abbiamo ancora molte cose da vedere da queste parti. È molto lontana Siena?

PASCOLO: Appena un centinaio di chilometri. Ci[43] si arriva in meno di due ore. E, se loro permettono, li accompagnerò io.

CARLO: Sa, caro ingegnere, che noi siamo forse i più fortunati turisti che siano mai venuti in Italia?

PASCOLO: Come mai?

CARLO: Perchè tanto a Napoli come a Roma abbiamo avuto la fortuna di incontrare dei buoni amici che ci hanno fatto da guida.[44] E qui, a Firenze, abbiamo lei. Inutile dirle che accettiamo di tutto cuore[45] la sua gentile offerta.

PASCOLO: Li assicuro che sarà un gran piacere per me. E che cosa hanno intenzione di fare durante questi quattro giorni?

MARIA: Non mancherà certo il modo di occuparli. Domani vogliamo andare a Fiesole, a visitare quell'incantevole monastero di cui ho tanto sentito parlare.

PASCOLO: Non avranno a pentirsene. Fiesole è poco distante. Il monastero è situato in cima ad una collina, e di lassù avranno occasione di ammirare un panorama stupendo.

CARLO: Dopodomani andremo a Pisa che, secondo i miei calcoli, possiamo raggiungere in circa due ore.

MARIA: Sono molto ansiosa di vedere la famosa Torre Pendente. Si può salire sulla Torre?

PASCOLO: Certo. E anche dalla Torre potranno ammirare il magnifico panorama degli Appennini e delle verdi colline di

---

fire." *41.* See Note 51, Lesson 18. *42. Si svolge:* "takes place." *43. Ci:* "there." *44.* Idiom: "to act as a guide." *45. Di tutto cuore:* "wholeheartedly." *46.* "Law of falling bodies." *47. Allora siamo a posto:* "Then everything is

Livorno. Quando saranno sulla Torre si ricorderanno del grande astronomo, fisico e matematico Galileo, che proprio da quella torre dimostrò la legge della gravità dei corpi.[46] Visiteranno anche

il Duomo, che è bellissimo. Fu nel santuario del Duomo che Galileo, osservando l'oscillazione della grande lampada, scoprì la legge del pendolo.

CARLO: Galileo fu veramente un grande uomo. A lui dobbiamo, fra tante altre cose, l'invenzione del termometro, del telescopio e del microscopio.

MARIA: Dopo la nostra visita a Pisa sai che cosa mi piacerebbe di fare?

CARLO: Non lo so. Dimmelo, e sarai accontentata.

MARIA: Mi piacerebbe andare a fare i bagni. Sono sicura che ci deve esser qualche bella spiaggia non molto lontano da Pisa.

PASCOLO: Infatti, cara signora, a solo pochi chilometri da Pisa si trova Viareggio, senza dubbio una delle più belle stazioni balneari del mondo.

CARLO: Allora siamo a posto.[47] Quando saremo a Pisa, invece di far ritorno a Firenze, andremo direttamente a Viareggio e vi rimarremo un paio di giorni. Poi ritorneremo qui per fare la nostra gita a Siena con il gentilissimo signor Pascolo.

MARIA: Benone,[48] mio caro!

CARLO: Ed ora, dopo questo delizioso pasto, andiamo a fare quattro passi.[49] E più tardi andremo a visitare la bella chiesa di San Lorenzo dove si trovano le tombe dei Medici, scolpite da Michelangelo. Cameriere, il conto per piacere.

PASCOLO: Se permettono . . .

O.K." 48. *Benone* is an augmentative of *bene*. 49. "Let's go for a stroll."

CARLO: Niente affatto,[50] caro ingegnere, oggi lei è nostro ospite.

PASCOLO: Allora ci rivedremo stasera. In quale albergo alloggiano?

CARLO: Al Grand Hotel.

PASCOLO: Verrò a prenderli alle otto. A stasera dunque.

CARLO E MARIA: Arrivederla. *(Tutti e tre si alzano ed escono.)*

---

50. *Niente affatto!:* "Don't even think of it!"

20 Ventesima Lezione

NELL'ITALIA SETTENTRIONALE

MARIA: Mio caro sposo, sarebbe impossibile dirti quanto sono felice. Questo viaggio, che purtroppo volge alla fine,[1] mi ha riempito il cuore di una gioia infinita. Non avrei mai potuto, nemmeno lontanamente, immaginare che l'Italia fosse così bella.

CARLO: Sì, il buon Dio è stato molto generoso verso l'Italia. Adesso capisco le parole di Longfellow che disse: "Aprite il mio cuore e vi troverete incisa la parola *Italia*." Portiamo con noi molti ricordi di questo "Bel Paese." Che cosa ti è piaciuto[2] di più, Maria?

MARIA: Questa è la domanda più difficile che tu possa[3] farmi. Ti risponderò semplicemente: tutto! Le bellissime città di Napoli, Roma, Firenze, Pisa; e poi Siena. Chi avrebbe mai potuto credere che la Festa del Palio fosse così bella? E poi la città che più di ogni altra volevo vedere: Venezia, la città romantica, la città dei sogni e della poesia, che sorge dalla laguna.

CARLO: Hai ragione, mia cara; Venezia è fantasticamente bella. Quel labirinto di canali, quelle graziose gondole[4] che scivolano silenziosamente sull'acqua, destramente spinte[5] dai gondolieri che stanno sempre ritti in piedi[6] dietro ai passeggieri. È incredibile che si sia potuto costruire[7] una città così bella su centinaia di isolette rocciose.

MARIA: Chissà per quale bizzarra idea la costruirono proprio in mezzo al mare.[8]

FOOTNOTES: *1. Volge alla fine:* "Is coming to an end." *2.* See Note 56, Lesson 17. *3.* Subjunctive of *potere*. Subjunctive is required by the relative superlative. *4.* At the time of the Venetian Republic the luxury of the gondolas and the rivalry of the owners were so great that the Doge ordered an end to all that, and since

CARLO: Non fu per bizzarria, mia cara, ma per assoluta necessità. Devi sapere che dopo la caduta dell'Impero Romano molte persone dovettero rifugiarsi sulle piccole isole della laguna per sfuggire all'oppressione degli invasori, Poco a poco[9] essi costruirono le prime case ed i primi ponti. Fu così che sorse[10] Venezia, che più tardi divenne una potente repubblica navale.

MARIA: Bravo il mio Carlo![11] Par i da uomo dotto.[12] C'è una gran differenza fra le prime case di allora ed i sontuosi palazzi di adesso, specialmente quelli che si trovano ai due lati del Canal Grande.

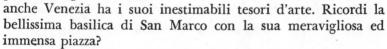

CARLO: Il tutto[13] sembra veramente un sogno incredibile, non è vero?

MARIA: Quel che è ancora più meraviglioso è il fatto che anche Venezia ha i suoi inestimabili tesori d'arte. Ricordi la bellissima basilica di San Marco con la sua meravigliosa ed immensa piazza?

CARLO: Non potrei immaginare una piazza più bella di quella di San Marco, con quell'imponente Campanile.

MARIA: Il Campanile mi è sembrato di costruzione recente.

CARLO: Lo è infatti. Nel 1902 avvenne un disastro! Il bellissimo Campanile crollò! Ma gli orgogliosi veneziani, addolorati ma non scoraggiati, lo ricostruirono "com'era, dov'era."[14]

MARIA: Non è interessante anche la Torre dell'Orologio con quelle due gigantesche statue dei mori che battono le ore sulla campana coi loro pesanti martelli? E il Lido, non è anche quella una spiaggia magnifica?

CARLO: Veramente stupenda. Tutto è bello a Venezia. Io non

---

that time gondolas have been painted black.   *5.* "Skillfully driven."   *6. In piedi:* "standing."   *7.* See Reference Grammar.   *8. In mezzo al mare:* "In the middle of the sea."   *9.* Idiom: "little by little."   *10. Sorse* is past definite of *sorgere* (to rise).   *11.* "Good for you, Charles!"   *12. Da uomo dotto:* "like a

credo ci sia al mondo una città che possa paragonarsi[15] a Venezia, giustamente chiamata "La Regina dell'Adriatico."

MARIA: È interessante il fatto che a Venezia non ci sono nè automobili, nè biciclette. La gondola è l'unico mezzo[16] di trasporto.

CARLO: Hai notato che in alcune parti d'Italia si fa ancora grande uso della bicicletta? Dico "in alcune parti" perchè la bicicletta in molti luoghi è già stata sostituita da migliaia e migliaia di piccole motociclette. Ma è pittoresco delle volte vedere centinaia e centinaia di bicilette per[17] le strade.

MARIA: È il mezzo di trasporto più economico, a meno che[18] non si voglia[19] andare a piedi, che è un mezzo ancora più economico, ma più sicuro.

CARLO: E più lento. E a Milano, che cosa ti è piaciuto di più?

MARIA: Anche Milano è una città molto interessante.

CARLO: Dal punto di vista economico e commerciale Milano è senza dubbio la più importante città d'Italia. Ciò è principalmente dovuto alla sua favorevole posizione nella pianura del Po,[20] che ne fa[21] un grandissimo centro di comunicazioni.

MARIA: Ma anche a Milano ci sono dei tesori d'arte d'inestimabile valore, come "Il Cenacolo"[22] di Leonardo Da Vinci, nella chiesa di Santa Maria delle Grazie. Quando ho visto questo famosissimo affresco il mio cuore ha palpitato d'emozione.[23] Che lavoro stupendo! Il tempo però lo aveva un po' rovinato, ma, grazie alla tecnica moderna, è stato restaurato alla perfezione. Che genio quel Leonardo da Vinci!

CARLO: Per me Leonardo da Vinci fu il genio più grande e più completo dell'umanità. E pensa che egli non fu soltanto un

man of learning." *13. Il tutto:* "the whole thing." *14.* "As it was, where it was." *15.* "That could be compared." *16. L'unico mezzo:* "the only means." *17. Per* in this case means "in." *18. A meno che* is an idiom: "unless." *19.*

pittore incomparabile. Oltre ad essere un ottimo architetto, scultore, matematico, scrittore, musicista, anatomico, geologo, egli fu un grande scienziato ed un grande inventore. Sai che egli ideò[24] l'aeroplano ed il sottomarino, convinto che un giorno l'uomo avrebbe volato come gli uccelli, ed esplorato le profondità degli oceani come i pesci. È mai vissuto al mondo un uomo più grande?

MARIA: Una cosa mi ha fatto dispiacere.[25]

CARLO: Veramente? Che cosa?

MARIA: Il fatto che a Milano non siamo potuti andare alla Scala.

CARLO: Hai ragione, cara. Purtroppo, durante la stagione estiva il teatro è chiuso. È un vero peccato[26] che tu non lo abbia visto. Io ebbi[27] il piacere di assistere a diverse rappresentazioni l'ultima volta che fui[28] in Italia. La Scala come sai, è il più famoso teatro d'opera del mondo. Qualsiasi artista che ottiene un successo[29] alla Scala vede la gloria spalancargli tutte le porte.

MARIA: Non fu in questo teatro che Verdi ottenne il suo primo successo?

CARLO: Sì, egli incominciò la sua illustre carriera alla Scala, quando, all'età di ventisei anni, presentò la sua prima opera, "l'Uberto." Verdi fu un compositore prolifico. Immagina—ventotto opere, fra le quali "Aida," "Rigoletto," "La Forza del Destino," "Il Trovatore," "La Traviata," "Otello," una più bella dell'altra. E sai quando compose "Falstaff," la sua ultima opera ed una delle più belle? All'età di ottantaquattro anni!

MARIA: Straordinario! Mi piace moltissimo la musica di Verdi perchè è bella, melodiosa, commovente, facile a ricordarsi. Chi,

---

Subjective of *volere*. *20. Pianura del Po:* "the plain of the Po." The Po Valley, the most fertile part of Italy, is called the "breadbasket of Italy." *21. Ne fa:* "makes it (of it)." *22.* "The Last Supper." *23.* "With emotion." *24.* "Con-

avendo sentito un'opera di Verdi, non esce dal teatro canterellando un'aria di quell'opera?

CARLO: E dire che al giovane Verdi fu rifiutata una borsa di studio[30] al Conservatorio di Milano perchè i professori non credevano che avesse abbastanza talento per la musica! E il Duomo di Milano, che impressione ti ha fatta?

MARIA: Caro mio, l'impressione non può essere che una: divinamente bello! Quello stile gotico così festoso e gaio, tutte quelle guglie e quelle statue danno al Duomo l'apparenza di un gigantesco e bellissimo ricamo. Tutte quelle magnifiche vetrate istoriate[31] sono sicuramente fra le più belle del mondo. Dopo avere viste tante chiese, una più bella dell'altra, si penserebbe che nessun'altra chiesa potrebbe farti impressione.[32] Eppure, vedi il Duomo e non puoi fare a meno[33] di domandarti: ma non finiscono mai le meraviglie di questa incantevole Italia?

CARLO: Anche a Genova, l'ultima grande città che visiteremo, avremo molto da vedere. Il treno arriverà fra una diecina di minuti.

MARIA: Sai, Carlo, che mi piacciono molto i treni italiani? Sono alquanto differenti dai nostri. Ogni carrozza ha diversi scompartimenti separati, ognuno di otto posti. E per andare da uno scompartimento all'altro c'è quel piccolo corridoio da un lato della carrozza.

CARLO: Sai chi troveremo alla stazione? Il mio carissimo amico, il dottor Barletta.

MARIA: Lo sa che arriviamo con questo treno?

CARLO: Certo, gli ho telegrafato!

MARIA: Ah, sì; ricordo. Siete buoni amici?

CARLO: È uno dei miei amici più cari. Siamo come fratelli.

IN CASA DEL DOTTOR BARLETTA A GENOVA

CARLO: Carissimo Totò, noi apprezziamo la tua gentile ospitalità, ma volerci in casa tua per tutto il tempo che saremo qui mi pare approfittare un po' troppo da parte nostra. Perchè non ci hai prenotata una camera all'albergo?

---

ceived the idea of." 25. "Has displeased me." 26. "It's really too bad!" 27. *Ebbi* is past definite of *avere*. 28. *Fui* is past definite of *essere*. 29. "Who

Totò: Ma che albergo? Scherzi? La mia casa è casa tua. Come vedi abbiamo abbastanza spazio qui. Avete la vostra camera e nessuno vi disturberà. Dopo tanti anni di attesa vorresti negarmi il piacere di averti con me? E poi sai bene che dobbiamo continuare le nostre battaglie.

Maria: Oh, Dio, delle battaglie?

Totò: Sì, dobbiamo continuare le nostre partite a scacchi.[34] Non so se tuo marito te lo ha detto, ma questo era il nostro passatempo prediletto quando egli era qui. E debbo confessare che allora il tuo maritino[35] ebbe quasi sempre la fortuna dalla sua parte.[36] Adesso voglio la rivincita e spero che il risultato sia alquanto diverso.

Olga (*moglie di Totò*): Ma tu scherzi. Credi che Carlo abbia fatto questo viaggio per venire a sprecare il suo tempo a giocare a scacchi[37] con te?

Carlo: Cara Olga, il tempo impiegato a fare una partita a scacchi non è mai sprecato. E poi, se tuo marito vuole ancora qualche lezione, io non posso negargli questo piacere.

Totò: Vedremo, vedremo. Questa volta la vittoria mi arriderà.[38] Dunque, parliamo adesso delle altre cose che faremo. Dico faremo perchè fortunatamente ho potuto ottenere la mia vacanza adesso, e quindi potremo passare quasi tutto il tempo insieme.

Maria: Prima di tutto voglio vedere tutto ciò che c'è d'interessante a Genova, questa orgogliosa città dove nacque il grande e intrepido navigatore Cristoforo Colombo. Esiste ancora la sua casa?

Totò: La casa propriamente no.[39] Ma si possono ancora vedere i ruderi della sua umile casetta,[40] che i genovesi considerano come una preziosa reliquia. Tanti e tanti turisti accorrono e fanno sempre delle fotografie.[41]

___

is successful." *30. Una borsa di studio:* "a scholarship." *31.* "Stained-glass windows." *32.* "Could impress you." *33. Non puoi fare a meno:* "You can't

MARIA: Vengono molti turisti a Genova?

OLGA: Sì, da ogni parte del mondo.

TOTÒ: Prima di tutto dovete sapere che Genova è il porto più importante non solo d'Italia, ma di tutto il Mediterraneo.

CARLO: I francesi probabilmente non sono d'accordo[42] con te su questo punto.

TOTÒ: Lo so, ma non importa. La più grande attrazione è forse il clima, che anche d'inverno è molto mite e piacevole. Sulla costa ligure si può dire che la primavera sia eterna.

MARIA: La costa ligure è famosa per le sue numerose e bellissime spiagge, non è vero?

OLGA: E andremo a visitarne parecchie: Santa Margherita, Rapallo, Chiavari e Portofino fra quelle che si trovano sulla Riviera di Levante;[43] Pegli, Arenzano e Alassio sulla Riviera di Ponente.[44] Naturalmente parlo di quelle più vicine a Genova. Ovunque vedrete dei panorami gloriosi, delle scene di incomparabile bellezza.

CARLO: So che la vegetazione sulla costa ligure è molto rigogliosa: dei lussureggianti giardini di aranci, di limoni e di olivi, e dei bellissimi fiori dappertutto. Ovunque ci sono palme in abbondanza, anche nelle vie di Genova che è molto più a nord di New York.

MARIA: Genova mi ha fatto una bella impressione. Ci sono molti palazzi veramente stupendi.

TOTÒ: Sono prova perenne della sua antica gloria e ricchezza. Avete notato il bel palazzo del Banco di San Giorgio? È quasi tutto di marmo. Come sapete, una volta Genova era una potente

help." *34.* "Games of chess." *35. Maritino* is diminutive of *marito. 36. Dalla sua parte:* "on his side." *37.* An idiom: *"to play chess." 38.* "Victory will smile upon me." *39. Propriamente no:* "Not exactly." *40. Casetta:* "little

repubblica navale, ma in continua lotta contro altri stati d'Italia, specialmente Pisa e Venezia.

CARLO: Peccato[45] che quegli stati erano sempre in lotta fra di loro.[46] Se invece fossero stati uniti, la storia d'Italia probabilmente sarebbe stata molto diversa e non si sarebbero combattute le sanguinose guerre dell'Indipendenza.

MARIA: Non fu da questa città che il grande liberatore Giuseppe Garibaldi iniziò la spedizione dei Mille?[47]

OLGA: Sì, dalla piccola rada di Quarto, qui vicino.

TOTÒ: Sapete che proprio a Genova nacque Giuseppe Mazzini, che fu l'anima del Risorgimento?[48]

CARLO: Sono stato sempre un ammiratore di questo grande pensatore e apostolo della libertà. Dobbiamo andare a Staglieno, dove si trova la sua tomba.

MARIA: Sì, dobbiamo vedere Staglieno. Ho sempre sentito dire[49] che è il più bel cimitero del mondo.

TOTÒ: Staglieno, miei cari, non è soltanto un cimitero, ma un immenso museo dove si trovano delle statue, delle cappelle ed altri lavori d'arte veramente meravigliosi.

CARLO: Allora uno di questi giorni vi andremo per ammirare questi altri capolavori del genio italiano.

MARIA: E così, ben presto, avrà fine[50] come un sogno, questo nostro incantevole viaggio. Quanti bei ricordi porteremo con noi. Ovunque abbiamo trovato bellezza, arte e generosa ospitalità. Ricorderò sempre gli italiani; questo popolo buono, generoso, ospitale, laborioso ed intelligente. Mi sento commossa al pensiero che dobbiamo presto dire addio a questa bella Italia.

---

house." Diminutive of *casa*. *41. Fare una fotografia:* "to take a picture." *42. Non sono d'accordo:* "Do not agree." *43.* "Of the east." *44.* "Of the west." *45.* "Too bad!" *46.* "At war against each other." *47.* Garibaldi, with his 1000

Reference Grammar

ALTHOUGH ALL the necessary grammatical explanations for each of the Twenty Lessons have been provided in the footnotes of the lessons, a complete REFERENCE GRAMMAR is provided here for the convenience of the student. Each part of speech (the Article, Noun, Verb, etc.) is explained thoroughly in all its uses. Therefore, should the student wish complete information about any point of grammar, he can easily find it in this handy REFERENCE GRAMMAR.

Study Plan for Reference Grammar

SINCE THE MATERIAL of the REFERENCE GRAMMAR is not arranged in order of difficulty or frequency of occurrence but is classified by subjects (the Article, Noun, Adjective, etc.), it is suggested that the student refer to and study the following paragraphs along with each lesson, for guidance in the grammatical points covered in each lesson. The easiest way of locating any paragraph (§) is to flip through the pages of the grammar watching for the § number which is in bold face alongside of the page number.

Lesson I   The definite article §1. Special uses of the definite article §2. The present indicative tense §54. Possessive adjectives §16. Gender of nouns §7. First conjugation §48.

Lesson II   Comparison of adjectives §17. Imperative mood §64. Personal subject pronouns §19. Second conjugation §49. -*isco* verbs §50. Direct object pronouns §20.

Lesson III   The indefinite article §4. Position of adjectives §11. Agreement of adjectives §10. Imperfect tense §56. The verb *avere* §47. Demonstrative pronouns §25. The preposition *da* §34. The preposition *di* §35.

Lesson IV   Reflexive verbs §52. Reflexive pronouns §28. Future tense §60. Present perfect tense §55. Past participle §45. Plural of nouns §8.

Lesson V   Interrogative adjectives §15. Interrogative pronouns §23. Comparison of equality §17-2. Disjunctive pronouns §22. Verbs with the auxiliary *essere* §51. Irregular adjectives §18.

Lesson VI   Present participle §45-1. Masculine and feminine nouns ending in *a* §7-4, 5. Classes of adverbs §30.

Lesson VII   The preposition *a* §33. Present subjunctive tense §65. Omission of definite article §3. Double pronouns §29. Formation of adverbs §31.

Lesson VIII   The verb *stare* §54-3. Indefinite pronouns §26. Contractions §6.

Lesson IX   Impersonal expressions §53. The subjunctive with certain expressions §65-1,d. Intransitive verbs §42.

Lesson X   Verbs that take the preposition *a* §33-5. *Loro* as possessive §16-6,9. The infinitive §43. Plural of adjectives §12.

Lesson XI   Demonstrative pronouns §25. Future of probability §60-4. Impersonal verbs §53. Indirect object pronouns §21.

Lesson XII   Comparison of adverbs §32. Relative pronouns §24. Irregular verbs §55-4. Servile verbs §66.

Lesson XIII   Present conditional tense §62. Irregular comparison of adjectives §17-3,d, 18. Indirect object pronoun §21.

Lesson XIV   Omission of possessive adjective §16-13. Subordinating conjunctions §39. Indefinite adjectives §14.

Lesson XV   Agreement of past participle §45-5. Transitive verbs §41. Conjugation of verbs §46.

Lesson XVI   Interrogative pronouns §23. Diminutive suffixes §9. Repetition of prepositions §37.

Lesson XVII   Interjections §40. Past definite tense §56.

Lesson XVIII   Past conditional tense §62. Coordinating conjunctions §38. The gerund §44.

Lesson XIX   Future perfect tense §61. Indefinite pronouns §26. Past anterior tense §57.

Lesson XX   Pluperfect indicative tense §59. Past conditional tense §63. Review irregular verbs.

REFERENCE GRAMMAR

Table of Contents

THE ARTICLE

THE NOUN

THE PRONOUN

THE ADVERB

THE PREPOSITION

The Article (L'Articolo)

§ 1 The Definite Article

1. The definite article ("the" in English) agrees in gender and number with the noun it modifies.

2. There are seven ways of saying "the" in Italian:

a. *il* is used before singular masculine nouns, except as explained in *c* and *d* below:

il libro	*il* padre
the book	*the* father

b. *la* is used before singular feminine nouns, except as explained in *d*:

la penna	*la* classe
the pen	*the* classe

c. *lo* is used before singular masculine nouns beginning with *z* or *s-impura* (*s* followed by a consonant):

lo zio	*lo* studente
the uncle	*the* student
lo specchio	*lo* zucchero
the mirror	*the* sugar

d. *l'* is used before singular nouns (masculine or feminine) beginning with a vowel:

*l'*aeroplano	*l'*opera
the airplane	*the* opera

e. *i* is used before plural masculine nouns, except as explained in *g*:

i libri	*i* padri
the books	*the* fathers

f. *le* is used before feminine plural nouns:

le penne	*le* classi
the pens	*the* classes

NOTE: Even though you will occasionally see *l'* used before plural feminine nouns beginning with a vowel, good usage

199

does not permit the dropping of the *e*. Thus it is better to say *le opere* than *l'opere*.

g. *gli* is used before plural masculine nouns beginning with *z*, *s-impura*, or a vowel:

gli **zii**	*gli* **studenti**	*gli* **orologi**
the uncles	*the* students	*the* watches

NOTE: *gl'* may be used before plural masculine nouns beginning with *i*. Thus you may say *gl'italiani* or *gli italiani*.

§ 2 Special Uses of the Definite Article

1. Before nouns used in an abstract or in a general sense:

La **salute è importante.**	*Il* **ferro è utile.**
Health is important.	Iron is useful.

2. Before names of continents, countries, states, provinces, large islands, rivers:

*l'***Italia**	*l'***Europa**	*il* **Tevere**
Italy	Europe	*the* Tiber
la **Sicilia**	*gli* **Stati Uniti**	
Sicily	*the* United States	

3. Before titles or professions followed by a person's name:

Il **presidente Martino**	*Il* **professore Di Giacomo**
President Martino	Professor Di Giacomo
La **signorina Borgese**	
Miss Borgese	

NOTE: The definite article, however, is omitted, when addressing a person:

Si accomodi, signorina Borgese.
Make yourself comfortable, Miss Borgese.

More normally, however, proper names are not used with titles in direct address. It is better to say:

Buon giorno, signor professore.
Good morning, Professor.

4. Before names of languages, except when the language is preceded by *parlare:*

Io studio *l'***italiano e** *lo* **spagnuolo.**
I study Italian and Spanish.

BUT:

Io parlo italiano.
I speak Italian.

5. Before a proper noun when preceded by an adjective:

la **cara Maria**
dear Mary

6. Before possessive adjectives and possessive pronouns:

il **mio libro**	*i* **suoi amici**
my book	his friends

NOTE: The definite article is omitted when the possessive adjective comes before a singular, unmodified noun denoting a member of the family or a relative:

mio zio
my uncle

tua madre
your [familiar] mother

However, the definite article must be used when the possessive adjective is *loro* (your [polite pl.], their) and before the words *babbo* (dad) and *mamma* (mother).

il **loro padre**
their father

la **mia mamma**
my mother

il **mio babbo**
my dad

7. In a series of nouns the definite article must be used before each noun:

Ho portato *la* **penna,** *il* **quaderno ed** *i* **libri.**
I brought *the* pen, *the* notebook, and *the* books.

8. In telling time:

È *l'***una e mezzo.**
It is half past one.

Sono *le* **tre e dieci.**
It is ten after three.

9. Before days of the week, when a regular occurrence is implied:

Io non vado a scuola *il* **sabato.**
I don't go to school on Saturday.

10. In dates:

il **quindici maggio**
May fifteenth

11. Before a noun expressing quantity, to translate the English word *per* or *a*:

Il caffè costa un dollaro *la* **libbra.**
Coffee costs one dollar a pound.

12. The definite article is used in place of the expected possessive adjective with parts of the body or personal articles of clothing when there is no ambiguity as to the possessor:

Io alzo la mano.
I raise my hand.

Egli si toglie *il* **cappello.**
He takes his hat off.

§ 3 Omission of the Definite Article

The definite article is omitted:

1. Before a proper noun followed by a numeral:

Vittorio Emanuele Terzo
Victor Emanuel the Third

2. Before a noun used in apposition:

Roma, capitale d'Italia
Rome, (the) capital of Italy

3. Before a possessive adjective, in direct address:

Ragazzo mio, fa attenzione!
Pay attention, my boy!

4. When the possessive adjective comes before a singular, unmodified noun denoting a member of the family or a relative [see note of § 2-6 above].

mio zio	mia sorella
my uncle	my sister

5. When the possessive stands alone as the predicate in a sentence:

Questo danaro è tuo.
This money is yours.

6. After the prepositions *in* and *di* before an unmodified name of a feminine country, continent, region, or large island ending in *a*:

Io andrò in Italia.	Essi sono in America.
I shall go to Italy.	They are in America.

BUT:

Io andrò *nell'*Italia Settentrionale.
I shall go to Northern Italy.

§ 4 The Indefinite Article

1. The indefinite article (sing. "a, an;" pl. "some," in English) agrees in gender and number with the noun it modifies.

2. There are seven indefinite articles in Italian:

a. *un* is used before singular masculine nouns, except as explained in *c* below:

un libro	*un* padre	*un* amico
a book	a father	a friend (m.)

b. *una* is used before singular feminine nouns, except as explained in *d* below:

una penna	*una* classe
a pen	a class

c. *uno* is used before singular masculine nouns beginning with z or *s-impura*:

uno specchio	*uno* zero	*uno* studente
a mirror	a zero	a student

d. *un'* is used only before singular feminine nouns beginning with a vowel:

*un'*amica	*un'*opera
a friend (f.)	*an* opera

e. *dei* is used before plural masculine nouns, except as explained in *g* below:

dei libri	*dei* maestri
some books	*some* teachers

f. *delle* is used before plural feminine nouns:

delle penne	*delle* classi
some pens	*some* classes

NOTE: It is better usage to write *delle opere* than *dell'opere*.

g. *degli* is used before plural masculine nouns beginning with *z, s-impura,* or a vowel:

degli zii   **degli** studenti   **degli** amici
some uncles   *some* students   *some* friends

NOTE: The *i* of *degli* may be replaced by an apostrophe when the following noun begins with *i*:

degli italiani or **degl'**italiani
some Italians

3. In a series of nouns the indefinite article must be used before each noun:

Ho comprato *una* penna, *un* quaderno e *dei* libri.
I brought *a* pen, *a* notebook, and *some* books.

§ 5   Omission of the Indefinite Article

The indefinite article is omitted:

1. Before the words *cento* and *mille*:

Io ho guadagnato *cento* dollari.
I earned *one hundred* dollars.

Io ho letto più di *mille* libri.
I have read more than *one thousand* books.

2. In exclamations, with nouns preceded by *che* and *quale*:

Che bel fiore!   **Quale disgrazia è questa!**
What a beautiful flower!   What a misfortune this is!

3. Before a noun used in apposition:

Questo è Carlo, amico di mio figlio.
This is Charles, a friend of my son.

4. Before a noun preceded by *da,* when *da* means "like, in the manner of":

Egli ha parlato da uomo.
He spoke like a man.

5. Before an unmodified predicate noun:

Egli è falegname.
He is a carpenter.

BUT:

Egli è *un* buon falegname.
He is *a* good carpenter.

§ 6   The Contractions

A contraction results when a preposition unites with the definite article.

1. The following five prepositions contract with each one of the definite articles: *a* (to, at), *da* (from, at, by), *in* (in, into), *di* (of), *su* (on, upon) as shown in the following table:

TABLE OF CONTRACTIONS OF PREPOSITIONS WITH
DEFINITE ARTICLES

	il	*lo*	*la*	*l'*	*i*	*gli*	*le*
a	al	allo	alla	all'	ai	agli	alle
da	dal	dallo	dalla	dall'	dai	dagli	dalle
di	del	dello	della	dell'	dei	degli	delle
in	nel	nello	nella	nell'	nei	negli	nelle
su	sul	sullo	sulla	sull'	sui	sugli	sulle

2. The preposition *con* contracts only with *il* and *i* and the results
are *col* and *coi*:

Io cammino *col* ragazzo.   **Io cammino *coi* ragazzi.**
I walk with the boy.   I walk with the boys.

BUT:

I scrivo *con la* penna.
I write *with the* pen.

Contractions of *con* with *la (colla), gli (cogli), lo (collo), l' (coll'), le
(colle)* are now considered obsolete.

3. The preposition *per* no longer contracts with the definite articles. The contractions *pel, pei, pella,* etc. are considered obsolete.
They are however used in poetry.

4. The contractions are used in exactly the same manner as the
definite articles:

dello zio, *agli* studenti, *nello* specchio, *dall'*America, etc.

5. The contractions *dal, dalla, dalla,* etc., besides meaning "from
the," also mean "at" or "to someone's home, place, office," etc.

Iersera sono andato *dalla* zia.
Last night I went *to* aunt's.

6. The contractions *del, della, dello, etc.,* besides meaning "of the,"
also mean "some," and are, therefore, considered partitive articles:

Ella compra *della* carne.   **Egli ha portato *dei* fiori.**
She buys *some* meat.   He brought *some* flowers.

The same contractions also denote possession:

L'amico *del* ragazzo è partito.   **Ecco i libri *degli* studenti.**
The boy's friend has left.   Here are the students' books.

The Noun (Il Nome)

§ 7   The Gender of Nouns

1. All nouns in Italian are either masculine or feminine. There is
no neuter gender.

2. Practically all nouns ending in *-o* are masculine. There are very

few exceptions to this rule; the following two common words are feminine even though they end in *o*:

la mano
the hand

la radio
the radio

3. The great majority of nouns ending in -*a* are feminine. The following common nouns are masculine, even though they end in -*a*:

il poeta
the poet

il dramma
the drama

il duca
the duke

il poema
the poem

il vaglia
the money order

il pianeta
the planet

il tema
the theme

il sistema
the system

il Papa
the Pope

il problema
the problem

il panorama
the panorama

il cinema
the motion picture theater

il diploma
the diploma

il profeta
the prophet

4. The following is a partial list of nouns ending in -*a* which are masculine when they refer to a man and feminine when they refer to a woman:

il *or* **la pianista**
the pianist

il *or* **la dentista**
the dentist

l'artista
the artist

il *or* **la musicista**
the musician

l'atleta
the athlete

l'organista
the organist

il *or* **la farmacista**
the pharmacist

il *or* **la suicida**
the suicide (the person)

il *or* **la giornalista**
the journalist

il *or* **la socialista**
the socialist

5. Some nouns are feminine, even though they usually refer to a man:

la spia
the spy

la guardia
the guard

la guida
the guide

6. Many Italian nouns end in -*e*. Some of them are masculine, and some are feminine:

il cane
the dog

il ponte
the bridge

la carne
the meat

il pane
the bread

la classe
the class

la lite
the quarrel

7. There are a few nouns in Italian which end in -*i* in the singular. Almost all are feminine:

la metropoli
the metropolis

la parentesi
the parenthesis

la paralisi
the paralysis

la tubercolosi
tuberculosis

l'eclissi
the eclipse

l'analisi
the analysis

la crisi
the crisis

l'ipotesi
the hypothesis

EXCEPTION:

il brindisi
the toast

8. Some words ending in -o also have a form ending in -a, but the two words have different meanings. Here is a partial list:

il collo the neck	**la colla** the glue	**il mento** the chin	**la menta** the mint
il colpo the blow	**la colpa** the fault	**il modo** the manner	**la moda** the fashion
il costo the cost	**la costa** the coast	**il pianto** weeping	**la pianta** the plant
il filo the thread	**la fila** the row	**il punto** the dot	**la punta** the point
il foglio the sheet	**la foglia** the leaf	**il porto** the port	**la porta** the door
il fosso the ditch	**la fossa** the grave	**lo scalo** the dock	**la scala** the stairs
il manico the handle	**la manica** the sleeve		

9. Some words end in -e in both the masculine and feminine, but have different meanings:

il fine
the aim

la fine
the end

il fronte
the front

la fronte
the forehead

10. Several masculine nouns have irregular feminine forms. Here is a partial list:

MASCULINE	FEMININE	MASCULINE	FEMININE
il dottore the doctor	**la dottoressa**	**il leone** the lion	**la leonessa**
il poeta the poet	**la poetessa**	**l'attore** the actor	**l'attrice**
il principe the prince	**la principessa**	**lo scrittore** the writer	**la scrittrice**
il duca the duke	**la duchessa**	**il pittore** the painter	**la pittrice**
il barone the baron	**la baronessa**	**il re** the king	**la regina**
il conte the count	**la contessa**	**il gallo** the rooster	**la gallina**
lo studente the student	**la studentessa**	**l'eroe** the hero	**l'eroina**

11. Some masculine nouns have an entirely different word for the feminine counterpart. Here is a list of the most common ones:

il marito
the husband

la moglie
the wife

il padre the father	**la madre** the mother
il genero the son-in-law	**la nuora** the daughter-in-law
l'uomo the man	**la donna** the woman
il maschio the male	**la femmina** the female
il babbo dad	**la mamma** mother
il bue bull	**la vacca** the cow

12. There are some nouns of animals which have no feminine form:

il topo the rat	**il coniglio** the rabbit

13. There are some nouns of animals which have no masculine form:

la volpe the fox	**la balena** the whale
la scimmia the monkey	**la rondine** the swallow

14. The names of the months are masculine in Italian.

15. The names of the days of the week, except *domenica* (Sunday), are masculine in Italian.

16. The names of most countries are feminine:

l'Italia Italy	**la Grecia** Greece	**l'Olanda** Holland
l'Inghilterra England	**la Francia** France	**la Russia** Russia
la Germania Germany	**la Spagna** Spain	

However, there are several that are masculine. Here is a partial list:

il Canadà Canada	**il Cile** Chile	**il Brasile** Brazil
il Messico Mexico	**il Giappone** Japan	**l'Egitto** Egypt
il Belgio Belgium	**il Perù** Peru	**gli Stati Uniti** the United States

§ 8   The Plural of Nouns

1. Masculine nouns, regardless of how they end in the singular, form their plural by changing the singular ending to *i*:

il libro the book	**il pittore** the painter	**il poeta** the poet
i libri	**i pittori**	**i poeti**

EXCEPTIONS:

il uaglia **i uaglia** the money order	**il cinema** **i cinema** the motion picture theater	

2. Feminine nouns ending in -*a* change to -*e* in the plural:

la porta	**la studentessa**
the door	the student
le porte	**le studentesse**

3. Feminine nouns ending in -*e* change to -*i* in the plural:

la classe	**la frase**
the class	the phrase
le classi	**le frasi**

4. Nouns ending in -*i* do not change in the plural:

la metropoli	**il brindisi**
the metropolis	the toast
le metropoli	**i brindisi**

5. The following two words do not change in the plural:

la specie	**la serie**
the species	the series
le specie	**le serie**

6. Nouns ending in -*io* drop the *o* when the *i* is unstressed:

il bacio	**il figlio**
the kiss	the son
i baci	**i figli**

However, when the *i* is stressed, the *o* changes to i:

lo zio	**il mormorio**
the uncle	the murmur
gli zii	**i mormorii**

7. Nouns ending in -*ca* and -*ga,* end in -*che* and -*ghe* in the plural if they are feminine, and in -*chi* and -*ghi* if they are masculine:

la bocca	**il duca**
the mouth	the duke
le bocche	**i duchi**
la riga	**il collega**
the ruler	the colleague
le righe	**i colleghi**

8. Nouns ending in -*cia* and -*gia* follow the general rule when the *i* is stressed:

la farmacia	**la bugia**
the pharmacy	the lie
le farmacie	**le bugie**

However, when the *i* is not stressed, they usually end in -*ce* and -*ge*:

la provincia	**l'arancia**	**la spiaggia**
the province	the orange	the beach
le province	**le arance**	**le spiagge**

EXCEPTIONS:

la camicia	**la valigia**	**la ciliegia**
the shirt	the valise	the cherry
le camicie	**le valigie**	**le ciliegie**

9. Nouns ending in -*co* usually end in -*chi* in the plural when the stress falls on the syllable preceding *co,* and in *ci* when the stress

falls on some other syllable. However, the exceptions are numerous. The following is a list of the more common nouns ending in *-co*, and their plural:

il fuoco fire **i fuochi**	**il fico** the fig **i fichi**	**il monaco** the monk **i monaci**
il manico the handle **i manichi**	**il bosco** the woods **i boschi**	**il porco** the pig **i porci**
lo stomaco the stomach **gli stomachi**	**l'amico** the friend **gli amici**	**l'equivoco** the misunderstanding **gli equivoci**
il cieco the blind **i ciechi**	**il nemico** the enemy **i nemici**	**il maniaco** the maniac **i maniaci**
il carico the load **i carichi**	**il greco** the Greek **i greci**	

10. Nouns ending in *-go* change to *-ghi* in the plural:

il borgo the hamlet **i borghi**	**il dialogo** the dialogue **i dialoghi**

Some nouns ending in *-go* form the plural in either *-ghi* or *-gi*:

l'astrologo the astrologer **gli astrologhi** *or* **astrologi**	**l'antropologo** the anthropologist **gli antropologhi** *or* **antropologi**

11. The following nouns have an irregular plural:

l'uomo the man **gli uomini**	**(il) Dio** God **gli Dei**	**la moglie** the wife **le mogli**
il bue the ox, bull **i buoi**	**mille** one thousand **mila**	

Notice the special use of *gli* before *Dei*.

12. The following nouns are used only in the plural:

le nozze the wedding	**le mutande** the underwear	**gli spinaci** spinach
gli sponsali the wedding	**le redini** the reins	**i viveri** the victuals
le busse the blows	**gli annali** the annals	

13. The following nouns are used mostly in the plural, very rarely in the singular:

i calzoni the trousers	(*sing.* il calzone)
i pantaloni the trousers	(*sing.* il pantalone)

le forbici   *(sing.* la forbice)
the scissors

gli spaghetti *(sing.* lo spaghetto)
the spaghetti

14. The following nouns are used only in the singular:

la fame hunger	il sangue blood	il miele honey	la requie the rest, requiem
la sete thirst	il fiele the gall	la prole the offspring	la senape mustard

15. The following nouns form their plural by changing the singular ending to *a,* and thus become feminine:

l'uovo the egg le uova	il grido the cry le grida	il ciglio the eyelid le ciglia
il dito the finger le dita	il lenzuolo the bed sheet le lenzuola	il ginocchio the knee le ginocchia *(also* i ginocchi)
il paio the pair le paia	il centinaio about a hundred le centinaia	
il miglio the mile le miglia	il migliaio about a thousand le migliaia	

16. The following nouns have both a feminine and a masculine plural, but with a difference in meaning:

il braccio the arm	le braccia i bracci (figurative)	il muro the wall	le mura (of a city) i muri (of a house)
il membro the member	le membra (of the body) i membri (of a club)	il corno the horn	le corna (of animals) i corni instruments
il riso rice, laughter	le risa laughter i risi rices	il filo the thread	i fili le fila (figurative)
il labbro the lip	le labbra (of man) i labbri (of animals, or figurative)	il frutto the fruit	la *(or* le) frutta (at the table) i frutti (figurative)
l'osso the bone	le ossa (of humans) gli ossi (of animals *or* in grease)		

17. Nouns ending with an accented vowel do not change in the plural:

il caffè coffee **i caffè**	**la virtù** virtue **le virtù**
la città the city **le città**	**la libertà** liberty **le libertà**

18. Monosyllabic nouns do not change in the plural:

il re
the king
i re

19. Surnames do not change in the plural:

il Barletta
i Barletta

20. Nouns ending in a consonant do not change in the plural:

il lapis the pencil **i lapis**	**il gas** the gas **i gas**

21. Nouns composed of a verb and a plural noun do not change in the plural:

il portalettere the letter carrier **i portalettere**	**il lustrascarpe** the shoeshine boy **i lustrascarpe**	**il tagliacarte** the paper cutter **i tagliacarte**

§ 9 Augmentatives and Diminutives

Many Italian nouns acquire different shades of meaning by the addition of suffixes, thus greatly enriching the language.

1. The suffix -*one* is attached to a noun (after the final vowel is dropped) to indicate bigness. The noun thus altered is always masculine, unless in the original form it has both a masculine and a feminine, in which case -*ona* is added to the feminine.

un palazzo a building **un palazz***one*	**un ragazzo** a boy **un ragazz***one*
un ladro a thief **un ladr***one*	**una ragazza** a girl **una ragazz***ona*

Likewise, adjectives are altered by adding -*one* to the masculine and -*ona* to the feminine:

stupido stupid **stupid***one* (m.) **stupid***ona* (f.)	**ricco** rich **ricc***one* (m.) **ricc***ona* (f.)

2. The suffix -*accio* (-*accia* in the feminine) conveys bigness also, but in a disparaging sense:

libro
book
libraccio

camera
room
cameraccia

3. The suffix -*otto* (f. -*otta*) denotes mediocre bigness:

un signore
a gentleman
un signorotto

una ragazza
a girl
una ragazzotta

4. The suffix -*ino* (f. -*ina*) denotes smallness often coupled with grace:

una stanza
room
una stanzina

una donna
lady
una donnina

un bicchiere
glass
un bicchierino

5. The suffixes -*ello, -etto, -uccio, -olino, -icino,* and their feminine forms ending in -*a,* have the same meaning as -*ino* above:

una stanza
room
una stanzetta

un vecchio
old man
un vecchietto

un libro
book
un libricino

un povero
poor man
un poverello

un pesce
fish
un pesciolino

The Adjective (L'Aggettivo)

§ 10   Classes and Forms of the Adjective

1. There are two classes of adjectives in Italian:

a. Those which end in -*o* in the masculine singular and have four forms:

il ragazzo *piccolo*
the *little* boy

la ragazza *piccola*
the *little* girl

i ragazzi *piccoli*
the *little* boys

le ragazze *piccole*
the *little* girls

b. Those which end in -*e* in the singular and have only two forms, the masculine and feminine forms being identical:

il ragazzo *grande*
the *big* boy

la ragazza *grande*
the *big* girl

i ragazzi *grandi*
the *big* boys

le ragazze *grandi*
the *big* girls

2. The adjective agrees in gender and number with the noun it modifies. See examples above.

3. An adjective which modifies two or more nouns is always masculine plural if at least one noun is masculine:

La cucina, il salotto e la sala da pranzo sono *piccoli*.
The kitchen, the living room, and the dining room are *small*.

§11 Position of Adjectives

1. In Italian the normal position of the adjective is after the noun. This is especially true when the adjective denotes color, shape, size, nationality, or religion:

un libro *rosso*
a *red* book

un ragazzo *italiano*
an *Italian* boy

una scatola *rotonda*
a *round* box

una ragazza *ebrea*
a *Jewish* girl

una matita *lunga*
a *long* pencil

2. Demonstrative adjectives precede the noun:

Quella signorina è molto simpatica.
That young lady is very charming.

Questo libro è di Giovanni.
This book is John's.

3. Numerals precede the noun:

Ho comprato *venti* libri.
I bought *twenty* books.

Egli occupa il *quinto* posto.
He occupies the *fifth* place.

4. The adjectives *molto* and *tutto* (the latter followed by the definite article) precede the noun:

Ci sono *molte* persone nella cucina.
There are *many* persons in the kitchen.

Egli ha bevuto *tutta* la birra.
He drank *all* the beer.

5. Possessive adjectives normally precede the noun:

Egli ha preso il *mio* libro.
He took *my* book.

6. The following common adjectives normally precede the noun unless they are modified by an adverb or special emphasis is desired:

grande big	**cattivo** bad	**bello** beautiful	**povero** poor
piccolo small	**giovane** young	**brutto** ugly	**santo** saintly
buono good	**vecchio** old	**ricco** rich	**ottimo** excellent

Ella è una *santa* donna.
She is a *saintly* woman.

Ho ricevuto un *piccolo* pacco.
I received a *small* package.

Hai parlato alla *vecchia* signora?
Have you spoken to the *old* lady?

But:

Ho ricevuto un pacco *molto piccolo*.
I received a *very small* package.

7. The following are some of the common adjectives which have a *figurative* meaning when placed before the noun, and a *literal* meaning when placed after the noun:

povero	**vecchio**	**grande**	**gentile**
poor	old	big	kind
nuovo	**dolce**	**piccolo**	**certo**
new	sweet	small	certain

Ella è una *povera donna*.
She is a *poor* (unfortunate) woman.

Ella è una donna *povera*.
She is a *poor* woman (financially).

NOTE: When an adjective precedes a noun, the article is determined by the adjective. Thus we say *il quadro*, but *lo splendido quadro*.

§ 12 Plural of Adjectives

1. For agreement with plural nouns, adjectives follow the same rules as the nouns.

2. For adjectives ending in *-co* see rule stated in § 8-9. The following three common adjectives are exceptions to that rule and form the plural in *ci*:

amico amici	**nemico nemici**	**greco greci**
friendly	unfriendly	Greek

3. The adjective *pari* (like, equal, even same) is invariable:

numeri *pari*
even numbers

§ 13 Demonstrative Adjectives

1. The demonstrative adjective *questo* (this) is used to indicate an object which is near the person who speaks. Since it ends in *-o* it has four forms:

questo   questa   questi   queste

2. The demonstrative adjective *codesto* (that) is used to indicate an object near the person addressed. It also has four forms:

codesto   codesta   codesti   codeste

3. The demonstrative adjective *quello* (that) is used to indicate an object which is far from both the person speaking and the person addressed. This adjective has various forms, similar to those of the contractions [See §6-1]:

***quel* ragazzo**	***quei* ragazzi**
that boy	*those* boys
***quella* lettera**	***quelle* lettere**
that letter	*those* letters
***quello* specchio**	***quegli* specchi**
that mirror	*those* mirrors

*quell'*uomo	*quegli* uomini
that man	*those* men
*quell'*amica	*quelle* amiche
that friend (f.)	*those* friends (f.)

4. The demonstrative adjectives *stesso* and *medesimo* (both meaning "same") are used to indicate something of which one has previous knowledge:

Egli dice sempre le *stesse* cose.
He always says the same things.

Tu ripeti il *medesimo* argomento.
You repeat the *same* argument.

5. The adjective *tale* (such) has the same meaning as *questo*, but refers to something previously mentioned:

Io non posso credere *tale* storia.
I can't believe *such a* story.

§ 14 Indefinite Adjectives

The following is a list of the more common indefinite adjectives:

1. Those that have four forms:

altro	**certo**	**troppo**
other	certain	too much
alcuno	**molto**	**poco**
some	much	little

Certe cose non le capisco.
I don't understand *certain* things.

Tu bevi *troppa* birra.
You drink *too much* beer.

2. Those that are invariable and are always used in the singular:

ogni	**qualunque**
every	any
qualche	**qualsiasi**
some	any

Hai *qualche* cosa per me?
Do you have *something* for me?

Egli ripete *qualunque* cosa sente.
He repeats *anything* he hears.

***Ogni* uomo ama la libertà.**
Every man loves liberty.

§ 15 Interrogative Adjectives

The following are the Italian interrogative adjectives:

1. *Che?* (what?) This adjective is invariable but the noun that follows it may be of either number or gender:

Che libri hai letto?
What books have you read?

Che lingua parla egli?
What language does he speak?

2. *Quale?* (*pl. quali*) (which?).

Quale lezione ha imparato lei?
Which lesson did you learn?

Quali amici verranno?
Which friends will come?

3. *Quanto?* (four forms) (how much?).

Quanta carne devo comprare?
How much meat must I buy?

Quante valigie ha lei?
How many suitcases have you?

4. *Di chi?* (Whose?).

Di chi è questa penna?
Whose pen is this?

Di chi sono questi libri?
Whose books are these?

§ 16 The Possessive Adjectives

1. The word "my" is rendered in Italian by *il mio, la mia, i miei, le mie.*

Il mio libro è qui.
My book is here.

Questa è la mia penna.
This is *my* pen.

Hai visto i miei amici?
Have you seen *my* friends (m.)?

Hai ricevuto le mie lettere?
Did you receive *my* letters?

2. The word "your" (familiar **singular, *tu*-form**) is rendered by *il tuo, la tua, i tuoi, le tue.*

Hai il tuo libro, Maria?
Do you have *your* book, Mary?

Ecco i tuoi guanti.
Here are *your* gloves.

Questa è la tua giacca.
This is *your* jacket.

Mi piacciono le tue cravatte.
I like *your* neckties.

3. The words "your" (polite singular, *lei*-form), "his," and "her" are rendered by *il suo, la sua, i suoi, le sue.*

Mi piace il suo cappello, signora.
I like *your* hat, madam.

Ecco Carlo ed i suoi amici.
Here is Charles and *his* friends (m.).

Sono queste le sue scarpe, signorina?
Are these *your* shoes, miss?

La sua casa è molto bella.
His (or *her, your*) house is very beautiful.

NOTE: You need not worry about any confusion arising about who is the possessor, as the last example above might seem to indicate. When you say *"La sua casa è molto bella"*, you will be able to tell by the context of the conversation to whom *la sua* refers. However, any possible ambiguity may be avoided by paraphrasing the sentence in which the possessive occurs. For example, instead of saying *"la sua casa"*, you may say *"la casa di Carlo"* if you mean Charles' house.

4. The word "our" is rendered by *il nostro, la nostra, i nostri, le nostre.*

Il nostro maestro è molto gentile.
Our teacher is very kind.

Noi amiamo la nostra bandiera.
We love *our* flag.

I nostri libri sono nuovi.
Our books are new.

Ecco le nostre amiche!
Here are *our* friends (f.).

5. The word "your" (familiar plural, *voi*-form) is rendered by *il vostro, la vostra, i vostri, le vostre.*

Io sono il vostro amico.
I am *your* friend.

Amate la vostra patria!
Love *your* country!

I vostri bicchieri sono vuoti.
Your glasses are empty.

Le vostre domande non sono difficili.
Your questions are not difficult.

6. The words "your" (polite plural, *loro*-form) and "their" are rendered by *il loro, la loro, i loro, le loro.*

Essi vogliono il loro denaro.
They want *their* money.

Gli uomini amano la loro libertà.
Men love *their* liberty.

I loro libri sono nuovi.
Their (or *your*) books are new.

Esse giocano con le loro amiche.
They play with *their* friends (f.)

7. The possessive adjectives agree with the *thing possessed* and not with the *possessor*. See the above sentences for examples.

8. The possessive adjectives are preceded by the definite article except when followed by a singular noun indicating a member of the family or a relative. If, however, this noun is modified by an adjective or a suffix, the definite article must be used.

Egli ama *sua* madre.
He loves *his* mother.

Io gioco con *mia* sorella.
I play with *my* sister.

BUT:

Egli ama *la sua* cara madre.
He loves *his* dear mother.

Io gioco con *la mia* sorellina.
I play with *my* little sister.

9. The word *loro* is always preceded by a definite article:

La loro zia è arrivata.
Their aunt has arrived.

10. With the words *mamma* (mother) and *babbo* (dad) the possessive adjective is always preceded by the definite article:

La sua mamma è molto gentile.
Your mother is very kind.

Il suo babbo è in America.
His dad is in America.

11. The possessive adjective is used without the definite article when it follows any form of the verb *essere*.

Questo denaro sarà *tuo*.
This money will be *yours*.

12. In direct address the possessive adjective follows the noun and is used without the definite article:

Amico *mio*, perdonami!
Forgive me, *my* friend!

13. The possessive adjectives are usually omitted, and the definite article is used instead, with parts of the body or personal articles of clothing:

Egli alzò *la* testa.
He raised *his* head.

Dammi *il* cappello, Carlo.
Give me *your* hat, Charles.

14. With expressions such as "a friend of mine", "a cousin of his", etc. the indefinite article is used instead of the definite article:

Ti presenterò ad *un mio* amico.
I shall introduce you to a friend *of mine*.

15. When a definite article preceding a possessive adjective is, in turn, preceded by a preposition, a contraction results [See § 6-1]:

Io scrivo *al mio* amico.
I am writing *to my* friend.

Egli gioca *coi suoi* amici.
He plays *with his* friends.

16. The possessive adjective *altrui* is invariable, and means "of others, other peoples'," etc.

Non rubare il denaro *altrui*.
Do not steal *other peoples'* money.

17. The possessives *i miei, i tuoi, i suoi* are, at times, used as nouns to indicate one's parents, and, in a broader sense, one's relatives.

Come stanno *i tuoi*?
How are *your* folks?

18. The words *proprio, propria, propri, proprie,* meaning "own", are often used to add emphasis to the other possessive adjectives:

Egli ha fatto questo con le sue *proprie* mani.
He did this with his *own* hands.

§ 17 Comparison of Adjectives

There are two grades of comparison in Italian — comparison of equality and comparison of inequality.

1. *Comparative of Equality*

a. A comparative of equality results when:

1) Two objects have the same quality in the same degree:

Maria è *tanto* bella *quanto* Lucia.
Mary is *as* beautiful *as* Lucy.

2) Two different qualities are found in the same degree in one object:

Ella è *tanto* buona *quanto* intelligente.
She is *as* good *as* she is intelligent.

3) Two distinct qualities are found in the same degree in two different objects:

Maria è *tanto* bella *quanto* Lucia è intelligente.
Mary is *as* pretty *as* Lucy is intelligent.

The English expressions "as . . . as," "so . . . as," "as much . . . as" are translated in Italian by *tanto . . . quanto* (see examples in *a, b, c* above) or *così . . . come*:

Il fratello è *così* buono *come* la sorella.
The brother is *as* good *as* the sister.

NOTE: The words in the first part of the comparison (*tanto* and *così*) may be omitted, and it is often desirable to do so. Thus the examples given above could read:

Maria è bella *quanto* Lucia.
Il fratello è buono *come* la sorella.

2. *Comparative of Inequality*

a. Inequality is expressed by the words *più* (more) and *meno* (less).

b. A comparative of inequality results when:

1) Two objects have the same quality in a greater or lesser degree:

Maria è *più* (or *meno*) *bella di Lucia*.
Mary is *more* (or *less*) beautiful than Lucy.

2) Two different qualities are found in a greater or lesser degree in one object:

Ella è *più* (or *meno*) buona che intelligente.
She is *kinder* (or *less* kind) than she is intelligent.

3) Two distinct qualities are found in a greater or lesser degree in two different objects:

Maria è più (or *meno*) bella che Lucia è intelligente.
Mary is *more* (or *less*) beautiful than Lucy is intelligent.

c. In the comparative of inequality the word *than* is translated by *di* before the following:

1) Nouns modified by an adjective:

Carlo è più alto *di* Enrico.
Charles is taller *than* Henry.

La terra è più piccola *del* sole.
The earth is smaller *than* the sun.

2) Pronouns modified by an adjective:

Io sono più povero *di* lui.
I am poorer *than* he.

3) Numbers:

Questo libro costa meno *di* dieci dollari.
This book costs less *than* ten dollars.

d. In the comparative of inequality the word "than" is translated by *che*:

1) When the comparison is between two nouns unmodified by an adjective:

Egli mangia più carne *che* pane.
He eats more meat *than* bread.

2) When the comparison is between two pronouns unmodified by an adjective:

Io amo più te *che* lui.
I love you more *than* I love him.

3) When the comparison is between two adjectives, two adverbs, or two verbs:

Tu sei più fortunato *che* prudente.
You are luckier *than* (you are) prudent.

Lei parla meglio italiano *che* inglese.
You speak Italian better *than* English.

Gli piace più mangiare *che* lavorare.
He likes to eat more *than* (he likes) to work.

4) When the second part of the comparison is preceded by a preposition or a contraction of the preposition with the definite article:

Lei ha dato più fiori a Maria *che* a me.
You gave more flowers to Mary *than* to me.

Egli gioca più col fratello *che* con la sorella.
He plays more with the brother *than* with the sister.

3. *The Relative Superlative*

a. When the comparison is between more than two persons or things we have the relative superlative.

b. The English words "the most" and "the least" are translated by *più* and *meno* preceded by the definite article.

c. The English word "in" is translated by *di* or a contraction of *di* with the definite article.

Carlo è il ragazzo più intelligente *della* classe.
Charles is the most intelligent boy *in the* class.

Maria è la meno studiosa *di* tutti.
Mary is the least studious *of* all.

Ho visitato le più belle città *del* mondo.
I have visited the most beautiful cities *in the* world.

Essi sono i più ricchi *della* città.
They are the richest *in the* city.

d. The following common adjectives have an irregular comparative and superlative in addition to the regular forms:

buono good	**migliore** better	**il migliore** the best
cattivo bad	**peggiore** worse	**il peggiore** the worst
grande big	**maggiore** bigger	**il maggiore** the biggest
piccolo small	**minore** smaller	**il minore** the smallest
alto high, tall	**superiore** higher	**il superiore** the highest
basso low, short	**inferiore** lower	**l'inferiore** the lowest

NOTES: (1) The final *e* of the comparative and superlative of the above adjectives is often dropped before a singular noun.

(2) *Maggiore* is used to mean "greater, older" rather than "bigger."

(3) *Minore* is used to mean "younger, minor" rather than "smaller."

(4) *Superiore* is used to mean "higher, superior, better" rather than "taller."

(5) *Inferiore* means "lower, inferior," never "shorter."

È la *miglior* cosa che tu possa fare.
It is the *best* thing you can do.

Essi sono i *migliori* alunni della classe.
They are the *best* pupils in the class.

Questo vino è *peggiore* dell'altro.
This wine is *worse* than the other.

Egli è il figlio *minore*.
He is the *youngest* son.

La signorina abita al piano *superiore*.
The young lady lives on the floor above *(higher)*.

Ti hanno venduto un vino *inferiore*.
They have sold you an *inferior* wine.

4. *The Absolute Superlative*

a. The absolute superlative is used to express a very high degree of a trait or characteristic of a person or thing, without any relation to other persons or things. It has no corresponding form in English, and can be translated only by using such words as "very, extremely, enormously," etc.

b. The superlative absolute is formed by adding *-ssimo* (or *-ssima, -ssimi, -ssime*) to the masculine plural form of the adjective. This rule automatically takes care of words ending in *-co, -go, -ca,* and *-ga.*

Egli è un uomo ricchi*ssimo*.
He is an *extremely* wealthy man.

I grattacieli di New York sono alti*ssimi*.
The skyscrapers of New York are *very* high.

La signora è stanchi*ssima*.
The lady is *extremely* tired.

Il delta di quel fiume è larghi*ssimo*.
The delta of that river is *enormously* wide.

c. The following common adjectives have irregular absolute superlative forms in addition to the regular forms:

buono good	ottimo	alto high, tall	supremo *or* sommo
cattivo bad	pessimo	basso low, short	infimo
grande big, great	massimo	celebre famous	celeberrimo (no regular form for this)
piccolo small	minimo		

Ecco un *ottimo* bicchier di vino!
Here is an excellent glass of wine!

Ti voglio dire una cosa di *somma* importanza.
I want to tell you something of *extreme* importance.

Questi sono gli ordini del comando *supremo*.
These are the orders of the *supreme* command.

È il *minimo* che tu possa fare.
It is the *least* you could do.

d. The absolute superlative is sometimes formed by simply repeating an adverb:

Egli cammina *piano* piano.
He walks *very* slowly.

Si mise a gridare *forte* forte.
He started shouting *very* loudly.

e. The absolute superlative is sometimes formed by having such adverbs as *immensamente, enormemente, estremamente* precede the adjective, or by having the expression *quanto mai* (*lit.*, as ever) follow the adjective:

Ella è *estremamente* felice.
She is *extremely* happy.

Egli è ricco *quanto mai*.
He is *enormously* rich.

§ 18   Some Irregular Adjectives

The four adjectives *bello, grande, buono,* and *santo* undergo the following changes when they are placed before a noun:

1. The adjective *bello* has all the forms of the contractions:

un *bel* cane
a *beautiful* dog

i *bei* fiori
the *beautiful* flowers

una *bella* ragazza
a *beautiful* girl

le *belle* città
the *beautiful* cities

un *bell'*uomo
a *handsome* man

i *begli* occhi
the *beautiful* eyes

un *bello* specchio
a *beautiful* mirror

2. The adjective *grande* (big, large, great) becomes *gran* before a singular masculine noun not beginning with *z, s-impura,* or a vowel. It becomes *grand'* before a singular noun (masculine or *feminine*) beginning with a vowel.

un *gran* palazzo
a *big* building

un *grand'* amico
a *great* friend

un *grande* scienziato
a *great* scientist

3. The adjective *buono* becomes *buon* before a singular masculine noun not beginning with *z* or *s-impura,* and *buon'* before a singular feminine noun beginning with a vowel.

un *buon* libro
a *good* book

un *buono* zio
a *good* uncle

un *buon* orologio
a *good* watch

una *buon'*amica
a *good* friend (f.)

4. The adjective *santo* (saintly, holy) becomes *san* before a singular masculine noun not beginning with *z, s-impura,* or a vowel, and *sant'* before a singular noun beginning with a vowel.

San Carlo
Saint Charles

Sant'Elena
St. Helen

Santa Maria
St. Mary

Sant'Angelo
St. Angel

Santo Stefano
St. Stephen

The Pronoun (Il Pronome)

§ 19 Personal Subject Pronouns

1. The personal pronouns, used as subjects of verbs, in Italian are:

io I	**noi** we
tu you, thou (familiar singular)	**voi** you (familiar plural)
lei you (polite singular)	**loro** you (polite plural)
egli he	**essi** they (masc.)
ella she	**esse** they (fem.)

2. Notes on the personal subject pronouns:

a. *Io* is never capitalized in Italian unless it begins a sentence.

b. *Tu* is the familiar form and is used only in speaking to a close friend, a relative, a child, or an animal.

c. The pronoun *lei,* which is used in polite, formal address, used to be capitalized even in the middle of a sentence. This, as a general rule, is no longer done, except when writing to someone in a very high and respected position, as a sign of respect.

d. *Ella* (capitalized) is often used instead of *lei* for the reason explained in *c* above. In such cases, of course, it means "you."

e. The word *essa* may be used instead of *ella* to mean "she."

f. The words *egli* and *ella* are used only to indicate persons. *Esso* and *essa* are used to indicate animals or objects, although more often than not, they are simply omitted.

g. The word "it" (*esso* or *essa*) usually is not translated when it is the subject of a verb:

Non è necessario.
It is not necessary.

h. *Voi* (which is a plural pronoun) is often used to address one person. In such cases, however, the verb is in the plural, but a qualifying adjective, if there be one, is singular:

Maria, *voi* siete molto generosa.
Mary, *you* are very generous.

i. The personal subject pronouns are often omitted when the verb ending clearly indicates what the subject is. Thus, instead of saying *noi balliamo* (we dance) we may simply say *balliamo,* because the verb ending, *-iamo,* refers only to *noi.*

§ 20 Direct Object Pronouns

1. The direct object pronouns in Italian are:

mi me	**ci** us
ti you (fam. sing.)	**vi** you (fam. plur.)
la you (pol. sing.), her, it (fem.)	**li** you (pol. pl. masc.), them (masc. pl.)
lo him, it (masc.)	**le** you (pol. pl. fem.), them (fem. pl.)

ne
some, some of it, some of them, any, any
of it, any of them, of it, of them.

2. The normal position of the direct object pronouns is before the verb:

Io *lo* vedo.
I see *him* (or *it*).

Ella *mi* chiama.
She calls *me*.

Io *li* compreró.
I shall buy *them*.

Egli non *ne* mangia.
He doesn't eat *any*.

3. In a compound tense the direct object pronoun is placed before the auxiliary, and the past participle agrees with it:

Io *li* ho comprati.
I have bought *them*.

Egli non *le* ha incontrate.
He has not met *them*.

4. Before a vowel or vowel sound *lo* and *la* become *l'*; the others remain unchanged:

Io *l'*ho incontrato.
I met *him*.

Io *l'*ho incontrata.
I met *her*.

5. The direct object pronouns are attached to the word *ecco*:

Ecco il libro becomes **Ecco*lo*.**
Here is the book.   Here *it* is.

Ecco le signore becomes **Ecco*le*.**
Here are the ladies.   Here *they* are.

6. The direct object pronouns are attached to an infinitive after the latter loses its final *e*:

Non è necessario far*lo* adesso.
It is not necessary to do *it* now.

NOTE: If the infinitive depends on another verb, the pronoun may be attached to the infinitive or precede the first verb:

Essi vogliono veder*la* or Essi *la* vogliono vedere.
They want to see *it*.

However, when the infinitive depends on *fare, vedere, sentire,* or *lasciare,* the pronoun must be placed before this verb.

Io *lo* vedrò partire.
I shall see *him* leave.

Ella *mi* lascia parlare.
She lets *me* talk.

Voi *li* sentirete cantare.
You will hear *them* sing.

Essi *ci* fanno aspettare.
They make *us* wait.

7. The direct object pronouns are attached to the *tu, noi,* and *voi* forms of the affirmative imperative:

tu form:	**Porta il libro.** carry the book.	**Porta*lo*.** Carry *it*.
noi form:	**Compriamo le arance.** Let us buy the oranges.	**Compriamo*le*.** Let us buy *them*.
voi form:	**Imparate la lezione.** Learn the lesson.	**Imparate*la*.** Learn *it*.

BUT:

Non compriamo i libri. **Non *li* compriamo.**
Let us not buy the books. Let us not buy *them*.

§ 21 Indirect Object Pronouns

1. The indirect object pronouns in Italian are:

mi   **ci**
to me   to us

ti   **vi**
to you (fam. sing.)   to you (fam. pl.)

le   **loro**
to you (pol. sing.), to her   to you (pol. pl.), to them

gli
to him

2. The indirect object pronouns are normally placed before the verb:

Io parlo al professore.   **Io *gli* parlo.**
I speak to the professor.   I speak *to him*.

3. The indirect object pronoun *loro* always follows the verb:

Io parlo alle signorine.   **Io parlo *loro*.**
I speak to the young ladies.   I speak *to them*.

4. In a compound tense the indirect object pronoun is placed before the auxiliary, but the past participle does not agree with it:

Perchè non *ci* hai scritto?
Why haven't you written *to us*?

5. The indirect object pronouns (except *loro*) follow the same rule as the direct object pronouns in reference to the infinitive [See § 20-6].

Voglio scrivere al mio amico.
I want to write to my friend.

Gli voglio scrivere *or*
Voglio scrivergli.
I want to write to *him*.

Voglio scrivere ai miei amici.
I want to write to my friends.

Voglio scrivere loro.
I want to write to *them*.

BUT:

Io gli farò vedere il quadro.
I shall let *him* see the picture.

6. The indirect object pronouns are attached to the *tu, noi* and *voi* forms of the affirmative imperative:

tu form:

Porta il libro a Giovanni.
Bring the book to John.

Portagli il libro.
Bring *him (to him)* the book.

noi form:

Mandiamo i fiori alla mamma.
Let's send the flowers to mother.

Mandiamole i fiori.
Let's send *her* the flowers.

voi form:

Date il denaro all'uomo.
Give the money to the man.

Dategli il denaro.
Give *him* the money.

BUT:

Non date il denaro all'uomo.
Don't give the money to the man.

Non gli date il denaro.
Don't give *him* the money.

Parlate a quelle ragazze.
Speak to those girls.

Parlate loro.
Speak *to them*.

NOTE: The indirect object pronouns are to be used even when the word "to" is understood in English:

Io gli ho mandato il libro.
I sent *him* the book.

§ 22 Disjunctive Pronouns

The following are called *disjunctive pronouns* because, unlike the other pronouns, they are used independently of the verb. They have special uses as explained in 2 below.

1. The disjunctive pronouns in Italian are:

me
me

noi
us

te
you (fam. sing.)

voi
you (fam. pl.)

lei
you (pol. sing.), her

loro
you (pol. pl.), them (persons

lui
him

essi
them (masc.) (objects)

esso
it (masc.)

esse
them (fem.) (objects)

essa
it (fem.)

sè
himself, herself, itself, themselves

2. The disjunctive pronouns are used:

a. After prepositions (*a, da, di, in, per, con,* etc.):

Egli parlava di *me*.
He was talking about *me*.

Io non voglio andare con *lui*.
I don't want to go with *him*.

Egli fa questo per *loro*.
He is doing this for *them*.

b. After the verb, for contrast or emphasis:

Ella ha chiamato *te*.
She called *you*.

Egli ama lei, non *lui*.
He loves her, not *him*.

c. In exclamations:

Fortunato *me!*
Lucky *me!*

3. *Lui* and *lei* may be used instead of *egli* and *ella* when greater emphasis is desired:

Lui (instead of *egli*) ha fatto questo.
He did this.

Lei (instead of *ella*) ha detto ciò?
Did *she* say that?

4. The adjective *stesso* is often used after the disjunctive or other pronouns if greater emphasis is desired:

Egli parla sempre di sè *stesso*.
He always speaks of *himself*.

Noi *stessi* andremo là.
We *ourselves* shall go there.

5. The disjunctive pronouns *lui, lei, loro* are used:

a. Only for persons.

b. After any form of the verb *essere*:

Era *lui!*
It was *he!*

Non è stata *lei* che ha fatto questo.
It wasn't *she* who did this.

c. In a compound subject:

Tu e *lui* andrete a Roma.
You and *he* will go to Rome.

6. The disjunctive pronouns *esso, essa, essi, esse* are more commonly used for animals or objects.

§ 23 Interrogative Pronouns

1. The interrogative pronoun *chi?* (who? whom?) is of both genders,

and is usually followed by a singular verb. Only when *chi?* is used with any form of *essere* (to be) may the verb be plural:

> **Chi vuole mangiare?**
> *Who* wants to eat?

> **Con *chi* parlavi?**
> With *whom* were you talking?

> **Chi sono quegli uomini?**
> *Who* are those men?

2. *Che cosa?* (what?) is always singular, and refers only to things. In lieu of *che cosa?*, *che?* or *cosa?* may be used alone:

> **Che cosa ha detto? *or* Che ha detto? *or* Cosa ha detto?**
> *What* did he say?

3. *Quale?* (which? which one?) and *Quali?* (which? which ones?):

> **Ecco i libri. *Quale (or quali)* vuoi?**
> Here are the books. *Which (one* or *ones)* do you want?

> **Di quelle attrici, *quale* è la più bella?**
> Of those actresses, *which one* is the most beautiful?

4. *Di chi?* means "whose?":

> **Di chi è questa borsetta?**
> *Whose* handbag is this?

> **Di chi sono queste sigarette?**
> *Whose* cigarettes are these?

§ 24 Relative Pronouns

1. *Che* (who, whom, that, which) is the most common of the relative pronouns. It is used both as the subject or the direct object of a verb. It should not be used after a preposition.

> **L'uomo *che* parla è mio zio.**
> The man *who* is talking is my uncle.

> **Quelli *che* studiano imparano.**
> Those *who* study learn.

> **Mi piace il libro *che* mi hai dato.**
> I like the book *(that)* you gave me.

Notice in the above sentence that the word "that", which may be and is often omitted in English, may not be omitted in Italian.

2. *Cui* means "whom" or "which" when it is preceded by a preposition. It is used for both persons and things, and is both singular and plural.

> **I ragazzi di *cui* parlo.**
> The boys of *whom* I am talking.

> **La penna con *cui* scrivo è nuova.**
> The pen with *which* I am writing is new.

3. *Cui* preceded by the definite article or a contraction means "whose."

> **L'uomo il *cui* figlio è avvocato.**
> The man *whose* son is a lawyer.

L'uomo la *cui* figlia è qui.
The man *whose* daughter is here.

L'uomo i *cui* figli sono qui.
The man *whose* sons are here.

L'uomo del *cui* figlio io parlo.
The man of *whose* son I am speaking.

4. *Il quale* and its variations, *la quale, i quali, le quali,* mean "who, whom, which." More often than not they are used after a preposition, which may contract with the definite article. They are used rather sparingly in place of *che* and *cui* when there is a possibility of ambiguity.

Quel libro e la penna con *la quale* scrivo sono miei.
That book and the pen with *which* I am writing are mine.

Il nipote di Carlo, *il quale* è arrivato poco fa.
Charles' nephew, *who* arrived a short while ago.

5. *Ciò che* means "what," but must be used only when the word "what" means "that which."

Non mi piace *ciò che* hai fatto.
I don't like *what* you have done.

Ciò che egli dice non è vero.
What he says is not true.

NOTE: *Quel che* or *quello che* may be used instead of *ciò che.*

Ti darò *quel che* vuoi.
I shall give you *what* you want.

Quello che voi dite è giusto.
What you are saying is just.

6. *Chi* means "he who, him who, the one who." It is always used with a singular verb, even though the English translation may be "those who, the ones who," etc.

Chi studia impara.
He who studies learns. Or, *Those who* study learn.

Chi visita l'Italia è colpito dalla sua bellezza.
He who visits Italy is struck by its beauty.

NOTES: a. *Colui che* (masc.) or *colei che* (fem.) or *coloro che* (the latter being plural, the verb must also be plural) may be used instead of *chi.*

Colui che parla sarà punito.
The one who talks shall be punished.

Colei che ama sarà amata.
She who loves will be loved.

Coloro che studiano imparano.
Those who study learn.

b. *Chi* is at times used as a correlative pronoun, repeated before each verb. In such cases it is translated by "some, those who."

Che bella festa! *Chi* balla, *chi* canta, *chi* mangia!
What a nice party! *Some* dance, *some* sing, *some* eat.

§ 25 Demonstrative Pronouns

1. There is no difference in form between the demonstrative pronouns *questo, quello,* and *codesto* and the corresponding demonstrative adjectives [See § 13].

Quei ragazzi sono studiosi; *quello* non studia affatto.
Those boys are studious; *that one* doesn't study at all.

NOTE: It should be noted, however, that *quello* as a pronoun has only four forms—*quello, quella, quelli,* and *quelle.*

2. The demonstrative pronouns *questi* (this one, the latter) and *quegli* (that one, the former) are commonly used in sentences with two substantives. They refer only to persons (masc. sing.), and are used only as subjects of the verbs:

Conosco bene Carlo e Luigi: *questi* è intelligente, *quegli* è uno stupido.
I know Charles and Louis: *the latter* is intelligent, *the former* is a dunce.

3. The demonstrative pronoun *ciò* (this, that) may be used as subject or as object of the verb, and refers to something which has already been said or which is going to be said. It never refers to persons.

Non hai studiato? *Ciò* è molto male.
You haven't studied? *That* is very bad.

È inutile ripeter *ciò.*
It's useless to repeat *that.*

NOTE: At times *ciò* is replaced by the particle *ci:*

Ha detto questo? Io non *ci* credo.
Did he say that? I don't believe *it.*

§ 26 Indefinite Pronouns

The most common indefinite pronouns in Italian are:

1. *Nessuno* Nobody, no one

Nessuno verrà a cercarti qui.
No one will come to look for you here.

2. *Nulla* or *niente* Nothing

Nulla mi impedisce di far ciò.
Nothing prevents me from doing that.

NOTE: *Nessuno, nulla,* and *niente* require the negative particle *non* when preceded by the verb:

Non verrà a cercarti *nessuno.*
Nobody will come to look for you.

3. *Ognuno* Anybody, any one, everyone, everybody

Ognuno può fare quel gli piace.
Anybody can do as he pleases.

4. *Qualcuno*　Some one, somebody

Qualcuno è entrato nella mia stanza.
Somebody entered my room.

5. *Chiunque*　Whoever, anybody who

Chiunque mi cerchi, ditegli che non ci sono.
Whoever looks for me, tell him I am not in.

6. *Tutto, tutti*　All, everything

Tutto è facile quando si sa come.
Everything is easy when you know how.

Tutti viaggerebbero se avessero denaro.
All would travel if they had money.

7. *Alcuni*　Some (normally used in the plural)

Dei miei amici, *alcuni* sono sotto le armi.
Of my friends, *some* are in the army.

8. *Altri*　Others. Refers only to persons. As a subject *altri* usually is singular and requires a singular verb; as an object it may be singular or plural.

Altri farebbe questo, ma io non posso farlo.
Somebody else would do this, but I cannot do it.

Io non voglio uscire con *altri*.
I don't want to go out with *others*.

9. *Checchè*　Whatever

Checchè succeda, dovete andarci.
Whatever happens, you must go there.

§ 27　The Possessive Pronouns

The possessive pronouns (mine, yours, his, hers, etc.) are exactly like the possessive adjectives (my, your, his, her, etc.) [See § 16].

NOTE: The definite article is always used before the possessive pronouns, even when they refer to a member of the family or to a relative:

Ho perduto i meie libri ed i *tuoi*.　　**Mia sorella e la *tua* sono uscite.**
I lost my books and *yours*.　　　　　　My sister and *yours* went out.

§ 28　Reflexive Pronouns

1. The reflexive pronouns in Italian are:

mi　　　　　　　　　　　　　　**ci**
myself　　　　　　　　　　　　　ourselves

ti　　　　　　　　　　　　　　**vi**
yourself (fam. sing.)　　　　　　　yourselves (fam. plural)

si
yourself (pol. sing.), himself,
　herself, itself, themselves,
　yourselves (pol. pl.)

2. The reflexive pronouns always precede the verb, except for the infinitive and *tu, noi,* and *voi* forms of the affirmative imperative [See § 20-3, 6, 7].

Io *mi* lavo la faccia.
I wash *my* face.

Essi *si* alzano di buon'ora.
They get up early.

Allontanate*vi*!
Move away!

Divertiamo*ci*!
Let's have a good time (Let's enjoy *ourselves*)!

Egli vuole alzar*si*.
He wants to get up.

NOTE: The reflexive pronouns are always used in Italian, whereas they are often omitted in the English translation, as may be seen in the examples above.

§ 29 The Double Pronouns

1. Both a direct and an indirect object are often used with the same verb.

Io mando il *libro* a *Carlo*.
I send the *book* to *Charles*.

When the object nouns are replaced by pronouns we get the following combinations:

TABLE OF DOUBLE PRONOUNS

MEANING	it (m.), him	it (f.), her	them (m.)	them (f.)	of him, of her, of it, of them, any, some
to me	me lo	me la	me li	me le	me ne
to you *(lei)*	te lo	te la	te li	te le	te ne
to him, to her	glielo	gliela	glieli	gliele	gliene
to us	ce lo	ce la	ce li	ce le	ce ne
to you *(voi)*	ve lo	ve la	ve li	ve le	ve ne
to you *(loro)*, to them	lo . . . loro	la . . . loro	li . . . loro	le . . . loro	ne . . . loro
to himself, to herself, to themselves	se lo	se la	se li	se le	se ne

2. Notice from the above table that the indirect object pronouns *mi, ti, ci, vi,* and *si* change to *me, te, ce, ve,* and *se* before the direct object pronouns.

Egli *mi* dà il denaro.   **Egli *me lo* dà.**
He gives *me* the money.   He gives *it to me*.

Essi ci mandano delle ciliegie.   **Essi *ce ne* mandano.**
They send us some cherries.   They send *us some*.

3. The indirect object pronouns *gli* (to him) and *le* (to her, to you) become *glie* and combine with the direct object pronouns.

Io porto i fiori alla mamma.   **Io *glieli* porto.**
I bring the flowers to mother.   I bring *them to her.*

4. The double pronouns normally precede the verb except an infinitive and the *tu, noi,* and *voi* forms of the affirmative imperative, in which cases they are attached to the end of the verb [See § 22-3, 6, 7].

Porta questo regalo al tuo amico.   **Porta*glielo*.**
Bring this present to your friend.   Bring *it to him.*

Mandate*mi* quelle sigarette.   **Mandate*mele*.**
Send *me* those cigarettes.   Send *them to me.*

Vogliamo dar*gli* quelle arance.   **Vogliamo dar*gliele*.**
We want to give *him* those oranges.   We want to give *them to him.*

Remember that when you attach a single or a double pronoun to a verb form the stress of the verb remains unchanged in pronunciation.

5. The pronoun *loro* always follows the verb and never combines with the verb or with another pronoun:

Noi scriviamo le lettere ai nostri amici.   **Noi le scriviamo *loro*.**
We write the letters to our friends.   We write them *to them.*

Offrite i dolci alle signore.   **Offriteli *loro*.**
Offer the candies to the ladies.   Offer them *to them.*

6. Sometimes in English the word "to" as part of the indirect object pronouns has the meaning of "for," but the indirect object is still used in Italian.

Il babbo *mi* comprerà il cavallo.   **Il babbo *me* lo comprerà.**
Dad will buy *me* the horse.   He will buy it *for me.*

The Adverb (L'Avverbio)

§ 30   Classes of Adverbs

1. There are several classes of adverbs in Italian:

a. Adverbs of quality or manner, the most common of which are:

bene	**peggio**	**anche**	**invano**
well	worse	also, too	in vain
meglio	**così**	**pure**	**altrimenti**
better	thus	also, too	otherwise
male	**come**	**insieme**	
badly	as, like	together	

b. Adverbs of time, the most common of which are:

sempre	**domani**	**talvolta**
always	tomorrow	sometimes

mai never	**dopodomani** the day after tomorrow	**ancora** yet, still
ora now	**ieri** yesterday	**a tempo** on time
adesso now	**l'altro ieri** the day before yesterday	**spesso** often
allora then	**stasera** tonight	**presto** early, soon
poi then, afterwards	**stamani** or **stamane** this morning	**tardi** late
dopo afterwards	**per tempo** early	**oggi** today
prima before		

c. Adverbs of place, the most common of which are:

lontano far	**dove** where	**avanti** forward
vicino near	**altrove** elsewhere	**indietro** backward
presso near	**dappertutto** everywhere	**davanti** before, in front of
qua or **qui** here	**dentro** inside, within	**dietro** behind
lì or **là** there	**fuori** outside, without	

d. Adverbs of quantity, the most common of which are:

assai much	**troppo** too much	**abbastanza** enough	**quasi** almost, nearly
molto much	**tanto** so much	**solo** or **soltanto** only	**più** more
poco little	**altrettanto** as much	**circa** nearly, about	**meno** less

e. Adverbial phrases, the most common of which are:

di tanto in tanto once in a while	**di bene in meglio** better and better	**di buona voglia** willingly
delle volte at times, sometimes	**di male in peggio** from bad to worse	**a malincuore** unwillingly, reluctantly
qualche volta sometimes	**ad un tratto** suddenly	**per lo più** mostly
a poco a poco little by little	**all'improvviso** suddenly, unexpectedly	**per lo meno** at least

f. Affirmative and negative adverbs, the most common of which are:

sì yes	**senza dubbio** undoubtedly	**forse** perhaps
certo certainly	**neppure** or **nemmeno** not even	**niente** or **nulla** nothing

davvero	**no**	**niente affatto**
really	no	not at all
nemmeno	**non**	
not even	not	

§ 31 Formation of Adverbs

1. Many adverbs of manner are formed by adding -*mente* to the singular feminine forms of adjectives:

ADJECTIVE	SING. FEM. FORM	ADVERB
ricco	**ricca**	**riccamente**
rich		
divino	**divina**	**divinamente**
divine		
breve	**breve**	**brevemente**
brief		

However, adjectives which end in -*ale, -ele, -ile, -ole, -are,* and -*ore* drop the final *e* before adding -*mente*:

generale	**inutile**	**particolare**
general	useless	particular
generalmente	**inutilmente**	**particolarmente**
fedele	**debole**	**maggiore**
faithful	weak	greater
fedelmente	**debolmente**	**maggiormente**

2. Several adjectives may be used as adverbs without changing form, although the alternate adverbial form may also be used:

Parlate *chiaro or chiaramente.*
Speak *clearly.*

Ella mi guardò *fisso or fissamente.*
She stared (*lit.,* looked *straight*) at me.

§ 32 Comparison of Adverbs

1. Most adverbs are compared in the same manner as the adjectives. The words *più* and *meno* are used for the comparative, and *il più* and *il meno* for the superlative:

Vi prego di parlare *più lentamente.*
I beg you to speak *more slowly.*

So che egli mi serve *meno fedelmente* del padre.
I know he serves me *less faithfully* than the father.

Vi prego di parlare il *più lentamente* possibile.
I beg you to speak *as slowly* as possible.

2. Adverbs, like adjectives, also have an absolute superlative form. Simply add -*mente* to the singular feminine form of the absolute superlative of the adjective:

Egli imparava tutto *facilissimamente.*
He learned everything *very, very easily.*

3. The following adverbs have irregular comparatives:

bene well	**meglio** better	**molto** much	**più** more
male badly	**peggio** worse	**poco** little	**meno** less

4. The relative superlatives of the above four adverbs are:

il meglio   il peggio   il più   il meno

NOTE: These relative superlatives are normally used as substantives:

È *il meglio* che egli possa fare.
It is *the best* he can do.

5. The absolute superlative of *bene* is *ottimamente* or *benissimo*, and that of *male* is *pessimamente* or *malissimo.*

Egli scrive *ottimamente* (or *benissimo*).
He writes *exceptionally well.*

6. Some adverbs may take a diminutive or augmentative ending:

benino well	**benone** pretty well	**poco** little	**pocchetino** a very little
	piano slowly	**pianino** rather slowly	

7. The superlative of some adverbs may be formed by simply repeating them:

È uscito *subito subito.*
He went out *immediately.*

The Preposition (La Preposizione)

§ 33   The Preposition *a*

The preposition *a* (meaning "to" sometimes "at, in, for," etc.) or a contraction of *a* with the definite article [See § 6] is used:

1. Before indirect object nouns:

Io parlo *a* Carlo.
I speak *to* Charles.

Io parlo *ai* ragazzi.
I speak *to the* boys.

NOTE: Frequently the preposition "to" is omitted in English, but it cannot be omitted in Italian:

Egli dà il libro *a* Maria.
He gives (to) Mary the book.

2. Before disjunctive pronouns [See § 22]:

Egli parla *a* me, non *a* lui.
He is speaking *to* me, not *to* him.

3. Before names of cities, in which case it may also mean "in:"

Noi andremo a Napoli.
We shall go *to* Naples.

A Firenze ci sono molti tesori d'arte.
In Florence there are many art treasures.

NOTE: The preposition *in* may used instead of *a* in the sense of "within:"

Egli vive a (or in) Roma.
He lives *in* Rome.

4. In a number of idioms where a different preposition or none at all might be expected in English (see list of idioms at end of Reference Grammar):

Ti aspettano a braccia aperte.
They are waiting for you *with* open arms.

Egli non è buono a nulla.
He is good *for* nothing.

Si gettò a capofitto nel lago.
He threw himself headlong into the lake.

5. Before a number of infinitives depending upon *insegnare, imparare,* and other verbs usually denoting motion, progress, beginning, remaining, etc. Here is a partial list of such verbs:

aiutare a to help	**mettersi a** to start, begin	**esitare a** to hesitate
acconsentire a to consent	**riuscire a** to succeed	**imparare a** to learn
abituarsi a to get accustomed to	**stare a** to remain, wait, stay	**incominciare a** to begin
andare a to go	**tardare a** to be late	**insegnare a** to teach
continuare a to continue	**venire a** to come	**invitare a** to invite
divertirsi a to enjoy oneself		

Adesso incomincio a capire.
Now I am beginning to understand.

Egli è venuto a vederla.
He came to see her (*or* it).

Ella aiuta la mamma a pulire la casa.
She helps mother to clean the house.

6. To indicate price of items:

Ho comprato queste cravatte a cento lire l'una.
I bought these ties *at* a hundred lire each.

7. To indicate time:

Lo spettacolo comincia alle otto.
The show starts *at* eight.

Carlo verrà a mezzogorno.
Charles will come *at* noon.

8. In a number of adverbial locutions, the most common of which are:

A poco a poco impariamo.
Little by little we are learning.

Attorno alla casa c'è il giardino.
Around the house there is the garden.

Dietro a me siede Lucia.
Behind me sits Lucy.

Il negozio è dirimpetto alla posta.
The store is opposite the post office.

Ti aspetterò fino alle sei.
I shall wait for you until six.

Rispetto a questo non so che dire.
Concerning this I don't know what to say.

La signorina abita vicino a noi.
The young lady lives near us.

Ho trovato una palla in mezzo alla strada.
I found a ball in the middle of the street.

Le rose sono accanto all'albero.
The roses are at the side of the tree.

NOTE: a may become ad before a vowel:

Dietro ad Anna.
Behind Anne.

§ 34 The Preposition da

The preposition da (meaning "from," also "at, for, by, with, as", etc.) or a contraction of da with the definite article [See § 6] is used:

1. To indicate movement from a place:

Egli viene da Roma.
He comes from Rome.

2. To indicate "to or at a person's place," the nature of the place not being specified:

Io vado dal dottore.
I am going to the doctor's.

Andrò da lui stasera.
I shall go to his place tonight.

Lo troverete da Giovanni.
You will find him at John's.

3. To indicate a person, place, or object from which something comes or originates:

Ho ricevuto una lettera da Carlo.
I received a letter from Charles.

Il carbone si estrae dalla terra.
Coal is extracted from the earth.

L'ho preso dall'armadio.
I took it from the closet.

4. Before an infinitive or a noun to indicate purpose, convenience, capacity, duty:

Scarpe *da* passeggio.
Shoes *for* walking

Sala *d'*aspetto.
Waiting room

Quest'acqua non è *da* bere.
This water is not *for* drinking.

Non sono cose *da* dirsi.
These things are not to be told.

Non c'è tempo *da* perdere.
There is no time to lose.

5. To indicate cause, reason, or an agent:

Io tremavo *dal* freddo.
I was shivering *because of the* cold.

Ho fatto questo *da* me.
I did this *by* myself.

Abele fu ucciso *da* Caino.
Abel was killed *by* Cain.

6. To indicate a trait or characteristic of a person or thing:

L'uomo *dalla* barba lunga.
The man *with a* long beard.

La casa *dalle* persiane verdi.
The house *with* green shutters.

***Dal* rumore si sa che ci sono dei bambini.**
From the noise one knows that there are children.

7. To translate the English expressions "as, like, in the manner of:"

Egli parla *da* ragazzo intelligente.
He speaks *like an* intelligent boy.

Egli vive *da* re.
He lives *like a* king.

Notice the omission of the indefinite article before *ragazzo* and *re* [See § 5-4].

8. To indicate a place where an action occurs:

Si buttò *dalla* finestra.
He threw himself *out of the* window.

***Dalla* montagna si vede un panorama bellissimo.**
From the mountain one sees a beautiful panorama.

Il prete predica *dal* pulpito.
The priest preaches *from the* pulpit.

9. To indicate age or condition, in sentences such as these:

***Da* bambino avevo i capelli biondi.**
As a child (when I was a child) I had blond hair.

***Da* studente egli era svogliato.**
As a student he was unattentive.

10. In certain adverbial locutions such as:

lontano da
far from

da ora in poi
from now on

fin (or fino) da
since, from

Fin da*ll'***infanzia egli è stato sempre fortunato.**
Since childhood he has always been lucky.

NOTE: *Da* hardly ever becomes *d'* before a vowel.

§ 35 The Preposition *di*

The preposition *di* (of, by) or a contraction with the definite article is used:

1. To indicate possession:

La casa *dello* zio
Uncle's house

L'automobile *di* Giovanni
John's automobile

2. Material of which something is made, or contents:

Un orologio *d'oro*
a gold watch

Una veste *di* seta
a silk dress

Un bicchiere *di* latte
a glass *of* milk

3. In a sense of literary or artistic authorship:

Un romanzo *di* Manzoni
a novel *by* Manzoni

Un quadro *di* Michelangelo
a painting *by* Michaelangelo

4. In comparisons (see § 17-B-3 and § 17-C-3).

5. If, in the equivalent English, a noun is used as an adjective to modify another noun, the tendency in Italian is to place the modifying noun in a prepositional phrase with *di*:

Una lezione *di* francese
a French lesson

6. With infinitives depending upon an adjective:

Egli è contento *di* andare là.
He is glad to go there.

Sei felice *di* rivedermi?
Are you happy to see me again?

Io sono orgoglioso *di* fare questo lavoro.
I am proud to do this work.

7. Before certain nouns or pronouns depending upon an adjective:

Tu sei invidioso *di* lui.
You are envious *of* him.

Noi siamo orgogliosi *della* nostra patria.
We are proud *of* our country.

Non siete sicuri *di* me?
Aren't you sure *of* me?

8. Before a large number of infinitives depending upon other verbs. Here are some examples:

Io *penso di* andar via.
I *am thinking of* going away.

Egli non *desidera di* fare ciò.
He doesn't *wish to* do that.

Non ti *permetto di* uscire.
I do not *permit* you *to* go out.

Ella *offrì di* accompagnarmi.
She *offered to* accompany me.

***Hai paura di* rimanere qui?**
Are you afraid to remain here?

Other verbs are:

avere ragione di to be right	**proibire di** to prohibit	**rifiutare di** to refuse
avere torto di to be wrong	**promettere di** to promise	**finire di** to finish
dire di to tell	**dimenticare di** to forget	**pregare di** to pray, to beg
ordinare di to order	**ricordare di** to remember	**cercare di** to try

9. To indicate time:

Egli partì *di* mattina.
He left *in the* morning.

10. To indicate manner:

Ella lo fa *di* buona voglia.
She does it willingly.

Io mangio *di* buon appetito.
I eat *with a* good appetite.

Essi si alzano *di buon'ora*.
They get up early.

11. Contracted with the definite article [see § 6-16] to mean "some:"

Ci sono *degli* uomini.
There are *some* men.

Ho mangiato *del* pane.
I ate *some* bread.

12. Between the expressions *qualche cosa* or *nulla* and a modifying adjective:

Non c'è nulla *di* nuovo.
There is nothing new.

Ti ha dato qualche cosa *di* buono?
Did he give you something good?

13. In a number of adverbial locutions, the most common of which are:

a favore di in favor of	**di tanto in tanto** once in a while	**a forza di** by dint of
invece di instead of	**di bene in meglio** better and better	**ad onta di** in spite of

per mezzo di by means of	**di male in peggio** from bad to worse	**fuori di** out of
prima di before	**di gran lunga** by far	**al di là di** on that side of
dopo di after	**a causa di** because of	

§ 36 Other Common Prepositions

1. The preposition *in* (or a contraction of *in* with the definite article), meaning "in, into," is used:

a. To indicate location, real or figurative:

Egli abita *in* Roma.
He lives *in* Rome.

Ella vive *nei* sogni.
She lives *in* dreams.

b. To indicate time:

Dante nacque *nel* 1265.
Dante was born *in* 1265.

In tre mesi finirò il lavoro.
In three months I shall finish the work.

c. To translate the word "to" in a verb of motion before names of countries:

Io ritornerò *negli* Stati Uniti.
I shall return *to the* United States.

La signora va *in* America.
The lady is going *to* America.

2. The preposition *con* or a contraction of *con* with *il* and *i* [See § 6-2], meaning "with," is used mostly as in English. These special uses, however, are of interest:

a. *Con* sometimes means "against":

Egli combatteva *col* nemico.
He was fighting *against the* enemy.

b. *Con* sometimes means "toward":

Egli è giusto *con* tutti.
He is just *toward* everybody.

c. *Con* sometimes means "in spite of":

Con tutta la sua intelligenza egli non è riuscito.
In spite of all his intelligence he did not succeed.

3. The preposition *per* (for, through, by) is mostly used as in English:

Passarono *per* Firenze.
They passed *through* (or *by*) Florence.

La notizia si sparse *per* tutta la città.
The news spread *through* the whole city.

It is also used in the Italian expressions meaning "to be about to":

L'attrice stava *per* partire.
The actress was *about to* leave.

Il ladro stava *per* confessare.
The thief was *about to* confess.

4. The preposition *su* (or a contraction of *su* with the definite article), meaning "on, upon" is mostly used as in English. These special uses, however, are of interest:

a. *Su* means "about" in sentences such as these:

Era un uomo *sulla* sessantina.
He was a man of *about* sixty.

Ella ha scritto un libro *sulla* vecchiaia.
She has written a book *on (about)* old age.

b. In the idiomatic expressions *dare su* (to face, to open upon) and *su due piedi* (right there and then, on the spot).

La finestra *dà sul* giardino.
The window *faces* the garden.

***Su due piedi* mi disse che non l'avrebbe fatto.**
Right there and then he told me he wouldn't do it.

§ 37   Repetition of Prepositions

When one preposition governs two words connected by a conjunction, such preposition must be repeated before each word in the Italian sentence:

Parlerò *a* Carlo e *a* Maria.
I shall speak *to* Charles and Mary.

Egli ha parlato *dell'*Italia e *della* Francia.
He spoke *of* Italy and France.

The Conjunction (La Congiunzione)

§ 38   Coordinating Conjunctions

Coordinating conjunctions may join two sentences or two parts of a sentence. The most common ones in Italian are:

e and	**però** however	**cioè** that is
o or	**dunque** therefore	**nè . . . nè** neither . . . nor
ma but	**perciò** therefore	**infatti** in fact

L'uomo studia *e* apprende.
Man studies *and* learns.

Carlo *nè* studia, *nè* apprende.
Charles *neither* studies *nor* learns.

È partito, *ma* ha dimenticato il biglietto.
He left, *but* forgot the ticket.

Penso, *dunque* esisto.
I think, *therefore* I exist.

§ 39 Subordinating Conjunctions

Subordinating conjunctions establish dependence between two verbs. The most common ones are:

che that	**quindi** therefore	**giacchè** inasmuch as
come how, as	**malgrado** in spite of	**dovunque** everywhere
perchè because	**mentre** while	**purchè** provided
per for	**benchè** although	**a patto che** on condition that
quando when	**sebbene** although	**nonostante** notwithstanding
dove where	**invece di** instead of	**neppure** *or* **nemmeno** neither, not even
se if		

Non è giusto *che* lei faccia questo.
It is not right for you to do this.

Sono venuto *per* salutarti.
I have come *to* (*for to*) greet you.

Egli gioca, *mentre* dovrebbe studiare.
He plays *while* he ought to be studying.

È venuto *perchè* ha bisogno del tuo aiuto.
He came *because* he needs your help.

NOTE: The conjunction *che* (that) is never omitted in Italian, as is often done in English:

Credo *che* Maria verrà.
I think (*that*) Mary will come.

The Interjection (L'Interiezione)

§ 40 Some Common Interjections

The interjection or exclamation is an invariable part of speech which, in itself, has no particular meaning, but which, in a sentence, serves to express such basic feelings as joy, pleasure, astonishment, grief, disgust, etc. Here are some of the more common interjections in Italian and their approximate English meanings:

ah! ah! oh!	**evviva!** hurrah! long live!	**perbacco!** by Jove!
oh! oh!	**viva!** hail!	**perdinci!** by Jove! dear me!
ahi! ouch! oh dear!	**guai!** woe!	**accidempoli!** the deuce!
ahimè! alas!	**caspita!** what the deuce!	**peccato!** too bad!
ecco! there!		

The Verb (Il Verbo)

§ 41   The Transitive Verbs

1. A transitive verb is one that takes a direct object:

> **Io *prendo* il libro.**
> I *take* the book.

2. There are a number of verbs which are transitive in Italian but intransitive in English. Some of these are:

> **Egli *guarda* il libro.**
> He *looks at* the book.
>
> **Io *cerco* il libro.**
> I *look for* the book.
>
> **Essi *aspettano* il treno.**
> They *are waiting for* the train.
>
> **Noi *ascoltiamo* la musica.**
> We *listen to* the music.

3. Transitive verbs are always conjugated with *avere*.

§ 42   The Intransitive Verbs

1. An intransitive verb is one which does not have a direct object. It may express an action which:

a. Is reflected on an indirect object introduced by a preposition:

> **Io *parlo* al mio amico.**
> I *speak* to my friend.

b. Remains on the subject itself, or expresses a state or condition of the subject:

> **La signorina *studia*.**
> The young lady *is studying*.
>
> **Il bambino *dorme*.**
> The child is sleeping.

2. There are a number of verbs which are intransitive in Italian but transitive in English. Some of these are:

> **Io *entro nella* stanza.**
> I *enter* the room.
>
> **Egli *rispose alla* mia lettera.**
> He *answered* my letter.
>
> **Questo non *mi conviene*.**
> This does not *suit* me.
>
> **Il pollo arrosto non *piace a* Carlo.**
> Charles doesn't *like* roast chicken.
>
> **Io mi *ricordo di* lei.**
> I *remember you*.

(*Mi ricordo* is a form of *ricordarsi*, which is reflexive. However, the verb *ricordare* does take a direct object and is, therefore, transitive.)

§ 43 The Infinitive

1. The infinitive is the basic form of the verb, from which all other forms (in the case of the regular verbs) are derived. In English the infinitive is distinguished by the preposition "to" which precedes it. In Italian the infinitive is identified by its characteristic ending. There are three infinitive endings in Italian, and each one identifies its conjugation:

FIRST CONJUGATION ENDING: -*are*

parl*are*, cant*are*
to speak, to sing

SECOND CONJUGATION ENDING: -*ere*

perd*ere*, vend*ere*
to lose, to sell

THIRD CONJUGATION ENDING: -*ire*

dorm*ire*, fin*ire*
to sleep, to finish

2. The infinitive may be used in the function of a noun as the subject of a verb, as an object, or as a predicate noun. It may or may not be preceded by the definite article.

***Godere* la vita è il desiderio di tutti.**
To enjoy life is everybody's wish.

***Il dormire* fa bene a tutti.**
Sleeping does everybody good.

3. The infinitive is often used after prepositions when in English we would normally use a gerund (-*ing*). In these cases the infinitive is preceded by the definite article (or a contraction) except when it follows *prima di* (before), *dopo di* (after), and *senza* (without).

***Col viaggiare* si imparano molte cose.**
Traveling one learns many things.

***Prima di rispondere* voglio rileggere la sua lettera.**
Before answering I want to read his letter again.

Uscì *senza dire* niente.
He went out *without saying* anything.

4. An infinitive often depends on a noun. In these cases it is preceded by *da* if use or purpose is implied; otherwise *di* is used.

Mi dia dell'acqua *da bere*.
Give me some *drinking* water.

Il suo *desiderio di aiutare* gli altri è grande.
His *desire to help* others is great.

5. An infinitive depending on an adjective may be introduced by the preposition *di, a,* or no preposition at all.

Sono *felice di fare* questo per lei.
I am *happy to do* this for you.

Queste cose sono *facili a fare.*
These things are *easy to do.*

È *difficile imparare* **tante cose.**
It is *difficult to learn* so many things.

6. An infinitive depending on another verb may be introduced:

a. By the preposition *a* [See § 33-5].

b. By the preposition *di* [See § 35-8].

c. By no preposition. The following is a list of the most common of these verbs:

fare to do, make	**dovere** must, ought to	**lascire** to allow, let
sentire to hear	**preferire** to prefer	**parere** to seem
volere to want	**desiderare** to wish	**sembrare** to seem
potere to be able, can	**osare** to dare	**giovare** to be advantageous
vedere to see	**ardire** to dare	**bisognare** to need (impersonal)
sapere to know	**bastare** to suffice	**amare** to love, like

L'ho *vista* **piangere.**
I *saw* her cry.

Essi non *sanno* **nuotare.**
They don't *know how* to swim.

Voi dovete *partire* **subito.**
You must *leave* right away.

7. The English expression "in order to" (or "to" alone, if it means "in order to") is rendered by *per* before an infinitive.

Per comprare queste cose ci vuole molto denaro.
In order to buy these things you need a great deal of money.

8. Direct, indirect (except *loro*), and reflexive pronouns are attached to an infinitive after the latter loses its final *e*.

9. The past infinitive is formed by the infinitive of the auxliary verb and the past participle of the desired verb [See § 48, § 49, § 50].

10. Direct, indirect, and reflexive pronouns are attached to the auxiliary verb, which, as you already know, loses its final *e*:

Dopo di esser*mi* **alzato uscii.**
After I got up I went out.

Lacerò la lettera senza aver*la* **letta.**
He tore the letter without having read *it.*

§ 44 The Gerund

1. The present gerund of regular verbs is formed as follows:

FIRST CONJUGATION: Drop -are and add -ando
> parlando, ballando

SECOND CONJUGATION: Drop -ere and add -endo
> perdendo, leggendo

THIRD CONJUGATION: Drop -ire and add -endo
> sentendo, dormendo

2. The present gerund translates the English present participle whether preceded by a preposition or not.

> **Leggendo si imparano molte cose.**
> By reading one learns many things.

> **L'appetito viene mangiando.**
> Appetite comes while eating.

> **Vedendo che non c'era, andai via.**
> Seeing that he wasn't there, I went away.

NOTE: The present gerund is often called the present participle.

3. The past gerund is formed by the present gerund of the auxiliary verb and the past participle of the desired verb.

4. The past gerund is used as in English.

> **Essendo arrivato prima del tempo, dovetti aspettare.**
> Having arrived before time, I had to wait.

> **Non avendo studiato, egli non potè rispondere bene.**
> Not having studied, he was unable to answer well.

5. Direct, indirect (except loro), and reflexive pronouns are attached to the present gerund, whether used alone or as an auxiliary:

> **Mettendomi in commercio, spero di fare fortuna.**
> By going into business, I hope to make a fortune.

> **Avendola vista (la casa), decise di comprarla.**
> Having seen it (the house), he decided to buy it.

§ 45 The Participle

1. The present participle is formed as follows:

FIRST CONJUGATION: Drop -are and add -ante
> parlare   parlante
> to speak

SECOND CONJUGATION: Drop -ere and add -ente
> perdere   perdente
> to lose

THIRD CONJUGATION: Drop -ire and add -ente
> dormire   dormente
> to sleep

NOTE: Some third conjugation verbs add *-iente* instead of *-ente*:

ubbidire ubbid*iente*   **nutrire**   nutr*iente*
to obey   to nourish

2. The present participle is rarely used, and a good many verbs do not have one. When used, the present participle has the function of an adjective or a noun:

Un buon *cantante*   **Il grillo *parlante***
a good *singer*   the *talking* cricket

L'*insegnante* d'italiano   **La Torre *Pendente***
the Italian *teacher*   the *Leaning* Tower

3. The past participle of regular verbs is formed as follows:

FIRST CONJUGATION: Drop *-are* and add *-ato*

     parlare   parl*ato*

SECOND CONJUGATION: Drop *-ere* and add *-uto*

     perdere   perd*uto*

THIRD CONJUGATION: Drop *-ire* and add *-ito*

     dormire   dorm*ito*

4. The past participle is mainly used in the formation of compound tenses.

5. The past participle is often used in an absolute construction; that is, without the auxiliary verb. In such cases it agrees with the subject if the verb is intransitive, and with the object if the verb is transitive.

Imparata la poesia, egli uscì contento.
Having learned the poem, he went out happy.

Partiti alle nove, essi arrivarono a mezzogiorno.
Having left at nine, they arrived at noon.

6. Direct, indirect (except *loro*), and reflexive pronouns are attached to the past participle used in an absolute construction. This, however, is not a frequent occurrence.

Lavatesi le mani, incominciò a mangiare.
Having washed his hands, he began to eat.

7. The past participle used in compound tenses agrees with the preceding direct object, which may be a noun or a pronoun:

La *signorina* che ho invita*ta*.
The young lady I invited.

Ho comprato i libri.   *Li* ho comprat*i*.
I bought the books.   I bought *them*.

§ 46 The Conjugation of Verbs

The complete conjugation of a verb includes:

1. The indicative mood, which indicates certainty or reality, and which has eight tenses—four simple tenses and four compound tenses:

SIMPLE TENSES	COMPOUND TENSES
presente present	**passato prossimo** present perfect
imperfetto imperfect	**trapassato prossimo** pluperfect
passato remoto past definite	**trapassato remoto** past anterior
futuro future	**futuro anteriore** future perfect

2. The conditional mood, which expresses or implies a condition, and which has two tenses:

presente present	**passato** past

3. The imperative, which expresses a command or exhortation, and which has only one tense.

NOTE: There is no imperative form for the first person singular (*io*).

4. The subjunctive mood, which is the mood of doubt, possibility, emotion, etc., and which has four tenses:

presente present	**passato** past
imperfetto imperfect	**trapassato** pluperfect

5. The infinitive, which has two forms:

presente present	**passato** past

6. The participle, which has two forms:

presente present	**passato** past

7. The gerund, which has two forms:

presente present	**passato** past

§ 47 Conjugation of the Verbs *Essere* and *Avere*

Before discussing the uses of the different tenses let us first learn the complete conjugation of *avere* (to have) and *essere* (to be), which are the auxiliary verbs, and of the three regular conjugations.

Inasmuch as the singular forms for *lei* (you, polite), *egli* (he), *ella* (she), and the plural forms for *loro* (you, polite), *essi* (they, masc.) and *esse* (they, fem.) are the same, only one form will be given, except in the compound tenses of *essere*, where the past participle agrees with the subject.

avere	essere
to have	to be

INDICATIVE MOOD

PRESENT

io *ho*	io *sono*
I *have*, I *am having*, I *do have*	I *am*
tu *hai*	tu *sei*
you *have*, you *are having*, you *do have*	you *are*
egli *ha*	egli *è*
he *has*, he *is having*, he *does have*	he *is*
noi *abbiamo*	noi *siamo*
we *have*, we *are having*, we *do have*	we *are*
voi *avete*	voi *siete*
you *have*, you *are having*, you *do have*	you *are*
essi *hanno*	essi *sono*
they *have*, they *are having*, they *do have*	they *are*

PRESENT PERFECT

io *ho avuto*	io *sono stato* (or *stata*)
I *had*, I *have had*	I *was*, I *have been*
tu *hai avuto*	tu *sei stato* (*stata*)
egli *ha avuto*	egli *è stato*
	ella *è stata*
noi *abbiamo avuto*	noi *siamo stati* (*state*)
voi *avete avuto*	voi *siete stati* (*state*)
essi *hanno avuto*	essi *sono stati*
	esse *sono state*

IMPERFECT

io *avevo*	io *ero*
I *had*, I *used to have*, I *was having*	I *was*, I *used to be*, I *was being*
tu *avevi*	tu *eri*
egli *aveva*	egli *era*
noi *avevamo*	noi *eravamo*
voi *avevate*	voi *eravate*
essi *avevano*	essi *erano*

PLUPERFECT

io *avevo avuto*
I *had had*

tu *avevi avuto*

egli *aveva avuto*

noi *avevamo avuto*

voi *avevate avuto*

essi *avevano avuto*

io *ero stato (-a)*
I *had been*

tu *eri stato (-a)*

egli *era stato*

ella *era stata*

noi *eravamo stati (-e)*

voi *eravate stati (-e)*

essi *erano stati*

esse *erano state*

PAST DEFINITE

io *ebbi*
I *had*

tu *avesti*

egli *ebbe*

noi *avemmo*

voi *aveste*

essi *ebbero*

io *fui*
I *was*

tu *fosti*

egli *fu*

noi *fummo*

voi *foste*

essi *furono*

PAST ANTERIOR

io *ebbi avuto*
I *had had*

tu *avesti avuto*

egli *ebbe avuto*

noi *avemmo avuto*

voi *aveste avuto*

essi *ebbero avuto*

io *fui stato (-a)*
I *had been*

tu *fosti stato (-a)*

egli *fu stato*

ella *fu stata*

noi *fummo stati (-e)*

voi *foste stati (-e)*

essi *furono stati*

esse *furono state*

FUTURE

io *avrò*
I *will* (or *shall*) *have*

tu *avrai*

egli *avrà*

noi *avremo*

voi *avrete*

essi *avranno*

io *sarò*
I *will* (or *shall*) be

tu *sarai*

egli *sarà*

noi *saremo*

voi *sarete*

essi *saranno*

FUTURE PERFECT

io *avrò avuto*
I will (or *shall*) *have had*

tu *avrai avuto*

egli *avrà avuto*

noi *avremo avuto*

voi *avrete avuto*

essi *avranno avuto*

io *sarò stato (-a)*
I *will* (or *shall*) *have been*

tu *sarai stato (-a)*

egli *sarà stato*

ella *sarà stata*

noi *saremo stati (-e)*

voi *sarete stati (-e)*

essi *saranno stati*

esse *saranno state*

CONDITIONAL MOOD
PRESENT

io *avrei*
I *would* (or *should*) *have*

tu *avresti*

egli *avrebbe*

noi *avremmo*

voi *avreste*

essi *avrebbero*

io *sarei*
I *would* (or *should*) be

tu *saresti*

egli *sarebbe*

noi *saremmo*

voi *sareste*

essi *sarebbero*

PAST

io *avrei avuto*
I *would* (or *should*) *have had*

tu *avresti avuto*

egli *avrebbe avuto*

noi *avremmo avuto*

voi *avreste avuto*

essi *avrebbero avuto*

io *sarei stato (-a)*
I *would* (or *should*) *have been*

tu *saresti stato (-a)*

egli *sarebbe stato*

ella *sarebbe stata*

noi *saremmo stati (-e)*

voi *sareste stati (-e)*

essi *sarebbero stati*

esse *sarebbero state*

THE IMPERATIVE

abbi (tu)
have

abbia (lei, egli, ella)
have, let him have, let her
have

abbiamo (noi)
let us have

abbiate (voi)
have

abbiano (loro, essi, esse)
have, let them have

sii
be

sia
be, let him be, let her be

siamo
let us be

siate
be

siano
be, let them be

NOTE: Normally the personal pronouns are not used in the imperative.

SUBJUNCTIVE MOOD
PRESENT

che io *abbia*
I *have*, I *may have*

che tu *abbia*

che egli *abbia*

che noi *abbiamo*

che voi *abbiate*

che essi *abbiano*

che io *sia*
I *be*, I *may be*

che tu *sia*

che egli *sia*

che noi *siamo*

che voi *siate*

che essi *siano*

PAST

che io *abbia avuto*
I *had*, I *might have*

che tu *abbia avuto*

che io *sia stato (-a)*
I *have been*, I *may have been*

che tu *sia stato (-a)*

che egli *abbia avuto*	che egli *sia stato*
	che ella *sia stata*
che noi *abbiamo avuto*	che noi *siamo stati (-e)*
che voi *abbiate avuto*	che voi *siate stati (-e)*
che essi *abbiano avuto*	che essi *siano stati*
	che esse *siano state*

IMPERFECT

che io *avessi*	che io *fossi*
I *had*, I *might have*	I *was*, I *might be*
che tu *avessi*	che tu *fossi*
che egli *avesse*	che egli *fosse*
che noi *avessimo*	che noi *fossimo*
che voi *aveste*	che voi *foste*
che essi *avessero*	che essi *fossero*

PLUPERFECT

che io *avessi avuto*	che io *fossi stato (-a)*
I *had had*, I *might have had*	I *had been*, I *might have **been***
che tu *avessi avuto*	che tu *fossi stato (-a)*
che egli *avesse avuto*	che egli *fosse stato*
	che ella *fosse stata*
che noi *avessimo avuto*	che noi *fossimo stati (-e)*
che voi *aveste avuto*	che voi *foste stati (-e)*
che essi *avessero avuto*	che essi *fossero stati*
	che esse *fossero state*

NOTES: 1. The subjunctive is usually introduced by the word *che*.

2. The meanings given for the subjunctive are not complete. They can best be learned when the uses of the subjunctive are taken up.

THE INFINITIVE

PRESENT

avere	**essere**
to have	to be

PAST

avere avuto	**essere stato**
to have had	to have been

THE PARTICIPLE

PRESENT

avente	(missing)
having	

PAST

avuto	**stato**
had	been

THE GERUND
PRESENT

avendo
having

essendo
being

PAST

avendo avuto
having had

essendo stato
having been

§ 48 The First Conjugation

amare to love

INDICATIVE MOOD

PRESENT	PRESENT PERFECT
io *amo*	io *ho amato*
I *love,* I *do love,* I *am loving*	I *loved,* I *have loved*
tu *ami*	tu *hai amato*
egli *ama*	egli *ha amato*
noi *amiamo*	noi *abbiamo amato*
voi *amate*	voi *avete amato*
essi *amano*	essi *hanno amato*

IMPERFECT	PLUPERFECT
io *amavo*	io *avevo amato*
I *loved,* I *used to love,* I *was loving*	I *had loved*
tu *amavi*	tu *avevi amato*
egli *amava*	egli *aveva amato*
noi *amavamo*	noi *avevamo amato*
voi *amavate*	voi *avevate amato*
essi *amavano*	essi *avevano amato*

PAST DEFINITE	PAST ANTERIOR
io *amai*	io *ebbi amato*
I *loved*	I *had loved*
tu *amasti*	tu *avesti amato*
egli *amò*	egli *ebbe amato*
noi *amammo*	noi *avemmo amato*
voi *amaste*	voi *aveste amato*
essi *amarono*	essi *ebbero amato*

FUTURE	FUTURE PERFECT
io *amerò*	io *avrò amato*
I *will* (or *shall*) *love*	I *will* (or *shall*) *have loved*
tu *amerai*	tu *avrai amato*
egli *amerà*	egli *avrà amato*
noi *ameremo*	noi *avremo amato*
voi *amerete*	voi *avrete amato*
essi *ameranno*	essi *avranno amato*

Conditional Mood

PRESENT	PAST
io amerei I *would* (or *should*) *love*	**io avrei amato** I *would* (or *should*) *have loved*
tu ameresti	**tu avresti amato**
egli amerebbe	**egli avrebbe amato**
noi ameremmo	**noi avremmo amato**
voi amereste	**voi avreste amato**
essi amerebbero	**essi avrebbero amato**

Imperative

ama love	**amiamo** let us love
ami love, let him love, let her love	**amate** love
	amino love, let them love

Subjunctive Mood

PRESENT	PAST
che io ami I *love*, I *may love*	**che io abbia amato** I *have loved*, I *may have loved*
che tu ami	**che tu abbia amato**
che egli ami	**che egli abbia amato**
che noi amiamo	**che noi abbiamo amato**
che voi amiate	**che voi abbiate amato**
che essi amino	**che essi abbiamo amato**

IMPERFECT	PLUPERFECT
che io amassi I *loved*, I *might love*	**che io avessi amato** I *had loved*, I *might have loved*
che tu amassi	**che tu avessi amato**
che egli amasse	**che egli avesse amato**
che noi amassimo	**che noi avessimo amato**
che voi amaste	**che voi aveste amato**
che essi amassero	**che essi avessero amato**

The Infinitive

PRESENT	PAST
amare to love	**avere amato** to have loved

The Participle

PRESENT	PAST
amante loving, lover	**amato** loved

THE GERUND

PRESENT	PAST
amando	avendo *amato*
loving	having loved

Verbs of the first conjugation have certain peculiarities:

1. Verbs which in the infinitive end in *-care* and *-gare* take an *h* between the stem and the ending when the ending is or begins with *e* or *i*.

PRESENT

cercare	pagare
to look for	to pay
io cerco	io pago
tu *cerchi*	tu *paghi*
egli cerca	egli paga
noi *cerchiamo*	noi *paghiamo*
voi cercate	voi pagate
essi cercano	essi pagano

FUTURE

io *cercherò*	io *pagherò*
I *shall look for*	I *shall pay*
tu *cercherai*	tu *pagherai*
egli *cercherà*	egli *pagherà*
noi *cercheremo*	noi *pagheremo*
voi *cercherete*	voi *pagherete*
essi *cercheranno*	essi *pagheranno*

CONDITIONAL

io *cercherei*	*io pagherei*
I *should look for*	I *should pay*
tu *cercheresti*	tu *pagheresti*
egli *cercherebbe*	egli *pagherebbe*
noi *cercheremmo*	noi *pagheremmo*
voi *cerchereste*	voi *paghereste*
essi *cercherebbero*	essi *pagherebbero*

IMPERATIVE

cerca	paga
look for	pay
cerchi	*paghi*
cerchiamo	*paghiamo*
cercate	pagate
cerchino	*paghino*

PRESENT SUBJUNCTIVE

che io *cerchi* I *look for*	che io *paghi* I *may pay*
che tu *cerchi*	che tu *paghi*
che egli *cerchi*	che egli *paghi*
che noi *cerchiamo*	che noi *paghiamo*
che voi *cerchiate*	che voi *paghiate*
che essi *cerchino*	che essi *paghino*

2. Verbs which in the infinitive end in *-ciare* and *-giare* drop the *i* before *e* or *i*. This occurs in the *tu* and *noi* forms of the present indicative, in the *lei, noi,* and *loro* forms of the imperative, and the whole future, conditional, and present subjunctive tenses.

3. Other verbs which end in *-iare* drop the *i* only when the ending is or begins with *i*, except when in the first person singular of the present the stress falls on the *i*, as in *inviare* (to send) and *spiare* (to spy):

> **Che cosa mi *consigli?***
> What *do you advise* me?
>
> **Perchè vi *annoiate?***
> Why *are* you *bored?*
>
> **Egli ti *consiglierà* di fare questo.**
> He *will advise* you to do this.

BUT:

> **A chi *invii* questa lettera?**
> To whom *are you sending* this letter?

§ 49   The Second Conjugation

temere   to fear

INDICATIVE MOOD

PRESENT

io *temo*
I *fear,* I *do fear,* I *am fearing*

tu *temi*

egli *teme*

noi *temiamo*

voi *temete*

essi *temono*

PRESENT PERFECT

io *ho temuto*
I *feared,* I *have feared*

tu *hai temuto*

egli *ha temuto*

noi *abbiamo temuto*

voi *avete temuto*

essi *hanno temuto*

IMPERFECT

io *temevo*
I *feared,* I *used to fear,* I *was fearing*

tu *temevi*

egli *temeva*

noi *temevamo*

voi *temevate*

essi *temevano*

PLUPERFECT

io *avevo temuto*
I *had feared*

tu *avevi temuto*

egli *aveva temuto*

noi *avevamo temuto*

voi *avevate temuto*

essi *avevano temuto*

PAST DEFINITE	PAST ANTERIOR
io *temei* or *temetti* I *feared*	io *ebbi temuto* I *had feared*
tu *temesti*	tu *avesti temuto*
egli *temè* or *temette*	egli *ebbe temuto*
noi *tememmo*	noi *avemmo temuto*
voi *temeste*	voi *aveste temuto*
essi *temerono* or *temettero*	essi *ebbero temuto*

FUTURE	FUTURE PERFECT
io *temerò* I *will* (or *shall*) *fear*	io *avrò temuto* I *will* (or *shall*) *have feared*
tu *temerai*	tu *avrai temuto*
egli *temerà*	egli *avrà temuto*
noi *temeremo*	noi *avremo temuto*
voi *temerete*	voi *avrete temuto*
essi *temeranno*	essi *avranno temuto*

CONDITIONAL MOOD

PRESENT	PAST
io *temerei* I *would* (or *should*) *fear*	io *avrei temuto* I *would* (or *should*) *have feared*
tu *temeresti*	tu *avresti temuto*
egli *temerebbe*	egli *avrebbe temuto*
noi *temeremmo*	noi *avremmo temuto*
voi *temereste*	voi *avreste temuto*
essi *temerebbero*	essi *avrebbero temuto*

IMPERATIVE

temi fear	temiamo let us fear
tema fear, let him fear, let her fear	temete fear
	temano fear, let them fear

SUBJUNCTIVE MOOD

PRESENT	PAST
che io *tema* I *fear*, I *may fear*	che io *abbia temuto* I *have feared*, I *may have feared*
che tu *tema*	che tu *abbia temuto*
che egli *tema*	che egli *abbia temuto*
che noi *temiamo*	che noi *abbiamo temuto*
che voi *temiate*	che voi *abbiate temuto*
che essi *temano*	che essi *abbiano temuto*

IMPERFECT	PLUPERFECT
che io *temessi* I *feared*, I *might fear*	che io *avessi temuto* I *had feared*, I *might have feared*
che tu *temessi*	che tu *avessi temuto*
che egli *temesse*	che egli *avesse temuto*
che noi *temessimo*	che noi *avessimo temuto*
che voi *temeste*	che voi *aveste temuto*
che essi *temessero*	che essi *avessero temuto*

THE INFINITIVE

PRESENT	PAST
temere to fear	avere temuto to have feared

THE PARTICIPLE

PRESENT	PAST
temente fearing	temuto feared

THE GERUND

PRESENT	PAST
temendo fearing	avendo temuto having feared

§ 50 The Third Conjugation

The third conjugation verbs are of two kinds: the normal ones, like *dormire* (to sleep), and the *-isco* verbs, like *finire* (to finish). The *-isco* verbs have this peculiarity: in the singular and in the third person plural of the present indicative, imperative, and present subjunctive they take *-isc* between the stem of the verb and the ending. You can identify a verb as an *-isco* verb if only one consonant precedes the infinitive ending *ire*. If two or more consonants precede the infinitive ending *-ire* then it is not an *-isco* verb. There are exceptions, however.

finire   to finish

PRESENT INDICATIVE

io *finisco* I *finish*, I *do finish*, I *am finishing*	noi *finiamo*
tu *finisci*	voi *finite*
egli *finisce*	essi *finiscono*

IMPERATIVE

finisci finish	finiamo let us finish
finisca let him finish, let her finish	finite finish
	finiscano let them finish

Present Subjunctive

che io *finisca* I *finish*, I *may finish*	che noi *finiamo*
che tu *finisca*	che voi *finiate*
che egli *finisca*	che essi *finiscano*

In all the other tenses the -*isco* verbs follow the pattern of *dormire*.

dormire   to sleep

Indicative Mood

PRESENT	PRESENT PERFECT
io *dormo* I *sleep*, I *do sleep*, I *am sleeping*	io *ho dormito* I *slept*, I *have slept*
tu *dormi*	tu *hai dormito*
egli *dorme*	egli *ha dormito*
noi *dormiamo*	noi *abbiamo dormito*
voi *dormite*	voi *avete dormito*
essi *dormono*	essi *hanno dormito*

IMPERFECT	PLUPERFECT
io *dormivo* I *slept*, I *used to sleep*, I *was sleeping*	io *avevo dormito* I *had slept*
tu *dormivi*	tu *avevi dormito*
egli *dormiva*	egli *aveva dormito*
noi *dormivamo*	noi *avevamo dormito*
voi *dormivate*	voi *avevate dormito*
essi *dormivano*	essi *avevano dormito*

PAST DEFINITE	PAST ANTERIOR
io *dormii* I *slept*	io *ebbi dormito* I *had slept*
tu *dormisti*	tu *avesti dormito*
egli *dormì*	egli *ebbe dormito*
noi *dormimmo*	noi *avemmo dormito*
voi *dormiste*	voi *aveste dormito*
essi *dormirono*	essi *ebbero dormito*

FUTURE	FUTURE PERFECT
io *dormirò* I *will* (or *shall*) *sleep*	io *avrò dormito* I *will* (or *shall*) *have slept*
tu *dormirai*	tu *avrai dormito*
egli *dormirà*	egli *avrà dormito*
noi *dormiremo*	noi *avremo dormito*
voi *dormirete*	voi *avrete dormito*
essi *dormiranno*	essi *avranno dormito*

CONDITIONAL MOOD

PRESENT	PAST
io *dormirei*	**io *avrei dormito***
I *would* (or *should*) *sleep*	I *would* (or *should*) *have slept*
tu *dormiresti*	**tu *avresti dormito***
egli *dormirebbe*	**egli *avrebbe dormito***
noi *dormiremmo*	**noi *avremmo dormito***
voi *dormireste*	**voi *avreste dormito***
essi *dormirebbero*	**essi *avrebbero dormito***

IMPERATIVE

dormi	**dormiamo**
sleep	let us sleep
dorma	**dormite**
sleep, let him sleep, let	sleep
her sleep	**dormano**
	sleep, let them sleep

SUBJUNCTIVE MOOD

PRESENT	PAST
che io *dorma*	**che io *abbia dormito***
I *sleep*, I *may sleep*	I *have slept*, I *may have slept*
che tu *dorma*	**che tu *abbia dormito***
che egli *dorma*	**che egli *abbia dormito***
che noi *dormiamo*	**che noi *abbiamo dormito***
che voi *dormiate*	**che voi *abbiate dormito***
che essi *dormano*	**che essi *abbiano dormito***

IMPERFECT	PLUPERFECT
che io *dormissi*	**che io *avessi dormito***
I *slept*, I *might sleep*	I *had slept*, I *might have slept*
che tu *dormissi*	**che tu *avessi dormito***
che egli *dormisse*	**che egli *avesse dormito***
che noi *dormissimo*	**che noi *avessimo dormito***
che voi *dormiste*	**che voi *aveste dormito***
che essi *dormissero*	**che essi *avessero dormito***

THE INFINITIVE

PRESENT	PAST
dormire	**avere dormito**
to sleep	to have slept

THE PARTICIPLE

PRESENT	PAST
dormente	**dormito**
sleeping	slept

THE GERUND

PRESENT	PAST
dormendo	**avendo dormito**
sleeping	having slept

§ 51　Verbs with the Auxiliary *Essere*

1. The great majority of Italian verbs are conjugated with the auxiliary verb *avere* in the compound tenses. However, there are several important verbs which take the auxiliary verb *essere*. The most common of these verbs are:

andare to go	**arrivare** *or* 　**giungere** to arrive	**essere** to be
venire to come	**ritornare** to return	**salire** to climb, to go up
entrare to enter	**diventare** to become	**scendere** to descend, to go down
uscire to go out	**nascere** to be born	**rimanere** to remain
cadere to fall	**morire** to die	**restare** to remain
partire to leave		

NOTES: a. *Morire* is commonly used only in the third person:

　　La povera vecchia è morta ieri.
　　The poor old lady died yesterday.

　b. *Salire* and *scendere* take the auxiliary verb *avere* if they have a direct object:

　　Ho salito le scale lentamente.
　　I climbed the stairs slowly.

BUT:

　　Sono salito lentamente.
　　I climbed slowly.

2. Reflexive verbs take the auxiliary *essere* [See § 52].

3. Verbs used in the passive voice take the auxiliary *essere*:

Questa canzone è conosciuta dappertutto.
This song *is* known everywhere.

NOTE: The passive voice is used rather infrequently in Italian. More often than not the impersonal expression is used instead when no subject is mentioned. Thus the above example would be written:

Questa canzone si conosce dappertutto.

4. Impersonal verbs (used only in the third person singular) take the auxiliary *essere*:

È necessario fare questo.
It *is necessary* to do this.

Era impossibile partire a quell'ora.
It *was impossible* to leave at that hour.

However, most impersonal expressions denoting metereological facts may take either *essere* or *avere*:

È piovuto (or *ha* **piovuto**) **tutta la notte.**
It rained the whole night.

5. The past participle of verbs conjugated with *essere* agrees in gender and number with the subject:

> **Esse sono *andate* a casa.**
> They went home.
>
> **I ragazzi si sono *divertiti*.**
> The children enjoyed themselves.
>
> **Maria è *arrivata* questa mattina.**
> Mary arrived this morning.
>
> **Quando è *nato* questo ragazzo?**
> When was this boy *born?*

6. Here is the complete conjugation of the compound tenses of *andare,* one of the verbs that takes the auxiliary *essere*:

PRESENT PERFECT	PLUPERFECT INDICATIVE
io *sono andato (-a)*	io *ero andato (-a)*
I *went,* I *have gone*	I *had gone*
tu *sei andato (-a)*	tu *eri andato (-a)*
lei *è andato (-a)*	lei *era andato (-a)*
egli *è andato*	egli *era andato*
ella *è andata*	ella *era andata*
noi *siamo andati (-e)*	noi *eravamo andati (-e)*
voi *siete andati (-e)*	voi *eravate andati (-e)*
loro *sono andati (-e)*	loro *erano andati (-e)*
essi *sono andati*	essi *erano andati*
esse *sono andate*	esse *erano andate*

PAST ANTERIOR	FUTURE PERFECT
io *fui andato (-a)*	io *sarò andato (-a)*
I *had gone*	I *shall have gone*
tu *fosti andato (-a)*	tu *sarai andato (-a)*
lei *fu andato (-a)*	lei *sarà andato (-a)*
egli *fu andato*	egli *sarà andato*
ella *fu andata*	ella *sarà andata*
noi *fummo andati (-e)*	noi *saremo andati (-e)*
voi *foste andati (-e)*	voi *sarete andati (-e)*
loro *furono andati (-e)*	loro *saranno andati (-e)*
essi *furono andati*	essi *saranno andati*
esse *furono andate*	esse *saranno andate*

PAST CONDITIONAL	
io *sarei andato (-a)*	noi *saremmo andati (-e)*
I *would* (or *should) have gone*	
tu *saresti andato (-a)*	voi *sareste andati (-e)*
lei *sarebbe andato (-a)*	loro *sarebbero undati (-a)*
egli *sarebbe andato*	essi *sarebbero andati*
ella *sarebbe andata*	esse *sarebbero andate*

PAST SUBJUNCTIVE	PLUPERFECT SUBJUNCTIVE
che io *sia andato (-a)* that I *have gone,* that I *may have gone*	che io *fossi andato (-a)* that I *had gone,* that I *might have gone*
che *tu* sia andato *(-a)*	che tu *fossi andato (-a)*
che lei *sia andato (-a)*	che lei *fosse andato (-a)*
che egli *sia andato*	che egli *fosse andato*
che ella *sia andata*	che ella *fosse andata*
che noi *siamo andati (-e)*	che noi *fossimo andati (-e)*
che voi *siate andati (-e)*	che voi *foste andati (-e)*
che loro *siano andati (-e)*	che loro *fossero andati (-e)*
che essi *siano andati*	che essi *fossero andati*
che esse *siano andate*	che esse *fossero andate*

PAST INFINITIVE

essere andato
to have gone

PAST GERUND

essendo andato
having gone

§ 52   The Reflexive Verbs

1. The infinitive of reflexive verbs in Italian ends in *-si*: *lavarsi* (to wash oneself), *sedersi* (to sit), *pentirsi* (to repent).

2. A reflexive verb is conjugated like any active verb. Each verb form, however, must be preceded by the reflexive pronoun (except as explained in 5 below):

io *mi* lavo I wash *myself*	noi *ci* laviamo
tu *ti* lavi	voi *vi* lavate
lei *si* lava	loro *si* lavano
egli *si* lava	essi *si* lavano
ella *si* lava	esse *si* lavano

3. In the compound tenses reflexive verbs take the auxiliary *essere*, and the past participle agrees with the subject, unless it is followed by a direct object:

io *mi sono lavato (-a)* I have washed *myself*	noi *ci siamo lavati (-e)*
tu *ti sei lavato (-a)*	voi *vi siete lavati (-e)*
lei *si è lavato (-a)*	loro *si sono lavati (-e)*
egli *si è lavato*	essi *si sono lavati*
ella *si è lavata*	esse *si sono lavate*

4. When a reflexive verb is followed by a direct object the past participle agrees with the direct object:

Io mi sono *lavate* le mani.
I washed my hands.

5. The reflexive pronouns are attached to the *tu, noi,* and *voi* forms of the affirmative imperative, to the infinitive, to the past participle when used alone, and to the gerund:

Alza*ti*, Carlo.
Get up, Charles.

Alziamo*ci* insieme.
Let's get up together.

Alzate*vi* presto.
Get up early.

Alzato*si*, prese il cappello ed uscì.
After he got up he took his hat and went out.

Alzando*mi* di buon'ora io riesco a fare molto lavoro.
By getting up early I succeed in doing a great deal of work.

Essendo*si* alzato incominciò subito a lavorare.
Having gotten up he quickly began to work.

6. The reflexive pronouns *mi, ti, si, ci,* and *vi* become *me, te, se, ce,* and *ve* when used in combination with another pronoun [See § 29]:

Io *mi* sono lavate le mani; io *me* le sono lavate.
I washed my hands; I washed them.

Egli *si* è pentito di ciò che ha fatto; egli *se* n'è pentito.
He has repented for what he did; he repented for it.

7. Many reflexive verbs in Italian are not reflexive in English. Here is a list of some of the most common Italian reflexive verbs:

accontentarsi di
to be satisfied

abituarsi
to get accustomed

addormentarsi
to fall asleep

affrettarsi
to hurry

allontanarsi
to move away

alzarsi
to get up, to rise

annoiarsi
to feel annoyed, bored

arrabbiarsi
to get angry

asciugarsi
to dry oneself

avvicinarsi
to approach

bagnarsi
to get wet, bathe

chiamarsi
to be called

coricarsi
to go to bed

divertirsi
to enjoy oneself, to have a good time

fermarsi
to stop

fidarsi
to trust

innamorarsi
to fall in love

ingannarsi
to be mistaken

lavarsi
to wash oneself

lamentarsi
to complain

meravigliarsi
to wonder

mettersi a
to start, to begin

pentirsi
to repent

pettinarsi
to comb (oneself)

radersi
to shave (oneself)

raffreddarsi
to get cold, to catch a cold

rallegrarsi
to rejoice

ricordarsi
to remember

sbagliarsi
to be mistaken

scusarsi
to excuse oneself

sedersi
to sit

sentirsi bene
to feel well

spaventarsi
to be frightened

spogliarsi
to undress

svegliarsi
to wake up

vergognarsi
to be ashamed

vestirsi
to dress

voltarsi
to turn (oneself)

§ 53 Impersonal Verbs

1. Impersonal verbs are so called because they have no definite subject. Impersonal verbs are used only in the third person singular. Impersonal verbs express a fact, a phenomenon, or a condition. In English the subject of an impersonal verb is "it."

2. Several impersonal expressions refer to weather conditions. Here are the most common:

fa bel tempo the weather is fine	**lampeggia** it is lightning
fa cattivo (*or* mal) tempo the weather is bad	**gela** it is freezing
fa caldo it is hot *or* warm	**grandina** it is hailing
fa freddo it is cold	**tira vento** it is windy
fa fresco it is cool	**si scivola** it is slippery
piove it is raining	**c'è fango** it is muddy
nevica it is snowing	**c'è umidità** it is damp, humid
tuona it is thundering	

3. Of the above expressions, those with *fare* take the auxiliary *avere* in the compound tenses; the others may take either *avere* or *essere*:

Ha fatto freddo. It has been cold.	**Ha piovuto *or* è piovuto.** It has rained.
Ha nevicato *or* è nevicato. It has snowed.	

C'è fango and *c'è umidità,* of course, have the verb *essere*.

4. There are many other impersonal verbs. Here is a partial list of the most common ones. All of these take *essere* in the compound tenses.

accade it happens	**basta** it is enough	**è meglio** it is better
bisogna it is necessary	**occorre** it is required	**è certo** it is certain
importa it matters	**vale la pena** it is worth while	**è impossibile** it is impossible
conviene it is proper, fitting	**è necessario** it is necessary	**è giusto** it is right
piace it is pleasing	**è possibile** it is possible	**è tempo** it is time
sembra it seems	**è probabile** it is probable	**è evidente** it is evident

§ 54 The Present Indicative Tense

1. The present indicative of regular verbs is formed as follows:

FIRST CONJUGATION: Drop -are and add: -o, -i, -a, -iamo, -ate, -ano [See § 48]

parlare io parlo

SECOND CONJUGATION: Drop -ere and add: -o, -i, -e, -iamo, -ete, -ono [See § 49]

perdere io perdo

THIRD CONJUGATION: Drop -ire and add: -o, -i, -e, -iamo, -ite, -ono [See § 50]

dormire io dorno

2. The present indicative in Italian is used to express the three forms of the English present:

Io compro il giornale. { I *buy* the newspaper. (Habitual Present)
I *do buy* the newspaper. (Emphatic Present)
I *am buying* the newspaper. (Progressive Present)

3. However, there is a progressive present in Italian also. It is formed by using a form of the verb *stare* before the present gerund of the desired verb. This progressive present is used mostly for emphasis:

Io sto leggendo il giornale.
I *am* reading the newspaper.

Il babbo stava scrivendo una lettera.
Dad *was* writing a letter.

4. In addition to its normal function, the present tense is used in Italian to indicate an action begun in the past but continuing in the present.

Io aspetto da un'ora.
I *have been waiting* for an hour.

Da quanto tempo sei qui?
How long *have* you *been* here?

§ 55 The Present Perfect Tense

1. The present perfect is formed by the present indicative of the auxiliary verb and the past participle of the desired verb. The past participle of regular verbs is formed as follows:

FIRST CONJUGATION: Drop -are and add -ato

parlare io ho parlato

SECOND CONJUGATION: Drop -ere and add -uto

perdere io ho perduto

THIRD CONJUGATION: Drop -ire and add -ito

dormire io ho dormito

2. The present perfect is used to express an action that took place recently or within a period of time not yet completed, such as this week, this month, this season, this year, this century.

Egli *ha comprato* un'automobile.
He *bought* a car (recently, understood).

Quest'anno *ho guadagnato* poco.
This year I *earned* little.

3. With such expressions as *ieri* (yesterday), *la settimana scorsa* (last week), and *il mese scorso* (last month), the past definite may be used, but in common usage the present perfect is preferred:

La settimana scorsa *siamo andati* (or *andammo*) in campagna.
Last week we *went* to the country.

4. Although all the important irregular verbs are listed in the table of irregular verbs, the student ought to familiarize himself with the present perfect of the most common irregular verbs, here listed:

bere	**essere**	**rompere**
to drink	to be	to break
io ho *bevuto*	io sono *stato*	io ho *rotto*
aprire	**fare**	**scegliere**
to open	to do, make	to select
io ho *aperto*	io ho *fatto*	io ho *scelto*
apprendere	**leggere**	**scendere**
to learn	to read	to descend, go down
io ho *appreso*	io ho *letto*	io sono *sceso*
chiudere	**mettere**	**scrivere**
to close	to put	to write
io ho *chiuso*	io ho *messo*	io ho *scritto*
coprire	**offendere**	**spendere**
to cover	to offend	to spend
io ho *coperto*	io ho *offeso*	io ho *speso*
correggere	**offrire**	**tradurre**
to correct	to offer	to translate
io ho *corretto*	io ho *offerto*	io ho *tradotto*
decidere	**prendere**	**vedere**
to decide	to take	to see
io ho *deciso*	io ho *preso*	io ho *visto*
dire	**ridere**	**vincere**
to say, tell	to laugh	to win
io ho *detto*	io ho *riso*	io ho *vinto*
dividere	**rispondere**	
to divide	to answer	
io ho *diviso*	io ho *risposto*	

§ 56   The Past Definite Tense

1. The past definite of regular verbs is formed as follows:

FIRST CONJUGATION: Drop *-are* and add: *-ai, -asti, -ò, -ammo, -aste, -arono* [See § 48]

parlare   io parl*ai*

SECOND CONJUGATION: Drop *ere* and add: *-ei, -esti, -è, -emmo, -este, erono* [See § 49]

    perdere io perdei

THIRD CONJUGATION: Drop *ire* and add: *-ii, -isti, -ì, -immo, -iste, -irono* [See § 50]

    dormire io dormii

2. The past definite is used to express an action which took place long ago, in narratives, and in expressions indicating elapsed time, such as *l'anno scorso* (last year), *due anni fa* (two years ago), etc.

    I soldati attaccarono la fortezza.
    The soldiers attacked the fortress (a considerable lapse of time understood)

    Cinque anni fa *comprai* una casa.
    Five years ago I bought a house.

The past definite *is not used* when the verb expresses:

    a. a continued action in the past.

    b. a habitual or customary action in the past.

    c. a description in the past [See §58 below].

§ 57 The Past Anterior Tense

1. The past anterior is formed by the past definite of the auxiliary verb and the past participle of the desired verb [See § 48, 49, 50].

2. The past anterior is used to express something that *had happened,* usually after the words *appena* (as soon as), *quando* (when), and *dopo* (after). Otherwise the pluperfect is used in preference to this tense.

    Dopo che *ebbi finito* il lavoro egli mi pagò.
    After I *had finished* the work he paid me.

    Appena essi *furono partiti* noi andammo a letto.
    As soon as they *had left* we went to bed.

§ 58 The Imperfect Indicative Tense

1. The imperfect indicative of regular verbs is formed as follows:

FIRST CONJUGATION: Drop *-are* and add: *-avo, -avi, -ava, -avamo, -avate, -avano* [See § 48]

    parlare io parlavo

SECOND CONJUGATION: Drop *-ere* and add: *-evo, -evi, -eva, -evamo, -evate, -evano* [See § 49]

    perdere io perdevo

THIRD CONJUGATION: Drop *-ire* and add: *-ivo, -ivi, -iva, -ivamo, -ivate, -ivano* [See § 50]

    dormire io dormivo

2. The imperfect is used:

a. To indicate an incomplete or continuing action in the past:

Il professore *spiegava* la lezione.
The professor *was explaining* the lesson.

A quell'epoca l'Italia non *era* una nazione unita.
At that time Italy *was* not a united nation.

Io *suonavo* il pianoforte mentre ella *cantava*.
I *played* (or *was playing*) the piano while she *sang* (or *was singing*).

b. To express customary, habitual, or continually recurring actions .These notions are usually conveyed in English by the phrase "used to" or "kept (doing)." Even though a different form of the verb may be used in English, the imperfect must be used in Italian if the phrase "used to" or "kept (doing)" can be substituted:

Io mi *alzavo* alle sette ogni mattina. { I *got up* at seven o'clock every morning.
{ I *used to get up* at seven o'clock every morning.
{ I *would get up* at seven o'clock every morning.

NOTE: "Would" is the characteristic word of the conditional. However, if it means "used to," the imperfect must be used, not the conditional.

c. In description in the past, no matter what tense is used in English:

Tutti gli alberi *erano* in fiore.
All the trees *were* in bloom.

Il castello *dominava* il villaggio.
The castle *overlooked* the village.

Quando *ero* bambino *avevo* i capelli biondi.
When I *was* a child I *had* blond hair.

§ 59 The Pluperfect Indicative Tense

1. The pluperfect is formed by the imperfect of the auxiliary verb and the past participle of the desired verb [See § 48, § 49, § 50].

2. The pluperfect in Italian has the same function as the pluperfect in English and presents no problem in translation. It expresses something that *had happened,* the same as the past anterior [See § 57 above].

La moglie *aveva parlato* troppo.
The wife *had spoken* too much.

Esse *erano arrivate* prima di noi.
They *had arrived* before us.

§ 60 The Future Tense

1. The future of regular verbs is formed as follows:

FIRST CONJUGATION: Drop *-are* and add: *-erò, -erai, -erà, -eremo, -erete, -eranno* [See § 48]

parlare   io parlerò

SECOND CONJUGATION: Drop -ere and add: -erò, -erai, -erà, -eremo, -erete, -eranno [See §49]
> perdere   io perderò

THIRD CONJUGATION: Drop -ire and add: -irò, -irai, -irà, -iremo, -irete, -iranno [See § 50]
> dormire   io dormirò

2. The future is used to express an action that will happen at some future time:
> Essi *partiranno* domani sera.
> They *will leave* tomorrow night.

3. The future is also used after the words *se* (if), *quando* (when), and *appena* (as soon as) when a future action is implied, even though in English the present is used:
> Noi pranzeremo appena il babbo *verrà*.
> We shall have dinner as soon as dad *comes.*
>
> Quando *leggerai* il libro *vedrai* che ho ragione.
> When you *read* the book you *will see* that I am right.
>
> Se lei *canterà* io *suonerò* il violino.
> If you *sing* I *shall play* the violin.

4. The future is also used to express probability in the speaker's mind:
> Ella *sarà* ammalata.
> She *is probably* ill.

5. The expression "to be about to" is translated by *stare per*:
> Io *stavo* per uscire.
> I *was about to* go out.

6. All the important irregular verbs are listed and conjugated in the table of irregular verbs. However, the student ought to familiarize himself with the future of the most common irregular verbs, here listed:
> **andare**
> to go
> **andrò, andrai, andrà, andremo, andrete, andranno**
>
> **avere**
> to have
> **avrò, avrai, avrà, avremo, avrete, avranno**
>
> **bere**
> to drink
> **berrò, berrai, berrà, berremo, berrete, berranno**
>
> **dare**
> to give
> **darò, darai, darà, daremo, darete, daranno**
>
> **dire**
> to say, tell
> **dirò, dirai, dirà, diremo, direte, diranno**

dovere
to have to, must
dovrò, dovrai, dovrà, dovremo, dovrete, dovranno

essere
to be
sarò, sarai, sarà, saremo, sarete, saranno

fare
to do, make
farò, farai, farà, faremo, farete, faranno

potere
to be able to, may, can
potrò, potrai, potrà, potremo, potrete, potranno

rimanere
to remain
rimarrò, rimarrai, rimarrà, rimarremo, rimarrete, rimarranno

sapere
to know
saprò, saprai, saprà, sapremo, saprete, sapranno

stare
to stay
starò, starai, starà, staremo, starete, staranno

tenere
to hold
terrò, terrai, terrà, terremo, terrete, terranno

vedere
to see
vedrò, vedrai, vedrà, vedremo, vedrete, vedranno

venire
to come
verrò, verrai, verrà, verremo, verrete, verranno

volere
to want
vorrò, vorrai, vorrà, vorremo, vorrete, vorranno

§ 61   The Future Perfect Tense

1. The future perfect is formed by the future of the auxiliary verb and the past participle of the desired verb [See § 48, § 49, § 50].

2. The rules for the use of the future perfect are the same as those given for the use of the future:

> **Uscirò dopo che *avrò finito* di mangiare.**
> I shall go out after I (shall) *have finished* eating.

> **Ella *sarà stata* ammalata.**
> She *has probably been* ill.

§ 62 The Present Conditional

1. The present conditional of regular verbs is formed as follows:

FIRST CONJUGATION: Drop -are and add: -erei, -eresti, -erebbe, -eremmo, -ereste, -erebbero [See § 48]

parlare   io parlerei

SECOND CONJUGATION: Drop -ere and add: -erei, -eresti, -erebbe, -eremmo, ereste, -erebbero [See § 49]

perdere   io perderei

THIRD CONJUGATION: Drop -ire and add: -irei, -iresti, -irebbe, -iremmo, ireste, -irebbero [See § 50]

dormire   io dormirei

2. Whereas the conditional tense in English uses the auxiliaries "should" and "would", the Italian conditional consists of one word. Before deciding whether these auxiliaries in English are an indication of the Italian conditional, analyze them according to the following principles:

a. If "would" means "used to", the verb in question will be imperfect and not conditional [See Note, § 58-2-6].

b. If "would" means "wanted" the imperfect of *volere* is used:

Egli non *voleva* partire.   {He *would* not leave.
                                  {He *did not want* to leave.

c. If "should" means "ought" the conditional of *dovere* is used:

Voi *dovreste* studiare di più.
You *should (ought to)* study more.

3. Otherwise, the conditional is used in the same manner as in English.

Io *uscirei* volentieri con quella signorina.
I *would* willingly *go out* with that young lady.

Egli non *farebbe* mai una cosa simile.
He *would* never *do* such a thing.

4. The conditional is used to express probability in some one else's opinion:

Secondo lei io *sarei* ricco.
According to you I *am* rich.

§ 63 The Past Conditional Tense

1. The past conditional is formed by the present conditional of the auxiliary verb and the past participle of the desired verb [See § 39, § 40, § 41].

2. The rules for the use of the past conditional are the same as those given for the use of the present conditional.

Egli *sarebbe andato* là con piacere.
He *would have gone* there with pleasure.

Voi *avreste dovuto* studiare di più.
You *should (ought to) have studied* more.

§ 64 The Imperative Mood

1. The first person singular of the imperative does not exist. You cannot reasonably give yourself a command.

2. The *tu, lei, noi, voi,* and *loro* forms of the imperative express direct command, whereas the *egli, ella, essi,* and *esse* forms express indirect commands.

3. The imperative of regular verbs is formed as follows:

FIRST CONJUGATION: Drop *-are* and add: *-a, -i, -iamo, -ate, -ino* [See § 48]

    parlare parla

SECOND CONJUGATION: Drop *-ere* and add: *-i, -a, -iamo, -ete, -ano* [See § 49]

    perdere perdi

THIRD CONJUGATION: Drop *-ire* and add: *-i, -a, -iamo, -ite, -ano* [See § 50]

    dormire dormi

4. The personal pronouns are usually omitted in the imperative.

5. The negative forms (*non* before the verb) of the imperative are the same as the positive forms except the *tu* form, in which case the infinitive is used instead.

    Carlo, *mangia* la carne.
    Charles, *eat* the meat.

    Carlo, *non mangiare* la carne.
    Charles, *don't eat* the meat.

BUT:

    Ragazzi, *mangiate* la carne.
    Children, *eat* the meat.

    Ragazzi, *non mangiate* la carne.
    Children, *don't eat* the meat.

6. The *noi* form of the imperative is translated by "let us (let's)".

    Andiamo in campagna.
    Let's go to the country.

7. The *egli, ella, essi,* and *esse* forms of the imperative are translated by "let him, let her, let them."

    Consulti un avvocato.
    Let him (her) consult a lawyer.

    Vendano la casa.
    Let them sell the house.

§ 65   The Subjunctive Mood

The subjunctive mood in Italian is used in dependent clauses in which action is presented as a possibility and not as a fact. The tenses of the subjunctive are the present, past or perfect, imperfect, and pluperfect.

1. *Uses of the Subjunctive*

The subjunctive is always used in a subordinate clause. It is the verb in the main clause that determines whether the verb in the subordinate clause should be subjunctive or not. The subjunctive must be used when the verb in the main clause is one of:

a. *Volition, Wishing, Desiring, Ordering:*

Egli *vuole* che io *compri* questo libro.
He *wants me to buy* this book.

Io *desidero* che voi *impariate* questa lezione.
I *want you to learn* this lesson.

Il generale *ordina* che i soldati *avanzino*.
The general *orders* that the soldiers *advance*.

b. *Doubt, Supposition, Hope, Belief:*

Io *dubito* che Giovanni *venga*.
I *doubt* that John *is coming*.

Crede lei che ella *sia* qui?
Do you *think* she *is* here?

Spero che ella *parli* allo zio.
I *hope* she *will speak* to (her) uncle.

Suppongo che egli *canti* bene.
I *suppose* he *sings* well.

c. *Emotion,* such as wonder, fear, personal feeling:

Mi dispiace che ella non *sia* qui.
I am sorry she *is* not here.

Egli *teme* che tu non *finisca* il lavoro.
He *is afraid* that you *will* not *finish* the work.

Ella è *felice* che io le *scriva* ogni giorno.
She *is happy* that I *write* to her every day.

d. The subjunctive is also used after impersonal expressions, except those which express certainty:

È necessario che *invitiate* anche il fratello.
It is necessary for *you to invite* the brother also.

È possibile che essi non *capiscano* l'italiano.
It is possible that they do not *understand* Italian.

È probabile che *vengano* anch'essi.
It is probable that they too *will come*.

È meglio che tu *spedisca* la lettera ora stesso.
It is better that you *send* the letter right now.

But:

È evidente che ella non *capisce* questa lingua.
It is evident that she *does* not *understand* this language.

È certo che egli non *lavora.*
It *is certain* that he *is* not *working.*

e. The subjunctive is used after an indefinite antecedent (that is, when the verb of the dependent clause refers to some person or thing which is not definite, certain or attained) and after such indefinite words as:

chiunque whoever	checchè whatever
qualunque whichever	qualsiasi cosa whatever
dovunque wherever	nessuno no one

Qui non c'è *nessuno* che *capisca* l'italiano.
There is *no one* here who *understands* Italian.

Dovunque egli *vada* c'è sempre *qualcuno* che lo conosce.
Wherever he *goes* there is always *someone* who knows him.

Checchè egli *dica,* non gli rispondere.
Whatever he *says,* don't answer him.

Voglio comprare *una casa* che non *costi* troppo.
I want to buy *a house* that *does* not *cost* too much.

Notice that in the last example, I have not bought the house yet, therefore *una casa* is an indefinite antecedent.

BUT:

Ecco una casa che non *costa* troppo.
Here is *a house* that *does* not *cost* too much.

Now the house is no longer indefinite, therefore no subjunctive is used.

f. The subjunctive is used after a relative superlative and after these words:

il primo the first	il solo the only
l'ultimo the last	l'unico the only

These words have the force of a superlative.

Egli è *il più ricco* uomo che ci *sia* al mondo.
He is *the richest* man (that there *is*) in the world.

Questo è *il libro più vecchio* che io *abbia.*
This is *the oldest book* I *have.*

Ella è *l'unica ragazza* che io *ami.*
She is *the only girl* I *love.*

Carlo e Maria sono *i soli* che *abbiano capito* quello che egli ha detto.
Charles and Mary are *the only ones* who *understood* what he said.

g. The subjunctive is used after adverbial expressions of time, purpose, condition, negation such as:

prima che before	a meno che unless	finchè until

affinchè in order that	**a patto che** on condition that	**in caso che** in case
di modo che so that	**benchè** although	**se mai** in case
senza che without	**sebbene** although	**perchè** in order that, so that
purchè provided that		

Voglio vederlo *prima che vada via.*
I want to see him *before he goes away.*

***Sebbene* egli *sia* ricco, non è felice.**
Although he *is* rich he is not happy.

Verrò *purchè venga* anche tu.
I *will come provided* you *come* too.

h. The imperfect or pluperfect subjunctive is used in *if* clauses which express a condition contrary to fact.

Se io *avessi* denaro farei quel viaggio.
If I *had* money I would take that trip.

(The implication is that I don't have the money, therefore a condition contrary to fact exists. Keep in mind that the verb of the main clause is in the conditional).

NOTE: The subjunctive is not used in simple conditions:

Se mi *scrivi sarò* molto felice.
If you write to me I shall be very happy.

2. *The Subjunctive Tenses*

THE PRESENT SUBJUNCTIVE

a. The present subjunctive of regular verbs is formed as follows:

FIRST CONJUGATION: Drop *-are* and add: *-i, -i, -i, -iamo, -iate, -ino* [See § 48]

parlare   io parl*i*

SECOND CONJUGATION: Drop *-ere* and add: *-a, -a, -a, -iamo, -iate, -ano* [See § 49]

perdere   io perd*a*

THIRD CONJUGATION: Drop *-ire* and add: *-a, -a, -a, -iamo, -iate, -ano.*

dormire   io dorm*a*

-isco verbs drop *-ire* and add: *-isca, -isca, -isca, -iamo, -iate, -iscano* [See § 50]

finire   io fin*isca*

b. The endings of the present subjunctive of all irregular verbs, regardless of what conjugation they belong to, are: *-a, -a, -a, -iamo, -iate, -ano.*

The above endings are added to the first person singular of the present indicative of the irregular verb, after the final o is dropped, to give the three persons of the singular and the third person plural. The first and second person plural (*noi* and *voi*) are formed from the first person plural of the irregular verb. Study the following:

	uscire	to go out (irreg. verb)
	PRES. IND.	PRES. SUBJ.
	io esco	che io esc*a*
	tu esci	che tu esc*a*
	lei esce	che lei esc*a*
	noi usciamo	che noi usc*iamo*
	voi uscite	che voi usc*iate*
	loro escono	che loro esc*ano*

EXCEPTION TO THE ABOVE RULE: The entire present subjunctive of the following five verbs is formed from the *noi* form of the present indicative:

	PRES. IND.	PRES. SUBJ.
avere to have	noi abbiamo	che io abb*ia*, che tu abb*ia*, etc.
essere to be	noi siamo	che io s*ia*, che tu s*ia*, etc.
dare to give	noi diamo	che io d*ia*, che tu d*ia*, etc.
stare to stay	noi stiamo	che io st*ia*, che tu st*ia*, etc.
sapere to know	noi sappiamo	che io sapp*ia*, che tu sapp*ia*, etc.

THE PAST SUBJUNCTIVE

c. The past subjunctive of regular verbs is formed by the present subjunctive of the auxiliary verb and the past participle of the desired verb.

d. When the verb of the main sentence is present or future, the past subjunctive is used if the action of the verb in the subjunctive clause occurred before the action of the verb in the main clause, no matter what the English says:

Io non *credo* che egli *sia partito.*
I *do* not *think* he *has left.*

Gli *dispiacerà* che tu non lo *abbia aspettato.*
He *will be sorry* that you *have* not *waited for* him.

However, if the action of the verb in the subjunctive clause did not occur before the action of the main verb, the present subjunctive is used even though the English may have a future:

Egli *dubita* che io *parta.* {He *doubts* that I *am leaving.* {He *doubts* that I *will leave.*

THE IMPERFECT SUBJUNCTIVE

e. The imperfect subjunctive of regular verbs is formed as follows:

FIRST CONJUGATION: Drop *-are* and add: *-assi, -assi, -asse, -assimo, -aste, -assero* [See § 48]

parlare **che io parl*assi***

SECOND CONJUGATION: Drop *-ere* and add: *-essi, -essi, -esse, -essimo, -este, -essero* [See § 49]

perdere **che io perd*essi***

THIRD CONJUGATION: Drop *-ire* and add: *-issi, -issi, -isse, -issimo, -iste, -issero* [See §50]

dormire **che io dorm*issi***

f. The imperfect subjunctive is used when the main verb is a past tense or conditional, and when the action of the subjunctive clause did not occur prior to the action of the main verb:

Egli *voleva* che io *cantassi*.
He *wanted me to sing.*

Egli *vorrebbe* che io *cantassi*.
He *would want me to sing.*

Io *ordinai* che essi *andassero* a dormire.
I *ordered them to go* to sleep.

THE PLUPERFECT SUBJUNCTIVE

g. The pluperfect subjunctive is formed by the imperfect subjunctive of the auxiliary verb and the past participle of the desired verb.

h. The pluperfect subjunctive is used when the main verb is a past tense or conditional and when the action of the subjunctive clause occurred before the action of the main verb:

Il prof*essore credeva* che noi *avessimo studiato*.
The professor *thought* we *had studied.*

Noi *avremmo studiato* se *avessimo avuto tempo*.
We *would have studied* if *we had had time.*

NOTES ON THE SUBJUNCTIVE:

i. If you study the examples given in the presentation of the subjunctive you will notice the different ways in which the Italian subjunctive can be translated into English. However, this should give you no reason for concern. Your first problem in translating into Italian is to determine whether conditions in the main verb require the use of the subjunctive in the subordinate clause. Your next problem is to select the proper verb and put it into the proper tense of the subjunctive according to the rules given, regardless of how the English sentence is worded.

j. Regardless of the rules, the subjunctive *is not used* when the verb in the subordinate clause indicates distant future or certainty. Thus, if you want to say: "I don't think he will go," if you want to imply that *his going* will take place at a future time, you will say in Italian: *"Non credo che egli andrà,"* even though *non credo* is a verb of doubt. Likewise, if you want to say: "She doesn't know that he has arrived," you will say: *"Ella non sa che egli è arrivato,"* because *è arrivato* is a certain, definite fact. But if you say: *"Ella non sa se egli sia arrivato,"* you are now implying a doubt or uncertainty because of the use of the word *se* (if).

k. The infinitive rather than the subjunctive is used in subordinate clauses when the subject of both the main and dependent verbs is the same:

> *Io* voglio partire.
> *I* want to leave.

But:

> *Io* voglio che *egli* parta.
> *I* want *him* to leave.

l. When the verb in the main clause is one of ordering or commanding the use of the subjunctive is often avoided by putting the subordinate verb in the infinitive and substituting an indirect object pronoun for the subject of the subordinate verb. This pronoun precedes the main verb. Thus, instead of saying:

> **Ordinai** che egli **venisse.**
> *I ordered* him *to come.*

you may say:

> *Gli* ordinai di *venire.*

§ 66 Servile Verbs

The verbs *volere* (to want), *potere* (to be able to, can), and *dovere* (to have to, must) are called servile verbs because when they are not used absolutely, that is, by themselves, they require an infinite as a predicate complement:

> Io *voglio* studiare.
> I *want* to study.
>
> Essi *devono* partire.
> They *must* leave.
>
> Tu non *puoi* uscire.
> You *cannot* go out.

When these verbs are used absolutely they require the auxiliary *avere.*

> Io non *ho potuto;* egli non *ha voluto;* etc.

But when they are followed by an infinitive, they require the auxiliary of the dependent infinitive:

Io non *ho potuto* **mangiare.**
I *was unable* to eat.

Io non *son potuto* **venire.**
I *was unable* to come.

(*Son* is often used instead of *sono*.)

Egli *ha dovuto* **lavorare.**
He *had to* work.

Egli *è dovuto* **partire.**
He *had* to leave.

Essi *sono dovuti* **andare.**
They *had to* go.

When these three verbs are followed by a reflexive verb they take the auxiliary verb *essere* if the reflexive pronoun precedes the verb, and the auxiliary *avere* if the reflexive pronoun is attached to the infinitive:

Egli non *si è potuto* **alzare.**
Egli non *ha potuto* **alzar***si***.** } He *was* un*able to* get up.

List of Irregular Verbs

The following list gives the hundred most common Italian irregular verbs. Of the simple tenses, only those which are irregular and those which might present some problems in spelling are given. Since the past participle is given, the compound tenses, which are made with the past participle, are not included. The following abbreviations are used:

P.P.—Past Participle
PRES.—Present Indicative
P. DEF.—Past Definite
IMPF.—Imperfect Indicative
FUT.—Future

COND.—Conditional
IMPV.—Imperative
PRES. SUB.—Present Subjunctive
IMPF. SUB.—Imperfect Subjunctive

Accendere
to light
  P.P. *acceso*
  P. DEF. *accesi, accendesti, accese, accendemmo, accendeste, accesero*

Accogliere
to receive, to welcome
  P.P. *accolto*
  PRES. *accolgo, accogli, accoglie, accogliamo, accogliete, accolgono*
  P. DEF. *accolsi, accogliesti, accolse, accogliemmo, accoglieste, accolsero*

Accorgersi
to notice, to perceive
  P.P. *accorto*
  P. DEF. *mi accorsi, ti accorgesti, si accorse, ci accorgemmo, vi accorgeste, si accorsero*

Accludere
to inclose
  P.P. *accluso*
  P. DEF. *acclusi, accludesti, accluse, accludemmo, accludeste, acclusero*

Affliggere
to afflict
  P.P. *afflitto*
  P. DEF. *afflissi, affliggesti, afflisse, affliggemmo, affliggeste, afflissero*

Andare
to go (takes auxiliary *essere*)
  PRES. *vado, vai, va, andiamo, andate, vanno*
  FUT. *andrò, andrai, andrà, andremo, andrete, andranno*
  COND. *andrei, andresti, andrebbe, andremmo, andreste, andrebbero*
  IMPV. *và, vada, andiamo, andate, vadano*
  PRES. SUB. *vada, vada, vada, andiamo, andiate, vadano*

Appartenere
to belong (conjugated like *tenere*)

Appendere
to hang
  P.P. *appeso*
  P. DEF. *appesi, appendesti, appese, appendemmo, appendeste, appesero*

Apprendere
to learn (conjugated like *prendere*)

Aprire
to open
  P.P. *aperto*
  P. DEF. *aprii* or *apersi, apristi, aprì* or *aperse, aprimmo, apriste, aprirono* or *apersero*

Ardere
to burn
  P.P. *arso*
  P. DEF. *arsi, ardesti, arse, ardemmo, ardeste, arsero*

Avere
to have
  PRES. *ho, hai, ha, abbiamo, avete, hanno*
  P. DEF. *ebbi, avesti, ebbe, avemmo, aveste, ebbero*
  FUT. *avrò, avrai, avrà, avremo, avrete, avranno*
  COND. *avrei, avresti, avrebbe, avremmo, avreste, avrebbero*
  IMPV. *abbi, abbia, abbiamo, abbiate, abbiano*
  PRES. SUB. *abbia, abbia, abbia, abbiamo, abbiate, abbiano*

Bere
to drink (conjugated from the old infinitive *bevere*)
P.P. *bevuto*
P. DEF. *bevvi, bevesti, bevve, bevemmo, beveste, bevvero*
FUT. *berrò, berrai, berrà, berremo, berrete, berranno*
COND. *berrei, berresti, berrebbe, berremmo, berreste, berrebbero*

Cadere
to fall (takes auxiliary *essere*)
P. DEF. *caddi, cedesti, cadde, cademmo, cadeste, caddero*
FUT. *cadrò, cadrai, cadrà, cadremo, cadrete, cadranno*
COND. *cadrei, cadresti, cadrebbe, cadremmo, cadreste, cadrebbero*

Chiedere
to ask
P.P. *chiesto*
P. DEF. *chiesi, chiedesti, chiese, chiedemmo, chiedeste, chiesero*

Chiudere
to close
P.P. *chiuso*
P. DEF. *chiusi, chiudesti, chiuse, chiudemmo, chiudeste, chiusero*

Cogliere
to pick (flowers, etc.), to gather
P.P. *colto*
P. DEF. *colsi, cogliesti, colse, cogliemmo, coglieste, colsero*

Compiere *or* **Compire**
to accomplish, to finish
P.P. *compito or compiuto*
PRES. *compio, compi, compie, compiamo, compite, compiono;* also *compisco, compisci, compisce, compiamo, compite, compiscono*
FUT. *compirò, compirai, compirà, compiremo, compirete, compiranno*
COND. *compirei, compiresti, compirebbe, compiremmo, compireste, compirebbero*
IMPV. *compi, compia, compiamo, compite, compiano*
PRES. SUB. *compia, compia, compia, compiamo, compiate, compiano;* also *compisca, compisca, compisca, compiamo, compiate, compiscano*

Concedere
to grant, to concede
P.P. *concesso*
P. DEF. *concessi, concedesti, concesse, concedemmo, concedeste, concessero*

Condurre
to lead, to conduct (conjugated from old infinitive *conducere*)
P.P. *condotto*
PRES. GERUND. *conducendo*
PRES. *conduco, conduci, conduce, conduciamo, conducete, conducono*
IMPF. *conducevo, conducevi, conduceva, conducevamo, conducevate, conducevano*
P. DEF. *condussi, conducesti, condusse, conducemmo, conduceste, condussero*
FUT. *condurrò, condurrai, condurrà, condurremo, condurrete, condurranno*
COND. *condurrei, condurresti, condurrebbe, condurremmo, condurreste, condurrebbero*
IMPV. *conduci, conduca, conduciamo, conducete, conducano*
PRES. SUB. *conduca, conduca, conduca, conduciamo, conduciate, conducano*
IMPF. SUB. *conducessi, conducessi, conducesse, conducessimo, conduceste, conducessero*

Conoscere
to know (usually a person)
P.P. *conosciuto*
P. DEF. *conobbi, conoscesti, conobbe, conoscemmo, conosceste, conobbero*

Coprire
to cover
P.P. *coperto*

Correggere
to correct
P.P. *corretto*
P. DEF. *corressi, correggesti, corresse, correggemmo, correggeste, corressero*

Correre
to run (conjugated with *essere* when it means from one place to another, otherwise it is conjugated with *avere*)
P.P. *corso*
P. DEF. *corsi, corresti, corse, corremmo, correste, corsero*

Crescere
to grow (conjugated with *essere* except when it has a direct object)
P.P. *cresciuto*
P. DEF. *crebbi, crescesti, crebbe, crescemmo, cresceste, crebbero*

Cuocere
to cook
P.P. *cotto*
PRES. *cuocio, cuoci, cuoce, cuociamo (cociamo), cuocete (cocete), cuociono*
P. DEF. *cossi, cocesti, cosse, cuocemmo, cuoceste, cossero*
PRES. SUB. *cuocia, cuocia, cuocia, cuociamo, cuociate, cuociano*

Dare
to give
P.P. *dato*
PRES. *do, dai, dà, diamo, date, danno*
P. DEF. *diedi, desti, diede, demmo, deste, diedero*
IMPF. *davo, davi, dava, davamo, davate, davano*
FUT. *darò, darai. darà, daremo, darete, daranno*
COND. *darei, daresti, darebbe, daremmo, dareste, darebbero*
IMPV. *dà, dia, diamo, date, diano*
PRES. SUB. *dia, dia, dia, diamo, diate, diano*
IMPF. SUB. *dessi, dessi, desse, dessimo, deste, dessero*

Decidere
to decide
P.P. *deciso*
P. DEF. *decisi, decidesti, decise, decidemmo, decideste, decisero*

Difendere
to defend
P.P. *difeso*
P. DEF. *difesi, difendesti, difese, difendemmo, difendeste, difesero*

Dipingere
to paint
P.P. *dipinto*
P. DEF. *dipinsi, dipingesti, dipinse, dipingemmo, dipingeste, dipinsero*

Dire
to say, to tell
(conjugated from old infinitive *dicere*)
P.P. *detto*
PRES. GERUND. *dicendo*
PRES. *dico, dici, dice, diciamo, dite, dicono*
P. DEF. *dissi, dicesti, disse, dicemmo, diceste, dissero*
IMPF. *dicevo, dicevi, diceva, dicevamo, dicevate, dicevano*
FUT. *dirò, dirai, dirà, diremo, direte, diranno*
COND. *direi, diresti, direbbe, diremmo, direste, direbbero*
IMPV. *di'* (or *dici*), *dica, diciamo, dite, dicano*

PRES. SUB. *dica, dica, dica, diciamo, diciate, dicano*
IMPF. SUB. *dicessi, dicessi, dicesse, dicessimo, diceste, dicessero*

Dirigere
to direct
P.P. *diretto*
P. DEF. *diressi, dirigesti, diresse, dirigemmo, dirigeste, diressero*

Discutere
to discuss
P.P. *discusso*
P. DEF. *discussi, discutesti, discusse, discutemmo, discuteste, discussero*

Dividere
to divide
P.P. *diviso*
P. DEF. *divisi, dividesti, divise, dividemmo, divideste, divisero*

Dovere
to have to, must
P.P. *dovuto*
PRES. *devo* (or *debbo*), *devi, deve, dobbiamo, dovete, devono* (or *debbono*)
P. DEF. *dovei* (or *dovetti*), *dovesti, dovè* (or *dovette*), *dovemmo, doveste, doverono* (or *dovettero*)
FUT. *dovrò, dovrai, dovrà, dovremo, dovrete, dovranno*
COND. *dovrei, dovresti, dovrebbe, dovremmo, dovreste, dovrebbero*
PRES. SUB. *deva, deva, deva* (or *debba, debba, debba*), *dobbiamo, dobbiate, devano* (or *debbano*)

Esprimere
to express
P.P. *espresso*
P. DEF. *espressi, esprimesti, espresse, esprimemmo, esprimeste, espressero*

Essere
to be (conjugated with itself as auxiliary)
P.P. *stato*
PRES. *sono, sei, è, siamo, siete, sono*
P. DEF. *fui, fosti, fu, fummo, foste, furono*
IMPF. *ero, eri, era, eravamo, eravate, erano*
FUT. *sarò, sarai, sarà, saremo, sarete, saranno*
COND. *sarei, saresti, sarebbe, saremmo, sareste, sarebbero*
IMPV. *sii, sia, siamo, siate, siano*
PRES. SUB. *sia, sia, sia, siamo, siate, siano*
IMPF. SUB. *fossi, fossi, fosse, fossimo, foste, fossero*

Fare
to do, to make (conjugated from the old infinitive *facere*)
P.P. *fatto*
PRES. GERUND. *facendo*
PRES. *faccio, fai, fa, facciamo, fate, fanno*
P. DEF. *feci, facesti, fece, facemmo, faceste, fecero*
IMPF. *facevo, facevi, faceva, facevamo, facevate, facevano*
FUT. *farò, farai, farà, faremo, farete, faranno*
COND. *farei, faresti, farebbe, faremmo, fareste, farebbero*
IMPV. *fà, faccia, facciamo, fate, facciano*
PRES. SUB. *faccia, faccia, faccia, facciamo, facciate, facciano*
IMPF. SUB. *facessi, facessi, facesse, facessimo, faceste, facessero*

Fingere
to pretend, to feign
P.P. *finto*
P. DEF. *finsi, fingesti, finse, fingemmo, fingeste, finsero*

Giungere
to arrive, to reach (conjugated with *essere*)
P.P. *giunto*
P. DEF. *giunsi, giungesti, giunse, giungemmo, giungeste, giunsero*

Leggere
to read
P.P. *letto*
P. DEF. *lessi, leggesti, lesse, leggemmo, leggeste, lessero*

Mantenere
to maintain, to keep, to support (conjugated like *tenere*)

Mettere
to put
P.P. *messo*
P. DEF. *misi, mettesti, mise, mettemmo, metteste, misero*

Mordere
to bite
P.P. *morso*
P. DEF. *morsi, mordesti, morse, mordemmo, mordeste, morsero*

Morire
to die (conjugated with *essere*)
P.P. *morto*
PRES. *muoio, muori, muore, moriamo, morite, muoiono*
FUT. *morrò, morrai, morrà, morremo, morrete, morranno*
COND. *morrei, morresti, morrebbe, morremmo, morreste, morrebbero*
NOTE: The regular forms for the future and conditional are also used.
IMPV. *muori, muoia, moriamo, morite, muoiano*
PRES. SUB. *muoia, muoia, muoia, moriamo, moriate, muoiano*

Muovere
to move (*not* to change residence)
P.P. *mosso*
PRES. *muovo, muovi, muove, moviamo, movete, muovono*
P. DEF. *mossi, movesti, mosse, movemmo, moveste, mossero*
IMPV. *muovi, muova, moviamo, movete, muovano*
PRES. SUB. *muova, muova, muova, moviamo, moviate, muovano*

Nascere
to be born (conjugated with *essere*)
P.P. *nato*
P. DEF. *egli nacque, essi nacquero*

Nascondere
to hide, to conceal
P.P. *nascosto*
P. DEF. *nascosi, nascondesti, nascose, nascondemmo, nascondeste, nascosero*

Offendere
to offend
P.P. *offeso*
P. DEF. *offesi, offendesti, offese, offendemmo, offendeste, offesero*

Offrire
to offer
P.P. *offerto*
P. DEF. *offrii* (or *offersi*), *offristi, offrì* (or *offerse*), *offrimmo, offriste, offrirono* (or *offersero*)

Perdere
to lose
P.P. *perduto* or *perso*
P. DEF. *persi* (or *perdei* or *perdetti*), *perdesti, perse* (or *perdè* or *perdette*), *perdemmo, perdeste, persero* (or *perderono* or *perdettero*)

Persuadere
to persuade
P.P. *persuaso*
P. DEF. *persuasi, persuadesti, persuase, persuademmo, persuadeste, persuasero*

Piacere
to like, to please, to be pleasing (conjugated with *essere*)
NOTE: This verb is used mostly in the third person singular and plural.
P.P. *piaciuto*
PRES. *piaccio, piaci, piace, piacciamo, piacete, piacciono*
P. DEF. *piacqui, piacesti, piacque, piacemmo, piaceste, piacquero*
PRES. SUB. *piaccia, piaccia, piaccia, piacciamo, piacciate, piacciano*

Piangere
to cry, to weep
P.P. *pianto*
P. DEF. *piansi, piangesti, pianse, piangemmo, piangeste, piansero*

Porre (Ponere)
to put, to place
P.P. *posto*
PRES. GERUND. *ponendo*
PRES. *pongo, poni, pone, poniamo, ponete, pongono*
P. DEF. *posi, ponesti, pose, ponemmo, poneste, posero*
FUT. *porrò, porrai, porrà, porremo, porrete, porranno*
COND. *porrei, porresti, porrebbe, porremmo, porreste, porrebbero*
IMPF. *ponevo, ponevi, poneva, ponevamo, ponevate, ponevano*
IMPV. *poni, ponga, poniamo, ponete, pongano*
PRES. SUB. *ponga, ponga, ponga, poniamo, poniate, pongano*
IMPF. SUB. *ponessi, ponessi, ponesse, ponessimo, poneste, ponessero*

Potere
to be able to, can, may
PRES. *posso, puoi, può, possiamo, potete, possono*
FUT. *potrò, potrai, potrà, potremo, potrete, potranno*
COND. *potrei, potresti, potrebbe, potremmo, potreste, potrebbero*
IMPV. *possa, possa, possiamo, possiate, possano*
PRES. SUB. *possa, possa, possa, possiamo, possiate, possano*

Prendere
to take
P.P. *preso*
P. DEF. *presi, prendesti, prese, prendemmo, prendeste, presero*

Produrre
to produce (conjugated like *condurre*)

Proteggere
to protect
P.P. *protetto*
P. DEF. *protessi, proteggesti, protesse, proteggemmo, proteggeste, protessero*

Radere
to shave
P.P. *raso*
P. DEF. *rasi, redesti, rase, rademmo, radeste, rasero*

Rendere
to render, to give back
P.P. *reso*
P. DEF. *resi, rendesti, rese, rendemmo, rendeste, resero*

Ridere
to laugh
P.P. *riso*
P. DEF. *risi, ridesti, rise, ridemmo, rideste, risero*

Rimanere
to remain
P.P. *rimasto*
PRES. *rimango, rimani, rimane, rimaniamo, rimanete, rimangono*
P. DEF. *rimasi, rimanesti, rimase, rimanemmo, rimaneste, rimasero*
FUT. *rimarrò, rimarrai, rimarrà, rimarremo, rimarrete, rimarranno*
COND. *rimarrei, rimarresti, riamarrebbe, rimarremmo, rimarreste, rimarrebbero.*
IMPV. *rimani, rimanga, rimaniamo, rimanete, rimangano*
PRES. SUB. *rimanga, rimanga, rimanga, rimaniamo, rimaniate, rimangano*

Rispondere
to answer, to reply
P.P. *risposto*
P. DEF. *risposi, rispondesti, rispose, rispondemmo, rispondeste, risposero*

Ritenere
to retain (conjugated like *tenere*)

Rompere
to break
P.P. *rotto*
P. DEF. *ruppi, rompesti, ruppe, rompemmo, rompeste, ruppero*

Salire
to go up, to climb, to ascend, to get on
PRES. *salgo, sali, sale, saliamo, salite, salgono*
IMPV. *sali, salga, saliamo, salite, salgano*
PRES. SUB. *salga, salga, salga, saliamo, saliate, salgano*

Sapere
to know, to know how (*never* to know a person)
PRES. *so, sai, sa, sappiamo, sapete, sanno*
P. DEF. *seppi, sapesti, seppe, sapemmo, sapeste, seppero*
FUT. *saprò, saprai, saprà, sapremo, saprete, sapranno*
COND. *saprei, sapresti, saprebbe, sapremmo, sapreste, saprebbero*
IMPV. *sappi, sappia, sappiamo, sappiate, sappiano*
PRES. SUB. *sappia, sappia, sappia, sappiamo, sappiate, sappiano*

Scegliere
to choose, to select
P.P. *scelto*
PRES. *scelgo, scegli, sceglie, scegliamo, scegliete, scelgono*
P. DEF. *scelsi, scegliesti, scelse, scegliemmo, sceglieste, scelsero*
IMPV. *scegli, scelga, scegliamo, scegliete, scelgano*
PRES. SUB. *scelga, scelga, scelga, scegliamo, scegliate, scelgano*

Scendere
to descend, to go down, to get down, to get off
P.P. *sceso*
P. DEF. *scesi, scendesti, scese, scendemmo, scendeste, scesero*

Sciogliere
to untie, to dissolve, to melt
P.P. *sciolto*
P. DEF. *sciolsi, sciogliesti, sciolse, sciogliemmo, scioglieste, sciolsero*
IMPV. *sciogli, sciolga, sciogliamo, sciogliete, sciolgano*
PRES. SUB. *sciolga, sciolga, sciolga, sciogliamo, sciogliate, sciolgano*

Scomparire
to disappear
P.P. *scomparso* or *scomparito*
PRES. *scompaio, scompari, scompare, scompariamo, scomparite, scompaiono*
P. DEF. *scomparii* (or *scomparvi* or *scomparsi*), *scomparisti; scomparì* (or *scomparve* or *scomparse*), *scomparimmo, scompariste, scomparirono* (or *scomparvero* or *scomparsero*)
IMPV. *scompari, scompaia, scompariamo, scomparite, scompaiano*
PRS. SUB. *scompaia, scompaia, scompaia, scompariamo, scompariate, scompaiano*

NOTE: Besides the forms given above, this verb also has the regular *-isco* forms in the present indicative, imperative, and present subjunctive [See §50].

Scoprire
to discover
P.P. *scoperto*
P. DEF. *scoprii* (or *scopersi*), *scopristi, scoprì* (or *scoperse*), *scoprimmo, scopriste, scoprirono* (or *scopersero*)

Scrivere
to write
P.P. *scritto*
P. DEF. *scrissi, scrivesti, scrisse, scrivemmo, scriveste, scrissero*

Sedere
to sit
PRES. *siedo* (or *seggo*), *siedi, siede, sediamo, sedete, siedono* (or *seggono*)
IMPV. *siedi, segga, sediamo, sedete, seggano*
PRES. SUB. *segga, segga, segga* (or *sieda, sieda, sieda*), *sediamo, sediate, seggano* (or *siedano*)

Soffrire
to suffer
P.P. *sofferto*
P. DEF. *soffrii* (or *soffersi*), *soffristi, soffrì* (or *sofferse*), *soffrimmo, soffriste, soffrirono* (or *soffersero*)

Sorgere
to arise, to rise
P.P. *sorto*
P. DEF. *sorsi, sorgesti, sorse, sorgemmo, sorgeste, sorsero*

Sorridere
to smile (conjugated like *ridere*)

Spargere
to spread, to scatter
P.P. *sparso*
P. DEF. *sparsi, spargesti, sparse, spargemmo, spargeste, sparsero*

Spegnere *or* **Spengere**
to extinguish
P.P. *spento*
PRES. (regular) also *io spengo, essi spengono*
P. DEF. *spensi, spegnesti, spense, spegnemmo, spegneste, spensero*
IMPV. *spegni, spenga, spegniamo, spegnete, spengano*
PRES. SUB. *spenga, spenga, spenga, spegniamo, spegniate, spengano*

Spendere
to spend
P.P. *speso*
P. DEF. *spesi, spendesti, spese, spendemmo, spendeste, spesero*

Spingere
to push, to shove, to thrust
P.P. *spinto*
P. DEF. *spinsi, spingesti, spinse, spingemmo, spingeste, spinsero*

Stare
to stay (sometimes, to be, to stand)
(conjugated with *essere*)
P.P. *stato*
PRES. *sto, stai, sta, stiamo, state, stanno*
P. DEF. *stetti, stesti, stette, stemmo, steste, stettero*
IMPF. *stavo, stavi, stava, stavamo, stavate, stavano*
FUT. *starò, starai, starà, staremo, starete, staranno*
COND. *starei, staresti, starebbe, staremmo, stareste, starebbero*
IMPV. *stà, stia, stiamo, state, stiano*
PRES. SUB. *stia, stia, stia, stiamo, stiate, stiano*
IMPF. SUB. *stessi, stessi, stesse, stessimo, steste, stessero*

Stringere
to hold fast, to squeeze, to grasp, to bind fast
P.P. *stretto*
P. DEF. *strinsi, stringesti, strinse, stringemmo, stringeste, strinsero*

Supporre
to suppose (conjugated like *porre*)

Svenire
to faint (conjugated like *venire;* takes the auxiliary *essere*)

Tacere
to be silent, to keep quiet
P.P. *taciuto*
PRES. *taccio, taci, tace, taciamo, tacete, tacciono*
P. DEF. *tacqui, tacesti, tacque, tacemmo, taceste, tacquero*
IMPV. *taci, taccia, taciamo, tacete, tacciano*
PRES. SUB. *taccia, taccia, taccia, tacciamo, tacciate, tacciano*
(may also be written with one *c*)

Tenere
to hold, to have, to keep
PRES. *tengo, tieni, tiene, teniamo, tenete, tengono*
P. DEF. *tenni, tenesti, tenne, tenemmo, teneste, tennero*
FUT. *terrò, terrai, terrà, terremo, terrete, terranno*
COND. *terrei, terresti, terrebbe, terremmo, terreste, terrebbero*
IMPV. *tieni, tenga, teniamo, tenete, tengano*
PRES. SUB. *tenga, tenga, tenga, teniamo, teniate, tengano*

Togliere
to take away, to remove, to take from
P.P. *tolto*
PRES. *tolgo, togli, toglie, togliamo, togliete, tolgono*
P. DEF. *tolsi, togliesti, tolse, togliemmo, toglieste, tolsero*
FUT. *torrò, torrai, torrà, torremo, torrete, torranno*
COND. *torrei, torresti, torrebbe, torremmo, torreste, torrebbero*
NOTE: Both the future and the conditional have the regular forms in addition to those given above.
IMPV. *togli, tolga, togliamo, togliete, tolgano*
PRES. SUB. *tolga, tolga, tolga, togliamo, togliate, tolgano*

Tradurre
to translate (from the old infinitive *traducere;* conjugated like *condurre*)

Trarre
to draw or pull out; to drag, to haul, to derive
P.P. *tratto*
PRES. GERUND. *traendo*
PRES. *traggo, trai, trae, traiamo, traete, traggono*
P. DEF. *trassi, traesti, trasse, traemmo, traeste, trassero*
IMPF. *traevo, traevi, traeva, traevamo, traevate, traevano*
FUT. *trarrò, trarrai, trarrà, trarremo, trarrete, trarranno*
COND. *trarrei, trarresti, trarrebbe, trarremmo, trarreste, trarrebbero*
IMPV. *trai, tragga, traiamo, traete, traggano*
PRES. SUB. *tragga, tragga, tragga, traiamo, traiate, traggano*
IMPF. SUB. *traessi, traessi, traesse, traessimo, traeste, traessero*

Uccidere
to kill
P.P. *ucciso*
P. DEF. *uccisi, uccidesti, uccise, uccidemmo, uccideste, uccisero*

Udire
to hear
PRES. *odo, odi, ode, udiamo, udite, odono*
FUT. *udrò, udrai, udrà, udremo, udrete, udranno*
COND. *udrei, udresti, udrebbe, udremmo, udreste, udrebbero*
NOTE: Both the future and the conditional have regular forms in addition to those given above.
IMPV. *odi, oda, udiamo, udite, odano*
PRES. SUB. *oda, oda, oda, udiamo, udiate, odano*

Uscire
to go out (takes the auxiliary *essere*)
PRES. *esco, esci, esce, usciamo, uscite, escono*
IMPV. *esci, esca, usciamo, uscite, escano*
PRES. SUB. *esca, esca, esca, usciamo, usciate, escano*

Valere
to be worth (takes the auxiliary *essere*)
P.P. *valso*
PRES. *valgo, vali, vale, valiamo, valete, valgono*
P. DEF. *valsi, valesti, valse, valemmo,*

valeste, valsero
FUT. *varrò, varrai, varrà, varremo, varrete, varranno*
COND. *varrei, varresti, varrebbe, varremmo, varrete, varrebbero*
IMPV. *vali, valga, valiamo, valete, valgano*
PRES. SUB. *valga, valga, valga, valiamo, valiate, valgano*
NOTE: Of this verb usually only the third person singular and the third person plural are used.

Vedere
to see
P.P. *visto* or *veduto*
P. DEF. *vidi, vedesti, vide, vedemmo, vedeste, videro*
FUT. *vedrò, vedrai, vedrà, vedremo, vedrete, vedranno*
COND. *vedrei, vedresti, vedrebbe, vedremmo, vedreste, vedrebbero*

Venire
to come (conjugated with the auxiliary *essere*)
P.P. *venuto*
PRES. *vengo, vieni, viene, veniamo, venite, vengono*
P. DEF. *venni, venisti, venne, venimmo, veniste, vennero*
FUT. *verrò, verrai, verrà, verremo, verrete, verranno*
COND. *verrei, verresti, verrebbe, verremmo, verreste, verrebbero*
IMPV. *vieni, venga, veniamo, venite, vengano*
PRES. SUB. *venga, venga, venga, veniamo, veniate, vengano*

Vincere
to win
P.P. *vinto*
P. DEF. *vinsi, vincesti, vinse, vincemmo, vinceste, vinsero*

Vivere
to live (*not* to reside)
NOTE: Takes the auxiliary *avere* if followed by a direct object, otherwise it takes the auxiliary *essere*.
P.P. *vissuto*
P. DEF. *vissi, vivesti, visse, vivemmo, viveste, vissero*
FUT. *vivrò, vivrai, vivrà, vivremo, vivrete, vivranno*
COND. *vivrei, vivresti, vivrebbe, vivremmo, vivreste, vivrebbero*

Volere
to want, to be willing, to desire, to wish

PRES. *voglio, vuoi, vuole, vogliamo, volete, vogliono*

P. DEF. *volli, volesti, volle, volemmo, voleste, vollero*

FUT. *vorrò, vorrai, vorrà, vorremo, vorrete, vorranno*

COND. *vorrei, vorresti, vorrebbe, vorremmo, vorreste, vorrebbero*

IMPV. (rarely used) *vogli, voglia, vogliamo, vogliate, vogliano*

PRES. SUB. *voglia, voglia, voglia, vogliamo, vogliate, vogliano*

Volgere
to turn, to revolve

P.P. *volto*

PRES. *volgo, volgi, volge, volgiamo, volgete, volgono*

P. DEF. *volsi, volgesti, volse, volgemmo, volgeste, volsero*

List of Common Italian Proverbs

Volere è potere.
Where there's a will there's a way.

Dove c'è fumo c'è fuoco.
Where there's smoke there's fire.

L'unione fa la forza.
In union there is strength.

Uomo avvisato è mezzo salvato.
Forewarned is forearmed.

Finchè c'è vita c'è speranza.
Where there is life there is hope.

Scopa nuova scopa bene.
A new broom sweeps clean.

Se son rose fioriranno.
Time will tell.

Ride bene chi ride l'ultimo.
He laughs best who laughs last.

Il riso abbonda in bocca degli sciocchi.
Laughter is abundant in the mouth of fools.

La miglior vendetta è il perdono.
Forgiveness is the best revenge.

L'ozio è il padre di tutti i vizi.
Idleness is the root of all evil.

Paese che vai, usanze che trovi.
When in Rome do as the Romans do.

Trova un amico e troverai un tesoro.
A good friend is a treasure.

La notte porta consiglio.
Night brings counsel.

Chi è causa del suo male piange se stesso.
He who has made his own bed must lie in it.

Chi ama il suo lavoro lo fa bene.
He who loves his work does it well.

Chi ben comincia è alla metà dell'opera.
Well begun is half done.

Chi asino nasce asino muore.
He who is born a fool dies a fool.

Chi cerca trova.
Seek and you shall find.

Chi va piano, va sano e va lontano.
He who goes slowly, goes safely and goes far.

Chi prima non pensa in ultimo sospira.
Look before you leap.

Chi troppo abbraccia nulla stringe.
He who grasps too much holds nothing.

Chi tardi arriva male alloggia.
The latecomer finds bad lodging.

Chi sa poco presto lo dice.
He who knows little soon reveals it.

Chi si contenta gode.
Contentment is better than riches.

Chi male fa male aspetti.
He who does evil must expect evil.

Chi la dura la vince.
Perseverance brings success.

Chi non semina non raccoglie.
As you sow, so shall you reap.

Chi s'aiuta Dio l'aiuta.
God helps those who help themselves.

Chi è paziente è sapiente.
He who is patient is wise.

Chi dorme non piglia pesci.
You can't catch fish while you are sleeping.

La bugia ha le gambe corte.
A lie is short lived.

A buon intenditore poche parole.
A word to the wise is sufficient.

Al bisogno si conosce l'amico.
A friend in need is a friend indeed.

Bisogna battere il ferro quando è caldo.
Strike while the iron is hot.

Ad ogni uccello il suo nido è bello.
There is no place like home.

Non c'è rosa senza spine.
There is no rose without thorns.

Oggi a me, domani a te.
Every dog has its day.

Meglio tardi che mai.
Better late than never.

La parola è d'argento, il silenzio è d'oro.
Speech is silver, silence is golden.

Cosa rara, cosa cara.
Something rare, something dear.

Contro la forza la ragion non vale.
Might is stronger than right.

Dimmi con chi vai e ti dirò chi sei.
A man is known by the company he keeps.

Giovane ozioso, vecchio bisognoso.
Lazy youth makes needy old age.

L'occhio del padrone ingrassa il cavallo.
Under the master's eye everything prospers.

Fra due litiganti il terzo gode.
While two dogs strive for a bone, a third one runs away with it.

Non tutto è oro quel che riluce.
All that glitters is not gold.

Una rondine non fa primavera.
One swallow does not make a spring.

Ogni bel gioco dura poco.
All good things come to an end.

Tutto è bene quel che finisce bene.
All is well that ends well.

Some Common Italian Idioms

Andare a casa
To go home

Andare a passeggio
To go for a walk

Andare a letto
To go to bed

Andare a teatro
To go to the theater

Andare a piedi
To go on foot; to walk (to)

Andare in automobile
To go by car

Andare in ferrovia
To go by railroad

Andare per mare
To go by sea

Andare per terra
To go by land

Andare in aereo
To go by plane

Andare in chiesa
To go to church

Andare via
To go away

Coll'andare del tempo
As time goes on

Va bene
That's fine

Avere da fare
To be busy

Avere ragione
To be right

Avere torto
To be wrong

Avere sonno
To be sleepy

Avere bisogno di
To need

Avere sete
To be thirsty

Avere voglia di
To feel like; to wish to

Avere caldo
To be (feel) warm, hot

Avere freddo
To be (feel) cold

Fare colazione
To have breakfast

Fare un regalo
To give a gift

Fare gli auguri
To express good wishes

Fare una fotografia
To take a picture

Fare una partita
To play a game

Fare un viaggio
To take a trip

Fare una passeggiata
To take a walk

Giocare a dama
To play checkers

Giocare agli scacchi
To play chess

Giocare a carte
To play cards

Voler bene a
To be fond of (*lit.,* to wish well to)

Stare bene (male)
To be well (ill)

Di buon'ora
Early

Essere in ritardo *or* **fare tardi**
To be late

Da ora in poi
From now on

Oggi ad otto
A week from today

Di tanto in tanto
Once in a while

Qualche volta
Sometimes

Proprio ora
Just now

Ad un tratto
Suddenly

All'improvviso
Suddenly, unexpectedly

Al contrario
On the contrary

A poco a poco
Little by little

Ad alta voce
Loudly

Un biglietto di visita
A visiting card

Dire di sì; dire di no
To say yes; to say no

Questa è bella!
That's a good one!

Vestire con gusto
To dress well, in good taste

A buon mercato
Cheaply

In fretta
In a hurry

In campagna
In the country, to the country

Stringere la mano (a)
To shake hands (with)

Cercare di
To try to

Gli affari vanno bene (male)
Business is good (bad)

Buono a nulla
Good for nothing

Stare in pensiero
To be worried

Ingannare il tempo
To kill time

Fare un buco nell'acqua
To accomplish nothing (*lit.*, to make a hole in the water)

Di seconda mano
Second hand, used

Di buon mattino
Early in the morning

Volta per volta
Time after time

Domandare scusa
To apologize

Un mal di testa
A headache

Meno male!
It's a good thing!

Di male in peggio
From bad to worse

Di bene in meglio
Better and better

Di buon (mal) umore.
In a good (bad) humor

Sano e salvo
Safe and sound

Tale e quale
Exactly like, exactly alike

Vale la pena
It's worth while

Che vale?
What's the use?

Fare un brindisi
To drink a toast

Al solito
As usual

Prima del tempo
Before time, ahead of time

Guadagnarsi la vita
To earn a living

Farlo apposta
To do it on purpose, for spite

Peccato!
Too bad (*lit.*, sin)

Ancora una volta
Once more

Fare la coda
To stand on line; to wait on line

A rotta di collo
At breakneck speed

In punta di piedi
On tiptoe

In fretta e furia
In a great hurry

A braccia aperte
With open arms

Un biglietto di andata e ritorno
A round trip ticket

Fare orecchio da mercante
To turn a deaf ear (*lit.*, to make a merchant's ear)

A quattr'occhi
Privately; face to face (*lit.*, with four eyes)

Fare finta di
To pretend; to make believe

Conoscere di vista
To know by sight

Detto, fatto
No sooner said than done

Dio me ne guardi!
God forbid!

Non c'è nulla di male!
No harm done!

Che c'è di nuovo?
What's new?

Che faccia tosta!
What nerve (*lit.*, what a hard face)!

Come se niente fosse
As if nothing had happened

Questo è un altro paio di maniche.
That's a horse of another color (*lit.*, that's another pair of sleeves)

Italian-English Dictionary*

A

a to, at
abbastanza enough
abbondanza abundance
abbracciare to embrace
abitante *m.* inhabitant
abitare to live, reside, dwell
abito suit
    ... a giacca tailored suit (for a
    woman)
abituato accustomed
abitudine *f.* habit
accanto beside
accettare to accept
accendere to light
accidempoli! the deuce!
accidente accident
accogliere to receive, to welcome
accomodarsi to make oneself
    comfortable
accompagnare to accompany
accontentato satisfied
aceto vinegar
acqua water
acquaio kitchen sink
acquazzone *m.* shower (rain)
acquistare to acquire, to purchase
addio goodbye, farewell
addolorato grieved
addormentarsi to fall asleep

adesso now
adorare to adore
adorata beloved
aereo, in by plane
aeroplano airplane
aeroporto airport
affari *m. pl.* business
    fare ... to do business
affascinare to fascinate
affatto at all
affittare to rent
affluenza influx
affollato crowded
affresco (*pl.* affreschi) fresco
agente *m.* agent, policeman
agenzia agency
aggiungere to add
agnello lamb
ago needle
agosto August
agricoltura agriculture
aiuto help
albergo hotel
albero tree
alberato tree lined
alcuni,-e some
alba dawn
alcuno,-a any
allarmare to alarm
    non si alarmi don't get alarmed

---

*In the Italian-English and English-Italian dictionaries that follow, parts of
speech are not indicated except in ambiguous cases. In the case of nouns, gender
is indicated only where the form of the noun does not clearly indicate masculine
(*m.*) or feminine (*f.*). Irregular plurals (*pl.*) of nouns are also given. The abbreviations *adj.* for adjective and *adv.* for adverb are used where it is necessary to
distinguish these parts of speech. Familiar forms are abbreviated *fam.*, polite
forms, *pol.*

299

allegramente cheerfully
allegrezza cheerfulness
alloggiare to stay, to lodge
alloggio lodging
allora then
almeno at least
alquanto somewhat, rather
alto high, tall
altro other, else
altrui others, of others
alzare to lift, raise
alzarsi to get up
amante lover
amare to love
amaro bitter
ambedue both
americano American
amicizia friendship
amico friend
ammalarsi to get sick
ammirare to admire
amministrare to manage
ammiratore *m.* admirer
ammobiliato furnished
ammontare amount
amore love
   amor mio my love
analogo matching
ananasso pineapple
anatomico anatomist
anche also, too
ancora yet, still
   non . . . not yet
andare to go
andata e ritorno round trip
angolo corner
anima soul
animale *m.* animal
anno year
annunciare announce
ansia anxiety
ansioso anxious, eager
antichità antiquity
anticipo, in in advance
antico ancient
antipasto appetizer
apostolo apostle
appagato satisfied
apparecchiare to set
apparire to appear
appartamento apartment
appassionato full of feeling

appena as soon as
appetito appetite
   avere . . . to be hungry
apprezzare to appreciate
approvare approve
appuntamento appointment
aprile *m.* April
aprire to open
arachidi peanuts
arancia (*pl.* arance) orange
architetto architect
architettura architecture
ardere to burn
argenteria silverware
Argentina Argentina
argento silver
aria air
   corrente d' . . . draft
   un soffio d' . . . a breath of air
arrabbiato angry
arrivo arrival
armadio closet
arredare to furnish
arrivare to arrive
arrivederci until we meet again
   (*fam.*)
arrivederla until we meet again
   (*pol.*)
arrostito roasted
arrosto roast
arte *f.* art
artista *m. & f.* artist
articolo article
artistico artistic
ascensore *m.* elevator
ascesa, in rising
asciugamano towel
aspettare to wait
   . . . oltre to wait any longer
   . . . a lungo to wait a long time
assaggiare to taste
asino donkey
assediato besieged
assegno check
   libretto di assegni check book
assicurare to assure, to insure
assistere to attend
assolutamente absolutely
assortimento assortment
astronomo astronomer
Atene Athens
attento! careful!

atterrare to land
attesa waiting
attraente attractive
attrazione *f.* attraction
attuale present, actual
audacia audacity
augurare to wish
auguri *m. pl.* good wishes
autentico authentic
autista chauffeur, driver
autobus *m.* bus
automobile *f.* automobile, car
autorità authority
autore *m.* author
autunno autumn, fall
avanti forward, ahead
avere to have
aviazione *f.* aviation
avverarsi to come true
avvertire to warn
avvicinarsi to draw near, approach
avvolgere to wrap
azione *f.* action
azzurro blue

B

baciare to kiss
bacio kiss
bagaglio baggage
bagno bathroom, bath
    fare il . . . to bathe
    fare i bagni to go bathing
ballo dance
    da . . . for dancing
bambino,-a child
banana banana
banca bank
bandiera banner, flag
barca boat
barometro barometer
basilica basilica
basso low, short
battaglia battle
battere to strike, beat, knock
baule *m.* trunk
bel, bella, bello beautiful
belga Belgian
Belgio Belgium
bellezza beauty
benchè although

bene well
    sto . . . I am well, I feel well
benedire to bless
benedizione *f.* blessing
beninteso of course
benone very well
bere to drink
berretto cap
biancheria linens
    . . . intima underwear
bianco white
biblioteca library
bicchiere *m.* glass
bicicletta bicycle
biglietteria ticket window
biglietto ticket
    . . . di visita visiting card
biondo blond
bisogna che it is necessary
bisogno need
    ho . . . di I need
bistecca steak
bizzarria whim
bizzarro whimsical
bollire to boil
bollito boiled
bollo stamp, rubber stamp
bontà kindness
bordo, a on board
borsa stock exchange, scholarship
borsetta handbag
bosco woods
bottega (*pl.* botteghe) shop, store
bottiglia bottle
bottone *m.* button
braccio (*pl.* le braccia) arm
Brasile *m.* Brazil
bravo! bravissimo! fine! excellent!
breve brief, short
    a . . . scadenza short term
brillante brilliant, sparkling
brodo soup
brutto ugly
bugia lie
bue *m.* beef, ox
buio dark
buono good
buon'ora, di early
burro butter
busta envelope

C

cabina cabin
caduta fall
caffè coffee
caffelatte coffee with milk
caffettiera coffee pot
calamaio inkwell
calcolo calculation
caldo hot, warm
   fa ... it is warm, hot
calendario calendar
calosce $f. pl.$ overshoes, rubbers
calza stocking
calzatura footwear
calzino sock
calzoni $m. pl.$ trousers, pants
cambio rate of exchange
cameriere $m.$ waiter
camera room, chamber
   ... da letto bedroom
camicetta blouse
camicia ($pl.$ camicie) shirt
cammin facendo on the way
cammino path, walk
campanello doorbell, small bell
campo field
Canadà $m.$ Canada
canale $m.$ canal
cane $m.$ dog
canterellando humming
cantare to sing
canzone $f.$ song
canzonetta popular song
capelli hair
capire to understand
capitale $f.$ capital (of a country)
   $m.$ capital (money)
capitano captain
capo head
capolavoro masterpiece
cappella chapel
cappello hat
carabiniere $m.$ military policeman
caraffa decanter, pitcher
carbone $m.$ coal
caricare to load, to wind (a watch)
carne $f.$ meat
caro dear, expensive
carriera career
carrozza railroad car, carriage

carta paper
   foglio di ... sheet of paper
   ... da lettere letter paper
   ... geografica map
   ... sugante blotter
cartoleria stationary store
casa house
caserma barracks
cassettone $m.$ the bureau
   (furniture)
cassiere $m.$ cashier
castagna chestnut
castrato mutton
catacombe catacombs
cattedrale $f.$ cathedral
cattivo bad
   fa ... tempo the weather is bad
cattolico catholic
cavallo horse
c'è there is
Ceco-slovacchia Czechoslovakia
cedere to yield, to cede
celebrare celebrate
celeste blue
cena supper
cenare to have supper
centesimo cent
centigrado centigrade
centinaia $f. pl.$ hundreds
centinaio about a hundred
cento one hundred
centrale central
centro center
cera appearance, look
   avere buona ... to look well
cercare to look for, seek
   ... di to try to
cereale $m.$ cereal
certamente certainly
certo certain, certainly
cesta basket
che who, that, whom, which, what,
   what a, than
   non (verb) ... only
che cosa? what?
chi who, whom
chiamare to call
chiamarsi to be called (name)
chiarore $m.$ light
chiave $f.$ key
chiedere to ask
chiesa church

chilo kilogram
chilogrammo kilogram
chilometro kilometer
chiudere to close
chiunque whoever
ci there; us, to us
cibo food
cima summit, top
cimitero cemetery
cinema *m.* motion picture theater
cintura belt, waist
cinquanta fifty
cinque five
ciò that
   dopo di . . . after that
cioccolata chocolate
cioè that is, that is to say
cipria powder
circa about
circolazione *f.* currency, circulation
città city
civiltà civilization
classe *f.* class
clima *m.* climate
clinica doctor's office, clinic
cognata sister-in-law
cognato brother-in-law
colazione *f.* breakfast
colle *m.* hill
colletto collar
collina hill
collo neck
colore *m.* color
coltello knife
comandante *m.* commander
come as, like
cominciare to begin
comico funny
commerciale commercial
commerciante *m.* merchant
commercio trade, commerce
commosso moved, touched
commovente moving, touching
comodino night table
comodo comfortable
   quando le fa . . . whenever it
   suits you
compagnia company
completamente completely
completo complete
compone, si is composed
compositore *m.* composer

composto composed
comprare to buy
con with
concedere to grant
   ti sarà concesso it will be granted
   to you
concerto concert
conciliazione *f.* conciliation
condimento seasoning
condito seasoned
condizione *f.* condition
confessare to confess
conforto comfort
congelare to freeze
connazionale *m.* fellow countryman
conoscenza acquaintance,
   knowledge
   fare la . . . to make the
   acquaintance
conoscere to know
conoscitore *m.* connoiseur
consegnare to deliver
conservare to keep, preserve
   . . . agli atti to keep on record
consigliare to advise
consiglio advice
consistere di to consist of
contabilità accounting
contadino peasant
contanti, in for cash
contare to count
contento glad
conto check, bill
contorno side dish
contrada quarter, section, (of a city)
contrario opposite, contrary
   al . . . on the other hand, on the
   contrary
contro against
controllo della dogana customs
   inspection
convincere to convince
conversazione *f.* conversation
convinto convinced
coperta blanket
   sopra . . . on deck
coperto cover, place setting
copia copy, duplicate
   in duplice . . . in duplicate
coppia couple
coprire to cover
coraggio courage

corpo body
correre to run
corrispondenza correspondence
 sbrigare la . . . to write the
 correspondence
corsa race
 fare una . . . to run a race
corso boulevard, course
cortesia courtesy
cortile *m.* courtyard, inner court
corto short
così thus, so
cosparso strewn
costa coast
costare to cost
costoletta chop
costruire to construct, build
costume *m.* costume, custom
cotone *m.* cotton
cotto cooked
 ben . . . well done, well cooked
cravatta necktie
creatura creature
creazione *f.* creation
credenza buffet
credere to believe
credito credit
 a . . . on credit
crema cream
 . . . a base d'olio cold cream
crescere to grow
crespo crepe
cristianesimo Christianity
Cristo Christ
crollare to collapse, to fall to pieces
crudo raw
cucchiaio spoon
cucchiaino teaspoon
cucina kitchen
cucinare to cook
cucire to sew
cucitura seam, sewing
cugino,-a cousin
cultura culture
cuoio leather
cuore *m.* heart
 nel . . . della città in the center of
 the city
cupo deep dark (in ref. to a color)
cupola cupola
cuscino pillow

D

da from
danaro money
dappertutto everywhere
dare to give
 . . . su to face, open upon
davanti in front
davvero really
decadenza decadence
decidere to decide
decimo tenth
decisione *f.* decision
decollare to take off (aviation)
definire to define
delizioso delicious
denaro money
dente *f.* tooth
dentifricio toothpaste
dentista *m. & f.* dentist
dentro inside
depositare to deposit, check
deposito di bagagli checkroom
 (for baggage)
descrivere to describe
descrizione *f.* description
desiderare to wish, to desire
desideroso desirous
destra, a to the right
destramente expertly, skillfully
detenuto prisoner
dettagliato detailed
devo I must
di of
diamante *m.* diamond
dicembre *m.* December
dichiarare to declare
diciotto eighteen
diciannove nineteen
diciassette seventeen
dieci ten
diecina about ten
dietro behind
differente different
differenza difference
difficile difficult
difficoltà difficulty
Dio God
dimenticare to forget
dimostrare to show
dipingere to paint
dire to say, tell

direttamente directly
direttore *m.* director
dirigente *m.* manager
disastro disaster
discesa, in dropping
discutere to discuss
disopra, al above
disotto, al below
dispiacere to displease
dispiace, mi I am sorry
disposizione *f.* disposition
  a sua ... at your service
disposto disposed
distante distant
distanza distance
distinguere to distinguish
disturbare to bother, to disturb
disturbo bother, disturbance
dito (*pl.* **le dita**) finger
ditta *f.* firm
divano sofa
diventare become
diversi several
diverso different
  diverse volte several times
divertente amusing
divertimento amusement
dividere divide
divinamente divinely
dizionario dictionary
doccia shower (bath)
dodici twelve
dogana customs house
doganiere *m.* customs officer
dolce *adj.* sweet; *n. m.* dessert
dollaro dollar
dolore *m.* pain, ache
doloroso painful
domandare to ask
domani tomorrow
domenica Sunday
domestica maid
domicilio, a at home, to the house
dominare dominate
donna woman
dopodomani the day after
  tomorrow
doppio *m.* double
dopo, dopo di after
dormire to sleep
dotto learned
dottore *m.* doctor

dove where
dov'è? where is?
dovere must, to have to, owe
dovere *m.* duty
dovunque anywhere, everywhere
dovuto due
dozzina dozen
dubbio doubt
due two
dunque therefore
durante during
durare to last
duraturo lasting
duro tough, hard

E

e, ed and
ebreo Jewish
eccellente excellent
eccetto except
ecco here is, here are; **there is,**
  there are
economico economical
edificio building
Egitto Egypt
egli he
eguale equal, even, alike
elegante elegant, stylish
elettricità electricity
elettrico electric
ella she
entusiasmo enthusiasm
entusiasta *m. & f.* enthusiastic
entrare to enter, come in
epoca epoch, era
eppure yet, nevertheless
eruzione *f.* eruption
esagerare exaggerate
esaminare to examine
esattamente exactly
esattezza exactness
esatto exact
esempio example
esistere exist
esplorare to explore
esportare to export
espressione *f.* expression
essa *f.* she, it
esse *f.* they, them
essenziale essential
essi *m.* they, them
estasiato ecstatic

estate *f.* summer
estero foreign
  ...,all' abroad
estivo *adj.* summer
età age (of a person)
eterno eternal
evento event
evitare to avoid

F

fabbrica factory
fabbricazione *f.* manufacture
faccia face
facile easy
fame *f.* hunger
  avere ... to be hungry
famiglia family
famoso famous
fango mud
  c'è ... it's muddy
fare to do, to make
  ... colazione to have breakfast
farmacia drugstore, pharmacy
fascino charm
favorevole favorable
favorisca! come in!
fazzoletto handkerchief
febbraio February
febbre *f.* fever
fedele faithful
felice happy
felicità happiness
feltro felt
fermare to stop
fermato stopped
ferrovia railroad
fervente burning, fervent
festa festival, holiday
fiamma flame
fianco (*pl.* **fianchi**) hip
fico (*pl.* **fichi**) fig
fidanzato fiance
figlia daughter
figlio son
figuri, si! of course! you can
  imagine!
fila row, line
  in ... on line
filetto filet, filet mignon
film *m.* film, motion picture
filo thread

finalmente finally
finestra window
finire to finish
fino a up to, until, as far as
fiore *m.* flower
firmare to sign
fisico physicist
fiume *m.* river
flanella flannel
folla crowd
fontana fountain
fonografo phonograph
forbici *f. pl.* scissors
forchetta fork
forestiero foreigner
formaggio cheese
formalità formality
formato format, shape
forse maybe, perhaps
forte loud, strong
fortuna luck
  per ... luckily
fortunato fortunate, lucky
fotografia photograph
  fare una ... to take a picture
fra between, among
francese *m. & f.* French
Francia France
fratello brother
frattempo, nel in the meantime
freddo cold
  fa ... it is cold
frequentemente frequently
fresco *adj.* fresh, cool
  fa ... it is cool
fretta hurry
  ho ... I am in a hurry
friggere to fry
frigorifero refrigerator
frittata omelet
fritto fried
frutta fruit (at the table)
frutto fruit
fumare to smoke
funicolare *f.* funicular, cable railway
funziona, non it is out of order

G

gabbia cage
gabinetto toilet
galante gallant

galanteria gallantry
galosce *f. pl.* overshoes, rubbers
gamba leg
gas *m.* gas
gatto cat
gelato ice cream
gelo frost
   si gela it's freezing
geloso jealous
generalmente ordinarily, generally, usually
genio genius
genitore *m.* parent
gennaio January
gentile kind
gentilezza kindness
geologo geologist
ghiaccio ice
già already
giacca jacket, coat
   ... lenta loose jacket
   ... aderente close fitting jacket
giacchè inasmuch as, since
giallo yellow
giardino garden
gigantesco gigantic
giocare to play
giocatore *m.* player
giocattolo toy
giogo yoke
gioia joy
giornale *m.* newspaper, journal (business)
giornata day (in its duration)
giorno day
giovane young
giovedì *m.* Thursday
gita trip
giugno June
giustizia justice
   palazzo di ... court house
gloria glory
golfo gulf
gomma rubber, eraser
gonnella skirt
governare to govern, rule
gradevole agreeable
grado degree
grande big, large
grano wheat
grasso fat

grato grateful
gratis free
grave serious, grave
gravità gravity
grazie thank you
grazioso pretty
Grecia Greece
gridare to shout, cry
grido scream
grigio gray
grillo cricket
gruppo group
guadagno profit, gain
guanto glove
guarnizioni *f. pl.* trimmings
guasto *n.* damage, something out of order
guerra war
guida guide
guidare drive
gusto taste

H

ha you *(pol. sing.)* have, he has, she has
hai you *(fam. sing.)* have
hanno you *(polite pl.)* have, they have
ho I have

I

idea idea
ideare to conceive
immensamente immensely
incantevole enchanting
incontrare to meet
incontro meeting
indossare wear
indubbiamente undoubtedly
ieri yesterday
ignorante ignorant
ignoranza ignorance
illustrazione *f.* illustration
illustre illustrious
imbarcarsi to embark, sail
immaginare to imagine
immediatamente immediately, at once
immortale immortal
imparare to learn

impermeabile *m.* raincoat
Impero Romano Roman Empire
impiegato employed; *n.* employee
imponente imposing
importa, non it doesn't matter
importare to import; to be of
   consequence
impossibile impossible
impossibilità impossibility
impressione *f.* impression
in in
incantevole enchanting
inchiostro ink
inciso engraved
includere include
indescrivibilmente indescribably
indicare to indicate, point
indietro behind
   va . . . it is slow (of a watch)
indimenticabile unforgettable
indirizzo address, direction
indovinare to guess
indubbiamente undoubtedly
industria industry
industriale industrial
inestimabile incalculable
infanzia childhood
infatti in fact
infinito infinite
informare inform
ingegnere *m.* engineer
Inghilterra England
inglese *m. & f.* English
ingrosso, all' wholesale
iniziare to start
innegabile undeniable
insalata salad
insegnare to teach
insieme together
insipido tasteless
intanto meanwhile
intellettuale intellectual
intelligente intelligent
intende, s'- of course, it's understood
interessante interesting
intero entire
interrogazione *f.* question
interrompere interrupt
intimo intimate
intrepido intrepid, fearless
intrusione *f.* intrusion
inutile useless

invano in vain
introduzione *f.* introduction
invaso taken hold, invaded
invasore *m.* invader
invece instead
inventore *m.* inventoɩ
inverno winter
invitare to invite
invitato guest
invocante invoking
io I
isola island
isoletta small island
ispirazione *f.* inspiration
Italia Italy
italiano Italian
itinerario itinerary

L

là there
labirinto labyrinth
laborioso hard working
laggiù down there
lagnarsi to complain
lago lake
lagrima tear
laguna lagoon
lametta razor blade
lampada lamp
lampadina lamp bulb
lampo lighting
lampeggia it's lighting
lana wool
lancetta hand (of a watch or clock)
lanciare to throw
lapis *m.* pencil
largo wide, large
lasciare to leave, to let, allow
lassù up there
lato side
latte *m.* milk
lattuga lettuce
lava lava
lavabo wash basin
lavanderia laundry
lavarsi to wash oneself
legale legal
legalizzare legalize
legge *f.* law
legno wood
legumi *m. pl.* vegetables, legumes

lei you *(pol. sing.)*
lento slow
lenzuolo *(pl.* **le lenzuola) bed sheet**
leone *m.* lion
lettera letter
 . . . **di cambio** letter of exchange
letteratura literature
letto bed
lezione *f.* lesson
lì there
liberazione *f.* liberation
libero free, unoccupied
libro book
 . . . **di cassa** cash book
 . . . **mastro** ledger
lido seashore
lieto glad
limone *m.* lemon
lingua language, tongue
lino linen
liscio smooth
 non se la passa liscia you won't
 get away with it
lista list
 . . . **delle vivande** menu
 . . . **dei vini** wine list
logico logical
Londra London
lontano far
loro you *(pol. pl.),* they, them
luce *f.* light
 . . . **elettrica** electric light
luglio July
luminoso bright
luna moon
 . . . **di miele** honeymoon
lunedì *m.* Monday
lungo long
 a . . . for a long time
luogo *(pl.* **luoghi) place**
lupo wolf
lusso luxury
lussureggiante luxurious,
 luxuriant

M

ma but, however
macchina machine, car
 . . . **cinematografica** movie camera
 . . . **da cucire** sewing machine

 . . . **da scrivere** typewriter
 . . . **fotografica** camera
madre *f.* mother
maestro teacher
maggio May
maggiore major
 la maggior parte most, the
 majority
magnifico magnificent, wonderful
mai never
 non . . . (verb) . . . **mai** never
maiale *m.* pork
mal di testa headache
malamente badly
malato ill
male bad
 non c'è . . . not bad
 sto . . . I am ill, I feel sick
mamma mother
mancia tip
mangiare to eat
manica *(pl.* **maniche) sleeve**
mantenere to keep
marciapiede *m.* sidewalk
mare *m.* sea
marina navy
marito husband
marmellata jam
marmo marble
martedì *m.* Tuesday
martello hammer
marzo March
massimo maximum
matematico mathematician
materasso mattress
matita pencil
mattina morning
 di or **la** . . . in the morning
mattino morning
me me
meccanismo movement (of a watch)
medicina medicine
medico doctor, physician
medioevale medieval
medio evo Middle Ages
meglio better
mela apple
melodioso melodious
meno less
 a . . . **che** unless

mensilmente monthly
mente *f.* mind
mentire to lie
mentre while
meraviglia marvel, wonder
meravigliosamente marvelously
meraviglioso wonderful, marvelous
mercato market
   a buon . . . cheap, inexpensive
merce *f.* merchandise
mercoledì Wednesday
meritare to deserve
merletto lace
mese *m.* month
messa Mass
messaggio message
metà half
mettere to put, put on
metro meter
mezzanotte *f.* midnight
mezzo middle, half, means
   non c'è altra via di . . . there is no
   other way
mezzogiorno noon
miei *m. pl.* my, mine
microscopio microscope
miei my, mine
miele *m.* honey
migliaia *f. pl.* thousands
migliorare to get better
migliore better
mila (*pl.* **mille**) one thousand
milione *m.* million
milite *m.* soldier
   Milite Ignoto Unknown Soldier
minacciare to threaten
minestrone *m.* minestrone, thick
   vegetable soup
minuto minute
minuto, al retail
mio my, mine
mischiare mix
misura measurement, measure, size
   prendere la . . . to take the
   measurement
mite mild
mobile *adj.* movable; *n. m.* piece of
   furniture
mobilia furniture

modello pattern, model
moderato moderate, reasonable
moda fashion
moderazione *f.* moderation
moderno modern
modesto modest
modo manner
   in ispecial . . . especially
mogano mahogany
moglie *f.* wife
molla spring
molo pier
moltissimo very much
molto *adj.* much, a great deal;
   adv. very
momento moment
   . . ., al at present
mondiale of the world
mondo world
montagna mountain
monumento monument
moro Moor
morso bite
mostrare to show
motocicletta motorcycle
motore *m.* motor
municipio city hall
muovere move
muro wall
museo museum
musica music
musicista *m. & f.* musician
mutande *f. pl.* underwear, shorts

N

nacque was born
nascere to be born
nascita birth
napoletano Neapolitan
nastro ribbon
naturalmente naturally
Natale *m.* Christmas
naturale natural
naturalmente naturally
nazione *f.* nation
nazionalità *f.* nationality
nè . . . **nè** neither . . . nor

nebbia fog
  c'è ... it's foggy
necessità necessity
negare to deny
negozio store
nemico (*pl.* **nemici**) enemy
nemmeno not even
nero black
nessuno nobody
neve *f.* snow
nevica it is snowing
niente nothing
  ... affatto not at all
nipote *m.* nephew; *f.* niece
no no
nobile *m.n.* nobleman; *adj.* noble
noce nut (tree *m.*; fruit *f.*)
  ... di cocco cocoanut
noi we
noleggio, prendere in to rent
nome *m.* name
nonna grandmother
nonno grandfather
nono ninth
nord *m.* north
normalmente usually, normally
nostalgia nostalgia, longing
nota note
notare to note, notice
notaio notary
notte *f.* night
novanta ninety
nove nine
novella short story
novembre *m.* November
nulla nothing
numero number, size
nuotare to swim
nuovamente again
nuovo new
nutriente nutritious
nuvola cloud
nuvoloso cloudy

O

o or
occasione *f.* occasion
  colgo questa ... I take this
  occasion

occupare occupy
occupato busy, occupied
odiare to hate
odorare to smell
offerta *n.* offer
offrire to offer
oggetto object
oggi today
  al giorno d'... nowadays
  ... ad otto a week from today
  ... stesso this very day
ogni each, every
ognuno everyone, everybody
Olanda Holland
olio oil
oliva olive
olivo olive tree
oltre more, beside
ombra shade, shadow
ombrello umbrella
onda wave
onesto honest
onorario fee
onore *m.* honor
  fare ... to honor
opera opera, work
  ... d'arte work of art
opinione *f.* opinion
oppure or, otherwise
opuscolo pamphlet
ora *n.* hour, time
  che ... è? what time is it?
ora *adv.* now
  da ... in poi from now on
  proprio ... just now
  fin da ... as of now
orario timetable
  in ... on time
orecchio ear
orgoglio pride
orgoglioso proud
origine *f.* origin
orlo edge
ormai (oramai) by now
oro gold
orologeria watchmaker's shop
orologiaio watchmaker

orologio watch
...a pendolo wall clock
...a sveglia alarm clock
...da polso wrist watch
...da tasca pocket watch
orrendo horrendous, horrible
oscillazione f. oscillation, swinging
oscurità darkness
ospedale m. hospital
ospitale hospitable
ospitalità hospitality
ospite $m. \& f.$ guest
ottanta eighty
ottavo eighth
ottimo excellent
otto eight
ottobre m. October
ovest west
ovunque anywhere, everywhere

P

pacco package
pacchetto little package
pace f. peace
padre m. father
paese m. country
Paesi Bassi Low Countries
pagamento payment
pagare to pay
paio pair
palazzo building, palace
palma palm tree, palm
panciera girdle
panciotto vest
pane m. bread
panino roll (bread)
panorama m. panorama, view
pantofola slipper
Papa m. Pope
paradiso paradise
paralume m. lamp shade
parapioggia m. umbrella
parata parade
parco ($pl.$ **parchi**) park
parente $m. \& f.$ relative
pari even
Parigi Paris
parlare to speak
parola word
parte f. part

la maggior ... the larger part, most
da questa ... this way
partenza departure
partire to leave, to depart
partita n. game, contest
Pasqua Easter
passaporto passport
passare to pass, to spend (time)
passatempo pastime
passeggiata walk
passeggio n. walk, walking
da ... for walking
pasticcino pastry
pasto meal
patata potato
purè di patate mashed potatoes
patria homeland, mother country
patriottico patriotic
paura fear
ho ... I am afraid
pecora sheep
pedone m. pedestrian
peggio worse
pelle f. leather, skin
pellicola film, motion picture
pena pain
non vale la ... it is not worthwhile
pendolo pendulum
penicillina penicillin
penna pen
...stilografica fountain pen
pensare to think
pensatore f. thinker
pensiero thought
pensione f. board, boarding house
pentirsi to repent, regret
pepe m. pepper
per for
per cento per cent
perchè because
perchè? why?
perdere to lose
perdonare to forgive, pardon
peregrinazione f. wandering
perenne perennial, everlasting
perfettamente perfectly
perfetto perfect
perfezione f. perfection
pericolo danger
pericoloso dangerous
periferia suburbs

solito usual
  più del ... more than usual
solo *adv.* only; *adj.* alone, only, single
soltanto only
sono, ci there are
sontuoso sumptuous
sopra on, over
soprabito overcoat
soprascarpe *f.pl.* overshoes, rubbers
sorella sister
sorgere to rise
sostituire to replace
sottana slip, petticoat
sottile thin
sotto beneath, under
sottomarino submarine
spaghetti *m. pl.* spaghetti
Spagna Spain
spagnuolo Spanish, Spaniard
spalancare to open wide
spalla shoulder
sparire to disappear
spaventarsi to get frightened
spazzola brush
spazzolare to brush
spazzolino tooth brush
specchio mirror
speciale special
specialmente especially
spedire to send
spedizione *m.* expedition
spegnere to extinguish
sperare to hope
spesso often
spettacolo spectacle
spiaggia beach
spiccioli *m. pl.* change (money)
spiegare to explain, unfold
spiegarsi to make oneself clear
spinaci *m. pl.* spinach
spinto driven, pushed
splendore *m.* splendor
sporco dirty
sportello window, pay window (of a bank)
sposa bride, wife
sposare to marry
sposina dear little wife
sposini newlyweds
sprecare to waste
spugna sponge

squadra team
squillare ring out
squisito delicious, exquisite
stabile *m.* building, house
stabilire to establish
stagione *f.* season
stagno tin
stanco tired
stare to stay
  ... a pennello to fit perfectly
  ... in piedi to stand up
  ... per to be about to
stasera tonight
Stati Uniti *m. pl.* United States
stato state
statua statue
stazione *m.* station
  ... balneare *f.* bathing resort
sterlina pound sterling
sternutire to sneeze
stesso same
stile *m.* style
stizzito angry
stoffa material, cloth
stomaco stomach
storia history, story
storico historical
strada street, road
strage *f.* slaughter
strano strange
stretto tight, narrow
studente *m.* student
studio study
stufa stove
stupendo stupendous
stupido stupid
sua *f.* his, her, hers, your, yours
subito at once; quickly
sublime sublime
successore *m.* successor
succursale *f.* branch (of a firm)
sud *m.* south
sudare to perspire
sudore *m.* perspiration
sigillo seal
suo his, her, hers, your, yours
suoi *pl.* his, her, hers, your, yours
suola sole (of a shoe)
suonare to ring; strike (the hour); to play (an instrument)
superfluo superfluous
supporre to suppose

svegliarsi to wake up
svestirsi to undress
sviluppo development
svizzero Swiss

T

tabacco tobacco
tacco (*pl.* tacchi) heel
tanti, tante many
tanto so, so much
tappeto rug
tardi late
   più . . . later
tasca pocket
tassa tax, duty
tassì *m.* taxi
tavola table
tazza cup
tè *m.* tea
teatro theater
tedesco (*pl.* tedeschi) German
telefonare to telephone
telefono telephone
telegramma *m.* telegram
telegrafare to telegraph
telescopio telescope
televisione *f.* television
temperatura temperature
tempesta storm
tempo time, weather
   in or a . . . on time
   fa bel . . . the weather is fine
   . . . disponibile free time
tendina curtain
tenere to hold, keep
   . . . il resto to keep the change
tenero tender
termometro thermometer
terra earth
terribile terrible
terzo third
tesoro treasure
tessuto cloth, fabric
testa head
testimonio witness
titolo title, security
toccare to touch
   ci toccherà we shall have to
togliere to take away from
toletta dressing table

tomba tomb
Torre Pendente *f.* Leaning Tower
torrenti, a pouring
torta cake
totale *n.m. & adj.* total
tovaglia tablecloth
tovagliolo napkin
tra between, among
tracciare trace, outline
tracciato outlined
tradurre to translate
traffico traffic
tramonto sunset
transazione *f.* transaction
trasportare to transport
trasporto transportation
tratta draft
trattenersi to remain
tre three
tredici thirteen
treno train
trenta thirty
tromba horn (of a car)
troppo too, too much
trovare to find
trovarsi to be; to be located; to find
   onself
trucidato slaughtered
truppe *f. pl.* troops
tu you (*fam. sing.*)
tuono thunder
   tuona it is thundering
Turchia Turkey
turista *m.* tourist
tutt'altro! on the contrary, anything
   but!
tuttavia nevertheless
tutto all, everything

U

uccello bird
udienza audience
udire to hear
ufficio office
   . . . postale post office
uguale alike, equal
ultimo last
umidità humidity, dampness
umido humid, damp
umile humble

undici eleven
unito united
università university
uno one
uomo (*pl.* **gli uomini**) man
uovo (*pl.* **le uova**) egg
uragano hurricane
urgente urgent
usanza custom
usare to use, employ
uscita exit
uso use, usage
utile useful
uva grape

V

va bene all right
vacanza vacation
valido valid
valigia (*pl.* **valigie**) valise, suitcase
valore *m.* value, security
vano room (empty, unfurnished)
vapore *m.* steamboat
varietà variety
vasca washtub
vasellame *m.* china
vasto large, vest
Vaticano Vatican
vecchio old
vedere to see
veduta view
veicolo vehicle
velluto velvet
veloce fast
vendere to sell
venerdì Friday
venire to come
venti twenty
ventina about twenty
vento wind
   tira . . . it is windy
venturo next
venuta *n.* coming
veramente really, truly
verde green

verdura green vegetables
verità truth
vero true, real
vertigini *f. pl.* dizziness
   avere le . . . to be dizzy
veste *f.* dress
vestiario clothing
vestirsi to dress (oneself)
vestito suit
   confezionare un . . . to make a suit
vetro glass, crystal
vettura car (of a train); carriage
via *n.* street, avenue; *adv.* away
   per . . . aerea by the mail
viaggiare to travel
viaggiatore *m.* traveler
viaggio trip, voyage
   . . . di nozze honeymoon trip
vicino near; *n.* neighbor
vigilia eve
vino wine
visibile visible
visita visit
visitare to visit
vita waistline, life
vitella veal
vittoria victory
vocabolario vocabulary
voce *f.* voice
voi you (*fam. pl.*)
volentieri willingly
volere to want, wish
volta turn; way; road
   una . . . once
   qualche . . . sometimes
   delle volte at times
voltare turn over
vulcano volcano
vuoto empty

Z

zero zero
zia aunt
zio uncle
zonzo, andare a to wander about
zuccheriera sugar bowl
zucchero sugar

English-Italian Dictionary

A

a, an uno, una, un
able, to be potere, essere capace
about circa
above sopra, al disopra
abroad all'estero
absolutely assolutamente
accept, to accettare
accident accidente
accompany, to accompagnare
according, to secondo
accustomed abituato
ache dolore
acquaintance conoscenza
action azione
add, to aggiungere
address indirizzo
admire, to ammirare
advance, in in anticipo
advice consiglio
advise, to consigliare
afraid, I am ho paura
after dopo, poi
afternoon pomeriggio
again nuovamente
against contro
age età (of a person)
agency agenzia
agent agente *m.*, rappresentante *m.*
agreeable gradevole, piacevole
agriculture agricoltura
ahead avanti
air aria
air mail posta aerea
airplane aeroplano
airport aeroporto
alarm, to allarmare

alike uguale, eguale, simile
all tutto, tutti, tutte
allow, to permettere
all right va bene
almost quasi
alone solo
already già
also anche, pure
although benchè, sebbene
always sempre
American americano
among fra, tra
amount ammontare *n. (m.) & v.*
amusement divertimento
amusing divertente
ancient antico
and e, ed
angry adirato, stizzito, arrabbiato, in collera
animal animale *m.*
announce, to annunziare
answer, to rispondere
answer riscontro, risposta
anxious ansioso
any alcuno
anyone chiunque, ognuno
anywhere dovunque, ovunque
apartment appartamento
appear, to apparire
appetite appetito
appetizer antipasto
apple mela
appointment appuntamento
appreciate, apprezzare
approach, to avvicinarsi
approve, to approvare
April aprile *m.*
arm braccio (*pl.* le braccia)

320

armchair poltrona
arrival arrivo
arrive, to arrivare
art arte *f.*
article articolo
artist artista *m. & f.*
as come
ask, to chiedere, domandare
asleep, to fall addormentarsi
assure, to assicurare, accertare
at a
at all affatto
at once subito
attend, to assistere
attraction attrazione *f.*
attractive attraente
August agosto
aunt zia
authentic autentico
author autore *m.*
authority autorità
automobile automobile *f.*
autumn autunno
avenue via
aviation aviazione *f.*
avoid, to evitare
away via
awaken, to svegliarsi

B

bad cattivo *m.*
 not . . . non c'è male
badly malamente
baggage bagaglio
bank banca
basket cesta, paniere
bath bagno
bathe, to fare il bagno
bathroom bagno, stanza da bagno
bathtub vasca
battle battaglia
be, to essere, trovarsi, stare
beach spiaggia
beat battere
beautiful bel, bella, bello
beauty bellezza
because perchè
become, to diventare
bed letto
bedroom camera da letto
bed sheet lenzuolo (*pl.* le lenzuola)

beef bue *m.*
before prima
begin, to cominciare, incominciare
behind dietro, indietro
Belgium Belgio
believe, to credere
bell campanello
below sotto, al disotto
belt cintura
beneath sotto
beside accanto, oltre
bet, to scommettere
better migliore *adj.;* meglio *adv.*
 to get . . . migliorare
between tra, fra
bicycle bicicletta
big grande
bill conto
bird uccello
birth nascita
bite morso
bitter amaro
black nero
blanket coperta
bless, to benedire
blond biondo
blood sangue *m.*
blouse camicetta
blue azzurro, celeste
boarding house pensione *f.*
boat barca
body corpo
boil, to bollire
book libro
born, to be nascere
both ambedue, tutti e due
bottle bottiglia
box scatola
boy ragazzo, fanciullo
brassiere reggipetto
Brazil Brasile *m.*
bread pane *m.*
break, to rompere
breakfast colazione *f.*
 to have . . . fare colazione
bride sposa
bridge ponte *m.*
brief breve
bright luminoso
brilliant brillante
bring, to portare
broad largo

brother fratello
brother-in-law cognato
brown bruno,-a, marrone
brunette brunetta
brush spazzola
brush, to spazzolare
build, to costruire
building palazzo, edificio, stabile *m.*
to burn ardere, bruciare
bus autobus
business affari
   to do . . . fare affari
busy occupato
but ma, però
butcher shop macelleria
butter burro
button bottone *m.*
buy, to comprare
by per
by means of mediante, per mezzo di
by chance per caso

C

cabin cabina
cake torta
calendar calendario
call, to chiamare
called, to be (name) chiamarsi
camera macchina fotografica
Canada Canadà *m.*
cap berretto
captain capitano
car (railroad) carrozza, vagone
   (automobile) macchina,
   automobile
card biglietto visita,
   carta da gioco
career carriera
carry, to portare, trasportare
cash, to riscuotere
cashier cassiere
cat gatto
catch, to pigliare, prendere
cathedral cattedrale *f.*
catholic cattolico, cattolici *m.pl.,*
   cattoliche *f.pl.*
celebrate, to celebrare
cemetery cimitero
cent centesimo, soldo

center centro
centigrade centigrado
central centrale
century secolo
cereal cereale
certain certo, sicuro
certainly certamente
chair sedia
change (money) spiccioli *m. pl.*
charm fascino
charming simpatico
chauffeur autista *m.*
cheap a buon mercato
check (bill) conto
   (money) assegno
check room (for baggage) deposito
   (di) bagagli
cheerfully allegramente
cheese formaggio
chestnut castagna
chicken pollo
child bambino,-a
childhood infanzia
chocolate cioccolata
choose, to scegliere
Christmas Natale *m.*
church chiesa
cigar sigaro
cigarette sigaretta
city città
city hall municipio
civilization civiltà
class classe *f.*
clean to, pulire
climate clima *m.*
climb salire
close, to chiudere
closet armadio
cloth tessuto, stoffa
clothing vestiario
cloud nuvola
cloudy nuvoloso
coal carbone *m.*
coast costa
coat giacca
coffee caffè *m.*
collapse, to crollare
cold freddo *n. & adj.*
   (illness) raffreddore *m.*
collar colletto

collection raccolta
color colore *m.*
comb pettine *m.*
come, to venire
come in, to entrare
come in! favorisca!
comfort conforto
comfortable comodo
  to make oneself . . . accomodarsi
commerce commercio
commercial commerciale
company compagnia
complain, to lagnarsi
complete completo
completely completamente
concert concerto
condition condizione *f.*
confess, to confessare
consist of, to consistere di
construct, to costruire
contrary contrario, opposto
  on the . . . al contrario
conversation conversazione *f.*
convince, to convincere
cook, to cucinare, cuocere
cooked cotto
cool fresco
copy copia
corner angolo
correspondence corrispondenza
cost, to costare
cotton cotone *m.*
count, to contare
country paese *m.,* campagna
couple paio, coppia
courage coraggio
course (of a dinner) pietanza
course, of si figuri, beninteso,
  s'intende
courtesy cortesia
cousin cugino,-a
cover, to coprire
cream crema
credit credito
cry, to gridare (shout), piangere
  (weep)
cuff (of a shirt) polsino
cup tazza
curtain tendina
custom usanza, costume *m.*

customs dogana
  . . . inspection controllo della
  dogana
  . . . officer doganiere *m.*
cut, to tagliare
Czechoslovakia Ceco-slovacchia

D

daily quotidiano
damage guasto
damp umido
dance ballo
  to . . . ballare
danger pericolo
dangerous pericoloso
dark scuro, buio
darkness oscurità
date appuntamento, data, dattero
daughter figlia
dawn alba
day giorno, giornata
dear caro
December dicembre *m.*
decide, to decidere
decision decisione
declare, to dichiarare
deep cupo, profondo
degree grado
delicious delizioso, squisito
deliver, to consegnare
demand, to domandare
dentist dentista *m. & f.*
deny, to negare
depart, to partire
departure partenza
deposit, to depositare
descend, to scendere, andar giù
describe, to descrivere
description descrizione *f.*
deserve, to meritare
desire, to desiderare
desk scrittoio, scrivania
dessert dolce *m.*
diamond diamante *m.*
dictionary dizionario
difference differenza
different differente, diverso
difficult difficile
difficulty difficoltà
dine, to pranzare

dining room sala da pranzo
dinner pranzo
direction indirizzo, direzione *f.*
directly direttamente
dirty sporco, sudicio
disappear, to sparire
discover, to scoprire
discuss, to discutere
dish piatto
distance distanza
distant distante
disturb, to disturbare
divide, to dividere
do, to fare
doctor dottore *m., medico*
dog cane *m.*
dollar dollaro
donkey asino
door porta
doorbell campanello
double doppio
doubt dubbio
    to ... dubitare
dozen dozzina
draft corrente d'aria; (commercial) tratta
dream sogno
dream, to sognare
dress veste *f.*
dressmaker sarta
dress (oneself), to vestirsi
drink, to bere
drive, to guidare
driver autista *m.*
drugstore farmacia
dry secco
during durante
dwell abitare

E

each ogni
eager ansioso
ear orecchio
early di buon'ora, presto
earth terra
Easter Pasqua
easy facile
eat, to mangiare
egg uovo, *pl.* le uova
eight otto

eighteen diciotto
eighty ottanta
electric elettrico
electricity elettricità
elegant elegante
elevator ascensore *m.*
eleven undici
embark, to imbarcarsi
embrace, to abbracciare
embroidery ricamo
empty vuoto
enchanting incantevole
enemy nemico, nemici *pl.*
engineer ingegnere *m.*
England Inghilterra
English Inglese *m.&f.*
enough abbastanza
enter, to entrare
enthusiasm entusiamo
enthusiastic entusiasta
entire intero
envelope busta
epoch epoca
equal eguale
error sbaglio, errore *m.*
escape, to fuggire, scappare
especially in ispecial modo, specialmente
essential essenziale
establish, to stabilire
eternal eterno
even pari
evening sera, serata
event evento
every ogni
everyone ognuno
everything tutto
everywhere dappertutto, dovunque, ovunque
exact esatto
exactly propriamente, precisamente, esattamente
exaggerate esagerare
examine, to esaminare
example esempio
excellent eccellente, ottimo
except eccetto
excuse me! scusi!
excuse, to scusare
exist, to esistere
exit uscita
expensive caro

explain, to spiegare
export, to esportare
expression espressione *f.*
extinguish, to spegnere

F

fabric tessuto
face faccia
factory fabbrica
faithful fedele
fall caduta
family famiglia
famous famoso
far lontano, distante
  as ... as fino a
farm podere *m.*
farmer contadino, agricoltore *m.*
fashion moda
fast veloce
fat grasso
father padre *m.*
favorable favorevole
fear paura
February febbraio
feel sentire
festival festa
fever febbre *f.*
field campo
fifth quinto
fifteen quindici
fifty cinquanta
fill, to riempire
film film *m.*, pellicola
finally finalmente
find, to trovare
finger dito (*pl.* le dita)
finish, to finire
first primo
first class prima classe
fish pesce *m.*
fish, to pescare
five cinque
flame fiamma
floor (of a house) piano
flower fiore *m.*
fly, to volare
fog nebbia
follow, to seguire
food cibo

foot piede *m.*
footwear calzature *f. pl.*
for per
foreign estero
foreigner straniero, forestiero
forget, to dimenticare
forgive, to perdonare
fork forchetta
fortunate fortunato
forty quaranta
forward avanti
fountain fontana
four quattro
fourteen quottordici
fourth quarto
France Francia
free gratis, libero
freeze, to congelare
French francese *m. & f.*
frequently frequentemente
fresh fresco
Friday venerdì *m.*
fried fritto
friend amico
friendship amicizia
frightened, to be spaventarsi
from da
front, in davanti
frost gelo
fruit la frutta (at the table), frutto
fry, to friggere
funny comico, buffo
furnish, to arredare
furnished ammobiliato, arredato
furniture mobilia
  piece of ... mobile *m.*

G

game partita
garage rimessa, autorimessa, **garage**
garden giardino
gas gas *m.*
gather, to radunarsi, riunirsi
gentleman signore *m.*
German tedesco, tedeschi *pl.*
get up, to alzarsi
girdle panciera
girl ragazza, fanciulla
give, to dare, porgere
glad lieto, contento

glass bicchiere *m.*, vetro
glove guanto
go, to andare
go up, to salire
God Dio
gold oro
good buono
goodbye addio
granddaughter nipote *f.*
grandfather nonno
grandmother nonna
grandson nipote *m.*
grapefruit pompelmo
grape uva
grateful grato, riconoscente
grave grave
gray grigio
Greece Grecia
green verde
greet, to salutare
greeting saluto
group gruppo
grow, to crescere
guess, to indovinare
guest invitato
guide guida

H

hair capello, *pl.* capelli; pelo
half metà, mezzo
hall sala
ham (Italian) prosciutto
hammer martello
hand mano *f.*, lancetta (of a watch or clock)
handbag borsetta
handkerchief fazzoletto
happiness felicità
happy felice
hard duro
hat cappello
hate, to odiare
have, to avere
have to, to dovere
he egli
head testa, capo
health salute *f.*
hear, to udire
heart cuore *m.*
heat riscaldamento, calore *m.*

heavy pesante
heel tacco (*pl.* tacchi)
help aiuto
her, hers il suo, la sua, i suoi, le sue
here qui, qua
here is ecco, c'è
high alto
hill colle *m.*, collina
his, il suo, la sua, i suoi, le sue
history storia
hold, to tenere
holiday festa
Holland Olanda
holy santo
homeland patria
honest onesto
honey miele *m.*
honeymoon luna di miele
honeymoon trip viaggio di nozze
honor onore *m.*
hope speranza
hope, to sperare
horn (of a car) tromba
horse cavallo
hospital ospedale *m.*
hospitality ospitalità
hot caldo
hotel albergo
hour ora
house casa, stabile *m.*
how come, quanto
how much? quanto?
however però, ma, tuttavia
humidity umidità
hundred cento
hunger fame *f.*
hungry, to be avere appetito, avere fame
hurry fretta
husband marito

I

I io
ice ghiaccio
ice cream gelato
idea idea
if se
ignorance ignoranza
ignorant ignorante
ill malato, ammalato
  I am ... sto male

imagine, to immaginare
immediately immediatamente
import, to importare
important importante
impression impressione *f.*
impossible impossibile
impossibility impossibilità
in in
inasmuch as siccome, poichè, dato che
include, to includere
incorrect, scorretto, sbagliato
indeed in verità
indicate, to indicare
industrial industriale
industry industria
inexpensive a buon mercato
inform, to informare
inhabitant abitante *m.*
ink inchiostro
inside dentro
instead invece
insure, to assicurare
intelligent intelligente
interesting interessante
interrupt, to interrompere
intimate intimo
introduce, to presentare
introduction introduzione *f.*
invite, to invitare
island isola
Italian italiano
Italy Italia
itinerary itinerario

J

jacket giacca
jam marmellata
January gennaio
jealous geloso
Jewish ebreo
joke, to scherzare
joy gioia
July luglio
jump, to saltare
June giugno

K

keep, to tenere, conservare, mantenere

key chiave *f.*
kilogram chilo, chilogrammo
kilometer chilometro
kind buono, gentile *adj.*
kind specie *f.*
kindness bontà, gentilezza
king re *m.*
kiss bacio
kitchen cucina
knife coltello
knock, to battere, bussare
know, to conoscere, sapere
knowledge sapienza, conoscenza

L

lady signora
lake lago
lamb agnello
lamp lampada
lamp bulb lampadina
language lingua
large largo, grande, vasto
last ultimo
last, to durare
last week la settimana scorsa
late tardi
later più tardi
laugh, to ridere
laughter riso, ilarità
laundry lavanderia
lavatory gabinetto
law legge *f.*
Leaning Tower Torre Pendente *f.*
learn, to imparare
least, at almeno
leather pelle *f.,* cuoio
leave, to lasciare (permit), partire (depart)
left sinistra
leg gamba
legal legale
lemon limone *m.*
lend, to prestare
less meno
lesson lezione *f.*
let, to lasciare, permettere
letter lettera
lettuce lattuga
library biblioteca

lie bugia
lie, to mentire, dire bugie
life vita
lift, to alzare
light, to accendere
lightning lampo
like, to piacere
line fila, linea
linen lino
linens biancheria
lion leone *m.*
list lista
literature letteratura
little poco, piccolo
live, to abitare, vivere
living room salotto
load, to caricare
located, to be trovarsi
lodging alloggio
logical logico
London Londra
loud forte, ad alta voce
longing nostalgia
look for, to cercare
lose, to perdere
loud forte, alto
love amore
love, to amare
lover amante
low basso
luck fortuna
lunch colazione *f.*
lunch, to have fare colazione
luxury lusso

M

machine macchina
madam signora
magnificent magnifico
mahogany mogano
maid domestica
mail posta
mailbox buca delle lettere
major maggiore
majordomo maggiordomo
make, to fare
man uomo *(pl.,* uomini)
manage, to dirigere, amministrare
manager dirigente *m.*
    amministatore *m.*

manner modo, maniera
many tanti,-e
map pianta, carta geografica
marble marmo
March marzo
market mercato
marry, to sposare
marvel meraviglia
marvelous meraviglioso
marvelously meravigliosamente
Mass Messa
mathematician matematico
material stoffa, materiale *m.*
mattress materasso
maximum massimo
May maggio
maybe forse
mayor sindaco
me me
meal pasto
meaning significato
means mezzo
meantime, in the nel frattempo
meanwhile intanto
measure misura
measurement misura
meat carne *f.*
medicine medicina
medieval medioevale
meet, to incontrare, riunirsi
melodious melodioso
menu lista della vivande
merchandise merce *f.*
merchant commerciante *m.*
message messaggio
meter metro
microscope microscopio
midday mezzogiorno
middle mezzo
Middle Ages medio evo
midnight mezzanotte *f.*
mild mite
milk latte *m.*
million milione *m.*
mine il mio, la mia, i miei, le mie
minute minuto *(n. & adj.)*
mirror specchio
Miss signorina
mistake sbaglio, errore *m.*
mistaken, to be sbagliarsi
mister signor
mix, to mischiare, mescolare

model modello
moderate moderato
moderation moderazione *f.*
modern moderno
modest modesto
Monday lunedì *m.*
money denaro, danaro
month mese *m.*
monthly mensilmente
monument monumento
moon luna
moor moro
more più
morning mattina
most la maggior parte
mother madre, mamma
**motion picture, motion picture
theatre** cinema *m.*
motor motore *m.*
motorcycle motocicletta
mountain montagna, monte *m.*
movable mobile
move, to muovere
movement (of a watch) meccanismo
movie camera macchina
cinematografica
Mrs. signora
much molto
mud fango
museum museo
music musica
musician musicista *m. & f.*
must dovere
mutton castrato
my il mio, la mia, i miei, le mie
myself me

N

name nome *m.*
napkin tovagliolo
narrow stretto
nation nazione *f.*
national nazionale
nationality nazionalità *f.*
natural naturale
naturally naturalmente
navy marina
near vicino
necessary necessario
   it is . . . è necessario, bisogna che
necessity bisogno, necessità

neck collo
necktie cravatta
need bisogno
needle ago
neighbor vicino
neither . . . nor nè . . . nè
nephew nipote *m.*
never mai, non . . . *(verb)* . . . mai
nevertheless tuttavia, eppure
new nuovo
newlyweds sposini, novelli **sposi**
newspaper giornale *m.*
next prossimo, venturo
   . . . week la settimana prossima
niece nipote
night notte *f.*
nine nove
nineteen diciannove
ninety novanta
no no
nobody nessuno
noon mezzogiorno
no one nessuno
north nord *n.*, settentrionale *adj.*
note nota
notebook quaderno
nothing niente, nulla
notice, to notare
November novembre *m.*
now adesso, ora
number numero
nut noce (tree *m.*, fruit *f.*)
nylon nylon

O

object oggetto
occasione occasione *f.*
occupy, to occupare
occur, to accadere, avvenire,
   capitare
October ottobre *m.*
of di
offer, to offrire
office sede *f.* ufficio
   main . . . sede centrale
   branch . . . succursale *f.*
often spesso
oil olio
old vecchio
olive oliva
on sopra, su

once una volta
one uno,-a
only solo, soltanto, solamente
open, to aprire
opinion opinione $f.$
opposite contrario, opposto
or oppure, o
orange arancia ($pl.$ arance)
other altro
otherwise oppure, altrimenti
our, ours nostro, nostra, nostri,
  nostre
ourselves noi stessi
out of order guasto
over sopra
overcoat soprabito
overshoes soprascarpe, calosce,
  galosce
owe, to dovere
own proprio
ox bue $m.$

P

package pacco
pain dolore $m.$, pena
paint pittura
paint, to dipingere, pitturare
painting pittura, quadro
pair paio ($pl.$, le paia)
palace palazzo
paper carta
parent genitore $m.$
Paris Parigi $f.$
park parco
part parte $f.$
pass, to passare
passport passaporto
pastime passatempo
path cammino
pattern modello
pay, to pagare
payment pagamento
peace pace $f.$
peasant contadino
pen penna
  fountain . . . penna stilografica
pencil matita, lapis $m.$
penicillin penicillina
people popolo, gente $f.$
pepper pepe $m.$

per cent per cento
perfect perfetto
perfectly perfettamente
performance rappresentazione $f.$
perfume profumo
perhaps chissà, forse
period periodo
person persona
personal personale
perspire, to sudare
perspiration sudore $m.$
petticoat sottana
phonograph fonografo
photograph fotografia
physician medico
picture quadro, fotografia
piece pezzo
pillow cuscino
pineapple ananasso
pitcher caraffa
place luogo, posto
plane, by in aereo
plant pianta
plate piatto
play, to giocare
play, to (an instrument) **suonare**
pleasant piacevole
please per piacere
pocket tasca
point punto
point, to indicare
Poland Polonia
police polizia
policeman agente $m.$
poor povero
Pope Papa $m.$
popular popolare
pork maiale $m.$
port porto
possible possibile
post office ufficio postale, **posta**
potato patata
powder cipria, polvere
powerful potente
pray, to pregare
precise preciso
prefer, to preferire
prepare, to preparare
prescription ricetta
present attuale (now)
  at . . . al momento

present, to presentare
preserve, to conservare
pretty grazioso, carino
price prezzo
prince principe *m.*
probably probabilmente
proceed, to procedere
profit guadagno
promise promessa
pronunciation pronuncia,
  pronunzia
protest protesta
protest, to protestare
public pubblico
punctual puntuale
purchase acquisto, compra
purchase, to acquistare, comprare
put, to mettere
put on, to mettersi, indossare

Q

quality qualità
quarter (of a city) contrada,
  quartiere *m.*
queen regina
question domanda
quick presto, subito
quickly presto, subito

R

race corsa
radio radio *f.*
railroad ferrovia
rain pioggia
rain, to piovere
raincoat impermeabile *m.*
raise, to alzare
rapid rapido
rare raro
rare (meat) al sangue
rate rata
rather alquanto, piuttosto
raw crudo
rayon rayon
razor rasoio
razor blade lametta
ready pronto
real proprio, vero

really proprio, propriamente,
  veramente, davvero
reason ragione *f.*
reasonable moderato, ragionevole
receipt ricevuta
receive, to ricevere, accogliere
recent recente
recently recentemente
red rosso
refrigerator frigorifero
refuse, to rifiutare
region regione *f.*
regret, to pentirsi
relative parente *m. & f.*
religion religione *f.*
religious religioso
remain, to rimanere, trattenersi,
  restare
remainder resto
remember, to ricordare,
  rammentare
remind, to ricordare, rammentare
Renaissance Rinascimento
rent pigione *f.*
rent, to prendere in affitto,
  prendere in noleggio
repair, to riparare
repeat, to ripetere
replace, to sostituire
representative rappresentante *m.*
republic repubblica
reserve, to prenotare
reservation prenotazione *f.*
rest, to riposarsi
restaurant ristorante *m.*
retail al minuto
return, to ritornare
ribbon nastro
rice riso
rich ricco
right, to the a destra
ring, to (the hour) suonare
rise, to sorgere, alzarsi
river fiume *m.*
road strada
roast arrosto
roast beef arrosto di bue
rob, to rubare
roll rullino (film); rullo panino
  (bread)
room camera, stanza, vano (empty),
  sala

rose rosa
round rotondo
round trip andata e ritorno
row fila
rubbers calosce, galosce, soprascarpe
rug tappeto
ruins rovine, ruderi
rule, to governare
Rumania Rumenia
run, to correre
Russia Russia
Russian russo

S

sacrifice sacrificio
sail imbarcarsi
saint santo
salad insalata
salt sale $m.$
salty salato
same stesso
satisfy, to soddisfare
Saturday sabato
sauce salsa
saucer piattino
save, to risparmiare
say, to dire
scene scena
school scuola
science scienza
scientist scienziato
scissors forbici $f.pl.$
scream grido
sea mare $m.$
seashore lido
season stagione $f.$
seasoning condimento
seat sedile $m.$
second secondo
section (of a city) quartiere $m.$
  contrada
see, to vedere
seek, to cercare
seem, to sembrare
sell, to vendere
send, to spedire, mandare, inviare
September settembre $m.$
serious grave
serve, to servire
set, to apparecchiare

seven sette
seventeen diciassette
seventh settimo
seventy settanta
several diversi, diverse $f.$
sew, to cucire
sewing machine macchina da
  cucire
shade ombra
shadow ombra
sharp piccante
shave, to radere, farsi la barba
she ella, essa
ship piroscafo, vapore $m.$, nave $f.$
shirt camicia ($pl.$ camicie)
shoe scarpa
shop bottega ($pl.$ botteghe)
short breve, corto, basso
shorts mutande $f. pl.$
show, to mostrare, dimostrare,
  far vedere
shower doccia, acquazzone
  (rain) $m.$
shoulder spalla
shout, to gridare
sick ammalato
  I feel . . . sto male
  to get . . . ammalarsi
side lato, parte $f.$
sidewalk marciapiede $m.$
sign segno, cartello
silence silenzio
silver argento
silk seta
similar simile
simple semplice
simply semplicemente
since siccome, poichè, giacchè
sing, to cantare
single solo, unico
sister sorella
sister-in-law cognata
sit, to sedersi
six sei
sixteen sedici
sixth sesto
sixty sessanta
size misura, numero
skin pelle $f.$
skirt gonnella

sleep, to dormire
 to go to . . . addormentarsi
sleeve manica (*pl.* maniche)
slip sottana
slip, to scivolare
slow lento
small piccolo
smell, to odorare
smile, to sorridere
smoke, to fumare
smooth liscio
sneeze, to starnutire, starnutare
snow neve *f.*
so così (therefore, thus)
 . . . much tanto
soap sapone *m.*
sock calzino
sofa divano
soldier soldato, milite *m.*
some alcuni,-e
some un po', un po' di
somebody qualcuno
someone qualcuno
sometimes qualche volta
something qualche cosa
somewhat alquanto
son figlio
song canzone *f.*
soon presto
 as . . . as appena
soup brodo, zuppa
south sud *n.,* meridionale *adj.*
souvenir ricordo
spaghetti spaghetti
Spain Spagna
Spaniard Spagnuolo
Spanish spagnuolo
speak, to parlare
special speciale
spend, to (time) passare,
 (money) spendere
sponge spugna
spoon cucchiaio
spring molla, primavera
square piazza
stairs scale
stairway scala
stamp francobollo, bollo
stand up, to stare in piedi
state stato
start, to iniziare, incominciare
station stazione *f.*

stay permanenza
stay, to alloggiare, stare
steak bistecca
steal, to rubare
steamboat vapore *m.*
steward maggiordomo
still ancora
stocking calza
stomach stomaco
stone pietra, sasso
stop, to fermare
store negozio bottega
storm tempesta
story storia
story (of a house) piano, (tale) storia
straight diritto, dritto
strange strano
street via, strada
strike, to battere
strong forte
study studio
study, to studiare
stove stufa
student studente *m.,* studentessa *f.*
stupid stupido
style stile *m.*
sublime sublime
sudden repentino, improvviso
sugar zucchero
suit abito, vestito
suitcase valigia (*pl.* valigie)
summer estate *f.,* estivo *adj.*
sun sole *m.*
Sunday domenica
sunset tramonto
supper cena
supper, to have cenare
suppose, to supporre
sure sicuro
sweet dolce
swim, to nuotare
Swiss svizzero

T

table tavola
tablecloth tovaglia
tailor sarto
tailor shop sartoria
take, to prendere
 . . . the measurement prendere
 la misura

take off, to (aviation) decollare
tall alto
taste gusto
taste, to assaggiare, gustare
tax tassa
taxi tassì *m.*
teach, to insegnare
teacher maestro
tear lagrima
tear, to lacerare, stracciare
teaspoon cucchiaino
telegraph to, telegrafare
telegram telegramma *m.*
telephone telefono
telephone, to telefonare
television televisione *f.*
tell, to dire, narrare
temperature temperatura
ten dieci
tenth decimo
than che, di
thank, to ringraziare
thank you grazie
that che *conj.*, quello *pro. & adj.*
the il, lo, la, i, gli, le
theater teatro
them loro, essi, esse, li, le
then poi, allora
there là, ci, vi
there are ci sono, ecco
there is c'è, ecco
therefore quindi, perciò, dunque
thermometer termometro
they loro, essi, esse
thin sottile, magro
think, to pensare
third terzo
thirteen tredici
thirst sete *f.*
thirty trenta
this questo
thought pensiero
thousand (*pl.* mila)
thousands migliaia
thread filo
threaten, to minacciare
three tre
throw, to lanciare, gettare, buttare
thunder tuono
Thursday giovedì
thus così

ticket biglietto
ticket window biglietteria
tight stretto
time ora, tempo
   on . . . a tempo, in tempo
timetable orario
tip mancia, punta
tired stanco
to a
tobacco tabacco
today oggi
together insieme, assieme
toilet gabinetto
tomato pomodoro
tomb tomba
tomorrow domani
tongue lingua
tonight stasera
too anche, pure
   too much troppo
tooth dente *m.*
toothbrush spazzolino
toothpaste dentrifricio
top cima
total totale
touch, to toccare
tough duro
tourist turista *m.*
towel asciugamano
trade commercio
traffic traffico
train treno
translate, to tradurre
transport, to trasportare
transportation trasporto
travel, to viaggiare
traveler viaggiatore
tree albero
trip viaggio, gita
trousers calzoni *m.pl.*
truck autocarro, camion
true vero
trunk baule *m.*
truth verità
try, to provare
try on, to provare
Tuesday martedì
Turkey Turchia
turn off the light, to spegnere la
   luce
turn over, to voltare
typewriter macchina da scrivere

typewrite, to scrivere a macchina
twelve dodici
twenty venti
two due

U

ugly brutto
umbrella ombrello, parapioggia *m.*
uncle zio
under sotto
understand, to capire
underwear biancheria intima,
    mutande
undoubtedly indubbiamente
undress, to svestirsi, spogliarsi
unfortunately purtroppo
united unito
United States Stati Uniti *m. pl.*
university università
unless a meno che
until fino a
up, to go salire, **andar sù**
upon sopra
urgent urgente
us ci
use uso
use, to usare
useful utile
useless inutile
usual solito
usually generalmente, di solito

V

vacation vacanza
vain, in invano
valid valido
value valore *m.*
variety varietà
Vatican Vaticano
vegetables legumi *m.pl.*, verdura
vehicle veicolo
very molto
vest panciotto
victory vittoria
view veduta, panorama *m.*
visit visita
visit, to visitare
voice voce *f.*
voyage viaggio

W

waist cintura, vita
waistline vita
wait, to aspettare
waiter cameriere *m.*
waiting room sala d'aspetto
wake up, to svegliarsi
walk passeggiata, passeggio
walk, to passeggiare, camminare
wall muro
want, to volere
war guerra
warm caldo
warn, to avvertire
wash, to lavare
wash oneself, to lavarsi
wash basin lavabo
waste, to sprecare
watch orologio
watchmaker orologiaio
water acqua
wave onda
way, this da questa parte
we noi
wealth ricchezza
weather tempo
Wednesday mercoledì
week settimana
weigh, to pesare
weigh oneself, to pesarsi
weight peso
welcome! benvenuto!
welcome, to accogliere
well bene
west ovest *m.*, ponente *m.*
what che, ciò che (that which)
what? che cosa?
whatever qualunque cosa
wheat grano
wheel ruota
when quando
whenever qualora
where dove
    . . . is? dov'è?
which che, quale
which? quale?
while mentre
white bianco
who che
who? chi
whoever chiunque

wholesale all'ingrosso
whom che, chi
why? perchè?
wide largo
wife sposa, moglie, signora
wind vento
wind, to caricare
window finestra
wine vino
winter inverno
wish desiderio, augurio
wish, to augurare, desiderare, volere
with con
within dentro
without senza
wolf lupo
woman donna
wonder meraviglia
wonderful meraviglioso, magnifico
wood legno
woods bosco
wool lana
word parola
work lavoro, opera
　. . . of art opera d'arte
world mondo
　of the . . . mondiale

worry preoccupazione *f.*
worse peggiore, *adj.* peggio *adv.*
wrap, to avvolgere
wrist polso
write, to scrivere
writer scrittore *m.,* scrittrice *f.*

Y Z

year anno
yellow giallo
yes sì
yesterday ieri
yet ancora
you tu, lei, voi, loro
young giovane
young lady signorina
your il suo, la sua, i suoi, le sue
　(pol. sing.)
　il loro, la loro, i loro, le loro
　(pol. pl.)
　il tuo, la tua, i tuoi, le tue
　(fam. sing.)
　il vostro, la vostra, i vostri,
　le vostre *(fam. pl.)*
zero zero